STOKVIS STUDIES IN
HISTORICAL CHRONOLOGY
AND THOUGHT
ISSN 0270-5338
Number 14

More Monumental Inscriptions

Tombstones of the British West Indies

by Vere Langford Oliver

BORGO PRESS / WILDSIDE PRESS

www.wildsidepress.com

Library of Congress Cataloging-in-Publication Data

Oliver, Vere Langford.
    [Monumental inscriptions of the British West Indies]
    More monumental inscriptions : tombstones of the British West Indies /
by Vere Langford Oliver ; introduction by Michael Burgess.
        p. cm. (Stokvis Studies in historical chronology and thought, ISSN
0270-5338 ; no. 15)
    Originally published: The monumental inscriptions of the British West
Indies. Dorchester : Friary Press, 1927. With new intro.
    Includes bibliographical references and index.
    ISBN 0-89370-322-2 (cloth). — ISBN 0-89370-422-9 (pbk.)
    1. Epitaphs—West Indies, British. 2. West Indies, British—Genealogy.
3. West Indies, British—History, Local—Sources. 4. Cemeteries—West
Indies, British. I. Title. II. Series: Stokvis studies in historical chronology
& thought ; no. 15.
CS261.W47O45 1993   93-90
929'.5'08920729—dc20   CIP

FIRST BORGO EDITION

PREFACE.

THE following monumental inscriptions were copied by me, during a visit to the West Indies in 1913—14, before the War. Those of Barbados were printed in a separate volume in 1915. The present collection completes the memorials of the Leeward Islands, those of Antigua having been included in a History of that Island, published in 1894—99. The Virgin Islands were not visited, and owing to lack of time, only a few relating to the Windward Islands, Trinidad and British Guiana are given. I wish to express my grateful thanks to the local clergy, officials and numerous friends for their unfailing help. I am also especially indebted to Mr. Algernon Aspinall, C.M.G., C.B.E., Secretary of the West India Committee, for keeping me informed of all official inquiries and reports.

Some of the records in the Islands are rapidly perishing, and require transcription, for which there is no money and no skilled staff. This is far from being a new complaint, for in the year 1714, my ancestor, Colonel the Hon. Richard Oliver, was appointed to inspect and report on the condition of the records in Antigua ; and in 1914, exactly 200 years later, I was engaged on the same work, though in a private capacity.

I am fully aware that H.M. Governors are anxious to preserve historic sites and naval and military monuments, which remain to us, as memorials of the achievements of gallant builders and defenders of the British Empire.

May the latter not have fought and died in vain, but in place of the bloodshed and ravages by disease in the past, may we look forward to a perpetual peace in these lovely Islands of the Caribbean.

V. L. OLIVER.

Weymouth.

INTRODUCTION

Monuments to Time

American genealogists have long been aware of the British West Indies's importance as a source of pre-Revolutionary War materials relating to the southern American colonies. Barbados and the other British-occupied islands were way stations for the transfer of slaves from Africa, tobacco from the Americas, and molasses from the Indies, to and from Great Britain and the New World. They also served as intermediate stops for many colonists who later moved on to Virginia and the Carolinas. Families which later became prominent in the American South often appear first in the records of Barbados, the Bahamas, Antigua, and the other plantation colonies. Sometimes their stay in the Caribbean was short, but a few remained in the West Indies for a generation or more.

The surviving parish registers of these islands were finally transcribed, indexed, and published within the last two decades, but V. O. Oliver's two collections of graveyard transcriptions have until now remained obscure. Based on visits to the West Indies in 1913-14, his work consists of hundreds of meticulously transcribed and copied records. These epitaphs were then compiled into two beautifully designed and typeset volumes privately issued by Oliver in 1915 and 1927, respectively, in 200-copy editions. Very few of the volumes found their way into American libraries. The first book, covering the Island of Barbados, was reprinted by The Borgo Press in 1989; the second, retitled *More Monumental Inscriptions* to avoid confusion with its companion work, is now being made widely available for the first time.

Many of the stones transcribed by Oliver have undoubtedly been lost to the elements in the ensuing eight decades since his original visit to the West Indies. We are indeed fortunate that his careful research has survived, and are pleased to present his work for a new generation of historians and genealogists.

—Michael Burgess
San Bernardino, California
1 March 1993

MONUMENTAL INSCRIPTIONS

IN THE

BRITISH WEST INDIES.

ANTIGUA.

ST. JOHN'S CATHEDRAL.

The following six tablets have been placed in the Church since I published my History of the Island.

1. On the north side of the Chancel is a brass tablet, fixed to one of the wooden pillars, near the organ, with this inscription :—

IN MEMORY OF
WILLIAM HENRY EDWARDS, F.R.C.S., ENG.
BORN AT FROGMORE DEVONSHIRE
ENGLAND 1ST AUGUST 1817
DIED AT ST JOHNS ANTIGUA 4TH JUNE 1899
RESIDENT IN ANTIGUA FOR 57 YEARS
SENIOR MEDICAL OFFICER FOR 21 YEARS.

2. On the south wall of the Chancel is a brass with a recumbent figure of the Bishop in his robes, the face taken from life.   Above in the dexter corner is a shield with the arms of the See and in the sinister corner another with the Bishop's family arms :—*Azure in pale three stags heads erased*; impaling, *on a chevron Azure between three crosses croslet fitchy Vert as many fleurs-de-lis.* Below is this inscription :—

In loving memory of
William Walrond Jackson D.D., Bishop of Antigua,
who was born 9th January 1811,
was consecrated 17th May 1860, and died 25th Nov. 1895.

In the parish church of Ealing, London, is a somewhat similar brass. 1808, May 14.   Mr. William Jackson, to Miss Walrond, daughter of Benjamin Walrond, Esq.   (*Barbados Mercury*).

3.   On a brass close to the preceding :—

**This Tablet is erected
In Loving Memory of the
Venerable James Clark, D.D., Ph.D.
Archdeacon of Antigua, Vicar General of the Diocese,
and for 19 years Rector of St. Philips.**

(Four lines omitted)

**He entered into rest on Dec. 4th, 1895,
Aged 59 years, and was buried in the
Chancel of St. Philips Church,
in this Island.**

---

4.   South Transept.   On a white and black marble tablet on the east
wall :—

IN
MEMORY OF
SIR ANTHONY MUSGRAVE G.C.M.G.
THIRD SON OF
ANTHONY MUSGRAVE M.D.
BORN IN ANTIGUA AUG. 31, 1828,
DIED IN BRISBANE OCT. 9, 1888,
HAVING BEEN SUCCESSIVELY
GOVERNOR OF S^T VINCENT, NEWFOUNDLAND,
BRITISH COLUMBIA, NATAL,
SOUTH AUSTRALIA,
JAMAICA AND QUEENSLAND.

5.

TO THE MEMORY OF
HENRY OGILVIE BENNETT,
1846—1895.
MERCHANT OF THIS ISLAND,
WHO DEVOTED MUCH TIME AND ENERGY TO PUBLIC AFFAIRS
TO THE CONSIDERABLE ADVANCEMENT OF THE WELFARE
OF THIS COMMUNITY.
FOR MANY YEARS HE WAS
PRESIDENT OF THE GENERAL LEGISLATIVE COUNCIL OF THE LEEWARD ISLANDS
AND OF THE LEGISLATIVE COUNCIL OF ANTIGUA : A MEMBER OF
THE EXECUTIVE COUNCILS OF THE LEEWARD ISLANDS AND ANTIGUA,
AND CHAIRMAN OF THE S^T JOHNS BOARD OF HEALTH.
THIS TABLET IS ERECTED BY A FEW FRIENDS
DESIROUS OF PRESERVING HIS MEMORY.

Mr. Bennett resided in a house on the road to Rat Island.   Both he and
his wife died of yellow fever, leaving a young family.

A marriage has been arranged, and will take place shortly, between Douglas
MacKinnie Bennett, of the Sudan Government, son of the late Hon. H. O.
Bennett, of St. John's, Antigua, British West Indies, and Cicely Olive, youngest
daughter of the late William Ansell Todd and Mrs. Todd, 4, Clifton Hill, Bristol.
(*Times*, 14 June, 1918)

---

6. On an upright bronze panel. Arms : Quarterly, 1 and 4, *Ermine, on a chief Sable, three lions rampant Argent* (Oliver) ; 2 and 3, *Gules a shoveller close Argent* (Langford).

Crest : *A lion's head erased Ermines, collared and ringed Argent* (Oliver).

SACRED | to the Memory of | RICHARD OLIVER Esquire | Planter Speaker of the | House of Assembly 1704 | Member of H.M. Council 1708 | & Colonel of Militia 1715 | Baptised at *S*ᵗ *Nicholas Bristol* | 14th August 1664 he was | here buried 29th May 1716 | also of | RICHARD OLIVER Esquire | his grandson an Alderman | & M.P. for the *City of London* | a strenuous Supporter of the | Constitutional Rights of the | American Colonies. Baptised in | this Parish 7th January 1734-5 he | died at sea off Nevis 16th April 1784 | also of | JONAS LANGFORD Esquire | Merchant of *Popeshead* and | *Cassada Garden* Plantations | (the first Quaker settler | here in 1660) who died at | an advanced age in 1712. |

This panel is dedicated by | VERE LANGFORD OLIVER | *in commemoration of his* | ANCESTORS *and* KINSFOLK | *who lie buried in the churchyard* | *or in their plantations A.D.* 1919.

WESLEYAN BURIAL GROUND, ST. JOHN'S.

7. On a head-stone at the end of a vault :—

𝔍n 𝔏oving 𝔐emory
OF THE
REVᴰ THOMAS BARRY NIBBS
WESLEYAN MINISTER
WHO FELL ASLEEP IN JESUS SEPᵀ 7ᵀᴴ 1897
AGED 83 YEARS

There is also adjoining the above a head-stone to JAMES DONALDSON infant son of WILLIAM LAMB NIBBS died April 1847.

I was told by an old resident that the Rev. Mr. Nibbs owned some landed property and that he was a white man. His name however does not appear in the Nibbs pedigree, though he may have been descended from Mr. Barry Nibbs of Sᵗ George's, who died 1756, leaving two sons John and Jeremiah.

JAMES FORT, ST. JOHN'S HARBOUR.

8. Fixed in the wall leading to the entrance, is a square cracked stone with this worn inscription, of which I could only read the following :—

This . . . . .was Laid by
. . . . SAAC MATHEW
. . . . The Right Worshipfull
. . he Prov . . . . . Grand Master
With His . . . . nd Officers
And
The Right W . rshipful the Masters
And
The Wardens . . . . . . Brothers
The three Lodges . . . ee & accepted Masons
of Antigua
November 15ᵗʰ 1739

A photograph of the above appeared in the West India Committee Circular vol. 23, p. 316. The fort was commenced about 1704-5, but additions were subsequently made, when this stone must have been inserted. Mr. R. H. K. Dyett informed me that the three Lodges referred to were : Parham Lodge, constituted Jan. 31, 1737 ; Baker's Lodge, March 14, 1738 ; and Court House, Nov. 22, 1738, afterwards known as the Great Lodge at St. John's.

The Circular also gave on the same page a photograph of the memorial obelisk at the Ridge to officers and men of the 54th regiment, now 2nd Dorsetshire, who died in these islands 1848-1851.

GOAT HILL, ST. JOHN'S.

9. This is a rocky eminence at the south side of the entrance to St. John's Harbour. It is now used as a signal station, but in former days there were guns on the stone platform. On the east side is the original powder magazine. At the entrance to the platform, fixed on either side, in the wall, are two oblong stone tablets. The one on the right has :—

> *GULIELMUS MATH : BURT*
> Imperator & Gubernator
> Insularum Charib :
> me posuit
> 1780

The tablet to the left has :—

> *LOUISA BURT*
> Nata Secunda
> *GULIEL : MATH : BURT*
> Imper : & Gubern ;
> me posuit
> 1780

See *Aspinall's Pocket Guide to the West Indies* p. 300, for the account of the storming of Goat Hill by Prince Rupert in 1652.

HODGES BAY PLANTATION, POPESHEAD.†

10. Mrs. Davis of New York who rented the house for the winter, 1913-14, pointed out to me old burial grounds on the estate.

The house is charmingly situated on the west coast, a stone's throw from the sea. In the open land to the south-east there is a large walled-in burial ground containing two very old tamarind trees. A negro told me that "Master" was buried here and that he once saw a large flat stone just beneath the surface, but that he did not know what had become of it. Farther south there are several headstones to slaves, and north again another ground, in which I saw a headstone with this inscription :—

CHRISTIAN | KING | *Died the 27ᵗʰ Jan.* | 1809 | *Aged 78 Years.*

He may have been an overseer or servant.

The negro also knew of slave headstones on land under Mount Jarvis, but I had not time to visit them.

PICCADILLY NEAR WILLOUGHBY BAY.†

11. At Indian Warner near the ruins of the Great House is a vault in which Col. Tho. Warner and others of his family were buried. (*Historic Sites*).

I did not visit this. The other family burial ground is at the Savannah.

---

† This burial ground is new to me and was not noticed in my History of the Island.

DOMINICA.

Dominica, now included in the government of the Leeward Islands, lies between its two French neighbours Martinique and Guadeloupe. It is 29 miles long and 16 broad, and is supposed to contain 275 square miles or 186,436 acres. Lofty mountains and deep valleys, cut out by torrents, abound, and the scenery is magnificent.

Although named in the grant of 1627 to the Earl of Carlisle, it was never settled by the English, but by the treaty of 1748 declared neutral and reserved to the Caribs.

Sir James Douglas and Lord Rolls having captured it in 1761, it was ceded by treaty in 1763, and next year Commissioners were sent out, who sold the lands in lots, of not more than 100 acres of cleared land, and 300 acres of wood, to any one person, and long leases were granted to the few old French settlers. (*Atwood's Dominica* p. 2)

Planters from Antigua and the other older colonies took up numerous grants, and sent their younger sons to develop the new country.

In 1778 the Marquis de Bouillé with 3 frigates and 30 sloops and over 4000 men attacked Roseau, and being in overwhelming numbers (the garrison consisting of only 100 men), Govr. Stuart was forced to capitulate.

After Rodney's decisive victory off here in 1782, the island was saved and restored the following year. Further predatory attacks were made by the French in 1795 and 1805.

Parishes were formed in 1764 of which there are to-day ten :—St. George, St. Mark, St. Luke, St. Paul, St. Peter, St. John, St. Andrew, St. David, St. Patrick, and St. Joseph, but owing to the lack of roads all social and official life is centred in Roseau.

This town is situated in St. George's parish on the south-west coast, where a small rapid river debouches from a deep narrow valley. Youngs Fort, built in 1775, stands on a bluff above the pier, and is now used as a police station. Opposite is the English Church, and behind that the Roman Catholic Cathedral. Next to the former are Government House and the Court House, and across the road on the cliff the Public Library. Beyond above the Savannah is the old burial ground, and below an ancient government building, formerly an ordnance store, built in 1784. This particular district was called Charlotteville, but in the map of Bryan Edwards it appears as Charlotte Town.

The great majority of the inhabitants are Roman Catholics many being of French descent, even the negroes speaking a patois.

Atwood wrote in 1791 :—

" The church is a large lofty building of wood, but it is at present much out of repair. It has a neat pulpit, reading desk and a few pews ; but neither altar-piece, hangings, baptismal font, belfry nor bell. This, the only Protestant church in the island, is built on a large lot of ground, has a good church-yard of very deep and excellent black mould ; but the yard is not inclosed." (p. 175).

John Matson in his letter of 1803 stated that the estimate for building the new church amounted to £6,500.

Langford Lovell wrote in 1818 :—

" The only protestant place of public worship in the island has been suffered to go to decay ; and not one stone, as I understand, is now remaining upon another . . . the people have never petitioned, as far as I can learn, either for repairing the old, or constructing a new church. That there never was more than one, will perhaps admit of some excuse. At Roseau there is a resident clergyman, etc." On account of the bad roads and often impassible rivers he advocated the attendance of missionaries at plantations, rather than the erection of more churches. (A letter to a friend relative to the present state of the Island of Dominica 8°. p. 35).

By Act of 1818 the present building was erected. In 1900 it was enlarged and repaired at a cost of £2,000, so that it is now one of the finest looking churches in the West Indies.

RECTORS.

In compiling the following list, the first nine names have been taken from Fothergill's *Emigrant Ministers* and the Fulham MSS., being clergy sent by the Bishop of London to this Island. They were probably all duly inducted, but a search through the minute books of the Council and Assembly would be necessary to obtain details.

Henry McLeane, 1 July, 1764
David Fullerton, 23 June, 1767
Austin Leigh, 16 Feb., 1771
James Macintosh, 29 Dec., 1771
Joseph Miller, 21 Sept., 1773
Isaac Mann, 24 Aug., 1774
George Green, 26 March, 1778
Francis Margaret, 10 Nov., 1785
John Nesbit Jordan[1], 11 Jan., 1790
David Ritchie[2], 3 June, 1801
John Audain[3], 1802
H. C. C. Newman[4], 1813—1829

George Clarke[5], 1829—1850
Marmaduke Martin Dillon, 1850—1852
W. T. Roper[6], 1855—1870
Henry Genever, 1871—1876
J. J. Hill, 1876
George Edward Elliot[7], 1877—1878
John Shaw, 1880
William Evered, 1883—1888
Thomas Dent[8], 1889—1905
Herbert Arthur Walton[9], 1905—1912
. . . . . . Boucher, 1913—1914
Percy Kennedy Pax Bolton[10], 1922

1　Son of John Morton Jordan of Annapolis Maryland. merchant, by Dorothy Darby his wife, of Antigua. Curate of Edburton co. Sussex 1791., R. of Halstead co. Kent 1801 and of W. Tarring co. Sussex 1803, until his death there 2 Nov., 1818, aged 55. He took a Lambeth degree 8 Oct. 1804, as of Emanuel Coll. Camb. M.A. Mr. Jarvis of Antigua wrote 2 Nov., 1791 : " Young Mr. Jordan. . . . . is starving on a curacy at Edburton in Sussex " and suggests that the first vacant living at Antigua should be obtained for him.

2　1801, Sept. 22. On the island of Dominica, the Rev. David Richie, a native of Perth. He had been appointed rector of Roseau, on that island, and fell a victim to the climate soon after his landing to take possession of his rectoriate (*Gent. Mag.* for 1802 p. 181).

3.　He was a native of St. Kitts, of Huguenot origin, started in life as a Midshipman, became Vicar of Charmouth in Dorset in 1783, and acted as curate of the parish of St. Thomas, St. Kitts 1786—1788. At the French attack on Dominica in 1805 he served a cannon and was wounded. He later owned a privateer and died at St. Eustatius 1 Oct., 1825. (Coleridge's *Six Months in the West Indies. Caribbeana* I. 223, IV. 212).

4　He was appointed Curate in 1809, was elected to the House of Assembly and chosen Speaker 1812, and was buried 16 Aug., 1829, aged 74.

5　He signed the Registers up to 24 April, 1845, followed by J. G. R. de Joux, then again 10 May, 1850, followed by Darius Davy. Officiating Minister 27 July, 1850.

6　Officiating Minister 1853, 1854, died 5 Nov. 1870.

7　At Codrington College 1871, from Tobago. S.P.G. Curate of St. John's, Antigua, 1876.

8　Curate of St. John's, Antigua 1886—1888. Vicar of Sutton Bridge diocese of Lincoln since 1917.

9　Rector of St. George's, Grenada, 1912—1922. Archd. 1915—1922.

10　Curate of St. John's, Antigua 1912—1922.

COMMUNION PLATE.

There are a large circular dish and flagon, both with the Hall-mark for the year 1763, and " G.R.", the royal crown and arms, evidently the gift of King George III. There was formerly another flagon, but this was exchanged in 1883 for two small modern chalices. There is also a large chalice.

PARISH REGISTERS.

Three volumes were provided in the year 1822, H. C. C. Newman, rector, but the first entries commenced in 1825. The books were damaged by the hurricane on 4 Sept., 1883.

BURIALS.

1828, June 5. John O'Driscol, Chief Justice[1] Roseau.

1829, Aug. 16. The Rev[d] H. C. C. Newman. Rector of the Parish of S[t] George and Town of Roseau. Rector. 74 years.

1830. Several soldiers of the 93[d] Regiment.

1831, Jan. 3. Leonard Coles Taylor, Doctor of Medicine, Williamsburg, Virginia. About Twenty-four years.

1834, Oct. 3. Edmund Plunkett Burke[2] Puisne Judge of y[e] island of S[t] Lucia. Morne Bruce. About thirty-two years.

The 7th Regiment here. In 1836 the 36th Regiment and in 1837 the 74th Regiment.

1838, June 2. Henry S. Elwin[3] son of the Rev[d] T. N. Elwin of East Barnet. Roseau. Eighteen years.

1841. The 92[d] Highlanders here.

1855, Dec. 2. Mary Ann Woodcock, wife of the Chief Justice, H.J.W., Roseau. 57 years.

BAPTISMS.

Blanc, Bertram, Bell, Doyle, Fadelle, Gordon, Humphreys and Stedman, occur frequently.

1843, June 22. Henry Philip (born 17th of May, 1843) s. of Thomas Shirley and Rebecca Warner. Roseau. Provost Marshal General.

1846. Several children about this period of Rich[d] Matson, Inspector of Police and Celeste his wife.

The first 204 pages to Oct. 1859 are perfect. After that date several pages are damaged. The last entry was on 15 Feb., 1885.

MARRIAGES.

1825, June 21. Regist S[t] Aromant of this P. and Marie Catherine Laurent of the P. of S[t] Joseph by Banns. Each signed by a cross.

1825, Aug. 2. Charles Brownlow Cumberland and Russell Brown both of this P. Licence.

---

1 1828, June 3.. In Dominica after a short illness, John O'Driscol, esq. late chief Justice of that Colony. His remains were consigned to the grave on the following day, attended by the Governor and all the public functionaries. Mr. O' Driscol was on the eve of returning to England to take out his family. (*Gent. Mag.* 94).

1842, Nov. 24. At Taunton, Edwin Wing, M.B., of Bourton-on-the-Water, Glouc. to Dorinda, eldest dau. of the late Hon. John O'Driscoll, Chief Justice of Dominica and Author of a " History of Ireland " and other works. (*Ib.* 197)

2 In consequence of injuries received in the late hurricane (*Court Mag.*)

3 See *Gent. Mag.* p. 342.

1830, Feb. 24.   Charles Digges Esquire of this P. and Mary Moore of S[t] Andrew's P. spinster. L.

1830, Aug. 31.   William Henry McCoy of this P., Merchant, and Mary Elizabeth Wilson of this P. spinster. L.

1832, Nov. 6.   Maurice Ogston of S[t] Luke's P., Esquire, and Amelia Grano of S[t] Luke's. spinster. L.

1832, Nov. 27.   Joseph Francois Beroard of this Island, Esquire, and Antoinette Coralie Roman of S[t] Patrick's P. spinster. L.

1834, June 24.   Charles Digges, Esquire, of this P., widower, and Latitia Constable of this P., spinster. L.

1841, Feb. 1.   William Henry Thornton of this P., bach., Lieutenant of the 89th Reg[t] and Rebecca Avis Lindsey of this P., spinster. L.

There are several other marriages of officers.

1851, Nov. 11.   Wilbraham Halliday of the P. of S[t] John in the Island of Antigua, Merchant, and Evalina McGregor of the P. of S[t] George in the I. of D., spinster. L.

1899, July 6.   William Robert Forrest of Saint John in the I. of A. Bach. and Anna Maynard Pemberton of this P., spinster. L.

1900, Nov. 29.   Thomas Leslie Hardtman Jarvis[1] of this P., bach. and Annie Mary McHattie spinster of the P. of Saint Mary, Ealing in the Co. of Middx. Eng. Banns.

ST. GEORGE'S CHURCH, ROSEAU.

1.   There are four tablets on the south wall of the Nave, seven on the west wall and four on the north wall, making fifteen.

On south wall of Nave east of door—Crest : *A dexter hand couped grasping a dagger* or *spear* (end broken and lost).   Arms : *Azure a chevron between three bezants.*

SACRED
TO THE MEMORY OF
THE HON[BLE] JAMES LAIDLAW
MEMBER OF HIS MAJESTYS COUNCIL
REGISTRAR SECRETARY AND CLERK OF THE
ENROLLMENTS OF THIS ISLAND
WHO IN THE 31ST YEAR OF HIS AGE
ON THE 1ST AUGUST 1841
DEPARTED THIS LIFE—MUCH AND DESERVEDLY LAMENTED.
THIS TABLET IS ERECTED
BY HIS AFFLICTED AND SORROWING WIDOW

1834, Feb. 2.   Rachel Laidlaw, Wall House Estate.   About Eighteen years.

1834, Feb. 4.   James Laidlaw, Wall House Estate.   Three years.

1841, Aug. 2.   James Laidlaw, Colonial Secretary, Wall House Estate. Thirty-one years.   (Bur. Reg.).

James Laidlaw, eldest son of | John of Dominica, esq. Trin. Coll. matric. 26 June 1827, aged 16.   (Foster's *Alumni Oxonienses*).

1847, April 27.   At Hythe, the Rev. John Innes, V. of Downe, to Eliza. Mary, dau. of the late John Laidlaw, President of Council in the Island of Dominica.   (*Gent. Mag.* 80).

1847, Nov. 25.   At Lewisham, Francis Head Brockman, youngest son of the late J.D.B. of Beachborough, Kent, to Ellen, relict of James Laidlaw, of Dominica.   (*Ib.* for 1848, p. 192).

---

1 Of a well-known Antiguan family, and after being Commissioner of the Virgin Islands was appointed to Montserrat in 1915 where he died soon after.

2. **Below No. 1**

IN MEMORY OF
DEPUTY COMMISSARY GENERAL
JOHN BANNER PRICE
WHO DIED AT SEA
ON 26TH NOVEMBER 1849.
HIS REMAINS WERE INTERRED
IN THIS ISLAND

1849, Nov. 26. John B. Price, Deputy Commissary General. Died on board the Steamer " Conway." 60 years. (Bur Reg.).

---

3. To the west of the south door :—

Above is the badge of his Regiment—St George and the Dragon with QUO FATA VOCANT & EGYPT. PENINSULA.

TO PERPETUATE THE MEMORY OF
THEIR BELOVED AND GALLANT COMMANDER
LIEUTENANT COLONEL THOMAS EMES,
OF THE 5TH REGIMENT
WHO DIED IN THIS ISLAND
ON THE 2ND DAY OF NOVEMBER 1824
IN THE 55TH YEAR OF HIS AGE.
THIS TABLET OF RESPECT AND ATTACHMENT
IS INSCRIBED BY HIS BROTHER OFFICERS.

---

4. **Below No. 3** :—

Arms : *In centre point a heart resting on a pair of wings, between three stars of six points.*

Motto : MENS CONSCIA RECTI CORLÆTUM FACIT

I. H. S.
TO THE MEMORY OF
THE HONOURABLE JAMES CORLEY,
SPEAKER OF THE HOUSE OF ASSEMBLY
IN THIS ISLAND ;
WHO
WHILE ON A VISIT TO ENGLAND
DIED ON THE 20TH SEPTEMBER 1840,
AGED 59 YEARS.
ALSO | TO THE MEMORY OF |
M^{RS} ANN CORLEY, HIS WIDOW
WHO SURVIVED HER HUSBAND ONLY ONE YEAR
AND DIED ON THE 21ST SEPTEMBER 1841

(Erected by a friend).

1829, Jan. 1. Barbara Corlet. Roseau. 100 years.
1834, Dec. 18. James Lucas Corlet, Esquire of this P., bach. and Jane Frances Court of the said p., spr. L.
1836, Ap. 3. James Lucas Corlet, Barrister, Roseau. Twenty-six years. (Bur. Reg.).
1840, Dec. Lately. James Corlet, of Dominica, Speaker of the House of Assembly, and Lt.-Col. of the St. George Reg^t of Militia, of that Island. (*Gent. Mag.* 676).

1799   Lately.   In Great Russell str., Bloomsbury, Wm. Burt Corlett, esq., of Dominica.   (*Ib.* 721).

Abr. Audain of St Kitts, uncle of the Rev. John Audain rector of Roseau, in his will dated 1770, names " My grandnephew John Corlet, son of John Corlet, of Sandy Point, Esq., and Mary his wife."

James Corlet of Dominica, gent.   Will dated 24 May, 1792.   My late brother John Corlet S^r of Trinidad planter deceased.   Several mulatto children named. (*Book of Wills* IV., 202).

---

5.   On the west wall of the Nave south of west door : —

SACRED | TO THE MEMORY OF | JOSEPH WETHERALL | MAJOR OF THE 1ST OR ROYAL REG^T OF FOOT | WHO DIED AT DOMINICA | ON THE 7TH OF AUGUST 1833 | AGED FORTY NINE YEARS | VIDUATI MONUMENTUM AMORIS.

1833, Aug. 8.   Major Joseph Wetherall, Roy^l Reg^t Morne Bruce.   Fifty years.   (Bur. Reg.)

---

6.   Below No. 5 :—

Motto : HONOR.
Crest : *A dragon's head couped, in its mouth a hand couped, dropping blood.*

IN MEMORY OF | THOMAS MACNAMARA ROSE PRICE, | THE ELDEST SON OF | THOMAS PRICE, ESQUIRE, | LIEUTENANT GOVERNOR | OF THIS ISLAND | WHOSE EARTHLY CAREER CLOSED ON THE 16TH | APRIL 1864, IN HIS EIGHTEENTH YEAR.   (Eight lines).

The above Tho. Price was sixth son of Sir Rose Price 1st. Bart. of Jamaica, born 3 Nov., 1817, of the 60th Rifles, married 26 May, 1845, Anne daughter of F. H. Macnamara. She died in the Virgin Islands, 1858, and he died 1865.

---

7.   Female and Urn at top :—

SACRED | TO THE MEMORY OF | CHARLES LEATHEM | WHO DEPARTED THIS LIFE ON THE 8TH DAY OF AUGUST 1867 | AFTER A BRIEF ILLNESS OF EIGHT DAYS| HE WAS BORN IN IRELAND ON THE 12TH OF APRIL 1803 | AND ARRIVED IN DOMINICA ON THE 23RD OF JAN^Y 1827 | (Twelve lines. He became the largest proprietor and a leading Merchant.   Erected by his wife and children).

ALSO | IN MEMORY OF | CHARLES AUGUSTUS LEATHEM | WHO DEPARTED THIS LIFE ON THE 12TH OF DEC^R 1854, AGED 14 DAYS | AND FANNIE THOMASINE, | WHO DEPARTED THIS LIFE ON THE 10TH OF MARCH, 1855, AGED 2 YEARS AND 9 MONTHS | THE BELOVED INFANTS OF | CHARLES AND ROSABELLA LEATHEM.

Below is Crest : *An eagle's head between two wings.*
    Arms : *A cross.*
    Motto : MAINTIEN LE DROIT.

1839, Oct. 22.   Charles Leathem of this P., bach., and Rosabella Humphrys of this P., spr.   L. in the presence of Nathl M. Humphrys, &c.

1840, Nov. 5.   Bap. Charlotte Elizabeth (born 16th Aug^t) daughter of Charles and Rosabella Leathem.   Roseau.   Merchant.

1867, Aug. 9.   Charles Leathem.   Roseau.   65 years.   (Bur. Reg.)

---

8. Below No. 7 :—

Above is Crest : *A boar's head erased over Wreath and Helmet.*

Arms : *Three boar's heads erased within a bordure engrailed Or*, impaling, Quarterly 1 and 4 *Azure, a lion rampant* (? Windle) ; 2 & 3 *Argent, a double-headed eagle displayed within a bordure Gules.* (Maxwell of Monreith Co. Wigtown, bart.)

Motto : CORDA SERATA PANDO.

SACRED TO THE MEMORY OF

THE HONORABLE JAMES POTTER LOCKHART,

PRESIDENT OF THE COUNCIL OF THIS ISLAND,
WHO DIED ON THE 22ND OF OCTOBER, 1837,
AGED 62 YEARS.

(Nine lines. He administered the government four times. Erected by the widow).

1837, Oct. 23.   The Hon. James Potter Lockhart.   Geneva Estate.   Sixty-five years.   (Bur. Regr.).

Sarah, wife of the Hon. Jas. Potter Lockhart d. 19 June, 1807 aged 31. M.I. at Montserrat.

John Dyer Lockhart, Esq., of Dominica, d. 15 Sept., 1809 ages 30, M.I. at Marylebone. (*Caribbeana* I., 227).

1811, Nov. 15.   At St. Andrew's, Holborn, James Potter Lockhart, Member of His Majesty's Council in the Island of Dominica, to Jane, eldest dau. of Tho. Windle, John st., Bedford row* (*Gent. Mag.*)

1813, Oct. 15.   At Dominica the wife of the Hon. James Potter Lockhart, a dau. (*Ibid.* 498).

1828, July 14.   At Plymouth, Dr. Wm. Bremner, late of Dominica. (*Ib.* 92)

1837, Oct. 22.   In Dominica, James Potter Lockhart many years senior member of H.M. Council, and late President of that island. (*Ib.* 1838, p. 222).

MARRIAGES AT ST. GEORGES, DOMINICA.

1843, Feb. 2.   Richard Hooton Lockhart of St. Patrick's Parish, bach. and Susanna Brackenbury of St. Patrick's, spinster. Lic.

1843, May 18.   Edward Lockhart of St. Patrick's Parish, bach. and Louisa Cumberland of this Parish, spinster. Lic.

1845, Dec. 9.   William Thomas Bremner Esquire, of this Parish, bachelor and Cora Lockhart of this Parish, spinster, by Licence.

1850, Sept. 18.   Edward Lockhart, widower, Coroner of the Island of Dominica, and Julia Matilda Woodcock, spr. Lic.

1880, July 3.   John Kemyss George Thomas Spencer Churchill, Bach., and Edith Maxwell Lockhart, spr. B. by Bishop Branch in the presence of J. M. Lockhart, A. W. Lockhart.

He was second son of Lord Charles Churchill, born 27 Dec. 1835, sometime President of Dominica, and died a few months ago. She was daughter of Edward Lockhart of Geneva estate.

———

9.   To the north of the west door :—

IN MEMORY OF

THE HONORABLE JOHN IMRAY, M.D.

BORN IN FORFARSHIRE SCOTLAND JANUARY 11TH 1811
DIED AT ST. AROMENT, DOMINICA, AUGUST 22ND, 1880,
THE DECEASED LEFT SCOTLAND IN 1832 AND ARRIVED
IN DOMINICA TOWARDS THE CLOSE OF THAT YEAR.

(Eight lines. Erected by W. Macintyre and W. Stedman his friends).

———

* and grandson of Alex[r]. Maxwell of Jamaica, Merchant who d. in 1797. (Note by Mrs. Sainthill).

He took the lead in establishing the cultivation of limes. St. Aroment the property and residence of the late Sir Henry A. A. Nicholls, C.M.G., is a charming spot on a bluff above the Roseau valley.

---

10.   Below No. 9 :—

I.H.S. | SACRED TO THE MEMORY | OF | BARBARA MURRAY MACGREGOR HORT, | WIFE OF HIS EXCELLENCY MAJOR HORT, | LIEUTENANT GOVERNOR OF THIS ISLAND | WHO | IN THE 34TH YEAR OF HIS AGE | WAS CALLED FROM THIS WORLD | ON THE 16TH OF AUGUST 1841.

She was buried 17 August, 1841.   See her tomb in the Churchyard, No. 19.
1841, Aug. 16.   At the Government House, Dominica, Barbara, wife of H. E. Major Hort, of the 81st Reg.   Lt. Gov. of the Island.   (*Gent. Mag.* 558).

---

11.   SACRED TO THE MEMORY OF THE LATE
ALEXANDER ROBINSON, ESQUIRE,
A MEMBER OF HIS MAJESTY'S COUNCIL OF DOMINICA,
WHO DEPARTED THIS LIFE ON THE 4TH DAY OF SEPTEMBER, 1839,
AT THE AGE OF 53 YEARS.
35 OF WHICH (WITH A FEW SHORT INTERVALS) WERE SPENT IN THIS ISLAND
WHERE HE ABLY DISCHARGED HIS DUTY IN PRIVATE LIFE
IN BOTH HOUSES OF THE LEGISLATURE
AND IN ACTION AGAINST THE FRENCH IN FEBRUARY, 1805.
WHEN SERVING IN THE ST GEORGES REGIMENT
OF MILITIA.
(Five lines.   Erected by his Brother, Skeffington Robinson, Esq., of London).

1839, Sept. 5.   Alexander Robinson.   Member of H.M. Council.   Rosalie Estate.   Fifty-six years.   (Bur. Reg).

On the north wall of Nave are four tablets :—

12.   TO THE MEMORY OF
WILLIAM FREDERICK SCOTT NICOLAY,
ELDEST SON OF HIS EXCELLENCY MAJOR-GENERAL NICOLAY, C.B.
GOVERNOR OF THIS COLONY.
HE WAS BORN THE 11TH OF JUNE, 1813
AND DIED ON THE 7TH OF SEPTEMBER, 1826.
HE WAS " *CUT DOWN LIKE A FLOWER.*"
ALSO IN MEMORY OF HIS AFFECTIONATE FRIEND
JOHN KER,
LIEUTENANT IN THE CORPS OF ROYAL ENGINEERS
WHO AT THE PREMATURE AGE OF 31 YEARS.
THOUGH OLD IN VIRTUES, WAS UNITED WITH HIM IN DEATH
ON THE 1ST OF OCTOBER, 1826.

1826, Sept. 7.   William Frederick Scott Nicolay, eldest son of Governor Nicolay, Roseau.   13 years and 2 Months.
1826, Oct. 2.   John Ker, Lieutenant in the Royal Engineers.   King's Hill, attached to the Garrison of Morne Bruce.   31 years.   (Bur. Reg.).
See " D.N.B." for notice of Sir Wm. Nicolay, Gov. of Dominica, Ap. 1824 to July 1831, of the Leeward I., 1831-2, Mauritius 1832-40. See *N. & Q.* 11s. IV, 407.

13. Below No. 12 :—

Crest : *A stag statant, guardant.*
Arms : *Argent, a chevron between three stags statant, guardant.*
Motto : QUALIS AB INCEPTO.

SACRED TO THE LAMENTED MEMORY OF
WILLIAM ROBINSON, EsQ^{RE}
WHO IN THE FORTIETH YEAR
OF AN HONORABLE AND USEFUL LIFE
IS SUPPOSED TO HAVE PERISHED IN THE BAY OF BISCAY
ON BOARD THE ENGLISH SHIP BROOKE
THE 12TH DECEMBER, 1821.
NO TIDINGS HAVING EVER BEEN RECEIVED
OF HIS MELANCHOLY FATE.

---

14. Above are a cannon, &c.

I.H.S. | SACRED TO THE MEMORY OF |
JOHN LONGLEY, ESQ^{RE}
MAJOR ROYAL ARTILLERY, LIEU^T GOVERNOR OF DOMINICA

(Seventeen lines. Died of fever one month after arriving at the time of apprenticeship to Freedom, and left a widow).
HE WAS BORN APRIL 23RD 1786. HE DIED AUGUST 5TH 1838

1838, Aug. 6. Major John Longley, R.A., Lieut. Governor of the Island Roseau. About fifty-four years. (Bur. Reg.)

1838, Aug. 5. At Dominica, Major John Longley, the newly arrived Lt. Gov. of that Island. (*Gent. Mag.* 566).

---

15. Below No. 14 :—

Crest : *A hand couped erect holding a dagger.*
Motto : LA VERTU EST LA SEULE NOBLESSE.

SACRED TO THE MEMORY OF
THE HON^{BLE} ## JAMES BROWN, M.D.
ONE OF HIS MAJESTY'S COUNCIL OF THIS ISLAND
WHO DEPARTED THIS LIFE JANUARY THE 26TH 1824
IN THE 42ND YEAR OF HIS AGE.

(Eight lines. Erected by his widow, Russel Brown).

---

16. On Chancel floor :—

I.H.S. | BENEATH THIS STONE
ARE DEPOSITED THE REMAINS OF
GEORGINA,
WIFE OF S. W. BLACKALL, ESQ.
L^T GOVERNOR OF THIS ISLAND,
WHO AFTER A SHORT RESIDENCE OF FIVE MONTHS
WAS CARRIED OFF BY THE PREVAILING EPIDEMIC
ON .THE 2ND MAY 1853,
AGED 39.

1853, May 4. Georgina Blackall wife of his Excellency S. W. Blackall Esqr Lieut-Govn^r. Government House, Roseau. 39 years. (Bur. Reg.).

17.   Chancel.   Stained-glass windows :—

In Memory of William Stedman.   Born 11th July, 1825.   Died 15th Aug., 1900.

In Memory of Hunter Stedman.   Born 20th December, 1812.   Died 2nd September, 1900, and of Marion his wife.   Born 11th May, 1816.   Died 25th August, 1898.

1844, Nov. 26.   Hunter Stedman of this P., bach., and Marion Taylor, spr. Lic.   (Mar. Reg.).

———

18.   Brass.   North wall of Chancel apse within the Communion Rails :—

IN EVER LOVING REMEMBRANCE OF
ELIZA ANN STEDMAN
WHO ENTERED INTO REST
NOV. 25 1889, AGED 70
THIS WINDOW OVER THE ALTAR HAS BEEN PLACED
BY HER DAUGHTER JESSIE.

———

CHURCH-YARD.

The Churchyard is small and has been used for very few burials.

19.   On the north side is a large vault within iron railing, on a white marble ledger :—

I. H. S.
BENEATH
ARE DEPOSITED THE REMAINS
OF BARBARA
MURRAY MACGREGOR HORT
WIFE OF HIS EXCELLENCY
MAJOR HORT
LIEUTENANT GOVERNOR OF
THIS ISLAND
SHE WAS REMOVED FROM THIS
WORLD HONOURED AND BELOVED
ON THE 16TH DAY OF AUGUST 1841
AT THE AGE OF 33.

———

20.   On a cross within railing :—

REV. W. T. ROPER, 5TH NOV., 1870.

———

21.   Aberdeen granite Cross within low iron railing on Curb :—

JOHN IMRAY, M.D.
BORN 11TH JANUARY, 1811
DIED 22ND AUGUST, 1880

———

22.   Granite tomb with Cross inserted.   Around the edge :—

ANNA MEADE THE BELOVED WIFE OF PRESIDENT ELDRIDGE DIED 17TH JUNE 1874.

Chas. Monroe Eldridge, Member of Assembly for St. John's, Antigua, 1852-63, and Member of Executive Council, 1863.   President of Dominica 1872 and 1882. Of St. Kitts, 1883.

1827, Aug. 4. Richard B. Eldridge and Harriot Branch of the p. of St. John's in the Island of Antigua by Lic.

In St. John's churchyard is the tomb of Tryphena, wife of Rd. Burroughs E., who died 24 Jan. 1826 aged 29. He was born 30 March, 1795, and died 13 Sept., 1852, aged 57 (*Antigua* III., 375).

---

23. White marble Cross against north wall of Chancel :—

MURIEL LOUISA FREDERICK | DAUGHTER OF | LIEUTENANT GOVERNOR | AND M^{RS} FREELING | BORN DEC. 20, DIED DEC. 28, 1870.

Sir Sanford Freeling, K.C.M.G., Capt. R.A. 1854, Lt. Gov. Dominica 1868, Lt. Gov. Grenada 1871, Gov. Trinidad 1880.

24.

SACRED
To the Memory of
CAPTAIN JOHN HALL
who departed this life 29th October
1804 Aged 6* Years.

---

25. Ledger in fragments :—

Anne Elizabeth Mackay Wife of
Mr Wm Mackay Born the 7th Aug^t
1766. Married the 29th July 1783, and
departed this life . . . .
1793 Aged. . . . .

26.

To the Memory of
Captn THOMAS SKOTTOWE
late of the 46th Regiment
who departed this Life
at *Morne Bruce Dominica*
on the 18th Day of July 1804
Aged 29 Years (3 lines)

At Morne Bruce are the old barracks now disused.

See *N. & Q.* 11S. x. 389 for inquiry about Tho. Skottowe, colonial secretary of South Carolina at the Rebellion.

---

27. Small white marble slab. The left-hand portion of the first four lines is worn away :—

. . . . . TO THE MEMORY
OF
. . . . . .AR INFANTS
. . . . . .E AND MARY
(blank)   A.D.
(blank)   1838

---

* crack.

BURIAL GROUND AT THE SAVANNAH, ROSEAU.

This is situated on a slope above an open square of grass land or common, at one time the centre of the old English quarter, about half a mile from the Church on the road to Wallhouse.

In *Porter's Views of the Island* published in 1849 is a drawing of it. The enclosure is walled in with good entrance gates and is well kept.

28. Sarcophagus within iron railing. At the west end on white marble :—

SACRED TO THE MEMORY OF
Mᴿ JAMES DALRYMPLE
WHO WAS CUT OFF
BY A MALIGNANT FEVER
ON THE 24ᵀᴴ OF SEPTEMBER 1821
AGED 25 YEARS.

---

29.   White marble :—

SACRED
TO THE MEMORY OF
Mᴿˢ MARY SISSON,
THE BELOVED AND DEVOTED WIFE OF
Mᴿ ANDREW SISSON *SURGEON,*
OF THIS ISLAND,
AND DAUGHTER OF
THOMAS AND ANN NEALE,
OF RIEGATE, (*sic.*)
IN THE COUNTY OF SURREY, ENGLAND ;
WHO FELL A VICTIM
TO THE YELLOW FEVER
ON THE 24ᵀᴴ OF AUGUST 1841,
FIVE MONTHS AFTER HER ARRIVAL
AGED 31 YEARS.

1841, Aug. 25.   Mary Sisson wife of Dr. Sisson, Roseau.   Thirty-one years. (Burial Register).

1841, Aug. 24.   At Roseau, Dominica, Mary, wife of A. Sisson, 3rd dau. of T. Neale, of Reigate, Surrey (*Gent. Mag.* 558).

---

30.   Sarcophagus (like No. 5) within iron railing.   At west end :—

SACRED TO THE MEMORY OF
Mᴿ THOMAS DALRYMPLE,
WHO BEING ATTACKED WITH FEVER
ON HIS PASSAGE
FROM Sᵀ BARTHOLOMEWS
ONLY SURVIVED TO ALLOW
HIS AFFLICTED FRIENDS
THE MOURNFUL SATISFACTION
OF SOOTHING HIS LAST
MOMENTS
HE DIED JUSTLY AND DEEPLY
LAMENTED
ON THE 11ᵀᴴ OF JUNE 1820
AGED 19 YEARS.

31. Stone slab over stone vault, within iron railing :—

DOMINICA
JOHN GREENWAY
SON OF
JOSEPH AND MARGARET GREENWAY
OF THE ISLAND OF *ANTIGUA*
WAS MARRIED TO MARGARET WARDROBE
DAUGHTER OF
DAVID AND JEAN WARDROBE
OF THE CITY OF *DINBURGH
ON THE 28ᵀᴴ DAY OF APRIL, 1788
MARGARET GREENWAY
WIFE OF JOHN GREENWAY DIED IN *ROSEAU*
ON THE 6ᵀᴴ OF MAY 1811

(Ten lines. Placed by husband).

He was baptised 3 June, 1760, see pedigree in *Antigua*, II., 36.

1828, Nov. 11. At Rosseau, Dominica, aged 69, Dr. John Greenway, one of the oldest inhabitants of that Colony, in which he had been a resident for upwards of 40 years (*Gent. Mag.* for 1829 p. 190).

---

32. White marble panel, urn above. Brick-work broken :—

FRANCES CAROLINE GRANVILLE
died Auguſt the 27ᵗʰ 1802,
Aged 17 Years.

33.

To the Memory | of |
C. W. Glanville Barrister at law
Died 16ᵗʰ of May 1825†
Aged 32 Years and 1 month.

(Four lines. By Widow and Children).

1831, Ap. 21. John Francis Pennington, Esquire, of St. Michael's, Barbados and Mary Glanville, spinster of St. George's by Lic.

1840, Feb. 6. Henry John Glanville of this Parish, widower and Eliz. Frances Righton of this P. spr. Lic.

1843, June 6. William Redhead of this P. bach. and Frances Glanville of this P. spr. Lic.

1847, Oct. 21. Henry Francis Glanville bach. and Elizabeth Martha Lloyd, spr. Lic.

The Glanvilles of Antigua appear to have disappeared about 1760. Perhaps one of them removed to Dominica.

1840. Mr. J. Glanville who married a dau., since dead, of Mr. Audains. Letter from Dominica. (*Caribbeana* I., 367).

---

* Oblong piece of stone cut out.

† 5 has been altered to 6. He is often named in the Chancery Minute Book, but I did not find his burial in the years 1825 or 1826 in Register.

34.   Up the hill.   Headstone within iron railing.

Sacred to the Memory | of
JOHN TENCH ESQ^{RE}
DEPUTY COMM^Y GEN^L
IN HER MAJESTY'S FORCES
BORN IN CHESTER
ENGLAND,
ON THE 21ST DECEMBER 1780
DIED AT DOMINICA
ON THE 13TH JANUARY 1857,
AGED 76 YEARS.

The burial entry has " Half Pay."

---

35.   Headstone within iron railing :—

IN MEMORY OF
THEODORE LEONARD
AND
JOHN MACFARLANE
SONS OF
THOMAS DAVID TENCH
MANAGER OF THE COLONIAL BANK, DOMINICA
BOTH OF WHOM DIED IN OCTOBER 1861 ;
THE FORMER ON THE 16TH AGED 12 YEARS.
AND THE LATTER ON THE 25TH AGED 15½ YEARS.
HIS ELDEST DAUGHTER
WHO DIED AT THE SAME PERIOD
LIES BURIED IN AN ADJOINING GRAVE

---

36.   White marble Cross within iron railing.

EMILY BLANCHE TENCH
Died January 10th 1881.
Aged | 22

---

37.   Slab of slate nearly all flaked away.
" Physic " and " 1798 " are legible and remains of eight lines of eulogy.

---

38.   Thomas Sebastinano Santorello
departed this life 22nd Septr 1804
Aged 15 Years and 10 Months.

---

39.   White marble Cross within iron railing roofed.

In | MEMORY OF | JESSIE MADELEINE HILL | WIFE OF CHARLES
HERBERT HILL | DIED 14TH JANUARY, 1911 |.

40.

To the Memory of
EDWARD HOLMES,
of Roseau, Dominica, Merchant
who died Septr 18th 1822
Aged *35 Years.

---

41. White marble headstone :—

ERECTED | BY | HIS BROTHER OFFICERS | TO THE MEMORY | OF | RICHARD
T. N. PEARCE | STAFF COMMANDER R.N. | WHO DIED ON BOARD | H.M.S. NORTH-
AMPTON | DECEMBER 20 A.D. 1882 |.

---

42. High up the hill :—

SACRED
TO THE MEMORY OF
JAMES INFANT SON AND OF
MARGARET
THE BELOVED WIFE OF
GEO. CHA. FALCONER ESQ^{RE}
WHO DEPARTED THIS LIFE
THE FORMER ON THE 27TH DAY
OF JUNE 1817 AGED 8 MONTHS.
AND 17 DAYS
AND THE LATTER ON THE 9TH
DAY OF AUGUST 1819
AGED 29 YEARS.

---

43. White marble headstone and vault within iron railing, near the top
boundary wall :—

IN LOVING MEMORY | TO ENID SIEBEL, | DIED 12TH APRIL 1882, | AGED
4 YEARS | HER FATHER, F. S. FADELLE

---

44. At the west end of the above vault :—

Sacred | TO THE MEMORY OF | MARY EMILY FADELLE, | BORN 6TH
JANUARY 1810 | DIED 10TH AUGUST 1864 |

(Erected by husband, Provost Marshal of the Island, married life 31 years).

Mr. Frederick Sterns Fadelle, B.A., resides at Cliff House, Roseau.
1833, July 17.   Joseph Fadelle, Bach. of this P. Clerk in the Treasurer's
Office, and Marie Emilie Dupigny, spr., of St. Mark's P. by Banns.
The above two are to the East of the main grass track running diagonally
up and across the ground.

Many stone and brick vaults have lost their slabs.

---

*Or 85

To the west of the above path are the following :—

On a white marble slab.

45.   Here lie the Remains of
                  HENRY DAVID WATT
            He died the 30th Jany 1801, aged 49.

---

46.   *JOHN POWELL, Efq^r*
                  Died 25th February, 1797
                        Aged 45.

1809, Nov. 3.   Thursday last was married, at St. Augustine's Bristol, Geo. Protheroe, esq. of that city, to Sarah, youngest dau. of the late John Powell, esq. of the Island of Dominica.   (*Dorchester & Sherborne Journal*).

---

47.   SACRED
                 TO THE MEMORY OF .
              THOMAS HENDERSON, Esq^n
           WHO DIED ON THE 10TH OF AUGUST
                        1816
             IN THE 42 YEAR OF HIS AGE.
         HE WAS FOR MANY YEARS A MEMBER
          OF THE HOUSE OF ASSEMBLY AND
           A MAGISTRATE OF THE *ISLAND*
                  OF DOMINICA.
            (Six lines.   Erected by Widow).

1822, April 5.   At Little Heath, near Woolwich, Mrs. Jane Henderson, relict of Thos. Henderson, esq. of Dominica.   Mr. Henderson was nephew of Mr. Laing. (*Gent. Mag.* 380).

---

48.   Foot-stone with " J. B. 1826," rests against No. 47.

---

49.   White marble slab within iron railing :—
               Sacreᵭ | to the Memory of |
                 JOHN LAING *Efquire.*

          He departed this Life on the 29th Augt 1808
                in the 29th Year of his Age
                        and has
            left a Widow, and four female Infants
                    to deplore his lofs.

1808, Aug. 30.   At Dominica, John Laing, esq.   (*Gent. Mag.* 1126).
1816, March 8.   Aged 61, Mrs. Eliza Laing, wife of James Laing esq., of Streatham-hill, Surrey, &c.   (*Ib.* 473).
1830, Aug. 28.   At Stonehouse Chapel, Devon, Assistant Com. Gen. John Lindsay, to Maria Lucas, 2nd dau. of the late John Laing, esq. of Dominica. (*Ib.* 270).

1853, Feb. 22. At St. Luke's, Jersey, aged 75, Maria, relict of John L., late of Dominica and Haddo, N.B. (*Gent. Mag.* 452).

Jas. Laing and Chas. Coleman Laing. (*West Indies Book-plates* Nos. 251 & 252).

Allan Stewart Laing, s. of James Laing of Dominica, esq. Trin. Coll. Oxf. matric. 26 Oct., 1805, a. 17, B.A. 1809, M.A. 1812, bar-at-l. Mid. T. 1812, a police magistrate at Hatton Garden, d. 12 Feb., 1862. (*Foster*).

"*Sketches and Recollections of the West Indies*" 1828, was dedicated to James Laing of Streatham Hill formerly of Dominica.

Sundry Accounts of the Estate of the late John Laing and Mrs. Mary Laing, with James Laing, from 1812 to 1828, and of Margaret Fry, of Stonehouse, in the county of Devon, and Dominica ; the whole nicely written in a book, folio, 10 pages, on 7 July, 1828. (*Coleman's Catalogue*).

---

50. White marble tomb within iron railing :—

IN MEMORY OF | CHARLES LEATHEM, | WHO DEPARTED THIS LIFE ON THE 8TH DAY OF AUGUST 1867, | AGED 64 YEARS | ALSO OF CHARLES AUGUSTUS AGED 14 DAYS | AND FANNIE THOMASINE, AGED 2 YEARS AND 9 MONTHS | BOTH THE BELOVED CHILDREN OF THE ABOVE-NAMED |.

---

51. White marble slab :—

SACRED TO THE MEMORY OF
MRS DUGALD STEWART LAIDLAW
WHO DEPARTED THIS LIFE
ON THE 24TH DAY OF JANUARY 1830,
IN THE 22ND YEAR OF HER AGE

(Seventeen lines. A few weeks after her marriage. Placed by husband).

1829, Dec. 10. The Honorable Dugald Stewart Laidlaw of this P. and Henrietta D'Anglebermes of St. Patrick's by Lic.

1830, Jan. 25. Henrietta Laidlaw, wife of ye Hon'ble Dugald Laidlaw, Goodwill Estate, 24 years.

1838, July 17. At St. Christopher, the Hon. Dugald Stewart Laidlaw, of Dominica to Meta-Jane, eldest dau. of Henry Trew, Collector of His Majesty's Customs. (*Gent. Mag.* 542).

---

52. Headstone :—

Sacred
TO THE MEMORY OF
CAPTN JAMES BROWN
LATE OF THE PETER PROCTOR
WHO DIED JULY 25TH 1826
AGED 31 YEARS.

1826, July 26. James Brown free Man of Color. R. 34 years. (Bur. Reg.)

---

53. Small slab :—

TO THE MEMORY | of |
LOUISA LOCKHART WHO
DIED ON THE
5TH OF AUGUST, 1843.
(Three lines by husband).

1843, Aug. 6. Louisa Lockhart. Geneva Estate. About thirty-two years. (Bur. Reg.)

1843, Aug. 5. In Dominica, Louisa, wife of Edward Lockhart. (*Gent. Mag.* 446).

---

54. Granite Runic Cross :—

IN LOVING MEMORY OF | WILLIAM POTTS REES WILLIAMS, | BORN IN CARNARVON, NORTH WALES | 29TH SEPT. 1853 | ENTERED INTO REST 19TH JUNE, 1910 | FOR 29 YEARS | MEDICAL OFFICER IN DOMINICA. (One line. Erected by friends).

---

55. Headstone :—

M.I.T. | Septr 11 | 1826 |.

1826, Sept. 11. Margaret Isabella Tulloh. R. 23 years (Bur. Reg).

1823, July 12. At Dominica after an illness of only three days, aged 21, Henry Bowyer Tulloh, esq. Colonial Secretary in the above island, and second son of Lieut.-Col. Tulloh, of the R.A. (*Gent. Mag.* 647).

1826, Sept. 11. In Dominica aged 22, Margaret-Isabella, wife of Lieut. Alex. Tulloh, of his M.R. reg. of Artillery, and dau. of the Hon. Wm. Bremner, President of H.M. Council of that Island. (*Ib.* 574).

56.

To the Memory of
JOHN WEIR VERE Efqr
of the City of *GLASGOW*
NORTH BRITAIN
Late his Majefty's Commiffary
of Stores in the ISLAND of DOMINICA
Born May 19th 1737
Died Febry 23rd 1789

1779, April. John Vere, Esq ; commissary gen. of his majesty's stores, at Dominica. (*Town & Country Mag.* 336). His will was proved in 1779 (331 *Warburton*) so that the year 1789 on the stone must be an error. He left a daughter Eliz. who married Hallen Bowman, Esq., and was living a widow in Glasgow in 1795, the date of the will of her aunt Eliz. Sherwood, formerly of Antigua last of Glasgow. Wm. Weir was Commissary of St. Vincent and had issue Tho. Capt. in the 60th regiment and Eliz. Walker.

---

57. Above is a female weeping over urn :—

Sacred
to the memory of
Capt GEORGE CUNNINGHAM
who departed this life the 10th
February in the year of our
Lord 1817 aged 43 years.

1817, Feb. 18. At Dominica, Capt. George Cunningham. (*Barbados Mercury*).

58.

Here rest the Remains of
HENRY GROVE Esq[R]
A Gentleman, who served many years
In the Army with a distinguished
Character Respected by his Superiors,
beloved by his Brother Officers, and
esteemed by the whole Corps. After a
general Peace being appointed Collector
of the Customs in this ISLAND He executed
that Office till the time of his Death which
happen'd the 22nd Day of February, 1788
(Nine lines. Ætat 48).

---

59. Headstone :—

Sacred
To the Memory of
ARISTARCHUS RUDOLPH
A Native of Lunenburg
Nova Scotia
who died 27th May 1837
Aged 21 Years.

1837, May 27. Aristarchus Rudolf native of Nova Scotia. Eighteen years. (Bur. Reg.)

---

60. Ledger cracked below the Monumental Inscription :—

. . . . . . Body of the late ·   (indistinct)
. . . . .JOHN CULPEPER
. . . . . this Life the 23 . . . . . .
. . . . . .1803 Aged . . .6 Years   (? 36 or 56)

1837, Dec. 20. Mrs. Elizabeth Culpeper of the Needsmust Estate St. Paul's Parish. About eighty years. (Bur. Reg.)

There was a family of this surname in Barbados.

---

61. Ledger on vault under a tree :—

Sacred to the Memory of
. . . . SUSANNA COLLINS
who departed this Life 19th Feb. 1800
In the 49th Year of her Age

(Several lines follow on which mortar has been mixed).

---

62. White marble headstone :—

HERE RESTS ALL THAT WAS MORTAL OF
THE Hon[BLE] BENOIT BELLOT,
DIED 29TH AUGUST 1880,
AGED 66 YEARS
(Six lines. A Wesleyan 40 years.)
ALSO THE REMAINS OF FREDERICK
HIS ELDEST SON
WHO DIED IN 1854 AGED 18 YEARS.

63.   Vault :—   " A A"   deeply cut.

---

64.   Large grave curbed.   Upright stone :—

Motto above : CUNCTA MEA MECUM—
Crest : *An anchor cabled.*
Arms : *Argent, a fess Vert. between two snails in their shells in chief and in base a thistle.*

3n Memory of

MARGARET LŒTITIA STEDMAN,
BORN 27 Decr 1843.   DIED 25 Jany 1845
HUNTER BURGOYNE STEDMAN,
BORN 5 June 1842,   DIED 9 Feby 1845.
ALICE IRMA THOMPSON,
BORN 16 Jan. 1852.   DIED 25 Nov. 1873
WILLIAM D. D. STEDMAN,
BORN 11 Nov. 1854.   DIED 19 Sep. 1884
ALSO

JAMES STEDMAN,
BORN 22 June 1806.   DIED 9 April 1862
AND

ELIZA ANN STEDMAN,
BORN 18 Nov. 1819   DIED 25 Nov. 1889
PARENTS OF THE ABOVE.   (One line).
JAMES MACFARLANE STEDMAN,
BORN 1st Oct. 1839.   DIED 9 June 1902. | R.I.P.

1845, Jan. 26.   Margaret Lœtitia Stedman.   R.   One-year.   (Bur. Reg.)
1845, Feb. 10.   Hunter Burgoyne Stedman.   R.   Two years.
There were Stedmans in St. Croix and I think St. Kitts.

---

65.   Headstone within iron rails :—

Olivia Bascome Astwood | Died 17th July | 1826 |

1826, July 18.   Olivia Bascombe Astwood.   R.   2 Years and 9 months (Bur. Reg.)

---

66.   SACRED
TO THE MEMORY OF
CATHERINE JANE
THE BELOVED WIFE OF
GEORGE STEPHENSON ESQUIRE
WHO DEPARTED THIS LIFE
AFTER A SHORT ILLNESS OF THIRTEEN DAYS
ON THE 7TH DAY OF NOVEMBER 1850
AT THE EARLY AGE OF 25 YEARS
ALSO
IN MEMORY OF THE SAID
GEORGE STEPHENSON, ESQUIRE
WHO DEPARTED THIS LIFE ON
THE 17TH DAY OF MAY 1852
AGED 47 YEARS.

(Eight lines.   Placed by his Brother Robert).

67. Ledger :—

SACRED

TO THE MEMORY OF

WILLIAM NAPIER JOHNSTON ESQ.

A NATIVE OF GREENOCK, SCOTLAND
BUT FOR MANY YEARS A RESIDENT
PLANTER IN THIS ISLAND
WHO DEPARTED THIS LIFE
ON THE 8TH MARCH 1862,
ON HIS ESTATE MOUNT EOLUS
IN THE PARISH OF ST JOHN
AFTER ONE DAYS ILLNESS AT THE
AGE OF FIFTY YEARS.

(Two lines.   Erected by widow).   DOMINICA

On an oblong white marble panel fixed lower down with metal letters :

ALSO OF
ANNE EMMA FRANCES TRAVERNIER
ELDEST DAUGHTER OF
GILLBANK AND MARY JANE BARNES
AND GRANDDAUGHTER OF THE ABOVE
DIED AUGUST 16TH 1885
AGED 28 YEARS.

68.

To
the Memory of
AUGUSTIN GOUJON Efq^r
He died the 8 June 1775
Aged 30 Years.

---

69. White marble ledger :—

MARY LE GALL
Obit 21st March
1807

70

Here lieth the Body of
JAMES BOSTOCK
who departed this Life
the 23rd of October 1787
in the 50th Year of his Age
In Youth he travell'd many a Mile
And eaf'd his Children of much Toil

---

71. White marble headstone enclosed by low iron rails already broken :—

JOSEPH BELLOT
DIED JANUARY 1885
AGED 77 YEARS.

72. Grey marble ledger :—

> SARAH BRIDGET PRINCE DULIEU
> the wife of JOSEPH DULIEU, Eſqʳ
> of *DOMINICA*
> Married the 1ˢᵗ of December 1792,
> Died the 13ᵗʰ September, 1793,
> Aged 23 Years.

---

73. White marble headstone within iron railing :—

SACRED | *to the memory of* | ELIZABETH ADIE | *Relict of* | DAVID STEDMAN | *Born in Glasgow Scotland* | Jany 12ᵗʰ 1785 | Died in Dominica | Jany 7ᵗʰ 1872 |

---

74. The following three are on wooden crosses enclosed by a wooden fence :

> In Loving Memory of
> OUR DEAR MOTHER
> C. H. SHEW,
> DIED 8ᵀᴴ MAY 1897,
> AGED 60

75.
> IN LOVING MEMORY OF
> THOMAS WILLIAM DOYLE
> DIED 30ᵀᴴ MAY 1878 AGED 86
> ALSO
> OF RACHEL SOPHIA DOYLE
> HIS DAUGHTER
> WHO DIED 10ᵀᴴ MARCH 1884
> AGED 63   R. I. P.

76.
> IN LOVING MEMORY OF
> SUSANNAH DOYLE
> DIED 20ᵀᴴ MAY 1879 AGED 85
> ALSO
> OF OUR DEAR " AUNT MARY "
> DAUGHTER OF THE ABOVE
> WHO DIED 9ᵀᴴ NOVEMBER 1912
> AGED 78

---

77. Inscription rather faint :—

> In Memory of
> Mᴿ MARTIN WALCH
> Master Mariner of this Island
> who departed this life
> June the 6ᵗʰ 1817 aged 37 Years.

78   ‫ﬣ‬ere Lies
the remains of
Mᴿ ROBERT BUNCH
who departed this Life
the 11th April 1786
Aged 74 Years
(Twenty-two lines.   Placed by Wife).

---

79.   ‫ﬣ‬ere Lies the Body of
Mᴿˢ CATHERINE MORSON
The Wife of
JAMES MORSON Junior
Obᵗ 13ᵗʰ Octʳ 1790 aged 34 years

Jas. Morson, senior, a leading Merchant had many land transactions with Langford Lovell of Antigua and Dominica.

---

80.   The following five white marble headstones are all enclosed by one iron railing :—

In Loving Memory
OF
WILLIAM HENRY
ELDEST SON OF
WILLIAM JOHN AND JANET S. JOHNSON
BORN MAY 22ᴺᴰ 1854,
DIED JANʸ 1ˢᵀ 1894

---

81.   SACRED TO THE MEMORY OF
WILLIAM JOHN JOHNSON
WHO DIED AUGUST 5ᵀᴴ 1879
AGED 74 YEARS.
ALSO | IN MEMORY OF
ELIZABETH ADIE JOHNSON
WHO DIED IN ANTIQUA   (sic)
DECEMBER 3ᴿᴰ 1864
AGED 13 YEARS
ALSO OF
JANET SYME JOHNSON
WIFE OF W. J. JOHNSON
BORN IN GLASGOW 18ᵀᴴ OCT. 1822
DIED 30ᵀᴴ MAY 1900

---

82. WILLIAM STEDMAN | BORN | JULY 11ᵀᴴ 1825 | DIED | AUGUST 15ᵀᴴ 1900 |

---

83.   JULIAN H. ARCHER | BORN BARBADOS | SEPTEMBER 8ᵀᴴ 1847 | DIED DOMINICA | JULY 8ᵀᴴ 1906. |

84.   HUNTER STEDMAN | BORN | DECEMBER 29TH 1812 | DIED | SEPTEM-
BER 2ND 1900 | MARION TAYLOR | WIFE OF | HUNTER STEDMAN | BORN
MAY 11TH 1816 | DIED AUGUST 25TH 1898 |.

85.   Ledger :—

SACRED To The MEMORY OF | WALTER BURKE LAUDER | BORN 13TH DECR.
1838 | DIED 26TH AUGUST 1845.   AGED | 6 YEARS AND 8 MONTHS.

86.   To the Memory of | MR GEORGE FITZ-GERALD | who died the 5TH
of Auguſt 1796 | Aged 55 Years.

87.   Headstone of white marble :—

CAPTAIN | WILLIAM LEWTHAITE | DIED 7TH MAY 1858 | (Two lines.   Placed
by a sister).

1858, May 8.   William Louthwaite.   R.   46 years.

88.   Dark ledger :—

Here lieth the Body of
Captain Samuel Bedfon of
Liverpool who departed this
life 21st January 1771.   In the 37th
Year of his Age.   (Nine lines.)

89.   A coffin-shaped slab :—

IN | Memory of | MARIA | *daughter of* | WILLIAM F. STEW* | *WHO
DIED* | 21st February 1842 | Aged 25 Years |
1842, Feb. 22.   Maria Stewart.   R.   Twenty-five years.

90.   White marble headstone :—

AGNES LEWTHAITE | DIED 12TH OCTOBER 1868 |

91.   The following two white marble crosses are within one iron railing :—

𝔍𝔫 𝔏𝔬𝔳𝔦𝔫𝔤 𝔐𝔢𝔪𝔬𝔯𝔶 𝔬𝔣 | ANNA, | WIFE OF | SHOLTO   THOMAS
PEMBERTON, | BORN AUGt 20TH 1838, | DIED SEPTR 29TH 1910 |.

She was daughter of Stedman Akers Rawlins of St. Kitts.   He died at
Nevis in 1889.   (See pedigree in *Caribbeana* I., 266.)

1868, Aug. 30.   Stedman Bates son of Sholto Thomas and Anna Pemberton.
Roseau.   Chief Justice of Dominica.   Bapt.   (This page has been much repaired).

92.   IN LOVING MEMORY OF | JAMES PEMBERTON | INFANT SON OF |
JAMES F. AND GRACE | W. JOHNSON | BORN SEPTR 19TH 1902. | DIED NOVR
25TH 1902 |

Grace Vancourt daughter of above Sholto Tho. P. married 10 Ap. 1901,
Mr. J. F. Johnson a planter.

---

* flaked.

93. Ledger :—

In Memory of
Mr. WILLIAM DODDS
Who departed this Life
the 10th day of July 1793
Aged 30 Years.

---

94. Marble ledger within iron railing :—

Sacred to the Memory of
the Hon. JAMES DODDS
late Member of His Majestys Council
of this Island and Major of
the Royal St Georges Regt of Militia :
He departed this life the 10th of Nov. 1810
Aged 52 Years.

---

95. A loose headstone, the right-hand edge broken off :—

SACRED
TO THE MEMORY OF
. . ELINA MARY BEDINGFE . .
ELDEST DAUGHTER OF
FRANCIS
. . HILIP BEDINGFELD ESQR
WHO DIED
SEPTEMBER 30TH 1849
AGED 3 YEARS
ALSO OF
WILLIAM FRANCIS
BALTHAZAR BLANC
. . E TO THE ABOVE AND ELD . . .
SON OF THE HONORABLE
WILLIAM FRANCIS
BALTHAZAR BLANC

1826, March 7. William Francis Balthazar, Son of William Francis
Balthazar and of Selina Augusta Blanc. Roseau. Attorney General (Bapt.)
1843, Feb. 23. Francis Philip Bedingfeld of this P. bach. and Myra Jane
Blanc of this P. Spr by Lic.
1841, March 1. William Blanc, son of the Hon. W. Blanc, Roseau. Eighteen
years.

---

96. Long loose slab :—

SACRED
To the Memory of
HENRY *de* LONGUEVILLE
Second Son of
FRANCIS P. BEDINGFELD
Died November 12th 1815
Aged 7 Months

97.   Grey marble slab :—

> In full hopes of Bleffed Immortality
> here lieth interred the Remains of
> Mⁿ JOHN VINGS, who died the 5ᵗʰ of Febʳʸ
> Anno Domini 1797 aged 50 Years

98.   Loose panel up the hill :—

> April 6
> 1816
> Aged 50.

99.   Iron cross with glazed white china plaque :—

> IN MEMORY OF
> SAMUEL
> MERCHANT SHERIFF, M.D.
> AND
> ANN SHERIFF
> HIS WIFE   (no dates)

1839, Jan. 16.   Samuel M. Sheriff, M.D. Roseau. Forty years.   (Bur. Reg.)

1825, July 21.   Samuel Marchant Sheriff and Ann Eliza Constable both of this P. by L. with consent of Parents in presence of Daniel C., etc.

He was eldest son of Sam. Harman Sheriff of Antigua, and was born 14 Jan., 1799.

They had two sons Wm., Puisne Judge of B. Guiana 1893, and Robert, Attorney Gen. of the Leeward Islands 1892.   (See *Antigua* iii., 85).

100.   Ledger on stone vault within iron railing :—

> SACRED
> TO THE MEMORY OF
> DENIS BOWES DALY
> WHO DEPARTED THIS LIFE
> ON THE 9ᵗʰ OF FEBRUARY 1844
> AGED 35 YEARS
> (Eight lines. Placed by Widow).

1844, Feb. 9.   Dennis B. Daly Merchant, R.   About thirty-eight years. (Bur. Reg.).

There was a family of this surname in Montserrat, Barbados and British Guiana.

101.   Headstone :—

In | Memory of | JOHN CORNEY CROMPTON, | WHO DIED IN THIS ISLAND | 20 FEBRUARY 1865, AGED 46 | AS ALSO OF | HIS BELOVED WIFE | WHO DIED AT MARTINIQUE 4ᵗʰ JANʳʸ 1863 |

1844, Oct. 31.   John Corney Crompton of this P. bach. & Marianne Félicité Renault of this P. spr.   Lic.

1877, Sept. 6.   Henry Alford Nicholls of this P. Bach. & Marion Crompton of this P. spr.   Lic.

Dr. Nicholls had filled many public offices.   On retiring recently from the position of Principal Medical Officer, he was knighted, but died on 9 Feb., 1926.

102.   Inter'd here
William Son of I. & E. Sanderson
of Ulverstone who died 28th Sep^t
1791 aged 27 Years. his Father
Capt I. Sanderson loft his life
near Lytham Hall 23^d Oct^r
1766 aged 42 Years
(Seven lines. Erected by Mother and Sister).

---

103. White marble headstone within iron railing :—

Sacreƌ | TO THE MEMORY OF | JAMES M^c FADZEAN | AGED 32 |
BORN IN NEWTON ON AYR, SCOTLAND | DIED IN THIS ISLAND 2ND DEC^R 1867 |
AFTER A RESIDENCE OF TEN YEARS |

---

104. Flat stone vault with a cross on it " J.R.B. 1911."

---

105. Headstone within iron railing :—

IN | MEMORIAM | DR EDMUND M. WILSON, | OF GLASGOW, | DIED 12TH
AUG^T 1869, | AGED 22.|

---

106. Oblong narrow loose stone :—
J. W.
1833

---

107. White cross :—

ℑn | LOVING MEMORY OF | JAMES FERDINAND KIRTON | BORN 24TH
OCT. 1860, | DIED 20TH SEP. 1900.

---

108.   *SACRED*
TO THE MEMORY OF
LIEUT COLONEL EMES
OF THE 5TH REGIMENT
COMMANDANT OF THIS
ISLAND
DIED 11TH NOVEMBER 1824
AGED 50 YEARS

---

109.   SACRED
To Lieu^t OLIVER MILLS FRY,
of HIS MAJESTY'S 5th Reg^t of Foot,
who died in this Island
on the 7th day of February 1825,
Aged 28 Years
(Four lines. Erected by Widow).

---

110. Broken flat stone :—
SAMUEL EMLENGI*ON
Obiit January 22 5
Ætat 5 Years.
* Two letters missing owing to cracks.

111.   White marble ledger, the lower half broken off and lost :—

To the Memory of
EDWARD DOW ESQUIRE
Deputy Inspector General of Hospitals,
Aide-de-camp to the Governor,
and
Lieutenant Colonel of Militia.
who was killed by falling with his horse
over a precipice in this Island
on the 8th of April 1832.
THIS MEMORIAL IS RAISED
BY
SIR EVAN JOHN MURRAY MACGREGOR, BART.

1832, Ap. 9.   Edward Dow, Deputy Inspector General in the Medical Department H.P. Roseau.   About fifty-two years.   (Bur. Reg.).

---

112.   Thick headstone :—

DEP	COM
GENᴸ	PRICE
OBIIT	26 NOV.
	1849

There is no burial of this date.

---

113.   Large stone vault with ledger set in the top :—

SACRED | To | The Memory of Mʳˢ | Francefs Sophia Smith |
The Beloved & ever to be lamented Wife of Gaᵇˡ Smith |
Efqʳ Ordnance Storekeeper
She died the 17th of September 1814 at the early
age of 22 Years
Also of Robert their infant son whom they both
most dearly loved he died September 22nd 1814
Aged one year & eight Months

---

114.   Ledger much flaked, especially on the left edge to the 6th line from bottom :—

. . . . .TERRED
OF
. . . . S SARLE ESQUIRE
THE SPECIAL
. . . . RATES FOR DOMINICA
. . . . .IED IN THE 50TH YEAR
. . . IS AGE ON THE
. . . .TH OF MAY 1838.
ALSO
THE REMAINS OF
MARIA LONGLEY, GRAND
. . . .UGHTER OF THE SAID
. . . ARLES SARLE, ESQUIRE ;
AND DAUGHTER OF
HOWARD F. LLOYD ESQUIRE
AND EMMELINE ROGERS,
HIS WIFE WHO DIED
AGED 2½ YEARS ON THE
10TH OF SEPTEMBER 1840.

1838, May 10. Charles Sarle. Stipendiary Magistrate. Union Estate. Forty nine years.

1840, Sept. 11. Anna M. L. Lloyd. R. Three years. (Bur. Reg.)

115.

I. H. S.
SACRED TO THE MEMORY
OF
MAJOR JOHN LONGLEY
OF THE
ROYAL ARTILLLERY
LIEUTENANT GOVERNOR
OF THIS ISLAND,
WHO DIED
4 AUGUST 1838

---

116. White marble ledger :—

Here lay the remains
of
JOHN WATTLEWORTH
A NATIVE OF THE ISLE OF MAN
Obiit the 2nd of Novr 1786.

---

117. Two large stone vaults within iron rails without inscriptions.

---

118. White marble ledger cracked :—

In Memory | **of** | HENRY SECOND SON | OF | FRANCES MARTIN | AND | JOHN. B. RIGHTON | obiit 3rd April 1840 | Aged 8 Years and 8 months |

---

119. Ledger within iron rails :—

BENEATH | ARE LAID THE DEAR REMAINS | *of* | ALEXᴿ ELLIOTT TROTTER | BORN AT TIDENHAM | CHACE GLOUCESTERSHIRE | 6ᵀᴴ MAY 1829 | DIED 22ᴺᴰ AUGUST 1845 | ELDEST SON | *of* | ELIZABETH AND ALEXᴿ TROTTER, | Assᵗ Comʸ General |

---

120. White marble ledger within railing :—

SACRED TO THE MEMORY |*of* | MARIA CAMPBELL RAE JUSTICE | STEWART | Died 11ᵗʰ May 1844 Aged 42 |

(Three lines. By her husband, A. Stewart, M.D., staff surgeon).

---

121 White marble ledger within iron railing :—

SACRED | To the Memory of Gustavus H. Reilly, Esqʳ | Lieuᵗ 1ˢᵗ W.I. Regᵗ and late Fort Adjᵗ of this Garrison | Second Son of John Lushington Reily Esqʳ | *of Scarvagh, County of Down, Ireland* ; | Born Janʸ 1813, Died 29th July, **1841** |

---

122.   White marble ledger within same iron railing as No. 121. :—

TO THE MEMORY OF | LIEUTENANT | JAMES CAULFIELD GORDON, | 92ND HIGHLANDERS | WHO DIED ON THE 27TH AUGST 1841.

1841, Aug. 27.   Lieut. James Caulfield Gordon 92nd Highlanders. Morne Bruce.   About twenty-three years.   (Bur. Reg).

---

123.   Two large enclosures within iron railing—no vaults—and two curbed graves :—

---

124.   White marble cross :—

J. A. R. | " *SISTER ROPER* " | AT REST 13TH JULY 1909 | AGED 75 YEARS.

---

125.   White marble headstone within iron railing :—

IN MEMORY OF | WILLIAM REDHEAD ESQR | WHO DEPARTED THIS LIFE | ON THE 6TH DAY OF MARCH 1866 | AGED 49 YEARS | (Two lines.   By widow). ALSO | EMMELINE BAIRD | DAUGHTER OF THE ABOVE | WHO DIED 28TH JUNE, 1889 | AGED 42 YEARS.

1843, June 6.   William Redhead of this P. bach. & Frances Glanville, of this P. spr.   Lic.—Perhaps both from Antigua.

---

126.   White marble cross within white marble curb and iron railing :—

IN | LOVING MEMORY OF | JAMES GAFFYN | WHO WAS | BORN IN | ST LUCIA | 25TH JUNE | 1825.

---

127.   White wooden cross :—

W. H. SHEW | Died 2ND Nov. 1874 | Aged 68.   (One line.   A husband and father).

---

128.   White marble headstone within iron railing :—

SACRED | TO THE MEMORY OF | ARTHUR GEORGE GELLION | WHO DEPARTED THIS LIFE | THE 25TH OF APRIL 1858 | AGED 39 YEARS | (One line.   A husband and father).

1853, May 17.   Arthur George Gellion, Bach. of the P. of St. Andrew and Susan Mulloom.   L.

---

129.   White marble cross within iron railing :—

TO THE MEMORY | (no name) | WHO DEPARTED THIS LIFE | 17 DECEMBER 1855 |

---

130.   White marble cross within a white marble curb and iron railing :—

In Loving Memory | of | WILLIAM MACINTYRE | BORN 1 JANUARY 1823, | DIED 24 FEBRUARY, 1891. |

---

131.   White marble cross within a white marble curb and iron railing :—

In Loving Memory | of | CELIA MACINTYRE | BORN 25 MARCH 1837 | DIED 19 JANUARY 1910 |

---

132. White stone cross within iron railing :—

IN MEMORY OF | FLORESCA JOHN | DEPARTED THIS LIFE | 24TH JANUARY 1891 |

133. Two white marble crosses and curbed graves within iron railing and under tin roof :—

I.H.S. | IN | MEMORIAM | EDWARD SHERRIF DAWBINEY, | DIED | 27TH | JUNE | 1895.

134. I.H.S. | IN | MEMORIAM | MARY GARDNER DAWBINEY | DIED | 30TH | DECEMBER | 1877.

135. At end of stone vault :—

H. *de* L.R.
1845.

ROMAN CATHOLIC CATHEDRAL, ROSEAU.

136. White marble ledger near the west front :—

Sous ce Marbre Repose
Guilleaume Renault Briolland
Décedé le 28 Fevrier 1769
Agé de 18 Ans
Pafsant priez pour le repos de son Ame

137. This ledger is at the west entrance and has been much walked on ; it has also been chipped with a tool to render it less slippery—

Near this Stone
rests the remains of
WILLIAM ABLART *Esq.*
Merchant of this Ifland
Also Madam ABLART
Native of this . . . .
and Wife of the above
WILLIAM . . . . *Esq*
And also beneath this Stone
. . . . remains of
J . . . . .daughter of the
above and 25 Years the
beloved Wife of the Honorable
ROBERT REID   Member of
his . . .jesty's privy Council
of this Ifland who departed
this Life on the 12th July
1813 Age. . . . .2 Years
A . . . . .Woman

W. Ablart was named in a deed of 1766.

Bur. 14 July 1813 Mrs. Jeannette Ablart wife of Hon. Rob. Reid by whom she left a dau. Anne Rose, now married to Lt.-Col. Orounk, &c. (Abbreviated translation from the French R.C. Register).

Mary Eliz. Roger Bellair wid. of the late Mr. Wm. Renault Briolland, native of the Island of Martinico, Will dated 4 Oct. 1778, My 8 children, My yr Son Norbert Renault B., Mr. Arthur Myler my son-in-law. Proved and Recorded 24 Nov. 1778. (Book of Wills p. 135).

---

138. On a white stone cracked across :—

. . . corps de | . . . FOURNIER, ECUYER ; | Habitant et Proprietaire de Morne Saint Louis, | a Couliabone, Paroisse Saint George : | Né le 15ᵉ de Novembre 1740, | décedé le 6ᵉ de Septembre 1804, Agé de 64 Ans | Bon Chretien, bon Mari, | Bon pere, et bon Ami. | Monument erigé par son respectveux Fils | Henry Didier Fournier.

Buried 7 Sept. 1804 as Jean Louis Fournier &c. son of the late Jean Baptiste Fournier De Raveniere & of Mrs. Therese Latouche &c.   (R.C. Register).

Therese Latouche widow Desravinieres Planter of the Quarter of Couliabonne & p. of St. George. Will dated 18 Sept. 1788. My eldest son Fournier Desravinieres Exor. My dau. Latouche. Sworn 29 Dec. 1788. Pp. 412—18.

Bernard Chainellon Latouche. Will dated 12 June 1789. My wife Ann Rose Fournier. My brother in law, Jⁿ Lˢ Fournier Desravinieres. Bernard Francois my son. My wife Extrix & G. Testator could not sign on account of the small pox. Sworn 20 Oct. 1789.

---

139. White marble ledger, only the upper portion remaining :—
1801 | Valentine Quin.

---

140. On another white marble ledger over the same vault :—
MARY FRANCES GLANVILLE | OB. 27ᵀᴴ MAY 1822, | AGED 8 YEARS 5 MONTHS | AND 18 DAYS.

---

141. On a ledger :—
Sacred | TO THE MEMORY OF | JUSTIN McSWINEY ESQUIRE | LIEUT COLONEL OF | THE 3ᵀ GEORGES REGIMENT | OF DOMINICA MILITIA | WHO DIED ON THE 20ᵀᴴ JANUARY | 1853 | AGED 59 YEARS | ERECTED BY HIS SORROWING WIDOW.

---

142. On a white marble cross within a curbed grave :—
HONᴮᴸᴱ THEODORE FRANCIS | LOCKHART, M.E.C. | 1812—77.

---

143. On a grey marble ledger :—
THE REMAINS OF | MARY JUDAH THE WIFE OF | LEWIS ISAAC JUDAH Efqʳ | ARE HERE INTERRED. | She Died *May* the 21ˢᵗ 1875, | in the 45ᵗʰ Year of her Age | (11 lines—Placed by her daughter Mary Ann Boland).

There are a few stones to French families but none earlier than about 1825 and I did not copy them.

Pere Moris showed me the Registers kept in his house adjoining the French R.C. Cathedral. They were in a cupboard in his library, well cared for, but there was no iron safe.

The present Register dates from 1769, and the series is complete from that year. From a note it appears that the older Register commenced in 1730, but this no longer exists.

The Father told me the Jesuits had quite recently given in to his custody, a Register from Grande Bay and this we examined together. On a loose sheet is written :—

" Second Registre des Baptemes Mariages enterremens des personnes li (bres) du quartier de la grande Baye (de) l'Isle Dominique.

Commencé en l'année mille Sept. . . . Soixante-un. Contenant 147 feuilletts." I noticed a few entries of 1737, 1738, 1759, then gap to 1780. The paper is very rotten. There was an ancient burial ground at Grande Bay where there was a Jesuit settlement.

MILITARY BURIAL GROUND, MORNE BRUCE.

This is in perfect order, grass having been sown and palm trees planted. It lies in a hollow just beyond the old barracks.

144. On a tablet in the enclosing wall :—

CONSECRATED
by the
LORD BISHOP of ANTIGUA
Jan^ry 31, 1849

---

145. On a ledger over a stone vault enclosed by iron railings :—
This is the only grave left.

SACRED To THE MEMORY
OF
ALEXANDER TROTTER
OF
TIDENHAM CHASE
GLOUCESTERSHIRE
ASSISTANT COMMISSARY GENERAL
WHO DIED
26th JANUARY 1852
AGED 60 YEARS.

---

146. On a loose head stone. Above is the badge : G.R. in the centre and around it . . . nd BATTALION 68 REGIMENT.

Erected by Qu^r Master
James Nash in Memory
of His Son Robert, who
Departed this Life the
31st of July 1801 Aged 8 Y^rs

---

147. Loose headstone (flaked in patches) a square space at the top is where some metal plate has been inserted. On the left is a Sheraton Urn festooned above with compasses and square thereon. To the right is a similar urn and thereon :

Crest : *A cubit arm holding a dart.*
Arms : *A chevron between three Towers.*

> Long Long this Stone and pointed Clay,
> Shall melt the musing Briton's Eyes.
> Oh ! vales, and wild woods shall they say
> In yonder Graves some Masons (*sic*) lies
> May each Freemason Good and true,
>   In Britains Isles be found :
> And in Remotest Regions too,
>   May love and Harmony abound,
> And all confess true Wisdom's Power
>   Till Time and Masons are no more.

148.

> The Body of Elenor Bartlet
> Daughter to George & C. . . . .en
> Bartlet, who died the 24. Feb
> 1805 Aged 3 Years.

149. Slab :—

> I. H. S.
> **here Rest**
> THE MORTAL REMAINS
> OF THE LATE
> SERJEANT BENJAMIN JONES
> 54TH REGIMENT WHO DIED
> SEPTEMBER 19TH 1848
> A . . . .* 27 Y. . . . *

150. Slab broken in two. Draped urn at top :—

> SACRED
> TO
> THE MEMORY OF
> CAPTAIN HENRY BROWN
> LATE OF THE 54TH REGIMENT
> WHO DEPARTED THIS
> LIFE ON THE 19TH SEPTEMBER
> 1849 AGED 41 YEARS.

MORNE DESMOULINS.

151. In a lime piece is a brick vault surmounted by a small square stone :—
I.H.S. | BOMBR D. MCKAY R.A. | *DIED 2nd SEPTR 1853 AGED 35 Yrs*

Dominica being very mountainous, with practically no roads across it, only halter tracks, it is probable that there are private burial grounds in distant estates, but nobody in Roseau seemed to know anything about them.

* flake.

MONTSERRAT.

This island lies 27 miles south-west from Antigua and 33 from Nevis. Its area has been variously estimated as 47 to 56 square miles, or about the same as Nevis, but no accurate survey has ever been made.

It is very mountainous with deep ravines and much wood. Little sugar is now produced, but limes have been extensively grown.

Former writers, who copied each others errors, and had little original information, have stated that the colony was settled by Sir Tho. Warner in 1632 (*Oldmixon and others*).

Col. John Cormick, a Member of Council, in his deposition of 1675-6, swore that " he is now aged 68 and has lived here 50 years," which would give the date of his arrival 1625-6.

The earliest Deputy Governor mentioned in the State Papers was Capt. Anthony Brisket, whose first commission had been signed by James, Earl of Carlisle (died March, 1636).

He writes that year " that he has come to England to carry more planters and necessaries thither, where he is erecting a church of stone and brick." In a petition of 1669, Anthony Bryskett, Junr., states that his father, by commission from the Earl of Carlisle, at his own great cost, gained from the Indians and planted the Island of Montserrat, where petitioner had a valuable estate, destroyed at the capture by the French, on 30 January, 1666.

Rochefort wrote in 1658 " what is most considerable in this Island is a very fair Church, of a delightful structure, built by the contributions of the Governor and Inhabitants. The Pulpit, the Seats, and all the Joyners and Carpenters work within it, are of the most precious and sweet-scented wood growing in the Country." (*Davies*, 19).

The first Census of 1677-8, has been printed (*Caribbeana*, II., 316), and there were then nine Companies or Divisions and one parish—St. Peter's, with a total of 1,148 men, comprising 346 English, 769 Irish, and 33 Scotch. Many Irish had been transported to the Plantations by Cromwell, and most of them seem to have been sent here ; other Papists were encouraged to also settle here, as they were not liked in the neighbouring islands.

In 1712 the French pillaged the colony a second time, the losses being sworn at £209,749.

Governor Walter Douglas wrote 5th April, 1714 about—" the distressed Ministers of Montserrat . . . . the only decent church they had was much defaced by the Enemy . . . . ye Ministers robbed of all they were masters of." (*Ibid*. III., 206, 341).

In 1782 the French captured the Island for the third and last time and it was finally restored in 1784.

There are now five parishes all with churches (which was not always the case), viz. : St. Anthony, St. Patrick, St. Peter, St. George, and St. John's, the last, I think, a new one. I have never seen any list of the plantations nor any map shewing the parish boundaries.

ST. ANTHONY'S PARISH.

Plymouth, the capital and only town is in this parish, which is situated on the south coast in an open roadstead.

The oldest public building appeared to be the prison, over the gateway of which is cut the year ' 1664.' Close by is an old powder magazine with bomb-proof stone roof; both this and the prison being probably part of the old fort which stood near to " Fort Gut." The Court House is less ancient, as when Coleridge visited the Island in 1825, there was none. The records are housed there, the top floor being used as a public library.

On rising ground, east of the town, just beyond the Gut, spanned by Houston's Bridge, stands Coco-nut Hill House, the very comfortable little boarding house* owned by Mr. Dudley Johnson, and farther on is Government House, recently built (1914) under the supervision of the Commissioner, Lt.-Col. W. B. Davidson-Houston. Some old cannon from Fort Barrington have been appropriately placed on the lawn near the edge of the cliff.

About half-a-mile west of the town one arrives at the Church and adjoining Rectory, which stand back a few hundred yards from the sea. Both structures suffered from the hurricane of 1899 which carried away their roofs. The present Rector, Canon Haynes, and his family had a marvellous escape, but the thick walls saved them. The recent hurricane in 1924, also caused much damage.

The churchyard is very extensive, having been enlarged at different periods to include all denominations.

A short distance north is St. George's Hill, at one time an important fortress, which I was told still contained a few guns, but scarcely any masonry.

ISLAND CLERGY.

The following clergy cannot be placed under their respective benefices—

Jonathan Yate Gifford went out 1 March, 1710-11.

Rev. Tho. Allen wrote in 1724 that all the records were destroyed by the French in 1712 as well as the contents of the Churches.

Rees Daly went out 18 Dec., 1735. As son of John Daly of Montserrat, esq., he matriculated from Exeter Coll., Oxf., 13 July, 1731, aged 18. (*Foster*).

Edward Gaillard went out 1 June, 1742, , as son of Lewis Gaillard of Hampstead, co. Middx., gent., he matriculated from Queen's Coll., Oxf., 17 Dec., 1734, aged 16 ; B.A. 6 March, 1738-9.

Rev. William Blair was licensed 27 Sept., and went out 18 Oct., 1750. (*Caribbeana* III., 325).

1775, Mrs. Barbara Davis, relict of the late Revd. Mr. Davis, of the Island of Montserat in America, died at Miss Dennis's in King's Bench Walks in the Inner Temple, 18 Sepr., 1775, and was buried near the Altar in St. Giles' Church, Cripplegate, 24 Sepr. following. (*Temple Church*).

Rev. Geo. Young, licensed 28 Dec., 1775, went out 26 Jan., 1776. (*Caribbeana* III., 325).

Rev. Geo. Collins went out 2 Dec., 1802.

---

* An excellent photograph of this appeared in the *West India Committee Circular*, Vol. XXX., p. 370.

RECTORS OF ST. ANTHONY.

Richard Molineux, 1678.   As son of the Rev. R. Molineux of Garsington. co. Oxford, he matriculated from. Trin. Coll., Oxf., 25 Oct., 1672, aged 16, B.A. 1676.   *(Foster)*.   The Bishop of London sent him out in 1677, and Governor Stapleton presented him in 1678.   Member of Council 1697.   Buried at St. St. Peter's 8 Oct., 1721.

David Bethun, 1712-1715 or later.   He wrote in 1712 that the French robbed him, broke the bell and burnt the books.   He may have been of St. Kitts in 1724, though the letter of this year is in a different handwriting.

James Cruickshank wrote to the Bishop of London in 1724.   He was to receive 20,000 lbs. yearly and preach every Sunday until this Island is provided with another minister.   See his affidavit of 1713 in London, attached to the will of the Hon. Wm. Irish which he copied in Montserrat and brought to England.

John Symes licensed 21 Sept., 1767.   His death announced 6 May, 1777. Had been appointed Member of Council, 3 March, 1759.

Wm. Taylor, third son of Nich. Taylor, of St. Kitts was Rector here for many years and died 22 May, 1823, aged 77 M.I. at Swanage, co. Dorset.

In the parish register of St. Pauls, Charlestown, Nevis, is the following fragmentary entry :—

1812 (later than 6 Oct) . . . .(? John) . . . . .rinn Esqr. . . . . .spinster both of the Island of Montserrat, where there is at present no Clergyman, by Licence from the now president.   Duty performed by Rev. Saml. Lyons to whom the Licence was addressed.

Rev. Benjamin Luckock, Rector of St. Anthony and St. Peter, 1825.   He preached a sermon at St. John's, Antigua on 16 Sept., 1831, which was printed 8° pp. iv. and 31.   He is therein described as Rector of St. Anthony and Rural Dean.   Another sermon preached at St. Croix on 20 April, 1834, was also printed and he is therein entitled : Minister of the English Churches of St. John and St. Paul, St. Croix.

1846, Jan. 13.   At Dorchester Place, London, the Rev. Benj. Luckock, M.A. He was for several years successively Rector of St. Anthony and Rural Dean of Montserrat and minister of the English Churches of St. John and St. Paul, St. Croix, W.I. (*Gent. Mag.* 327).

J. C. Collins.   1833-1844.   Died 25 March, 1844, aged 37.   Rector 11 years. About this time St. Partick was included.

George Henry Todd.   1846-1869.   Died 26 Oct., 1869, aged 56 .   Rector 23 years.   M.I. No. 76.

Baptist Noel Branch, 1876.   Rector.

Henry Redmayne Holme, B.A., 1876.   (? Curate).

A. D. Jamison, 1883-1889.   See No. 75 for his grave.

William Evered, 1895.

Frederick William Haynes, 1896, of St. Augustines Coll., Cant., 1887 ; ordained 1891 by Bishop Branch ; Curate of St. John's, Antigua, 1890-95 ; Canon of ditto 1906.

The present parish register commences—Baptisms 1828, Marriages 1828, Burials 1830.   Transcripts for the years 1721-1729 and 1739-1745 were printed in *Caribbeana*, I., 86, 361.

ST. ANTHONY, MONTSERRAT.

In the Church on the north wall of the Nave are four tablets :—

1. A white and grey marble tablet, which has been damaged. A cherub with trumpet formerly stood at the top.

IN MEMORY OF
WILLIAM FURLONGE,
MEMBER OF HIS MAJESTY'S COUNCIL
AND KING'S ADVOCATE
FOR THE LEEWARD ISLANDS ;
WHO DEPARTED THIS LIFE
ON THE 7TH APRIL, 1813, AGED 52 YEARS.
AND OF
ELIZABETH MARY FURLONGE,
HIS RELICT ;
WHO AFTER A LONG AND PAINFUL ILLNESS
CLOSED A LIFE OF PIETY
AND EVERY CHRISTIAN VIRTUE
ON THE 31ST OF JULY, 1823
IN THE 56TH YEAR OF HER AGE.

1813, April 7. In the Island of Montserrat, Wm. Furlonge, jun., esq., member of H.M. council for that island (*Gent. Mag* 660.). He married the only daughter of Dr. Michael Dardis and erected a monument to the latter in 1797 in the Roman Catholic burial ground in St. Patricks, which see later.

Tho. Furlonge, Esq., married Sarah Sophia, second daughter of Henry Dyett. She died 17 March, 1852, aged 71.

Michael Furlonge, Esq., of Guilford Street, later of this Island, married 22 May, 1800, at St. George's, Hanover Square, Mary Jane De Mattos. Others of the name were settled in St. Mary's Parish, Antigua in or before 1739.

————

2. Small white and black marble :—

SACRED TO THE MEMORY OF
EMMA SAUNDERS,
(THE BELOVED DAUGHTER OF RICHARD SAUNDERS ESQRE
COLLECTOR OF H.M. CUSTOMS)
WHO DEPARTED THIS LIFE ON THE 24TH FEBY 1846
IN THE 15TH YEAR OF HER AGE,
ALSO TO HENRY G. SAUNDERS, HER BROTHER
WHO DIED ON THE 16TH JULY, 1852
AGED 26 YEARS.
THIS TABLET IS ERECTED BY
A FOND AND BELOVED MOTHER.

————

3. An urn of Sheraton style with ribbon and festoon :—

HENRIETTA | CORNELIA | SKERRETT,
COADE, LONDON, 1797.

She was daughter of Edward Frye, Esq. Her husband Walter Skerrett of Montserrat, Esq., make his will 7 Aug., 1769, bequeathed her £171 a year and his estate to his son Walter. The latter was, I think, Walter Frye Skerrett of Heckfield Park, Hants, who died in 1828.

Titham Skerrett, Esq., had a lease for 15 years from 1 Jan., 1743, of a plantation at £400 a year rent from Patrick Blake, Esq., and dying was succeeded by Robert Skerrett, Esq., before 1763. Others of the name were in Antigua, from Galway.

---

4. Above is an urn on an Egyptian pedestal. On the face of this latter is a woman kneeling, weeping over an altar, on which is a spade shield with the arms painted thereon, now almost worn away. There are traces of : *Per fess Sa. and Arg. a pale counterchanged* ; impaling : ? *Vert, part of a bendlet.*

Sacred to the Memory of
THE HON^{ᴮᴸᴱ} RICHARD SYMMONS
a native of the City of Bristol,
of an ancient and respectable Family
Senior member of His Majesty's Counsel
and Collector of the Customs for this Island
who resigned a well spent life
in the active discharge of his duties on the
31st day of Decr 1820. Aged 81 Years.
(seven lines ; erected by his sister).

A copy of the above Inscription appeared in *Caribbeana* I., 46.

His sister Elizabeth m. firstly, Tho. Goodall of Bristol, b. about 1730, by whom she left descendants in Montserrat. She m. secondly, the Rev. Alex. Adams and d. 15 Oct., 1830. Will dated 9 Dec., 1820 then of Stapleton, Bristol, widow, buried in St. Paul's Church, Bristol. (Pedigree from R. H. K. Dyett).

In the north Transept are two tablets.

5. On the west wall :—

SACRED TO THE MEMORY OF
CLAUD MACKECHNIE, M.D., M.R.C.S.E..
WHO DEPARTED THIS LIFE
ON THE 15TH OF AUGUST, 1853
IN THE 34TH YEAR OF HIS AGE.
(Erected by his widow).

---

6. On the east wall :—

To the Memory of
The Honble ALEXANDER GORDON, Efq^r
President of this Ifland
and thirty Years Collector of
His Majefty's Revenue
By a Stroke of the Sun
in the Improvement of the Roads
he met his Fate
and departed this Life the 16th of June, 1790,
in the 52nd Year of his Age.
beloved and lamented,

7.   On the north wall of the Nave, near the Organ is a large urn of Sheraton style with drapery above—lower is an oblong of white marble bearing this inscription :—

THIS MONUMENTAL RECORD IS DEDICATED BY THE PIETY OF
WILLIAM LAFFOON *ESQ*ᴿ the only furviving Son of
CHARLES and MARY LAFFOON
To the Memory of his Sifter SARAH ANNE ALLEN LAFFOON,
who departed this Life the 1ᶠᵗ of June, 1772.
Alfo to the venerable Memory of MARY LAFFOON, his Mother,
who departed on the 21ᶠᵗ of June, 1773.
Alfo to the loved Memory of three Brothers, Vizᵗ
JOHN LAFFOON, who departed on the 16ᵗʰ of January, 1785.
THOMAS LAFFOON, who departed on the 1ᶠᵗ of December, 1787.
And CHARLES LAFFOON, who departed on the 11ᵗʰ of January, 1789

1785, Aug. 2.   Wm. Laffoon of St. Anthonys his bond of £8000.   Laffoon's plantation of 84 acres.   No. 3465.

---

8.   On the north wall of the Chancel, white and black marble :—

IN MEMORY OF
THE REVᴰ J. C. COLLINS
FOR THREE YEARS THE DEVOTED PASTOR
OF THE UNITED PARISHES OF Sᵀ ANTHONY
AND OF Sᵀ PATRICK IN THIS ISLAND
WHO DIED AGED 37 YEARS
ON THE 25ᵀᴴ MARCH, 1844
AT Sᵀ JOHN'S, ANTIGUA
WHITHER HE HAD GONE FOR THE PURPOSE OF
PREACHING AN ORDINATION SERMON ON THAT DAY.
HIS MORTAL REMAINS
REST IN Sᵀ JOHN'S CATHEDRAL CHURCH YARD
(Erected by Parishioners)

For his Monumental Inscription at St. John's see *Antigua* I., 176.   It is therein stated that he was Rector 11 years.

---

9.   On the south wall of the Chancel :—

SACRED | TO THE MEMORY OF | GEORGE HENRY TODD | FOR 23 YEARS THE BELOVED RECTOR OF | THESE PARISHES | WHO DIED OCTOBER 26ᵀᴴ 1869 | AGED 56 YEARS. |

---

10.   On the south wall of the Nave, east of Transept, white and black marble :—

SACRED | TO THE MEMORY OF | MARY FRANCIS AND ANN IRISH, | WHO DIED 16ᵀᴴ SEPᴿ 1866 | AGED 59 AND 54 YEARS.
(Seven lines—Erected by their only surviving Brother)

See pedigree in *Caribbeana* IV., 359.

---

11.   On the east wall of the south Transept white and black marble :—

TO THE MEMORY OF
THEIR BELOVED AFFECTIONATE &
UNIVERSALLY RESPECTED PARENTS
RICHARD DYETT
BORN SEPT^R 4TH 1775, DIED JAN^Y 11TH 1808
AGED 32 YEARS
AND FRANCES DYETT HIS WIFE
BORN NOV^R 30TH 1777, DIED AUG^T 17TH 1822
AGED 44 YEARS.
(Erected by their surviving children MARY and ANN DYETT)

12.   On west wall of the south Transept, white and black marble :—

SACRED | TO THE MEMORY OF | RICHARD WATSON YEARWOOD |
SON OF | JOHN RICHARD AND ELIZABETH ANN | YEARWOOD | OF THE ISLAND OF
BARBADOS) | WHO DEPARTED THIS LIFE OCT^R 2ND 1853 | AGED 11 YEARS, AND
6 DAYS. |

Mr. Graham Yearwood of Friendly Hall and his elder brother are both
Members of the Assembly of Barbados (1914).

13.   Chippendale white marble on south wall of the Nave :—

In vicino Cœmeterio
Molliter quiefcunt Reliquiæ
ELIZABETHÆ DANIEL :
Feminæ præcellentifsimæ,
Filiæ GEORGII WEBB,
In Infula Nevis,
Armigeri.
(Erected by her husband Edward Daniel).

Crest (carved) : *A lion rampant.*
Arms : Painted and much worn.
Quarterly 1 & 4, *Or, five barrulets, a bend Argent. 2 & 3 a lion rampant, Or.*
These arms do not appear in *Burke* under Daniel or Webb.

Josiah Webb of Stony Hill, Nevis, Esq. Will dated 20 Feb., 1767. My
niece Sarah Daniel £1200, my nephew Geo. Webbe Daniel £2500 in 3 years, my
niece Ann Daniel £1200 in 5 years and my niece Phoebe Daniel £1200 in 6 years,
all children of my late sister Elizabeth Daniel.

Nicholas Daniel appointed a Member of Council in 1743 and Edward in
1748. The latter was senior Member of Council 1764, but then residing in St.
Croix. His seat was vacated 1765, but he was re-instated 1768.

1748-9, Feb. 16.   Edward Daniel of Montserrat, Esq. and Elizabeth his
wife sell to Stapleton Dunbar of Nevis a parcel of land. (*Nevis Records* F. Vol.
III., p. 310).

Meade Daniel and Earle Daniel both Members of Council, 1760.

Meade Daniel. Will dated 17 March, 1762. Eldest son Nicholas Meade,
son William, my wife Elizabeth, my daughter Carolina. (*Montserrat Records.*
No. 2027).

Nicholas Mead Daniel d. 2 July, 1769. (*Cayon Diary*, St. Kitts)
See pedigree of Daniel in *Antigua* I., 188.

14.   On the base of the Font :—

> IN MEMORIAM MEÆ DELECTÆ FILIÆ
> LOUISA MARGARET DYETT TERTIO ÆTATIS
> ANNO OB.

Daughter of the late Richard Henry Dyett, Provost Marshal.   She died in 1884.

---

15.   On a chalice :—

MONTSERRAT, CHURCH OF Sᵀ ANTHONY | THIS CHALICE WAS PRESENTED BY THE FREE LABOURERS | OF THIS ISLAND AS A THANK-OFFERING TO GOD FOR THE | BLESSING OF FREEDOM VOUCHSAFED THEM ON THE | 1ˢᵀ AUGUST, 1838.

Plate marks of Birmingham for 1837-8.

---

16.   On the corner stone of the south aisle :—

REBUILT 1730 | ENLARGED 1893.

---

17.   On a square Sundial over the south Transept wall under the bell :—

TEMPUS VOLAT | EX DONO N. WEBB COM. SOM. ARM.

The Hon. Nath. Webb, Collector of Customs here died 1741 at Taunton, co. Somerset.   His second son Nath. Webb of the Grove plantation, baptised here in 1726, M.P. for Taunton, died in 1785.

---

18.   Stone vault.   On a stone roughly let into the centre of the top :—

TO THE MEMORY | OF JOHN | HELLEN | AND | MORRIS O'BRIEN |.

---

19.   Thick blue marble slab over stone vault :—

> In Memory | of |
> *The Hon*ᵇˡᵉ FRAˢ FARLEY, *Eſqʳ*
> one *of His Majesty's Council*
> *and*
> *Aſſiſtant Judge*
> *of*
> *Antigua*
> who Died *at Sea on the*
> 31ᶠᵗ *of March,* 1779
> Aged 60 Years.
> *This Stone is Inſcribed*
> **His Dutiful & Affectionate*
> *Daughter*
> ELINOR LAFOReY
> sic

He was son of John Farley of Antigua by Rebecca Christian his wife. Elinor his only surviving daughter married at St. John's 15 Feb., 1763, John Laforey later an Admiral and Baronet.

---

* Bush here.

20. Stone vault enclosed by iron railings :—

SACRED
TO THE MEMORY OF
GEORGE BRYAN JEFFERS Esq.
WHO DEPARTED THIS LIFE
ON THE 24 DAY OF JULY, 1841
AGED 60 YEARS.

*ST. GEORGE'S, MONTSERRAT.

1726, July 31.   John Jeffers and Sarah Bryan by Banns.
1728, Oct. 22.   Richd. Jeffers and Julian Mansfield by Banns.
1726-7, Jan. 15.   Thomas, son of John Jeffers and Sarah his wife, bap.
1729, May 25.   Eleanor, dau. of John Jeffers and Sarah his wife, bap.

It was only the poor settlers who were married by banns.

Henry Dyett, Esq., died 1804 having married Eleanor Jeffers who died March, 1834.   Aged 78.

---

21. Headstone very roughly executed :—

ELLENOR | MEERS | DEPARTED | DEC^{ER} 16 | 1769 AG^D 14 | YEARS.

---

22. Headstone :—

SACRED | TO THE MEMORY OF CAP^{TN} | JAMES PATERSON | who Departed this life MAR . . . . . . | AGED 33. . . . . .

---

23. A low stone obelisk.   On a white marbel tablet on the east side :—

TO THE MEMORY OF
MRS. SARAH LOCKHART,
WIFE OF THE HON. J^S P. LOCKHART,
OF DOMINICA.
WHO DEPARTED THIS LIFE
19TH JUNE, 1807,
AGED 31 YEARS.

1807, June 19.   At Montserrat. . . the wife of the Hon. Jas. Potter Lockhart of Dominica.   (*Gent. Mag.* 888).

1811, Nov. 15.   At St. Andrew's, Holborn, Jas. Potter Lockhart member of His Majesty's Council in the Island of Dominica, to Jane, eldest dau. of Tho. Windle, John Street, Bedford Row.

1813, Oct. 15.   At Dominica, the wife of the Hon. Jas. Potter Lockhart, a dau.   (*Ib.* 498).

1837, Oct. 22.   In Dominica, J. P. Lockhart, many years Senior Member of H.M. Council, and late President, of that Island.   (*Ibid.* for 1838, 222).

---

* From transcript in *Caribbeana* Vol. I.

24. Small white marble over cemented top of a stone vault :—

MARY ANN NIBBS
Daughter of
REV^D T. B. NIBBS
fell asleep in Jesus
December 11th, 1865.

The Rev. Tho. Barry Nibbs was a Wesleyan Minister, and died 7 Sept., 1897, aged 83. Monumental inscription in the Wesleyan Burial Ground at St. John's, Antigua. See *Ante* p. 3.

———

Four earth graves within low stone wall and wooden rails next to Lockhart, but without inscription.

———

25. Small headstone at east end of a rubble vault :—

SACRED | TO | THE MEMORY OF | ROBERT N. WOOD | who Departed this life | November 26th, 1826. Aged | (blank).

———

26. White marble ledger over stone vault with a few eighteenth century iron rails around it :—

To THE MEMORY OF
THE HONOURABLE ALEXANDE. . HO . . . .
A NATIVE OF *SCOTLAND*
WHO DURING A RESIDENCE
OF . . 8 YEARS IN THIS *ISLAND*
RENDERED HIMSELF
IN THE MEDICAL PROFESSION
EMINENTLY BENEFICIAL,
SUPPORTED IN SOCIETY A REPUTATION
HIGHLY RESPECTABLE,
AND DIED IN THE HONORABLE OFFICE
OF SPEAKER OF THE HOUSE OF ASSEMBLY
ON THE 17TH DAY OF AUGUST 1817
IN THE 80TH YEAR OF HIS AGE
AND OF MARTHA
HIS CONJUGAL ASSOCIATE
DAUGHTER OF RICHARD ILES *ESQUIRE*
WHO DEPARTED THIS LIFE
ON THE 18TH DAY OF SEPTEMBER, 1813.
AGED 77 YEARS.

1817, July 7. At Montserrat in his 80th year, Dr. Alexander Hood, Speaker of the Assembly, and 44 years a Member of that House. (*Gent. Mag.* 561).

He was Master and Examiner of the Court of Chancery and Member of the Assembly and J.P. (*Almanack of St. Kitts,* 1792).

In his will dated 18 July, 1817, he bequeathed his property to his sister Mary at Glasgow and appointed his friends Richd. Symons and Nath. Dyett Exors. (316 *Cresswell*).

1770, March 24.   Richard Iles of Montserrat, Esq., grandson and devisee of Rd. Iles Senr., Esq., recites the latter's will of 20 Sept., 1756, naming his wife Anne and his sons Wm. Tho. and Ellis.   Testator d. 28 Dec., 1759.   Anne d. in the lifetime of Rd. Iles and Wm. Iles is dead.   Quitclaim.   Registered 27 Jan., 1773.   (No. 2021).

1771, Sept. 6.   Marriage settlement between Martha Iles widow (*sic*) and Alex Hood, Surgeon.   (No. 2023).

Richard Iles matriculated from St. John's Coll., Oxf., 25 July, 1766, aged 19, was Member of Council 1774 and President 1792-8.

Edward Isles, Capt. 1st West Indies Regiment, by Christian his wife, had issue Edward Ellis Isles, Richd. Henry Oliver Isles, Wm John Isles and Tho. Augustus Isles.

Edward's sister Eliza m. Sept., 1805 at St. John's, Antigua, Richard Oliver, planter, a nephew of Tho. Oliver, Lt.-Gov. of Mass. and of Fryers Hill, Antigua.   Richard Oliver was buried 14 Nov. 1809, at St. John's, intestate.   His widow's will was dated 20 Aug., 1823.   See pedigree of Iles in *Antigua* II.

---

27.   Headstone :—

SACRED TO | THE MEMORY | OF WINIFRED |

---

28.   Stone slab over stone vault, wearing badly :—

𝕴𝖓 𝕷𝖔𝖛𝖎𝖓𝖌 𝕽𝖊𝖒𝖊𝖒𝖇𝖗𝖆𝖓𝖈𝖊 | OF | JOHN HENRY | SON OF | WILSON WATERALL | OF ROTHERHAM | ENGLAND | WHO DEPARTED THIS LIFE | ON THE | 22ND DAY OF SEPTEMBER, 1873 | AGED 26 YEARS |

---

29.   Grey granite tomb :—

JANE THE BELOVED WIFE OF
RICHARD HANNAM
DIED JANUARY 28, 1867

---

30.   Grave enclosed by a low iron rail on stone curb.

On a flat stone at the east end of the curb :—

M. SEMPER
E. M. BRAND   (no more)

Miss Elizabeth Mary Brand d. some years ago.   Her father was a planter of Antigua, manager of Betty's Hope, who m. a Miss Bird of Montserrat. (R. H. K. Dyett).

---

31.   Headstone of local work :—

TO THE MEMORY
of
ANN BRAMBLE WHO
DIED JANUARY 1811
AGED 16 YEARS

The year 1811 is doubtful.

---

32. Headstone :—

WILLIAM JEFFERS
SON of THO^S JEFFERS
DIED NOV^R 13, 1810
AGED 23 YEARS.

---

33. Small headstone close to the south wall. The dates uncertain :—

MARYE DYETT | Wife of ROB. DYETT | DIED JAN. 2 |, 1815.

---

34. On a headstone within a large space enclosed by a low stone wall :—

SACRED | TO | THE MEMORY OF | GEORGE IRISH WHO | DIED 26
1841 | AGED 39 YEARS.   See No. 10.

---

35. On an upright piece of wood in curbed grave :—

IN MEMORY | OF | ALLAN IRISH DIED 20TH DEC., 1908 | AGED 60 YEARS.

---

36. On a white marble cross at the west end of railed curb :—

CATHARINE MARY PENCHOEN 11TH FEBRUARY, 1873.
At the east end is :—K. P. PENCHOEN.

A Mr. King Pittman Penchoen is a leading planter at the present time (1914)
and correspondent of the West India Committee.

---

37. Headstone :—

This Stone
SERVES TO SHEW WHERE LIES
INTERRED THE REMAINS OF
JOHN DOBRIDGE
BORN ON THE 8TH OF SEPT^R 1830
DIED 18TH SEPTEMBER, 1831
AND
PERCY DOBRIDGE
BORN ON THE 30TH OF OCTOBER, 1832
DIED 7TH JULY, 1835
BROTHERS AND INFANT SONS
OF THE HONOURABLE
JOHN & ELIZABETH DOBRIDGE
OF THIS ISLAND.

Henry Dyett a lawyer and puisne judge of Montserrat, had a daughter
Elizabeth who married John Dobridge.   Elizabeth Dobridge married Sam.
Butler Goodall.

The name Duberry or Dubery is a very old one here.   There is a Duberys
Estate at the North of the Island and in going through the old records, I came
across a lease of Bugby Hole and Duberys from Mark Dyett as Exor of Henry
Dyett of London to Robert Dobridge.   The rent reserved was £1200 st., but up
to the present I have found no wills of Dubery or Dobridge.   (R. H. K. Dyett,
2 Sept., 1915, then Acting Commissioner of Montserrat).

38. White marble headstone at the west end of curbed grave :—

Sacred
to the Memory of
ALICIA W. CHAMBERS
who departed this life on the
16TH Oct., 1851
(Dedicated by her brother R. Piper)

39. White marble slab :—

SACRED
To the MEMORY of
SUSANNA LUTHER
who DIED Jany 10TH 1810
AGED 55 YEARS.
(Placed by her children).

Several headstones lie about without inscriptions.

40. Black marble ledger :—

Sacred to the Memory of
MRS. SARAH CHAMBERS
who departed this Life
on the 28TH day of January, 1812
Aged 85 Years
Alſo of her Son
JOHN CHAMBERS Eſquire,
who departed this Life
on the 25TH day of November 1796
Aged 48 Years.

In St. John's Churchyard Antigua is a Monumental Inscription to Tho. Chambers, Esq., of Montserrat, barrister-at-law, who died 20 July, 1828, in his 87th year leaving an only surviving child Eliza Robertson.

Charles Chambers was Member of Council 1792.

Twickenham. Will Chambers of Mountseratt, Esq., but now in England. Will dated 28 Sept., 1761 : funeral not to exceed £20. My plate and books to be sold. Before my marriage with my present wife Sarah I entered into a bond to Tho. Meade, Esq., since deceased in Trust for her then Sarah Blake for payment of £1000 c. but in lieu of this I give her one annuity of £120 st. and £100 c. immediately, her horse and jewels the use of my furniture and 2 negroes. To my Mother-in-law, Mrs. Mary Blake one annuity of £80 st. she to release all legacies and bequest of slaves under the will of her late husband John Blake, deceased, sufficient to secure annuities to be laid out in Montserrat or St. Christopher where the interest is 8 per cent., also £50 c. All residue of my estate to my friends Nich. Tuite and John Bradshaw both of London, Merchants in T. for my three sons, Thomas, John, and William at 21. My mulatto George, his freedom, he paying £100 st. To my Exors £50 c. for the poor. I appoint my Trustees, Guardians & Exors. and the Hon. John Dyer, Esq., Tho. Duberry & Tho. Dorsett Esq^rs all of Montserrat to be also Exors. 21 Sept., 1761. Codicil My wife to also have the use of any three of my house negroes, if she remain in the West Indies. My Mother-in-law to have the use of three others.

To my friend Mr. James Concannon £30 st. Nich. Tuite, £25, Mr. John Bradshaw £25. Proved 21 April, 1762 by Nich. Tuite and John Bradshaw, power reserved to the others. (143 *St. Eloy*).

41. Headstone against west wall :—

HENRY DYER

DIED FEB. 2, 1795.

The 5 is doubtful.

---

42. Yellow headstone :—

IN LOVING MEMORY OF | DIANA A. S. TUITT | WHO DEPARTED THIS LIFE | MAY 3, 1875 | AGED 40 YEARS | ERECTED BY HER DUTIFUL SON | R. BENJAMIN GARDSIDE DYETT. |

The preceding Monumental Inscriptions are to the left or south side of the walk going through the churchyard.

The following are on the north side of the ground :—

43. Headstone.

SACRED | *To The* MEMORY | OF | JOHN N. COLLINS | who died | *August 19th* 1857 | *Aged 54 Years.*

---

44. Headstone against the west wall :—

JOSEPH CORBETT | DEPARTED THIS LIFE | IN THE YEAR OF 1904 | FEB. 22 | 75 YEARS.

---

45. Headstone :—

SACRED | TO | THE | MEMORY | OF RICHARD WADE | Who | Departed this life | the 14th of October | in the year of our Lord | 1869.

---

46. Modern headstone :—

Sacred to the Memory of EDWARD J. AND ELIZA HALL | (no dates).

---

47. Sacred to the Memory | of (Right top corner broken off) ARTHUR A. AND SARAH HALL | (no dates).

---

48. Marble slab :—

SACRED TO THE MEMORY OF
ARCHIBALD BATHGATE,
FORMERLY OF FALKIRK IN SCOTLAND
AND LATE COMMANDER OF THE BRIG
ROBERT OF LONDON & MONTSERRAT
WHO DIED JUNE 18TH 1827 AGED 48 YEARS

---

49.   Black marble slab on stone vault :—

> UNDERNEATH THIS STONE
> ARE INTERRED THE REMAINS OF
> MISS ANN UNDERWOOD
> OF THIS *ISLAND*
> WHO DIED OCTOBER 25TH 1803,
> AGED 33 YEARS.

She was named as niece in the will of Henry Dyett dated 9 March 1803. Her brother Henry Iles Underwood of London, merchant and formerly of Demerara d. at Cheltenham 19 April 1818, very wealthy and single.   By his Will dated 12 May, 1815, he gave legacies to his cousins, the Dyetts, Musgraves, Duburys, and Mrs. Eliza Oliver widow of Richard Oliver, also to Miss Mary Underwood dau. of Tho. Underwood late of Montserrat, and niece of Mark Dyer, Esq., for attention to testator's late sister and made his cousins Walter Skerrett Morson and Henry Dyett joint heirs (255 *Cresswell*).

Sarah Underwood married in 1725 Richard Dyett, so the families were early connected.   In the census of 1730 Henry and George occur.

Tho. Underwood, gent., only son of John, late of Montserrat, Esq., deceased, was admitted at Lincolns Inn, 9 Oct., 1770.

Tho. Underwood of Suffolk aged 19, was admitted to Peterhouse, 17 May, 1759 ? son and heir of John and sold the advowson of Chevington the family living in 1770.   (*Admission Book of Peterhouse, Cambs.*, p. 318).

The Rev. Tho. Underwood went to Montserrat 15 Nov., 1791.   Tho. Underwood was Member of Council, 1792.

---

50.   Headstone :—

> IN MEMORY
> OF
> JOSHUA DYETT
> *Who* DIED *Octo*ʳ 19ᵀᴴ
> 1793
> AGED 7 . . . & 3 MS.

---

51.   Headstone.   The year 1803 is doubtful :—

> IN MEMORY OF
> ANN DYETT
> who DIED 3 0c 1793
> AGED   7 . . .
> AND
> NATH DYETT *who DIED*
> MARCH 27TH 1803

Four other headstones difficult to read :—

52. White marble ledger :—

> Here lie the Remains
> of
> . Mrs. MARY DYETT,
> Wife of MARK DYETT,
> of this ifland Efquire
> who departed this Life 21ᶠᵗ Janʸ 1807,
> Aged 54 Years.

Her husband was Chief Justice in 1804 and brother of Henry.

> SACRED
> TO THE MEMORY OF
> MRS. ANN DYETT
> WIFE OF NATHANIEL DYETT,
> OF THIS ISLAND ESQUIRE,
> WHO DEPARTED THIS LIFE
> ON THE 27ᵀᴴ DAY OF AUGUST 1807,
> IN THE 49ᵀᴴ YEAR OF HER AGE.

Her husband was brother of Mark and Henry.

---

54. White marble slab :—

> IN MEMORY of
> RICHARD DYETT
> of this Ifland Efquire,
> (eldeft Son of
> HENRY DYETT Efqʳ deceafed,
> late of *London*)
> Who died ON the 11ᵀᴴ of January 1808,
> Aged 31.
> And alfo in Memory
> of his two Infant Daughters
> both called ELLEN,
> who died at early Ages.
> (Two lines, by his Widow)

Richard Dyett, bap. in this parish 27 May, 1728, by the dau. of ... Blake his wife, had 5 sons Richard, Henry, Nathaniel, Mark, Joshua. The will of the above Henry dated 9 March, 1803 was proved 24 Nov., 1804. (768 *Heseltine*).

1804, June 16. At Brompton, Henry Dyett, esq. (*Gent. Mag.* 693) See pedigree in *Caribbeana* IV.

---

55. Headstone enclosed by iron railings :—

SACRED | TO | THE MEMORY | OF | WᴍHARPER | DEPARTED | THIS LIFE ON | THE 28ᵀᴴ OF JULY | 1834 | AGᴰ 40 YEARS.

---

56.   Marble slab :—

Here lies the Remains
of
Mifs ANNE HARCUM
Daughter of
WILLIAM HARCUM *late of this Ifland Efquire*
and
ANNE his Wife
She was born the 18ᵀᴴ of January, 1757
and
Died the 14ᵀᴴ of February, 1774
Aged
Seventeen Years and twenty seven days

57.   Within a stone curb :—

IN MEMORY OF
JOSEPH DALY
WHO DIED JULY 9 1867
AGED 76 YEARS.

58.   Headstone :—

GRAYSTON OCTAVIUS
BUCKE
Born November 22ᴰ 1778
Died September 9ᵀᴴ 1798
Of the Yellow Fever
In the 20ᵀᴴ Year of his Age.

59.   Headstone :—

Jn Loving Memory of
HENRY M. SHIELL
DIED FEB. 1st 1869, AGED 42
Also his wife
ROSETTA SHIELL
DIED SEP. 30th 1886 AGED 52.

1847, Nov. 27.   In Clarges Street, age 92, Queely Shiell, late of the Island
of Montserrat.   (*Gent. Mag.* 1848, 104).
1783, Dec. 18.   Queely Shiell of Montserrat, Esq., his deed.   No. 3484.

60.   Headstone in east wall :—

H. Banks
Depᵈ yˢ Life
Oct. 19 1753

This is the oldest Inscription in the place.

61. Blue marble ledger :—

Here lie the Remains | of |
Mrs. ELIZABETH HARCUM
wife of
THOMAS HARCUM Efquire
She was born the 1 . . . of February, 1744
and
Died fincerely and generally lamented
24ᵀᴴ day of May, 1774
Aged
30 Years, 3 Months and 5 days

The Hon. Thomas Harcum was Chief Justice and Speaker in 1792.

62. Headstone :—

In Memory of | HAROLD FRANCE Efqr. | Affistant Commifsary
General | who died | at the Island of Montserrat | in the West Indies | June the
20, 1820* | Aged 48 Years | Alfo near him are interred | two of his Daughters |
Emily Wigson | who died June the 3rd 1821 | Aged 14 Years | and Caroline
Elizabeth Herbert | who died April the 1ᵗ 1821 | Aged 11 Months.

63. Headstone :—

E. W. + F.
1821

64. Headstone :—

C. E. H. + F.
1821

65. Flat stone :—

T. A. Connell Johnson
Died 27 July
1870
Aged 86 days.

66. Square obelisk of stone. On the east face :—

To the Memory of the
Honᵇˡᵉ ANTHONY WYKE
Late Governor of this Island
Who died the 20ᵀᴴ of Novʳ 1777
Aged 39 Years.
In death lamented
As in Life Beloved

He m. 13 Jan., 1763, at St. John's, Antigua, Ann eldest dau. of Col. Wm.
Byam, by whom he left a numerous issue. Pedigree in *Antigua* III, 265.

* 20 altered to 1821.

67. Headstone :—

Sacred to the Memory | of | M^{RS} ANNE WELDON | wife of | N. P. WELDON, ESQ^R | who departed this life | December 14th 1814 | aged 42 Years |

68. Headstone :—

SACRED | TO THE MEMORY OF | SARAH POLHILL | WHO DIED ON THE 5TH JANUARY, 1838 | AGE 48 | ALSO OF FRANCIS POLHILL | HUSBAND OF THE ABOVE | WHO DIED ON THE 5TH SEPTEMBER, 1839 | AGE 61 |
ALSO OF FREDERICK POLHILL | SON OF THE ABOVE | WHO DIED ON THE 26TH SEPTEMBER, 1849 | AGE 24 | ALSO OF SARAH POLHILL | DAUGHTER OF THE ABOVE | WHO DIED ON THE 11TH DECEMBER, 1869 | AGE 38 | ALSO OF MARY HAMILTON | RELICT OF REV^D HENRY HAMILTON | WHO DEPARTED THIS LIFE ON THE 8TH DAY OF JULY, 1883 | AGED 72 YEARS.

1839, Sept. 6. Francis Polhill (Collector of H. M. Customs and Member of Council). Plymouth. 61 years. (Burial Register).

69. Headstone :—

SACRED | TO THE MEMORY OF | CHRISTOPHER WALTHAM WALTON | THE BELOVED SON OF | CHARLES WALTON ESQ. | MERCHANT OF LONDON WHO SENT HIM | (remainder illegible).

70. White marble slab on stone vault :—

Here lieth Interr'd the Remains of
Captain Gilbert Tarlton
of the Brigantine Jenny of Liverpool
who Died on this Ifland the 15th of June, 1769

71. Headstone :—

This Monumental Stone
Erected by their affectionate Parents
(MICHAEL and MARY JANE FURLONGE,
of this Island,
but formerly of Guildford Place, London)
Records the lamented Death
of five of their dear Children
whofe Remains
lie buried here and on either fide

ALFRED		12th Octr 1816 :		11 Weeks
EMMA RAINSFORD		8th May 1821 :		13 Years
MARY JANE	died	13th May 1821 :	Aged	12 Years
LOUISA MARY		25th June 1821 :		20 Years
ANNA DURBAN		13th Octr 1821 :		9 Months

The three Elder to the unfpeakable affliction
of their fond Parents,
were carried off by a dreadful Fever
that raged at the time in this Ifland
and which proved equally fatal
to many more of its Inhabitants

Wm. Furlonge, Jr., Master of Arts, barrister and J.P., and Michael Furlonge Attorney-at-law, 1792.

St. George's, Hanover Square, 1800, May 22. Michael Furlonge, Esqr. of this p. B., and Mary Jane Demattos, of St. Andrew, Holborn., Spr. Lic.

1802, April 13. In Upper Guildford-st, the wife of Michael Furlonge, esq., a son. (*Gent. Mag.* 373).

1803 ? May. Lately etc. . . . . .a son (*Ib.* 594).

1807, Sept. 25. The wife of Michael Furlonge, esq., of Guildford-pl., a dau. (*Ib.* 975).

1852, March 17. Aged 71, Sarah Sophia, widow of Thomas Furlonge, esq., formerly of Montserrat. (*Ib.* 531).

---

72. Red Granite Headstone :—

IN MEMORY OF | WILLIAM DARDIS FURLONGE | WHO DIED ON THE 19th FEBʸ 1867 |.

1830, Aug. 26. William Dardis Furlonge, Bach. of the P. of St. George, and Eliza Semper. Lic.

Three Headstones near, one of which is also to a Furlonge.

There is an extension of the old church-yard to the west and to the north is a burial ground for Roman Catholics and Dissenters.

---

73. White marble grave :—

SACRED TO THE MEMORY | OF | THE HONORABLE WILLIAM WILKIN | WHO DIED DECᴮ 2, 1883 | AGED 73 YEARS | HE WAS A NATIVE OF YORKSHIRE, ENGLAND, AND A MEMBER OF THE EXECUTIVE COUNCIL OF THIS ISLAND FOR 20 YEARS.

---

74. White marble grave adjoining preceding :—

𝔍n | 𝕷oving 𝕸emory of | SARAH EVELINA WILKIN | BORN 2ᴺᴰ DEC., 1832 | DIED 26ᵀᴴ DEC. 1904.

---

75. On stone curb of grave :—

A. D. JAMISON
RECTOR
1883—1889.

---

76. On stone curb of grave :—

G. H. TODD
1846—69 RECTOR

---

77.   White marble cross :—

In Loving Memory of | FRANCIS WELDON | INFANT SON OF | FRANCIS AND LOUISA WATTS, | WHO DIED APRIL 15ᵀᴴ 1884 |.

Sir Francis Watts is now Commissioner of Agriculture for the West Indies.

---

78.   On a thick slab set in the wall of the road opposite St. Mary's Chapel. The lettering is very coarsely cut, the surname doubtful and the last letter missing :—

HEARE LYETH | THE BODY OF A | NDEW (*sic*) ROIXIE | WHO DEPARTED | THIS LIFE THE 16ᵒ. | JANVARY 1720 | IN yᵉ 56 YEAR OF HIS | ADGE .

ST. PATRICK'S.

There is a large Roman Catholic Burial Ground in this Parish on the road to O'Garas.   It adjoins the sea, on which side there is a gate way for the use of funeral parties landing here from boats.   This Parish was always full of Papists. The English Church is quite modern.   The old windmills of Reads & Galways stand above the road.

The Parish is now united with St. Anthony.   There is no old register.   A transcript of the years 1721—29 appeared in *Caribbeana* I., 92.

79.   Headstone :—

Here lies
The Body of MICHAEL DARDIS, Esqʳ
who departed this Life on Thurſday
the 23 Day of Febʳʸ 1797 ; Aged 62 Years.
(Two lines)
He was born in *Galway* in the Kingdom of *Ireland*
and ſerved as SURGEON on Board the *Veſtal*
Capt. SAMUEL HOOD (now Lord HOOD,)
when ſhe engaged and took the *Bellona*
a French Frigate of ſuperior Force
after a ſevere and bloody Conflict,
upon which Occaſion
the following Epigram was written
In vain Bellona mounts the Gallic Gun,
To try the Honor of the Britiſh Nun
Chaſte as ſhe lived ſo bravely ſhall expire
Theres no extinguiſhing the Veſtal Fire !
He afterwards ſettled in this Iſland
where he practiſed PHYSIC
for upwards of thirty Years
with Credit and Reputation
His Character is compriſed in a few Words :
He was CHARITABLE to the POOR
HOSPITABLE to STRANGERS ; and the
FRIEND of MANKIND in General
He left an only Daughter
married to WILLIAM FURLONGE junior Eſqʳᵉ
who placed this humble Stone here.
(Four more lines partly effaced).

Capt. Tho. Nugent formerly of the Island, of Montnugent co. Bucks, Will dated 15 June, 1710.   Garret Dardis my nephew's bond.   (251 *Smith*).

---

80. Grey granite headstone :—

IN LOVING MEMORY | OF | ANN PERCY | WHO DIED ON THE | 5ᵀᴴ DEC. 1906 |
R.I.P.

81. Grey granite cross :—

IN | MEMORY OF | MARY M. FURLONG | WHO DIED ON 10 MARCH 1894 |
R.I.P.

82. Grey granite cross :—

IN MEMORY OF | HARRIET SEARL FURLONGE | WHO DIED ON THE 2ᴺᴰ
NOV. 1904 | ALSO EMILY FURLONGE | WHO DIED ON THE 27ᵀᴴ OCT., 1904 |
GREAT GRAND DAUGHTERS | OF MICHAEL DARDIS | OF GALWAY, IRELAND |
R.I.P.

83. Wooden cross at the head of a stone vault :—

IN MEMORY OF | HARRIET KIRWAN WHO | DIED MARCH 16ᵀᴴ 1846 HER |
REMAINS WERE REMOVED | FROM THE BURIAL GROUND | OF FARM ESTATE IN 1887 |
AND PLACED HERE WITH | HER HUSBAND | JOHN FRANK KIRWAN | WHO DIED
JUNE 4ᵀᴴ 1882 | R.I.P.

John Frank Kirwan was son of Clement Kirwan (eldest son of John Kirwan
of London, merchant, who died in 1799 aged 76). He went to Montserrat in 1839
married 3 Sept., 1853 Emily youngest daughter of John Russell of Summerhill,
Dartford, Kent, and secondly, a daughter of Henry Hamilton of Montserrat.
The Waterwork plantation is now owned by Miss Kirwan.

Bethells, The Farm and Trants are all in a small plain on the edge of the sea
facing Antigua. At the Farm the old Sugar Works and dwelling house are in
ruins, only cotton being now grown. On the Keystone of the mill is I.F.K.,
1858 for John Frank Kirwan.

84. Wooden cross at the head of a stone vault :—

IN MEMORY OF | FELIX GEORGE KIRWAN | WHO DIED MARCH 26ᵀᴴ 1884 | AGED
44 YEARS. R.I.P.

85. Grey granite headstone :—

IN MEMORY OF | ELIZA HAMILTON | WHO DIED | ON THE 27ᵀᴴ APRIL 1867 |
MARY ANN HAMILTON | 21ᵀᴴ OCT. 1867 | AUGUSTA HAMILTON | 15ᵀᴴ
JAN. 1905 | R.I.P.

86. Metal plate on a stone cross :—

S. M.
John Lindsay
Born in Scotland 1818
Died Oct. 22 1887
Aged 70 years 7 months
R. J. P.

87. Headstone of 177· Inscription illegible.

ST. PETER.

This church suffered from the Hurricane of 1899 when St. James, a chapel-of-ease was thrown down.

The Register commences in 1863. A transcript of the years 1721—1729 and 1739—1745 appeared in *Caribbeana* I., 90, 361.

RECTORS.

Thomas Underwood, licensed 6 Nov., 1791.   (*Ibid* III., 325)
Joseph Miller, Rector of St. Peter and St. George, 1792 (*Almanac*).
Joseph Shervington, 1863—1882.
Evan Evans, 1882—1899.
—— Easten, 1914, formerly Rector of Tortola, appointed Rector of St. Mary Cayon, St. Kitts, 1914.

88. On the north wall of the Chancel. Tablet of White marble on black :—

3n Memory of
THE REV^D JOSEPH SHERVINGTON
WHO FOR 20 YEARS WAS THE
BELOVED PASTOR OF THIS PARISH
HE WAS BORN IN ANTIGUA FEB^Y 1ST 1829,
DIED IN THIS ISLAND, DEC^R 27TH 1882.

His Tomb to the south of the Churchyard next Rev. E. Evans, bears a similar Inscription.

He was probably son of Joseph Shervington, Esq., of Antigua, by Louisa Appleton his wife. She d. 13 April, 1883, aged 28 and her gravestone is in St. John's Churchyard. (*Antigua* III, 87).

89. South wall of Chancel. White marble tablet :—

Sacred
TO THE MEMORY OF
RICHARD WYTHE CHALMERS
who departed this Life,
31st May, 1827,
in the 29th Year of his Age

90. South wall of Chancel. White marble lozenge on black. :—

3n | loving Memory of | FRANCIS BURKE | of Woodlands in this Island | he was born in London | Jany 19 1800 | died June 23 | 1862 |
(Four lines—erected by his children).

91. Headstone in the Churchyard :—

IN | MEMORY | OF | THE REV^D EVAN EVANS | FOR 18 YEARS RECTOR OF THIS PARISH | DIED 13TH AUGUST, 1899 | AGED 56 YEARS |.

A Portrait of Admiral Tucker of Bermuda is at *Gages* of which estate Mr. Wilkins is the owner.

ST. JOHN'S.

At Carrs Bay, where the French landed in 1706, there is a Burial Ground between a swamp and the beach with the three following tombs :

92. A large rifled mausoleum on the beach itself, without inscription.

---

93. Stone slab over a stone vault :—

Sacred
TO THE MEMORY OF
M^RS BARBARA DALY
WIFE OF MR JUSTIN DALY
WHO DEPARTED THIS LIFE
ON THE 26TH OF AUGUST, 1829
AGED 46 YEARS.

---

94. White marble slab over a stone vault :—
ELIZABETH
Wife of NATHANIEL BASS DALY Efq^r
was born January 31^ft 1762,
and departed this Life
January 10th 1793, much lamented
(Erected by her husband)

Nathaniel Bass Daly of St. Peter's planter, 6 Jan. 1785, deed of gift to his son, Wm. Collins Daly, infant and daughter Mary Alice Daly (No. 3848). See pedigree in *Caribbeana* I., 114.

1675-6. Daniel Daly aged 69, his deposition. (*Antigua* I., ii.).

Census of 1677-8, Lieut. Edmund Daley.

1702, Aug. 8. Major John Daly, in the army many years, who served in all the expeditions in the late war in those parts, is recommended for a seat in the Council. (*Col. Cal.* p. 512).

1754, Dec. 28. Richard Bass Daly and Margaret Crips (St. Michael's, Barbados).

There are also a few small illegible headstones.

ST. GEORGE.

A transcript of the parish register for the years 1721—1729 and 1739—1745 in *Caribbeana* I., 88, 362.

Jonathan Yate Gifford went out 1 March, 1710—11. In 1715 he is described as late Rector of St. George, when appointed Chancellor of the Court of Exchequer at Antigua. No list of the clergy is obtainable. The present church which is quite modern was formerly a chapel-of-ease to St. Peter's, and the Rector is now J. W. Leverock (S.P.G.)

FARM PLANTATION.

Formerly belonging to the Kirwan family. Here there is an old Roman Catholic Burial Ground but there were no Monumental Inscriptions.

RYLEYS.

This estate is at the top of a ridge, quite 800 feet up, on the road to St. George's.

On a white marble slab over a stone vault, in a cane piece. In a circle is an angel with trumpet.

ELEANOR MISSETT | Born in the Parifh of Cayon | in St. Chriftophers on the 24th Sep. | 1756 Died in Montferat 20th Dec. | 1760 Daughter of JOHN & | ANN MISSETT Grand-daughter to | EDMᴰ & WINEFRID MISSETT of Montferat | & to Collᵒ ROBᵀ & SUSANNAH HENVILL | of St. Chriftophers.

1751, Aug. 14. In the Court of K.B. & C.P. John Missett & others, Exors of the will of Edmund Missett of Montserrat, merchant as to claim of £1011.

Col. Robert Henvill was buried at St. Thomas, Middle Island, St. Kitts, 17 Sept., 1752 & Susannah his widow 18 Aug., 1754. A daughter, not named in the register, was baptised 14 Oct., 1726 at St. Anne's, Sandy Point.

The following from the *Gent. Mag.* for 1792, p. 884, appeared in *Caribbeana* I., 96. The stone is no longer to be seen. " Mr. Urban. Montserrat, July 26, 1792. As I have been long an admirer of your useful and learned Miscellanys I take the liberty of transmitting to you a very singular, and I believe, the oldest* inscription upon a tombstone in the West Indies ; by inserting which you will oblige, Wm. McKenly."

Sub hoc tumulo jacet
JOANNES DAVIES
vir integritate, industriâ, et benevolentiâ suis
quam alienis charissimus
Patriæ pro viribus minister,
nam in hâc insulâ Monserat pro multis annis
non tantum civilia sed etiam militaria
quædam erant illi officia :
præsertim fuif justiciarius pacis
qui post longum dolorem corpis tandem
quiete et libentur mortem obiit,
mense Septembris anno renovati hominis 1686.
Ita se totum unde exiit retribuit,
et vel in morte docuit,
suum cuique reddere

(eight lines in English omitted).

1677, Nov. 1. The Bishop of London writes Governor Stapleton that he has selected the following clergy :—Messrs. . . .Molineux, Davis . . ., who are embarking. (*Col. Cal.* p. 174).

1678, Jan. 24. Gov. Stapleton writes that he has presented Mr. Molineux to Montserrat (but he does not mention Davis). (*Ib.* p. 212).

---

* The Editor has seen dozens of older ones.

NEVIS.

Nevis is a small island of about 32,000 acres, two miles to the south-east of St. Kitts. A mountain, over 3,000 feet high, occupies the centre, the plantations sloping down to the coast all around it.

The exact date of settlement is uncertain, but Thomas Littleton of London, Merchant, stated that he sent out three ships in 1628, and his factor found Anthony Hilton then Governour under the patent of 1627 of the Earl of Carlisle. (*Caribbeana* II., 2).

Anthony Hilton signed Warner's Treaty with the French at St. Christopher on 13 May, 1627.   On Warner's Treaty of 8 Nov., 1628, is the signature " Captain Anthony Hylton, President of Mevis."

John Bourne dated a codicil 10   Sept., 1630 " now of Dulcina alias Neves in the province of Carliola " and gave to " Mr. Toby Rand, Minister Jesus Parish upon the said Island 100 lbs. weight of tobacco."

In 1655 the Island was so overcrowded, that 300 fighting men were enlisted for the Expedition under Penn and Venables, and the following year Governor Luke Stokes sailed for Jamaica, with 1,400 men, women and children, besides their servants from this and the neighbouring islands.   (*Ibid.* II, 45).

Charles De Rochefort in his History of 1658, after alluding to the mineral baths, stated that this island was the best governed in the Caribbees, justice being administered by a Council.   " There are in this Island three Churches, which have nothing extraordinary as to structure, but are very convenient as to the performing of Divine Service."

Act No. 1 of 1664 recites that King Charles II. having purchased Lord Carlisle's proprietary rights, had appointed Francis, Lord Willoughby of Parham, Capt.-General of Barbadoes and the other Caribbee Islands, and now made void the old tax of 20lbs of tobacco per pole, confirmed all titles, and settled an impost upon the native commodities of $4\frac{1}{2}$ per cent.   Col. Stapleton wrote in 1672 that some few ministers and schoolmasters were in Nevis, but none in the other islands.

The first Census of 1677—8 has been printed (*Caribbeana* III., 27), and the Island was then divided into 13 Companies or Divisions, each under a senior militia officer, and there were 1,541 white men.

Act No. 2 of 1680 recites that many planters having years ago deserted their plantations, and transported themselves to Jamaica, all titles to present possessors are confirmed.

By Act No. 8 of 1681, parishioners were to pay their Minister 16,000 lbs every year, also 2,000 lbs. to each clerk, " who is to keep a Register of all Christnings and Burials in each Parish."

An Act of 1681 refers to Charles Town and Morton's Bay.

In 1689 one half of the inhabitants are said to have died of small-pox and fevers.

An Act of 1700 names Charles Town, James Town, and Newcastle.

By Act No. 61 of 1705 the freeholders and householders were to meet in Easter week, and elect 12 vestrymen for each parish, and " in every Parish Church there shall be kept three large Paper Books for the publick Service of the said Parish, One whereof shall be kept for the Parish Accounts, the other for the Vestry Acts, and a Third as a Register for Christnings, Marriages, and Funerals ; the last of which to be kept by the Minister only." (See *State of the Church. Caribbeana* III., 321).

In 1706, the French captured the Island, committing much damage, towards which the English Parliament gave over £100,000. The census of 1707—8 was printed in *Caribbeana* III., 173.

The history of Nevis has never been written, nor is there any proper survey or map. In *Colonial Papers*, Vol. XXXIV., No. 85, reference is made to a map of Nevis sent home 9 June, 1675. The only old map I know is Bellin's, a French one of 1758 (reproduced in *Caribbeana* II., 6).

This shows only three parishes viz. : St. Thomas to the north-west, Ginger-land to windward, with a church marked at New River, and St. John to the south-west which includes Charlestown. These may have been the three ancient parishes alluded to by Rochefort 100 years earlier, but there must have been an error of omission for in 1724, and probably many years before, there were then as now, five parishes, viz. : 1—St. Paul's, Charlestown. 2—St. John's, Figtree. 3—St. George's, Gingerland. 4—St. James', Windward. 5—St. Thomas', Lowland.

Judging by the old wills it is evident that most of the early settlers were connected with Bristol, the merchants of that port, through its tobacco trade, being closely associated with Virginia and the Caribbees.

The numerous old " great houses," superior in style even to those in St. Kitts, and the abundant armorial slabs in the churches, point to the fact that many good families formerly settled here, men who appreciated artistic surround-ings in their homes. I saw many odd bits of Chippendale and Sheraton, Sheffield plate and old glass which were being collected by a dealer and despatched to U.S.A.

At the present day the white population seems to have dwindled to insignificant proportion. The ruins of sugar works, mansions, and windmills dotted about the lovely scenery engender a feeling of sadness and desolation. Cotton, bananas and coco-nut trees have been planted, but their cultivation can never be attended by the cheery animation, bustle and charm of the old sugar days.

———

The following Clergy were sent to Nevis by the Bishop of London, but it is not known which benefices they held.

Mr. Foster, 1678.
Mr. Tho. Sault, 1695. (*West Indies Calr.*, p. 440).
Tho. Winder, 1724.
John Langley, 1729. B.A., Oxf., 1728.
Colin Campbell, 1737—8.
Wm. Mc Kenly, 1773.
Wm. Vaughan Hamilton, 1805. Rector of Spanish Town, Jamaica, 1818.
Wm. Borrowdale, 1815.

ST. PAUL'S, CHARLESTOWN.

Charlestown, the capital and now the only town, is situated on a bay commanded by Fort Charles to the South. It directly faces St. Kitts, from which it is separated by the Narrows two miles across and is about twelve miles distant from Basseterre, with which town it is in close touch through a service of sloops, which sail there and back on market days.

There are the usual government buildings, including a fine old Court House where the Council and Assembly formerly sat, and the Courts meet and the records are kept. The foundation stone was laid 13 Feb., 1811. (MS. note in *Mr. Buck's Almanac*).

The church stands abutting the road leading North. It is impossible to judge its age, but a church probably stood here from the earliest days. In 1706 the French, besides robbing the interior, used it as a prison, and in 1712 it was rebuilt or renovated. Governor Walter Douglas wrote in 1714 that he had seen the greatest part of a very handsome church built in Nevis—probably referring to this one. The Rector, Rev. R. Robertson, wrote in 1724, that twelve years ago the parishioners built a neat church of brick costing £1,000. There seems a dearth of white clergy for the present rector (1914) is coloured and he was taking charge of two other parishes.

The old Government House, where H. N. Coleridge stayed in 1825, was sold to the parish in February, 1841, and has been lately converted into a hospital, and a new plain-looking building erected for the governor, on the hill above Bath House. The old West Indian style of architecture with its broad galleries and jalousies has been departed from, with poor result. There are several fine old houses and stores, with ruins of others, the old ovens and cisterns still conspicuous among the broken down walls.

Half-a-mile to the South stands Bath House, now a most comfortable hotel, with excellent baths and modern drainage. The mineral spring adjacent, in a separate building, is supposed to be as efficacious as the waters of Bath, and has been used for over 300 years.

The town was burnt in 1836 and again on 18 April, 1837.

For a list of plantations and other information see Mrs. Burden's Handbook.

PARISH REGISTERS.

The earliest volume commences in 1812 signed that year by Daniel G. Davis, Rector. The leaves are rotten, broken and loose, but they have been carefully inserted between the pages of an old account book. The baptisms, marriages and burials are written in three columns on each page (a most unusual arrangement). They are on very thin paper and written only on one side. At the end of this volume is " Finis 1823. Will Hendrickson, Curate."

In 1824 separate volumes for baptisms, marriages and burials containing printed forms were used.

The families more frequently named are Davis, Huggins, Bridgwater, Burke, Brodbelt, Lawrence, Maynard, New, etc.

For transcript of christenings and burials of the year 1726, see C.O. 152 in the P.R.O.

For notes of many of the following Monumental Inscriptions, see *Caribbeana* II., 168.

RECTORS.

John Huffam, 1673, in Southwark, January, 1676 (*Col. Cal.*) Given 5,000lbs. in the will of Jas. Hale but no parish named (*Caribbeana* IV., 110). He was a witness 1703 to the will of Henry Carpenter, Esq.

Robert Robertson presented 13 December, 1707, ordained at Fulham 9 February, 1706 (*Caribbeana* III., 323). He signed the Transcript in 1727 and was living in 1736. See No. 27.

Robert Pemberton, presented 22 Dec., 1785. He also held S. George. (*Ibid.* III., 325).

William Green, died 26 April, 1811, aged 37. See No. 5.

Daniel Gateward Davis, 1812-24.

1824, Aug. 9. Fred Huggins, churchwarden wrote to the Bishop of London that Daniel Gateward Davis, the Rector, is leaving for St. Christopher. (*Ibid.* III., 212). Later Bishop of the Leeward Islands.

See No. 7 for the Monumental Inscription to his wife.

Hamble James Leacock, 1828—35 and again 1849—52, died 20 Aug., 1856 in Sierra Leone.

Nicholas Rice Callender, B.A., died 27 May, 1836, aged 27. See No. 19.

F. M. Collins, 1879.

ST. PAUL'S CHURCH.

1. On the north wall of the Nave :—

Crest : *An arm couped at the shoulder, in the hand a short sword.*
Arms : *Gules, a lion couchant* ; impaling :—*Or, a crosspatonce, in chief five arrows banded.*
Motto : TIC E MO DAEICH.

SACRED | TO THE MEMORY OF | MARIA ELIZABETH | THE YOUNG AND MUCH LAMENTED WIFE OF | WILLIAM BUTLER URE MACPHAIL | OF THIS ISLAND, MERCHANT ; | SHE DEPARTED THIS LIFE | ON THE 22ND DAY OF JUNE | ANNO DOMINI 1846, ÆTATIS 21. (Two lines ; erected by her husband).

---

2. On the east wall of the north Transept, on a small oval tablet :—

SACRED | TO THE MEMORY OF | *JOHN RICHARDSON, ESQ*R | MANY YEARS A RESIDENT | OF THIS ISLAND | WHO DEPARTED THIS LIFE | THE 6TH DAY of SEPTEMBER 1816, | AGED 60 YEARS | AND IS INTERRED NEAR THIS PLACE |

He was probably son of the Hon. John Richardson by Elizabeth his wife. (See pedigree in *Caribbeana* V., 17).

---

3.   There are six tablets in the Chancel, three on each wall.

On the north wall :—

This *MONUMENT*
is erected by JOHN TOBIN CROSSE
in Memory of MARY CROSSE
His late Wife—She departed
this transitory Life
on the 26th Day of December
in the Year of our Lord, 1804,
and in the 44th Year of her Age.

1790, Aug. 26.   John Tobin Crosse, Planter to Polly Burke, spinster (St. John's, Figtree).

James Tobin of Nevis, now of Bristol, Esq.   Will dated 30 Oct., 1817.   To my sister Elizabeth Crosse, widow £100.   (549 *Effingham*).

John Tobin Crosse was second son of John Crosse, of Thurloxton Manor, co. Somerset, Esq., by Elizabeth, dau. of James Tobin Senior, of Nevis.   He was bap. at T. 16 February, 1761.

Administration of his goods as of Nevis, widower was granted 8 March, 1819 to Tho. Bickham Crosse and Andrew Moore Crosse, Esquires, the brothers.

----

4.   North wall :—

Underneath
lie the Remains of
SARAH CLAXTON,
Wife of BUTLER CLAXTON, deceased,
who departed this Life May 4th 1813.
(Four lines, placed by her surviving daughters).

----

5.   North wall.   Figure borne away by two angels :—

Near this Place | are deposited the remains | of the Revd WILLIAM GREEN | late Rector of the Parish of St. Paul | Charlestown | and of St. George's, Gingerland, | who departed this life | on the 26th April 1811, | in the 38th Year of his Age. |

William Green, son of Geo. Green of Newington, Surrey, cler. Q. Coll., matric. 22 Nov., 1791 aged 19 ; B.A. 1795.   (*Foster*).

----

6.   On the south wall :—

A man and woman kneeling over a bier.

Crest : *A pineapple with leaves*

Arms : *Party per pale Az. and Sa. three chevronels between as many covered cups all Or.*

(This coat seems to be a combination of the arms of Bowring & Butler).

Near this Sacred Monument are depofited the Remains of
WILLIAM BOWRIN who died on the 19th day of Decr 1816,
Aged 70 Years And of his Affectionate Wife JANE BUTLER,
who departed this Life on the 11th April 1777,
At the early Age of 30 Years.
Likewife the Remains of JOICE BUTLER Mother to the above JANE,
who died on the 22nd April 1798, Aged 85 Years
This Monument is erected by WILLIAM only Son of the above
WILLIAM & JANE BOWRING as a grateful teftimony of
the Affection he bore for the above Relatives.

1854, Jan. 1. At St. Kitts, aged 28, Grace Wilhelmina, only dau. of the late Wm. Bowrin, of the Paradise Estate, Nevis, and grand-daughter of Rear-Admiral Gourly, R.N. (*Gent. Mag.*, 329).

A pedigree of Butler appeared in *Caribbeana* II., 60, but Mrs. Joice Butler does not find a place in it.

In Westbury-upon-Trym, near Clifton is a stone to Mary, Wife of Wm. Butler, late of Nevis, died 1818 aged 41.

---

7. South wall :—

Within the Railing of the Altar in this Church
lie the remains of
ANNE, the Wife of the *Revd D. G. DAVIS*
Rector of this Parifh,
She departed this Life after a few days Illnefs
on the 16th Novr 1820, Aged 32 Years.

1813, Dec. 16. By Lic. The Rev. Daniel Gateward Davis, Rector of this Parish to Anne, Daughter of Butler Claxton, Esq.,, deceased, by the Rev. Wm. Davis at Figtree Church in this Island. (Par. Reg.) Daniel Gateward Davis was later Bishop of the Leeward Islands. and died in 1857.

In *Caribbeana* II., 169, the age was given as 52 but queried ; 32 is correct.

---

8. South wall :—

TO THE MEMORY OF
LIEUT. JOSEPH BAILEY, R.N.
MANY YEARS MASTER OF THE SHIP
" EARL OF LIVERPOOL "
TRADING TO THIS ISLAND.
HE WAS LOST IN THAT VESSEL'S PINNACE
IN THE NARROWS, ON THE 8TH MAY 1842,
AGED 47 YEARS

---

9. South wall of Nave :—

Sacred
TO THE MEMORY OF
DIANA MILLS POWELL,
NATIVE OF CHARMOUTH, DORSETSHIRE
WHO DEPARTED THIS LIFE,
ON THE 16TH OF SEPTR 1845,
AGED 31 YEARS.

On the floor of the Nave are four ledgers near the west door.

10. Blue marble ledger :—

HERE LIES THE BODY OF
JOHN HUGGINS ESQR
WHO DIED
THE 6TH DAY OF DECEMBER 1824
AGED 58 YEARS
HE BEGAN A CAREER OF USEFULNESS AS A
MERCHANT IN THIS TOWN.
IN PRIVATE LIFE HE WAS A FIRM FRIEND
AN AFFECTIONATE HUSBAND,
AND A SINCERE CHRISTIAN.
IN PUBLIC LIFE,
HE GAVE UNIVERSAL SATISFACTION
AS CLERK OF THE ASSEMBLY
AND DEPUTY TREASURER OF THE ISLAND.
NOT MANY YEARS BEFORE HIS DEATH HE BECAME
PROPRIETOR OF THE NEIGHBOURING HOT SPRINGS
OVER WHICH OUT OF GOOD WILL TOWARDS HIS
FELLOW CREATURES AND NOT FOR ANY ADVANTAGE
OF HIS OWN HE ERECTED CONVENIENT BATHS
AND AT A SHORT DISTANCE A LARGE AND
EXPENSIVE STONE EDIFICE FOR THE
ACCOMODATION OF INVALIDS.
THIS TOMB WAS PUT UP BY HIS WIDOW

1824, Dec. 6. At Nevis, John Huggins, Esq. (*St. Christopher Almanac*).

The Editor spent a most agreeable fortnight in the Bath House built by the above Mr. Huggins, now an hotel and owned by Messrs. W. Gillespie Bros., of London.

---

11. Blue marble ledger :—

Here lyeth the Body of Mrs JANE
MERRIWETHER late Wife of
Mr JEFFERY MERRIWETHER
of this Ifland Mercht fhe died April
the 24th 1750 Aged 68 Years.

---

12. Blue marble ledger, much worn and indistinct :—

> . . . . . of a Refurrection to Eterna . . . .
> lies here interr'd
> ANTHONY GILES
> late of PU . . . . * in Wiltfhire
> Who while living was defervedly belov'd
> and died lamented by all that knew him
> O . . . XX of January 1750
> . . . . of his Age
> *In refpect to whofe Memory*
> *This Tomb is erected*
> *by*
> (name illegible) *Merch* in *BRISTOL.*

13. White marble ledger :—

> Here lies all that was Mortal
> of MARY JONES an Infant Daughter
> of MATTHIAS JONES Merch: and
> SARAH his Wife Born July 18th
> 1753 & died ye 18th of Febry following.

In the cross-way of north Transept and Nave are five ledgers :—

14. Blue marble ledger with cherubs' heads at the four corners. In a sunk oval a Jacobean shield the Mantling much worn :—

Crest : *A lion's head couped over wreath and Helmet.*
Arms : *A chevron* (alone visible).
Band for Motto :

> HERE LYETH THE BODY OF Mr ARTHUR
> PLOMER OF THE CITY OF BRISTOLL
> MARCHANT WHO DEPARTED THIS LIFE
> THE 15 OF IVLY 1702 AGED 38 YEARS
> THO in ye GRAVE ye WIDOWD carcasse LYES
> HIS SOUL IS LIVING still yt never dyes,
> This TOO shaLL one day mount upon ye wing
> AS from dead winter dos ye VIGrous sprinG
> so both we hope wiLL meet at LAST in IOY
> And LIVE in pleasures yt have no ALLOy.

The will of Simon Plomer of Bristol, plomber was proved in 1670. (51 *Penn*).

---

* Perhaps Purton.

15.   Stone ledger :—

BENEATH THIS STONE
LIE THE REMAINS OF
THE HONOURABLE JAMES WATSON SHERIFF,
OF THE INNER TEMPLE, BARRISTER AT LAW,
AND PRESIDENT OF THIS ISLAND
FROM JULY 1864 TO MARCH 1866.
HE WAS A NATIVE OF ANTIGUA, WHERE FOR A SERIES
OF YEARS HE FILLED SUCCESSIVELY MANY OF THE MOST
IMPORTANT PUBLIC OFFICES AMONGST OTHERS THOSE OF
SPEAKER OF THE HOUSE OF ASSEMBLY, SOLICITOR GENERAL
AND ATTORNEY GENERAL BEING DISTINGUISHED BY HIGH
PROFESSIONAL ABILITIES AND. . . . . . . THE BAR
UNSULLIED. . . . . . ARACTE. : . . . . .CELLENCE
IN ALL . . . . OF LIFE

(Eight more lines, nearly all worn away).

1866, March 9.   At Nevis, West Indies from the effects of a severe carriage
accident James Watson Sheriff, esq., President administering the Government
of that island.   (Long notice in *Gent. Mag.* 755).

1775, Francis Sherriff b. in Nevis, eldest son of Alex. merchant there.
(*Glasgow University*).

He was born 5 Oct., 1803 at St John's, Antigua and in the Cathedral there is a
tablet to his memory.   (See pedigree in *Antigua* III., 85).

---

16.   Brown Stone ledger, much flaked :—

HERE LYETH Y^e BODY OF IOHN
COLE ES . . . . . . .THOMAS
COLE OF Y^e CITY OF BRISTOLL
WHO DEPARTED THIS
LIFE Y^e . . . . OF AVGVST 1705
AGED 57 YEARS.

Tho. Cole owned estates in St. Christopher and Nevis, and made his will in
1711.

Susannah Cole late of St. Christopher, then of St. Paul's Churchyard,
London, widow, made her will 1 Dec., 1732, proved 22 Feb., 1732-3 (35 *Price*),
and left all her estate to her nephew Tho. Bridgwater.

Stapleton Dunbar of Nevis in his will dated 6 April, 1759, named Master
Roger Cole son of Tho. Cole of Nevis.

Roger Cole, son of Thomas of Isle of Nevis, West Indies, gent. matriculated
from Corpus Christi Coll., Oxf., 29 Jan., 1768, aged 17.   (*Foster*).

---

17.   Blue marble ledger :—

CAP^T MATTHEW NEWTON
OB^T]4TH IUNE]724
ÆTATE 45.

There was a Wm. Newton, Esq., of St. Kitts.

---

18. Grey marble ledger :—

Here lieth the Body of
Mr MATHEW WALL who Departed
this Life the Third day of June
Anno Dom : 1733 in the Forty-first
Year of his Age

He and his wife Ann were Exors of the will of John Dowse in 1732.

———————

19. There are four White marble ledgers in the Chancel :—

BENEATH THIS STONE
REST THE REMAINS OF
THE REVEREND
NICHOLAS RICE CALLENDER
OFFICIATING MINISTER
OF THIS PARISH
AND A NATIVE OF THE ISLAND
OF BARBADOS
HE DIED ON THE 27th MAY 1836
AGED 27 YEARS.

1836, May 28. Nicholas Rice Callender, Off : Minister, Charles-town
27 years. (Burial Register).
He was a son of Lt.-Col. Nicholas Rice Callender of Barbados and matriculated from Queen's Coll., Oxf., 4 Nov., 1828, aged 19, B.A. 1832.

———————

20. White marble ledger.   In sunk oval is a Jacobean shield with
Mantling :—

Crest : *A cubit arm in armour couped, in the hand a broken spear.*
Arms : *A buck's head cabossed, on a chief a cross crosslet between two mullets
of six points pierced.*

Here lye interred the Bodies of
ANN and KATHARINE THOMSON,
Daughters of ARCHIBALD THOMSON Efq
of this *Ifland*
They died on the 24th day of October
in the Year 1774, ANN in her 18th, and
KATHARINE in her 15th Year
They were seized almoft in the same
hour by an unrelenting and fatal fever—
on the same day they both expired
And in the same Grave
they lye buried together

(No year, but on back of 1770). Nov. 28. Archibald Thomson, Esqr., to Mary
Abbot, spinster. (*St. Thomas Lowland Parish Register*).
1793, May 11. Mrs. Mary Thomas, wife of Archibald Thomson, Esq. (*St.
George Basseterre St. Kitts*).

The Jacobean shield does not suit the date 1774.

In a deed of 1769, Tower hill plantation of 240a. in the parish of St. Thomas was bounded north and west on lands of Archibald Thomson, Esq. (*Antigua* I., 89).

Wm. Hyndman of Nevis, Esq., Will dated 21 Dec., 1768. To Charles, Nancy and Catherine Thomson son and daughters of my friend Archibald Thomson of Nevis, Esq., £300 each. Archibald Thomson and Robert Thomson both of Nevis to be exors. (*Ibid.* II., 94).

Eliz. Thomson, widow, by her will dated 3 Jan., 1765, left her house and slaves for her two daughters, Mary wife of Wm. Smith, Esq., and their son Jas. Tobin Smith and Eliz. wife of the Rev. Edwin Thomas (Recorded at Nevis). These daughters were by her first husband Charles Bridgewater.

---

21.   On a small white marble lozenge :—

The Rev^d | WILLIAM GREEN | died 26th April, 1811 | in the 38th year | of his Age.

---

22.   White marble ledger :—

Hic Jacet Uxor optima, mater pientissima,
Filia Sororq obedientissima, MARIA BODDIE
Omnibus benevolens Omnibus dilectissima
tricefsimo die Novembris Anno MDCCLXIX.
Ætatis suæ vicesimo Sexto Fatis cefsit
Conjugis charifsimæ Memoriæ Sacrum,
Maritus superstes JOHANNES BODDIE
hocce posuit.

Below in a sunk oval is a Chippendale shield :—

Crest : *An eagle's head erased, in its beak an arrow.*
Arms : *On a chevron between three eagles' heads erased as many flowers* (? primroses) ; impaling, *Argent, A cross barbed.*
Motto : POST FUNERA VIRTUS

1768, May 3.   Dr. John Boddie passed his examination in physic and surgery and was licenced to practice. (*Minutes of Council of Nevis*).

John Boddy entered St. George's Hospital, Oct., 1768.

John Boddie of Nevis, surgeon, Will dated 17 April, 1777. My son John Ward Boddie and my daughter Mary Ward Boddie. Sworn 5 Aug., 1780. (*Book of Wills* p. 509).

---

23.   White marble ledger with Cherubs heads at the four corners. In a sunk heart-shaped depression is a Jacobean shield with wreaths below it. Above is a man with a scyth and on either side angels as supporters. Where the arms should be is this inscription :—

HORA RUIT.
IACOBUS EMRA *ARMIGER*
ANNOS. 58. NATUS
STABIT. VIRTUS

(Ten lines of Latin ; placed by his widow).

OBIIT IPSIS CALENDIS SEPTEMB : 1733.

He was a witness in 1705 to the will of Ph. Brome, Esq. of Nevis, was styled " Mr." in a deed of 1713, and was overseer 1716 of the will of John Thornton.

In a close roll of 1798 it is recited that Col. Wm. Ling's plantation of 60 acres in Charlestown was sometime since in the possession of James Emra, afterwards of James Cradock, late of Ralph Payne, and now or late of Rowland Oliver, Esq.

Jas. Emra owned 300 acres in St. Johns and 200 in St. Thomas, Lowland which descended equally to his two sons, viz. :—

The Hon. James Emra of Antigua who died 28 Dec., 1759, aged 37, and Thomas Emra of Nevis, Esq., who married in 1746 Eliz. Hudson.

Richard Emra of St. Christopher, aged 25 in 1707-8, may have been a brother of above James senior.

CHURCHYARD.

24.   South of chancel is a broken blue marble ledger in five pieces.   In sunk oval is a Jacobean shield with mantling.

The Crest has been lost and only the Helmet remains.
Arms : *Argent, a lion rampant between three annulets.*

(The Woodleys of St. Kitts used for arms : *a chevron between three owls*). The above coat may be that of the wife used in error.

> Here lieth the Body of MARY
> the Wife of JOHN WOODLEY, of
> this Ifland of NEVIS Merchant
> who Departed this Life April ye
> 7th]722 Aged 38 Years with 3
> of her Children viz.
> MARY WOODLEY born Jan : ye 25th
>]7]3, and died Sep. ye th following
> JOHN WOODLEY born June ye (piece gone here)
>]7]5 & died May ye]6 :]7]6
> IOHN VINSETTS WOODLEY born
> April ye 6th]720, and died Sept ye 4th
> following.

He was Member of the Assembly in 1718, 1724 & 1730-1 and was styled " Esq " in 1738.   He may have been son of Wm. Woodley of Nevis, 1677-8.

25.   On a very thick Blue marble ledger in two fragments :—

> Here Lyes Interr'd the Body of
> Mrs REBECCAH ALVAREZ
> who Departed this Life Augft 31ft
>]743 Aged 44 Years.

22 June, 1751.   Isaac Alvarez and Hester his wife for £108 sell a house in Charles Town.   (*Nevis Records*, Vol. IV., p. 253).

26. White marble tomb. On the top ledger :—

SACRED | To the Memory of ANNA, | the Daughter of | WILLIAM &
CHRISTIAN LAURENCE, | of this Island, | (Three lines) died at the early
Age of 19 Years, in May 23rd, 1801.   (Nine lines, by parents).

1814, Nov. 29.   Mrs. Christiana Lawrence wife of William Lawrence.
(Burial Register).

1823, Oct. 16.   William Garvey Lawrence, Jun., Esqr and Lucretia Woodley
Stanley, spinster.   Lic.

---

27. Blue marble ledger over brick vault.   Above in a Chippendale oval
is an arm cutting the trunk of a tree :—

Near this Stone lies what was Mortal
of MARY Eldeſt Daughter of ROBERT and
MARY ROBERTSON, born October 24th: 1711
Married to RICHARD MERRIWETHER July 2d: 1730
delivered of her Daughter MARY ROBERTSON
the 4th: of September 1731 died in Childbed,
the 18th: of the same Month.
ELIZABETH their Second Daughter born ye 29th:
of October 1713 Married to THOMAS WASHINGTON
Sept 19th: 1735 delivered of her Son THOMAS June 20th
1736 died in Childbed ye 27th of the same Month
MARY wife of ROBERT ROBERTSON
and Daughter of JOHN POGSON, Capt: of the
Independent Company in S. Christophers, in ye
Reigns of CHARLES & JAMES IId born Sept 15th 1675
Married November 13 1709, died April 6th 1739.
And what was Mortal of
ROBERT ROBERTSON Miniſter of St: Pauls
NEVIS from Decr: 1707 born at Edinburgh ye 18th
of March 168$\frac{1}{2}$ made some remarks which
were Publiſhed in LONDON in the Year 1730
1736 &c. on the Slaves and their Owners in ye
Sugar Iſlands of England and died   (sic—no more).

This Monumental Inscription from the *Gent. Mag.* appeared in *Caribbeana*
I., 9.

Richard Meriwether of London, Merchant.   Will dated 20 Dec., 1713.   My
moiety of Lady Bawdens & Sharlowes plantations in the Parish of St. Thomas.
(9 *Aston*).

Oldmixon writing of claying Muscovado, said :—" Sir John Bawdon order'd
his Overseers to attempt it, two or three & twenty Years since, in that Plantation,
in this Island, which is now Mr. Richard Merriweathers. (*British Empire in
America* 1st edition 1708, Vol. II., p. 197).

---

28. Blue marble ledger with Cherubs heads at the four corners over brick vault :—

Underneath this Tomb
lies all that was Mortal
of the much beloved and
Remarkably wife Child SARAH ROBERTSON
Daughter of MATTHIAS JONES Merchant
and SARAH his Wife who was born October 28th
1743 and Died the 25th of July 1748

29. Blue marble ledger with Cherubs heads at the four corners, over a brick vault :—

Under this Tomb
lies all that was Mortal
of the moft Beautiful and
dear-dear-dear Child MATHIAS JONES
Son of MATHIAS JONES Merchant
and SARAH his Wife who was Born
the 29th of Auguft 1746, and Died
on the 10th of October 1749

30. Stone slab :—

Sacred | To the Memory | of | *MARY WEEKS* | Relict of *W. WEEKS* | late of this Ifland | Gentleman | who departed this Life | the 2nd Day of April, 1784 | in the 97th Year of her Age |.

He was of Nevis in 1707-8 and gunner of Fort Charles in 1748. Major Wm. Burt Weekes was probably their son.

31. A Vault with " E R " cut on it.

32. Headstone close to the east end of the School :—

Sacred | To the Memory of | Mrs SARAH BRODBELT, | who died in Child-Bed | on the 5th July, 1802 | (Sixteen lines).

See pedigree of Brodbelt in *Caribbeana* IV., 19.

33.   West of the Church is a blue marble ledger over a stone vault :—
In sunk oval is a Chippendale shield

Crest : *Cut of a ducal coronet a demi lion rampant.*
Arms : *A saltire between four rustres* ; impaling—blank.

Here lies with her stillborn Child what was mortal of
MARY
Daughter of Capt. PETER MELOTE (a Native of New York) &
MARTHA his wife (a Native of this Place) & Wife of
SAMUEL NEW late Collector of the 4½ *pr cent* & Treaſurer of NEVIS
She was born in CHARLES TOWN the 12ᵗʰ Day of *Octʳ* 1715 married to Mʳ
SAMUEL NEW (from BRISTOL) Merchant *March* 27, 1733 and died in Childbed
in the Prime of her years *Feb.* 26, 174⅔
Of SAMUEL, the 2ᵈ Son of SAMUEL NEW & MARY his Wife, born the 15
Day of *Febʸ* 1737 & died *Decʳ* 28, 1739,
Of SAMUEL, their 4ᵗʰ⋮ Son, born the 2ᵈ Day of *March* 174⅘ &
died the 17ᵗʰ of *Jan.*, 174⅘
And of HENRY NEW (near this Stone) Comᵈʳ of a Merchant Ship,
born in the City of BRISTOL the   day of   17   & died *Sept* 2, 1743
in the 34ᵗʰ Year of his Age.
In memoriam Uxoris amantiſſimæ ac duorum
Filiorum amabilium atque Fratris chariſſimi,
Monumentum hoc (quale cunque)
Iuctuoſus poſvit,
SAMUEL NEW
Armige (*sic*)

Indrē made 25 June, 1711 between John Helden of St. Christopher, Esq.,
and Mr. Peter Mellotte of the same. (*St. Kitt's Records* A. No. 16).
   The will of Samuel New of Nevis was dated at Bristol 15 Feb. and proved
30 March, 1763 (145 *Cæsar*).   His eldest son, Rev. James New, B.A., Oriel Coll.,
Oxf., was Vicar of St. Philip and Jacob in that city and died 15 July, 1810, aged
74 and Descendants seem to have flourished in the neighbourhood down to 1851
or later.

---

34.   White marble ledger over brick vault.   In sunk oval is a Jacobean
shield with mantling :—

Crest : *An heraldic antelope's head couped over wreath and helmet.*
Arms : *A chevron chequy . . . between three greyhounds courant.*
Here Lyeth the Body of
Mᴿ⋮ IOHN DOWSE
who Departed this Life the
Fourteenth day of October
Anno Dom. 1733 in the Fortyeth
Year of his Age

A division of his estate sworn at £2316 was made 20 Geo. 3ᵈ between Robert
Cowley of London, gent. and James New, a minor, as son and heir at law of his
mother Mrs. Mary New deceased.   See the will in *Caribbeana* VI. 80, dated
30 Aug., 1731, wherein he desired a white marble tombstone to be put on
his grave.
   See a pedigree of Dowse of Broughton with these arms and crest in the *Visit.
of Hants*, and an illustration of the monument of Sir Edmund Dowce in Marylebone Chapel. (*Misc. G. et H.* 3ᵈ S. I., 129).

35. Adjoining above. Blue marble slab much flaked, over stone vault. In a sunk oval a Jacobean shield and mantling :—

Crest : *An heraldic antelope's head.*
Arms : (Dowse as above).

> . . . . . th the Body of
> . . . .   MELLOTTE
> . . . . . .d this life
> 718
> . . . . .rs

> hi . . . . ir Condv . . . .and Succefs
> . . . . .ral . . . . .att SEA . . . . . make them lefs
> . . . . is lies he proved
> of . . . . beloved
> . . . . tha . . there be
> . . . . men as he.
> *Lo ! he*   *Aims*
> *from.* . . . . *ger of Alarms*
> A. . here Lyeth the Body of THOMAS
> the. . . MR JOHN DOWSE and
> MA . . . . his Wife who dyed the
> 18th of . . . . .1724 aged two years
> 8 months and 13 days.

Mrs. Martha Dowse had previously married Mr. Peter Mellotte, by whom she had a daughter Mary.

---

36. At entrance of School house west end :—

> IN MEMORY
> OF
> DIANA MILLS POWELL
> DEPARTED THIS LIFE 15TH SEPTR. 1845
> AGED 31 YEARS.

---

37. Stone ledger :—

> SACRED
> TO THE MEMORY OF
> MARIA BENNETT
> OF THE COLONY OF BERBICE,
> AGED 21 YEARS 3 MONTHS AND 12 DAYS
> SHE QUITTED THIS SUBLUNARY LIFE
> ON THE 4TH OF AUGUST A.D. 1811

---

38. Old stone ledger over a stone vault. On a lozenge at the west end :—

> JAMES DUNBAR
> DIED 19 SEPTEMBER, 1838
> AGED 42 YEAR   (*sic*)

---

39. Old slate headstone with urn and leaves at the top :—

In
Memory of
Capt. Moses Morrill,
of Wells, in N° America,
Who died Augst 21st 1802
Ætat 26.

---

40. Stone ledger with very large lettering :—

JANE BROOKS
Died
April the 6th
1812

---

41. Slate ledger north-west corner of churchyard :—

HERE
REST THE REMAINS OF
WILLIAM NICHOLSON ESQ^{R}
WHO DEPARTED THIS LIFE,
18TH SEPTEMBER 1845,
AGED 66 YEARS.

---

42. Stone vault with white stone lozenge at its west end :—

HORATIO ILES
DIED 5TH JAN^{Y} 1834
IN THE 51^{t} YEAR
OF HIS AGE.

1862, Dec.   John Alex. Iles to be a Member of the Executive Council of Nevis.

The family was from Montserrat.   See pedigree in *Antigua* II., 95.

---

43. Below a window in the north wall of the chancel :—

TO THE MEMORY OF HAMBLE JAMES LEACOCK
MARTYR OF THE PONGAS

He was second son of John Wrong Leacock of Barbados.   His first wife and one child died here, and he then married Mrs. Beard who died of cholera Aug., 1854 in Bridgetown.

See the tablet to him in All Saints Chapel Barbados.   He died 20 Aug., 1856, aged 61, in Sierra Leone.   He was Rector here 1828-35 and a second time 1849-52.

---

44. Below a window over the altar, broken :—

𝔍𝔫 𝔐𝔢𝔪𝔬𝔯𝔶 𝔬𝔣 ELIZABETH BRIGGS, Wife of JOSEPH LYDER BRIGGS | who died February 14ᵗʰ 1859. Aged 59 years.

See *Barbados Monumental Inscriptions*, p. 154. Sir Thomas Graham Briggs owned estates in Nevis, and was a Member of Council there.

---

45. Below a window in the south wall :—

Above is a Bishop's Mitre.

Arms : *Argent, a long cross between a serpent on dexter side of base and a dove with sprig on the sinister side ; on a chief Gule a key and crozier saltire ways surmounted by a royal crown.*

The Inscription has been broken and part lost.

One piece has :—MEMORY : OF
  (CONSECR)ATED : 1842

Another fragment has . . . . . . WARD : DAVIS   with four crosses under.

---

46. On a brass shield fixed to the lectern :—

IN MEMORY OF | SIR ANTHONY | MUSGRAVE | G.C.M.G. | ADMINISTRATOR | OF | NEVIS | CIRCA 1860.

Third son of Dr. Anthony Musgrave of Antigua by Mary Harris Sheriff his wife, was baptised at St. John's, Antigua 10 Oct., 1828, Colonial Secretary 1854-60, K.C.M.G. 1875, G.C.M.G. 1885, died when Governor of Queensland, 9 Oct., 1888, aged 60.

---

47. On a clock in the north Transept :—" Presented to St. Paul's Church
  BY W. S. DANIELL."

ST. GEORGE, GINGERLAND.

This parish, beyond St. John's, is about four miles east or to windward of Charlestown and 700 feet above the sea. The church is cruciform, and the transepts being longer than the nave, made me think that the altar may have formerly stood to the North. The church was opened 30 April, 1848 (*Mr. Buck's Almanac*).

The Rev. Dr. Lawrence Buckley Thomas the last Rector was the only white one left in the Island, when I was there in 1914, and he died early in 1915 in New York. He was a very competent genealogist. A list of Rectors and the first few sheets of the parish register appeared in *Caribbeana* III., 215, 352 and some of the Monumental Inscriptions in II., 314.

By an Act, No. 60, of 1704-5, it was recited that great part of this parish remained still unmanured and inhabitants were quitting, therefore to encourage settlers and sugar-making Indian Castle Bay was to be a lawful place to ship produce.

In the map of 1758 the old church is marked at New River on the coast, but it is not known when that building was destroyed.

48. On the north wall of the Nave, close to the pulpit, is a tablet surmounted by a grey marble urn :—

(eight lines above by R. W.)
Near this spot lie the remains of
EDWARD PARR COTTLE,
who died the 17th Auguſt, 1811,
aged 10 months and 12 days.

---

49. On the north wall of the nave :—

SACRED | TO THE MEMORY OF | THE REV^D JOSEPH HERBERT PEMBERTON, | WHO WAS BORN | ON THE 10TH OF SEPTEMBER, 1787, | AND DIED | ON THE 10TH OF SEPTEMBER, 1870, | HAVING BEEN RECTOR OF THIS PARISH| NEARLY 60 YEARS | THIS TABLET | WAS ERRECTED BY HIS AFFECTIONATE PARISHIONERS |.

A complete pedigree of his family appeared in *Caribbeana* I.

---

50. A window on the same wall has :—

ERECTED IN MEMORY | OF THOMAS J. TYRRELL | BY HIS WIDOW (no date).

---

51. On the south wall of the Nave :—

JANE | WIFE OF | EDWARD HUGGINS, ESQ'R, | OF NEVIS W.I. | ELDEST DAUGHTER OF | MAJ. JUXON, DIED AUG. 24, 1840 | AT THE PAVILION, NEW HAVEN, U.S. | IN A FIT OF APOPLEXY, | AGED 48 YEARS, | (three lines) EDWARD HUGGINS ESQR., | OF NEVIS, W.I. | DIED OCT., 18, 1840, | AT THE PAVILION NEW HAVEN U.S. OF CONSUMPTION, | AGED 60 YEARS. | (Four lines, erected by her son).

1812, July 30. Edward Huggins, jun., Esq., of the Isl^d of Nevis and Jane Plastow Juxon, da. of Captain George Juxon of His Majesty's 25th Reg^t of Foot. (*St. Thomas Middle Island St. Kitts*).

Their son Geo. Juxon Huggins, only son and heir was baptised 1 June, 1821.

---

52. A window in the Chancel has :—

IN MEMORY OF ELIZABETH RAWLINS   (No date).

---

53. A pair of white marble tablets are on black marble touching each other :—

BENEATH THIS MONUMENT
REST THE MORTAL REMAINS OF
GEORGIANA ELIZA.
WIFE OF RICHARD LITCOTT HICKS, OF THIS ISLAND
SHE DEPARTED HENCE ON THE 5TH OF AUGUST 1835
AGED 21 YEARS ;

---

54. Above, the wreath remains but the crest lost :—

Arms : *Gules a chevron between three griffin's heads erased.*

IN THE SAME TOMB
ARE DEPOSITED THE EARTHLY REMAINS OF
RICHARD LYTCOTT HICKS, ESQ^R
WHO WAS CUT OFF IN THE BLOOM OF YOUTH
A FEW DAYS AFTER HAVING ATTAINED HIS TWENTY SIXTH YEAR
HE SURVIVED HIS BELOVED WIFE FIVE MONTHS,
HAVING DEPARTED THIS LIFE, ON THE 10TH JAN^Y 1836.

1786, April.   R. L. Hicks, esq., of the Island of Nevis, on his passage from the West Indies (*Town & Country Mag.* 279).   The above arms are not in Burke's Armory.   He was probably son of Thompson Hicks of Epsom in 1750, then of St. James, Nevis, last of London in 1760, by Sarah his wife, daughter and eventual sole heiress of Richard Lycott of Springfield, co. Essex in 1725, by Mary his wife, daughter and co-heiress of James Walker of the Leeward plantation, Nevis. Hicks and Hicks Village are adjacent to the church of St. James.

———

55.   On the same wall, the Gallery hiding part of the tablet :—

NEAR THIS MONUMENT LIE THE REMAINS OF
ELIZABETH HUGGINS,
WHO DIED JANUARY 3RD 1818,
AT THE ADVANCED AGE OF 101 YEARS
ALSO OF
HER SON EDWARD HUGGINS ESQUIRE
WHO DEPARTED THIS LIFE THE 3RD OF JUNE, 1829,
AGED 74 YEARS
LIKEWISE OF
JOHN HUGGINS ESQUIRE, SON OF
THE ABOVE EDWARD HUGGINS ESQUIRE
WHO WAS CUT OFF THE 17TH. OF JUNE 1822,
AGED 34 YEARS.
HE HAS LEFT A NUMEROUS FAMILY TO DEPLORE HIS LOSS.

Below are :—

Crest : *An eagle's head erased.*
Arms : *Argent, a chevron guttée between three trefoils on a chief Azure a lion passant.*
Motto : INDUSTRIA.

Burke's Armory does not give these arms.

I was told there were two distinct families of Huggins here.

———

56. On the south wall of south Transept close to the door is a curious lead plate with the following Inscription punched on it :—

SACRED TO THE MEMORY OF
. MARY E. MUNRO
WHO LEFT HER EARTHLY TAB
ERNACLE TO BE WITH CHRIST
ON THE 1ST SEPTR 1872 AGED 28 YRS
ALSO HER FAITHFUL NURSE
JEMIMA SARJEANT
DIED 21ST DECBR 1868 AGED 72 YRS
BOTH OF BARBADOES, W.I.
IDA CONSTANCE
DIED 28TH NOVBR 1868 AGED 18MTHS
PERCY RICHARD
DIED 28TH NOVBR 1872 AGED 7MTHS
THOMAS ALLAN
DIED 27TH JANRY 1874 AGED 5MTHS
THE BELOVED CHILDREN OF
T. H. HUTCHINSON.

J. T. BOURNE, BARBADOES.

Along the passage of this Transept are four ledgers :—

57. Blue marble one :—

In Memory of
Mrs MARY SYMONDS wife of IAMES SYMONDS Efqr
who departed this life ye J0th of Sept. 175J Aged 59.
Underneath this Stone also rest the Remains of her
Brother IOHN BUTLER Efq. who departed this Life
the 20th May J7J7.

See pedigree in *Caribbeana* II., 62.

58. Stone ledger :—

Under this Stone
lieth the Remains of
ELIZABETH HUGGINS
who died January 3rd 1818
at the advanced Age of
101 Years.
Alfo of her Son
EDWARD HUGGINS Esquire
who departed this life the
3rd of June 1829 in confequence
of a fall from his Carriage
Aged 74 Years.
Likewise of
JOHN HUGGINS Esquire
Son of the above
EDWARD HUGGINS Esquire
who died the 17th June 1822
Aged 34 Years

59. Blue marble ledger cracked across. In sunk oval a Jacobean shield blank :—

Here lieth Entomb'd M^{RS} DOROTHY HERBERT, wife | of MR THOMAS HERBERT, of this Ifland, Gen^t & Daughter | of Major HENRY LYTTON, of the fame Place deceafed.| When living she was an Ornament to ye Marriage state | in which she Virtuously liv'd Twenty-five years & Ten | Months, and had Ifsve... Sons & Seven Daughters.| But to the Jrreparable lofs of her Afflicted Family | Died in Childbed with her tenth Son.
She changed this Life for A Better JAN^{RY} J6th J724.| In the 42^d Year of her Age.

Mr. Tho. Herbert was eldest son and heir of Thos. Herbert of Nevis. See pedigree of Herbert in *Caribbeana* V., 223.

---

60.   Here lies the Body of
FRANCIS SANDERS Iunior who departed
this life the J8th of Iuly, 1742 Aged 51.
This put here by His Loving Widow
SARAH SANDERS.

He was probably son of Mr. Francis Sanders, Senior, of Nevis, planter, by Anne his wife.
His wife Sarah whom he married here 7 Sept., 1718, was a daughter of — Choppin and her sister Frances married John Williams and her sister Elizabeth married Tho. Stevens. Mrs. Sarah Sanders died at Antigua 22 Dec., 1748, intestate leaving 3 daughters and co-heiresses. See several entries to the family in *Caribbeana* I. & II.

---

61. In the central passage of Nave is a blue marble ledger :—

Here are deposited the Remains
of
SALLY MAYNARD DANIELL,
Infant Daughter,
of the Honourable
JAMES DANIELL, Esquire
who fell a victim
to a most malignant fever on
the 22nd of July, 1813
to the inexprefsible regret of
her Parents
Aged 3 Years 9 Months and 19 Days.
The Remains of her Infant Sister
SALLY MAYNARD DANIELL
who died on the 22nd of May, 1809,
Aged 11 Months and 17 Days
are buried with her.

Col. J. Daniell was President in 1833. He married Sarah daughter of William Archibald Maynard. She was baptised here 24 April, 1787.

---

62.   West of Churchyard.   Ledger on a stone vault :—

IN LOVING MEMORY OF
ELIZABETH RAWLINS
WIDOW OF STEDMAN AKERS RAWLINS
WHO FELL ASLEEP ON THE 23ᴿᴰ OF MARCH
A.D. 1891, AGED 76 YEARS

63.   On a Cross near by :—

IN | LOVING MEMORY | OF | STEDMAN AKERS RAWLINS | WHO DEPARTED
THIS LIFE | AUGUST 28 | A.D. 1850 AGED 43* YEARS |
ALSO OF STEDMAN RAWLINS.
SON OF THE ABOVE WHO DEPARTED THIS LIFE
FEBRUARY 5ᵀᴴ 1892 AGED 56

He was of the S. Kitts family, but his father and grandfather appear to have
been residents in Nevis.   See pedigree in *Caribbeana* V., 97.

64.   Over the west arch is :—

A.D.
1847

ST. JOHN'S, FIGTREE.

The Parish of St. John, Figtree, lies up the hill, about two miles to windward
of Charlestown.   The church abuts on the high road.   Illustrations of it, with a
transcript of the Parish Register to the year 1800, and a list of the
Rectors appeared in *Caribbeana* II., 369.

RECTORS.

Thomas Powers, Fellow of Trinity Coll., Cambridge.   Inducted Rector of
St. Mary's, Antigua, Jan 1695, died 14 Dec., 1698, buried and Monumental
Inscription at St. Johns in said island.   (*Antigua* III., 377).   He was Rector of
St. John's, Nevis, before Wm. Smith, but the date is unknown.

Theodore Heskith, M.A.   Went to the Leeward Islands 11 Nov., 1698.
Left Rectory in 1701.

Sermon of the Funeral of the Hon. Col. F. Collingwood, and of his Lady,
who were both interred in St. John's Church, in the Island of Nevis, in America,
May 29 and May 31, 1690.   By T. Heskith, 1700.   (*Bibliography of the West
Indies* by F. Cundall, No. 245).

Farewell Sermon preached in St. John's, at Nevis, in America, 25th May,
1701, by Theo. Heskith, 4°, pp. 30.   1702.   (*Ibid.* No. 246 and my copy).

William Smith, B.A., 1716—21.   Son of Josiah Smith of Yarmouth co.
Norfolk pleb. matriculated from Queens' College, Oxford 27 March, 1707, aged 17,
B.A. 16 Oct., 1710 ; went out to the Leeward Islands 3 Feb., 1715-16 ; Instituted
Rector here 18 April, 1716 ; left 1721 for England ; Rector of St. Mary's,
Bedford, 1745-49 and then left or died.   Author of a Natural History of Nevis.

---

* 43 is doubtful the figures having been altered.

William Wharton, 1729. Went out to Barbados 4 March, 1728-29, also Rector of St. Thomas, Lowland, 1735 ; died Feb., 1737-8. Will proved at York. (*N. & Q.* 11S. V., 127).

John Mackay, 1742-1750. Went out to the Leeward Islands, 31 May, 1739 ; Rector of St. George's, Gingerland, 1739-1740 and buried there 9 Sept., 1750.

Edwin Thomas, M.A., 1750-1764. Went out to Nevis 22 Dec., 1747 ; Rector of St. George's Gingerland, 1750-1763.   Rector of George's, Basseterre, St. Kitts, 1765 and died 19 Jan., 1789 aged 69.

John Bowen (?B.A., Oxford, 1753), 1765-1767. Went out to Antigua 9 Jan., 1760 ; Rector of St. John's, Antigua, 28 Jan., 1767 ; Rector of St. Thomas, Lowland, 1770 ; resigned St. John's, Antigua, June 1783, and died in London May, 1787. Will (198 *Major*).

William Scott, M.A., 1767. Ordained by Dr. Terrick, Bishop of London. Presented to St. John and St. James, 1767.

William McKenley, 1773. Also Rector of St. Thomas, Lowland.

William Jones, Rector of St. Thomas Lowland, 1787-90, dead 1800.

George Green, 1792-1800. ?Went out to St. Vincent, 1778. Rector of St. George's, Gingerland, 1783-99.

Thomas Mills, M.A., 1802-1803.

A. Hamilton, B.A., 1803. Probably Andrew Hamilton of the St. Kitts family, who held a living in the West Indies, and died Rector of Knipton, co. Leicestershire, to which he was instituted 1817.

Edward Brazier, M.A., 1808-11. Rector of St. Thomas, Middle Island, St. Kitts, 1811-18.   Son of Edward Brazier of St. Kitts, Esq., matriculated from Wadham College, Oxford, 22 May, 1792 aged 18 ; B.A. 1796, M.A. 1800   On 2 Nov., 1801, John Pinney writing from Somerton Early recommended him for holy orders.   See No. 76 inscription.

Joseph Herbert Pemberton, B.A., 1818-70. Also Rector of St. George's, Gingerland until his death 19 Sept., 1870.

John Mackechnie Collins, 1874-1890. Born 1835, of Codrington College, 1853.   Second son of Rev. John Cox Collins, Rector of St. Anthony, Montserrat. also Rector of St. George's, Gingerland.

John Jones, 1890-1898, also Rector of St. George's, Gingerland.   Rebuilt both churches.

Ifor James Jones, 1898-1899, brother of preceding.

(Alfred W. Watt, Priest-in-charge, 1900-1903).

Lawrence Buckley Thomas, D.D., 1903 until his death at New York early in 1915 ; also Rector of St. George's, Gingerland.

ST. JOHN'S CHURCH.

Along the Nave floor are nine ledgers all lying side by side across the passage.

65. White marble ledger. In sunk oval is a Jacobean shield with mantling :—

Crest : hidden by floor of pews.

Arms : *Argent three crosses crosslet fitchy, between as many crescents ;* on an inescutcheon : *Argent on a bend three pheons* (Helme).

The Inscription is a long one of forty-one lines in Latin, partly worn away.

1 Sub hoc marm. . . . . Viator
2   Iohann . . Pinne. . . . .
3   Azariæ Pinney. . . . .
4   . . . . haeres
                      (30 lines illegible)
35 Erat decefsus tempore in hae insulâ excellentissimo Regi Georgio
36 a consiliis, Capitalis Iusticiarius, & turmæ equitum tribunus.   Anno D.
37 1708vo uxorem duxit Mariam filiam & hœredem GULIELMI Helme
38 hujusce etiam Infulæ, armigeri, cumquâ duodecim felicis connubij
39 annos grate numerauit, conjugis optimæ maritus optimuse Septem=
40 liberis, tres tantum reliquit Superstites, puerulos duos, filiolam unam
41 Natus 3^{io} Maij an]686to Obiit]]^{mo} die Decembris an. dom. 1720mo
       ætatis Suæ.

He was only son and heir of Azariah Pinney who was sent as a convicted rebel to Nevis in 1685, after the Monmouth Rising.   He matriculated from Pembroke Coll., Oxf., 8 June, 1703, aged 17, barrister-at-law of the Middle Temple 1710, Member of Council 1717, Chief Justice 1720, died intestate in the Parish of St. Bennet Fink, London.

There was evidently a Rector c^a 1680 to 1690, a good classical scholar who wrote out this Epitaph as well as Nos. 68 & 75 and probably 75 & 88.

---

66. Blue marble ledger :—

Here lyeth the Body of FRANCES
BRODBELT late wife to Colonel
RICHARD BRODBELT of Nevis who
departed this life the 27th of Auguft
1725 Aged 37 Years
She was Humility Meeknefs
Conftancy and Evenefs of
Temper A Loving Wife and A
Tender Mother alfo two of her
Children IOSEPH HILL and
FRANCES HILL BRODBELT.

She was daughter and co-heiress of Joseph Hill planter.

He was brother of Laurence Brodbelt of Nevis and London, Merchant, was Brigadier and was buried here 4 Feb., 1755 aged 68.   See pedigree of Brodbelt in *Caribbeana* IV., 20.

---

67. Blue marble ledger :—

Here lies the Body of
Henrietta, Wife of John
Sanders who departed
this life 29th Decr 1746.

He was probably a son of Mr. Francis Sanders, senr., of Nevis, planter by Anne his wife.   Henrietta was daughter of James Bevon of Nevis, Esq., Speaker 1696, whose will was dated 1720 (153 *Marlboro*)   Her other sister Elizabeth was wife of Richard Abbot.   Their son James Bevon Sanders was born 21 July, baptised 29 Aug., and buried 11 Nov., 1733.   See pedigree in *Caribbeana* V., 263.

68   Blue marble ledger.   In sunk circle a Jacobean Shield with Mantling :—

Crest : *An animal's head couped over wreath.*
Arms : *Argent on a chief embattled three roundles.*

Hic situs est Philippus Lee
Familia ejusdem nominis infula Vectensi oriundus
In hac Insula natus A.D. MDCXLV
In eadem defunctus A.D. MDCLXXXVIIII

The arms are those of Leigh of North Court in the Isle of Wight, whose pedigree was entered in the *Visitation of Hampshire.*

---

69.   Beneath this Stone

rest the Bodies
of . . . . WAR WILLIAM
and A. . . . . BR . . . . ER

Perhaps Brazier.   Edward Brazier, Esq. and family were residents 1785—1800.

---

70.   White stone :—

Sacred to the Memory of
ANDREW HAMILTON Esqr
who died on the 3^d of April, 1808
in the . . . Year of his Age
(Erected by his wife MARTHA WILLIAMS HAMILTON)

He was a subscriber 1790 to Peterkin's *Book of Planting,* was President in 1798 of the General Council of the Leeward Isles, and resigned his seat on the Council of Nevis, 1 May, 1799.   She was daughter and heiress of John Richardson Herbert and was married here 18 May, 1787, and died 12 Aug., 1819. (MS. Note in Mr. Buck's *Almanac*).
Mr. Hamilton's first wife died in England 14 March, 1782.

---

71.   Blue marble ledger :—

Sacred to the Memory
of
SARAH HERBERT
Daughter of THOMAS & FRANCES *HERBERT*
and Sister
To the Honble *the PRESIDENT of this ISLAND*
who departed this Life *Sep*^{tr} 5th 1875
Aged 53

See pedigree in *Caribbeana* V., 223.

---

72.   White marble ledger with two cherubs heads at top corners—

Under this Stone
is Depofited
the Mortal part of
Mrs ELIZABETH HERBERT
Wife of the *Hon,ble*
JOHN RICHARDSON HERBERT *Esqr*
Prefident of this *Ifland*
She Died univerfally lamented
Sepr 29th 1769, in the 34th Year of her
Age, & the J7th of her Marriage.

She was daughter of Col. John Williams of Antigua and niece of Tho.
Williams Esq., of Nevis, and baptised at St. John's, Antigua.

---

73.   Brown ledger :—

There are traces of one or more lines under the pew.

. . . day of March, 1806 Aged 63 years
to enjoy the Rewards of a
happier State and to live
in the Memory of the Surviving.
An Affectionate Niece
hath paid this Tribute of
Refpect to her Remains.

---

74.   White marble ledger in front of the Communion Rails :—

Jacobean Shield bevelled or cut in at the edge.
Arms : *A lion rampant.*

Qui fi PROSAPIÆ Decus si VIRTVTIS Honos qua
Bellica qua Civilis fifpectata PROBITAS, fi
ERVDITIO fingularis, fi deniq Omniv qui norant
VOTA quidqua adverfus Moite valerent Vivcret
Heic Situs Eft
EDMVNDVS STAPLETON
Armiger ex antiquâ Familiâ in Agro
EBORACENSI oriundus ; Frater GVILIELMI
STAPLETON Baronetti, haru Infularum
Qua CARIBÆ vocantur, quot quot ad
BRITANNICVM Imperium fpectant, CAPITANEI
five Deputati REGII : a quo etiam, cum efset
Ipfi uti & Omnibus alijs Dilectifsimu^s Præfectus
erat hvic Infulæ MONTISERRATO dictæ
In qua poft quinquennalem Præfecturam,
Cœlebs & Ivvenis, undiquaq Defideratifsimus,
citra trigefsimum Ætatis Annum,
Diem Obijt XV. Kal
Sept. Anno Salutis
MDCLXXX

Henry Nelson Coleridge wrote in 1825, " There is also an old marble with the name of Stapleton Cotton engraved on it." (*Six Months in the West Indies*, p. 196.) This must have been an error on his part.

His ancestor settled in Ireland tem. Henry VI. Another [brother Col. Redmond Stapleton was Deputy Governor of Montserrat 1676 till his death about 1687.

There was a Knightly family of Stapleton in Yorkshire, whose pedigree was entered in the *Visitations*.

---

75. In the passage to the Vestry, with several cracks across it, is a blue marble ledger :—

In a sunk circle a Jacobean shield with Mantling, Helmet and Wreath but no Crest.

Arms : *Three mens heads with long curling hair couped at the shoulders* (Edye).

Here Ly's Interred the Body of
Cap[t] IOHN EDDY who Departed
this life the Second of April 1682
And In the thirty Sixth
year of his Age
Friendship and Courage Were in him Combind,
And equally Adorn'd his Virtuous Mind,
His friendſhip knew no Change his Courage no fear
But great & Matchleſs did in Both Appear,
With a kind wife and hopefull Iſue bleſt
Death snatch'd him hence to Everlasting reſt
Here alſo Ly's Interred the Body of
ANN CARPENTER late Wife of
HENRY CARPENTER and Daughter of
CAP[T] IOHN EDDY & PENELOPE his wife
Who departed this life the FOVRTEENTH,
day of IANVARY]702 And in the TWENTY,
THIRD year of her Age
Vertue and Beauty Join'd In her were Seen,
An Eaſy temper And a Charming Meen,
A conſtant Friendſhip, duty were twas due,
And Charity to all the poor She Knew,
Her Spotleſs life all poysn'd tongves Defy'd
Bemoan'd of all becauſe Belov'd ſhe Dyed

Penelope was daughter of Michael Smith of Nevis. She remarried Wm. Mead, President of St. Kitts, 1698-1701. His will was dated 1702 (36 *Ash*). She was aged 45 in 1707 and her will was dated 1733 (106 *Ducie*).

Henry Carpenter who was of Nevis in 1685, was appointed Secretary General in 1701. By his will in 1704 (227 *Ash*) he bequeathed to the Parish of St. Paul £200 for books and d.s.p. I think these books were a few years ago deposited in Codrington College Library.

In the book-plate No. 665 of Governor Wm. Mathew the coat of *Gules three mens heads couped affrontee*, attributed erroneously to Williams is that of Eddy.

On east wall of Chancel are three white and black marble tablets. A column between two oval tablets and below an oblong one.

76.   On the oblong tablet is the following :—

> Near this spot in the family burial place lies
> the Honble JOSEPH BRAZIER,
> Son of the late EDWARD BRAZIER
> who departed this life on the 24th July 1824, aged 42.

On the oval tablet above to the left is :—

> IN
> The same Burial place
> are interred the remains
> of HARRIET HOPKINS SLATER
> the aimable relict of
> WILLIAM SLATER Esqr
> and daughter of the late
> EDWARD BRAZIER
> who departed this life 11th July 1824
> aged 47 after eleven days illness of Fever !

On the right hand oval tablet is :—

> IN
> the same spot
> lie the remains
> of HARRIET SLATER
> youngest daughter of the said
> W^M & HARRIET HOPKINS SLATER
> who departed this life
> the 19th Decr 1824.
> aged 15.

On the south side of the east wall of Chancel are the two following tablets.

77.   On an oval tablet white marble on black :—

> *WILLIAM WOOLWARD*
> Of this Ifland *Efq^r*
> Died the 18th of February
> 1779
> Aged 53 Years
> He married *MARY* the Daughter of
> *THOMAS HERBERT Efq^rː*
> To whose joint Memory
> This Tablet is erected
> By their only Daughter
> *FRANCES HERBERT* :
> Who was first married to
> *JOSIAH NISBETT*, M.D.

And since to
Rear Admiral NELSON
Who, for his very distinguished Services
Has been successively created
A *Knight* of the *Bath* ;
And a *Peer* of GREAT BRITAIN
By the Title of
Baron NELSON
of the Nile

The above was copied on the spot on 28 Aug., 1899 by a Naval Officer of H.M.S. " Indefatigable " and sent to *The Times*. It was subsequently printed in *Misc. Gen. et H.*, Third Series, Vol. III., p. 299.

Hon. Wm. Woolward of Nevis, Esq. Will dated 5 Nov., 1778. Brother Tho. Woolward £100. All residue to my daughter Frances Woolward. The partnership of Herbert, Morton & Woolward. Sworn 20 May, 1779. Testator died 27 February, 1779. Administration to the creditors. (*Book of Wills* p. 465).

Josiah Nisbet, M.D., son of Walter Nibset of Nevis, born 7 Aug., 1747, was married here 28 June, 1779, and died intestate at Salisbury, 5 Oct., 1781. Their only son, Josiah, Capt., Royal Navy, died 1830. Mrs. Nisbet was married 11th March, 1787, to Capt. Nelson in a house in this parish long since in ruins. I walked all over its site in 1914. Lady Nelson was baptised May, 1761 at St. George's, Gingerland and died in London, 6 May, 1831 aged 73. Monumental Inscription at Littleham, co. Devon. (See *Antigua* III., 443).

Lord Nelson bore on an inescutcheon *Barry of six Azure and Argent three bucks' heads cabossed, on a chief Ermine a lion passant between two pheons* for *Woolward*

---

78   NEAR THIS MARBLE IN ONE GRAVE
LIE HUSBAND WIFE AND CHILD
WILLIAM BRAZIER DIED OF A FEVER
AT THE EARLY AGE OF 12 YEARS OCT^R 10TH 1794
M^{RS} ANNE BRAZIER OF FEVER
DEPARTED THIS LIFE AGED 47, 8TH DEC^R 1797.
EDWARD BRAZIER DIED SEPT^R 20TH 1819, AGED 83.

1785, Sept. 5. Betty, a Slave, the property of Edward Brazier, Esqr buried.
1793 (*sic*) Oct. 10. Willian Brazier, buried.
1797, Dec. 8. Ann Brazier, buried.

Edward, son of Edward Brazier of St. Kitts, esq., matriculated from Wadham College, Oxford, 22 May, 1792, aged 18 ; B.A. 1796 ; M.A. 1800 ; ordained 1801 ; Rector of St. Thomas, St. Kitts, 11 April, 1811 ; died 11 April, 1819.

On the south wall of Nave are three tablets :—

79. SACRED | TO THE MEMORY OF | *FANNY HENRIETTA PARRIS* | WIFE OF | *RICHARD NEAVE PARRIS, ESQ.* | OF THIS ISLAND | WHO DEPARTED THIS LIFE MARCH 19TH 1817, AGED 32 | LEAVING AN AFFLICTED HUSBAND AND FOUR FINE BOYS | (Erected by his brother-in-law).

1817, June. At Nevis, Mrs. Parris, wife of R. N. Parris, esq., of that island and late of Roath Villa, Cardiff (*Gent. Mag.* 646).
There was a family of Parris in Barbados.

---

80.   Sacred to the Memory of
                The Honble IOHN RICHARDSON HERBERT,
                       Prefident for 25 Years
                Of his *Majefty's Council* of this Ifland ;
        (Erected by his daughter MARTHA WILLIAMS HAMILTON, no date).

He died 18 Jan., 1793 and his will was dated 1788 (151 *Dodwell*).   Mrs. Wm.
Woolward was his sister and he states that having allowed his niece Frances
wife of Horatio Nelson, Capt. R.N., £100 a year he bequeathed her £3000 and to
Josiah Nisbitt her son £500 at 21.   By a Codicil of 5 Dec., 1792, he gave her
£1000 more.   All his property was entailed on his daughter, Mrs. Martha W.
Hamilton with reversion to his nephew Magnus Morton.

---

81.   SACRED TO THE MEMORY OF
                HENRY WILKINSON BAKER ESQ^{RE}
                         OF THIS ISLAND ;
                FORMERLY OF THE COUNTY OF SUFFOLK
        WHO DEPARTED THIS LIFE AFTER A FEW DAYS ILLNESS,
                ON THE 17TH DECEMBER 1833,
                       AGED 29 YEARS :
        AND WHOSE REMAINS WERE INTERRED IN THIS CH YD (*sic*)
                ALSO TO THE MEMORY OF
                M^{RS} MARY WILLIAMS SMITH,
                     OF CHARLES TOWN,
                  PARISH OF SAINT PAUL ;
            WHO DIED ON THE 21ST SEPTEMBER 1829,
                       AGED 63 YEARS ;
            AND WAS BURIED NEAR THIS PLACE

South side of Churchyard.

82.   A broken blue marble slab lying loose :—

Above is incised a Jacobean Shield with Mantling.

Crest : *A fleur-de-lis* over Wreath and Helmet.
Arms : *A chevron between three fleurs-de-lis* ; impaling, *a chevron between
as many portcullises.*   (Fishcocke).

The Inscription consists of six lines, all the lettering being raised instead
of incised.   I could not make out any name or date only the incomplete words :

" . . THOUT BLA . . . . " in the fifth line.   The dexter coat is too common a
one to identify.

83. Blue marble ledger :—

Sacred to the Memory of
EDWARD LAURENCE ESQ^R
of this Ifland,
who departed this Life
on the 8th of March, 1802
in the 72nd Year of his Age.
And alfo to the Memory of
FRANCES his only Daughter
who departed this Life on the 6th of
July 1795 in the 33rd Year of her Age.

1780. John Laurence, third son of Edward Laurence, merchant in Nevis.
(*Glasgow University Matriculations.*)

---

84. At the end of a large Vault :—

W. R
Æ 53

---

85. Two brown ledgers, side by side :—

Under this Stone
are Interr'd the Remains
of M^{RS} *MARY WEEKES,*
who departed this life on the 18th day.
of February, 1780
in the 38th Year of her Age.

1777, Aug. 21. William Burt Weekes to Mary Browne, Spinst. (*Par. Reg.*).
His first wife was Elizabeth. His will was dated 1796 (147 *Abercrombie*).
Dr. Tho. Pym Weekes was his only surviving son.
The first settler, Mr. Tho. Weekes was entered in the Census of 1677-8.

---

86. Brown slab :—

Under the Cover
of this Stone are the Remains
of *THOMAS BROWNE* who died the
19th day of November, 1779
in the Eleventh Year of his Age.

---

87. Broken blue marble slab lying loose :—

Hic me pofuit
felix Relicta SIMONIS BROWNE
de morte nimis tamen inopin . .
dum sim nescies Viator !
. . o Ælatis trigifimo octavo
. . . imo Julij die
1738.

1733, June 10.   Sarah daughter of Mr. Simon Browne and Sarah his wife born May 20 last past and Baptised this day. (*Par. Reg.*) She was living in 1751, but her three sisters Mary, Elizabeth and Frances were dead. "Ensine" Simon Browne was entered in the Census of 1677-8.

Col. John Netheway by his will of 1691 bequeathed to his godson Simon Browne, son of Simon Browne deceased 3000 lbs. at 18. (See pedigree of Browne in *Caribbeana* I., 35).

88.   Blue marble slab over stone vault :—

> HERE. . . . . OF . . . .
> RICHARD MADR. . . . 3 ACCIDEN. .
> . . . . ARTED THIS LIFE THE
> . . . . OF MARCH AN : 16
> . . . . 6 MO :
> ALSOE HERE LYE THE BODIES OF
> NICHOLAS SARAH AND MARY ONE OF
> HIS SONES & TWO OF HIS DAVGHTERS
> WHO ACCIDENTALLY WERE DROWNED
> THE 29 DAY OF MAY 1684
> NICHOLAS MADRIN AGED 9 YEAR 7 MO :
> ·   SARAH AGED 25 YEAR 5 MON :
> MARY AGED 18 YEAR 6 MON :
> (14 lines of Latin follow)

There is a pedigree of a family of this name in Dwnn's *Visitations of Wales* II., 177.

James Hale of Nevis Will dated 1673.   To the children of Lieut. Richard Mandrin 15,000 lbs. (*Caribbeana* IV., 110).

89.   Slate slab on stone vault :—

IN LOVING MEMORY | OF | MARY EMILY | WIFE OF CHARLES P. ESDAILE | BORN AUGUST 15th 1859 | DIED AUGUST 30th 1883 |.

There was a family of Esdaile resident in St. Kitts, the first of whom John Esdaile Senr., Esq., was aged 43 in 1707-8. Descendants are surviving. A Mrs. Esdaile resides with a daughter at St. John's, Antigua.

90.   Stone tomb.   On north Side of top :—

IN LOVING MEMORY | OF | PAITFIELD MILLS | DIED JANᴿʸ 1ˢᵀ 1854 | AGED 36 Yᴿˢ |.

He was of the Inner Temple and Chief Justice of Nevis, fifth son of John Colhoun Mills, President of Nevis.

On the south side of top :—

TO THE BELOVED MEMORY | OF | ANNE WIDOW OF JOHN COLQUHOUN MILLS | DIED DECᴿ 28ᵀᴴ 1872 AGED 88 Yᴿˢ

ST. JAMES, WINDWARD.

The old church was demolished and the present one built in 1830.

The early registers were burnt in Charlestown, perhaps in the great fire of 1837. A small book of marriages commences in 1830.

Three volumes, with printed forms for baptisms, marriages and burials, commence in 1839. The Vestry Minutes date from 1785.

The late Maj.-General R. Pemberton, who visited Nevis a few years ago stated that the registers began in 1787, but the coloured rector in charge in 1914 had no knowledge of any book so early.

RECTORS.

Rev. Mr. Gold arrived 25 April, 1684, and was presented to St. James' Parish. (*Col. Cal.* p. 625).

Mr. Johnson died 1719. The church going to decay ; no minister 1724. (*Caribbeana* III., 340).

Rev. Wm. Scott, M.A. was presented in 1767.

Rev. Henry Erskine Kirkpatrick ordained deacon and priest by the Bishop of London went out in 1768 and was presented by President R. H. Losack in 1770 to St. James.

ST. JAMES' CHURCH.

There are only two tablets.

91. At the west end of the Nave, partly covered by the Gallery :—

Beneath are the Remains of WALTER NISBETT *Efqr*
One of the Beft of Hufbands, the Beft of Fathers, and
Sincereft of Friends. He Departed this life on the 15th:
Day of June in the Year of our *LORD* 1765 in
(about three lines are here covered up by the joists).
JOSIAH WEBBE of New River *Efq* ; who Departed this
life on the 7th: Day of December, 1763.
Alfo Here Lie deposited, the Remains of WALTER NISBET,
Son to the above W. NISBET, *Efqr* ; who to the inexprefsible
grief of his Family and Friends, departed this Life the 8th
of Decr 1797 in the 53d Year of his Age.
Two Infant Children lie Buried with him.

Walter Nesbit, fifth child of Archibald Nesbit, II., of Carfin, Lanarkshire by Emilia daughter of Archibald Stuart, son of James, third Earl of Moray, was baptised 19 July, 1706. Under what circumstances he settled in Nevis I cannot say. He married in 1743, Mary, daughter of Josiah Webbe of New River who died 24 January, 1752, aged 28, leaving five children, as recorded on the floor stone over the vault. He was Colonel and Member of Council, 1759. Will dated 14 June, 1765. My sister Ann Nesbit. To Trustees £5000 for my four younger children viz. : two sons Josiah and James £1000 each and two daughters Ann and Mary Amelia £1500 each. All residue to my son Walter. Sworn 18 June 1765. (*Book of Wills* p. 31). They left issue :—

1.   Walter, born 3 Jan. and baptised 28 April, 1745 at St. James'.   Will (862 *Howe*) and left several children.

2.   Anne born 14 Febraury, 1746, died spinster, 7 July, 1833

3.   Josiah born 7 August, 1747, M.D., married 28 June, 1779 at St. Johns, Frances Herbert Woolward and died intestate, 5 October, 1781.   She remarried Lord Nelson.

4.   James Webbe, born 23 Aug., 1749 died bachelor.

5.   Mary Emilia born 4 February, 1751-2 married 17 July, 1773, James Lockhart.

Robert eighth child of Archibald Nesbit II., of Carfin baptised 19 Sept., 1712 also went to Nevis then to St. Kitts and died a bachelor 29 September, 1740. Will at Edinburgh.

1763, July 30.   Josiah Webbe of New River in the Parish of St. James, Nevis, Esq., for £3000 sells to Robt. Cooper of Sarum, draper, 4 parcels of land, containing 300 acres formerly the estate of Josiah Webbe the Elder, Esq. deceased.   (*Nevis Records* L. 73).

See a very good pedigree of Nesbit in *Misc. Gen. et Her*. 5S. Vol. II. p. 44.

---

92.   On the north wall of the north Transept :—

RICHARD CLEMENT
ELDEST SON OF RICHARD CLEMENT ESQ^R AND ELIZABETH HIS WIFE
OF BARBADOES,
BORN NOVEMBER VI. MDCCXCVIII.,
DIED IN THIS ISLAND NOVEMBER XXVII. MDCCCXXIII.
AFTER A FEVER OF EIGHTEEN DAYS
WHILST HONOURABLY EMPLOYED AS SECRETARY TO HIS MAJESTY'S COMMISSION
FOR INQUIRING INTO THE ADMINISTRATION OF CIVIL AND CRIMINAL JUSTICE
IN THE WEST INDIES.

He matriculated from Trinity College, 17 May, 1817, aged 18, B.A. 1821 (*Foster*).   The late Major Clement of Ascot, Berks, was of this family.

There are seven ledgers in the floor of the Nave.

93.   Grey marble ledger in central passage the left hand edge under a pew:—

In sunk oval is a fine Jacobean Shield with Mantling.

Crest : *A boar's head couped erect, over Wreath a Helmet.*
Arms : *Argent two chevronels within a bordure engrailed.*

Here are the remains of
. . . MOTHY TYRRELL ESQ^R
who departed this life
30th day of September, 1742
in the 66th Year of his Age.

Col. Sir James Russell, Knight, of Nevis married 13 Jan., 1675 at Camberwell, Penelope, daughter of Sir Timothy Tyrrell of Oakley, co. Bucks and Shotover, Oxfordshire, Knight.   She died in 1707 and the above may have been her nephew.   Her brother James, baptised 1642, married 1668-9 Mary Hutchinson.   (Chester's *Marriages in Westminster Abbey* and Blanch's *History of Camberwell*).

---

94.   Grey and blue marble ledger, alongside No. 93 :—

Inscription in border framewise.   This stone is like several in Barbados. In the centre are eight lines of religious poetry running lengthways.

H ERE LYETH THE BO
    ANNO DOM   1679
And in the 26 year of his ag

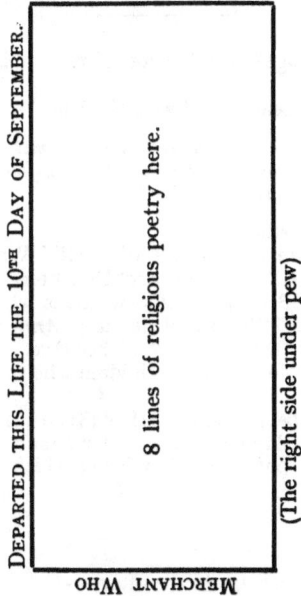

95.   In the floor of south Transept near the door is a blue marble ledger with the left hand top corner missing:—

In sunk circle a Jacobean shield with Mantling.

Crest : *A serpent, over wreath and helmet.*
Arms : *Argent four barrulets debruised of a sepent.*   (Not in Burke's Armory).

. . . . . lye . . . erred 3 of the *Daughters*
Thomas Belman Gent & Bridgett
his wife the firft *Elizabeth* Apr. y° 25
1699 in y° 4ᵗʰ year of her age y° fecond
Frances who died Sept y° 19ᵗʰ 1699 in
her fecond year, the third *Frances* who
died Auguft y° 20ᵗʰ 1700 being but four
Moneths old.

96. In the same passage is another blue marble ledger :—

Here lyeth the Body of
IOSEPH HAYTON GENT :
who. departed this Life the 15th
day of March in ye Year of Our Lord
17⅜⅝ Aged 37 Years.

97. In the same passage but in the north Transept is a blue marble ledger :

In sunk oval is a Jacobean Shield with Mantling.

Crest : *A boar's head erased, over wreath and helmet.*
Arms : *Three boars' heads, an annulet for a difference* ; impaling, *a cross
between four* (? *eagles* or *falcons*). (Webbe).

Motto : HIS FORTIBUS ARM (*sic*).
Here are the remains of MARY Wife of
Coll WALTER NISBET and Daughter to the late
JOSIAH WEBBE Efqr of new River who Departed
this Life the 24th Day of January *Ann. Dom.* 1752
In the 29th year of her Age.
(Six lines.   Mother of five children who survived her).

In the pedigree of Nisbet in *Antigua* III., 443 she has been incorrectly entered
as a daughter of Walter Maynard. Her sister Frances married in 1737 Wm.
Maynard whose grandson purchased New River which is still in the possession
of their descendants.

98. Brown ledger in passage to the altar :—

Here Lie the Mortal Remains of
EDWARD WILLIAMS
of Denbigh in North Wales born 27th
Octr 1784 died 28th Octr 1804.
(Eleven lines ; a Mother, Sister and Brother surviving).

99. Blue marble ledger near the Litany Stool :—

Here lye the Bodies of
ELIZABETH LEE who was born
Iune ye 9th 1716 & Died March ye : 15th : 171⅞.
JUDITH LEE who was born
Novr ye 26th : 1721 & Died Iuly ye :]0th : 1723
FRANCES LEE who was born
Decr ye :]0th : 1718 & Died Octr : ye : 21st : 1724
Also Mr THOMAS LEE their Father
who Departed this life Apll ye : 14th : 1729
in the 36 Year of his Age.

CHURCHYARD.

100. North side of Vestry :—

IN MEMORY OF THOMAS CHARLE, YOUNGEST SON OF THE VEN^{BLE} ISAAC WOOD | ARCHDEACON OF CHESTER AND MARY HIS WIFE | DIED NOVEMBER 4, 1864. | AGED 30.

101. On a fragment of blue marble lying loose :—

. . .ETH THE . . .
. . THE WIFE
. . . . PARTED THI
. . . . 6 YEARE OF
. . . . . DOM̄ 16 . .
(Traces of four lines following)

The lettering is in the style of the 17th century.

ST. MARK'S CHAPEL, ROUND HILL.

102. On the north wall of the Chancel is a tablet :—

SACRED TO THE MEMORY OF
OF M^{RS} FRANCES HUGGINS
(RELICT OF EDW^D HUGGINS ESQ^{RE} OF GOLDEN ROCK)
(SHE DIED) ON THE 11th DAY OF DEC^R
IN THE YEAR OF OUR LORD 1837
AGED 85 YEARS.

103. On the south wall of Chancel is a tablet :—

TO THE MEMORY OF
THOMAS JOHN COTTLE Esq^R
FOR MANY YEARS PRESIDENT OF THIS ISLAND
WHO DEPARTED THIS LIFE FEBRUARY 1st 1828
AGED 67 YEARS

Below is a shield of arms which was formerly between two festoons, the latter lost.

Crest : lost.
Arms : *Or, a bend Gules.*

See pedigree in *Caribbeana* IV., 210.

104. On the floor on an oblong piece of marble :—

M^{RS} FRANCES HUGGINS
AGED 86 YEARS ;
DIED 11TH DECEMBER
1837,

105. On a white marble lozenge like those in Bristol Cathedral :—

ANN PRENTIS PEMBERTON
DIED MAY 7TH ANNO DOMINI 1855
. AGED 64 YEARS

---

106. On a white marble lozenge :—

IN | MEMORY OF | ANNE SANDERS | BORN APRIL 9TH 1818 |
DIED AUGUST 26TH | 1881

---

107. On a white marble lozenge :—

WALTER PEMBERTON
DIED FEBRUARY 12TH A.D. 1849
AGED 29 YEARS.

In the passage from the north entrance door to the Nave are the three following :—

108. On a white marble lozenge :—

EDWARD PEMBERTON, M.D.
DIED AUGUST 12TH A.D. 1846
AGED 25 YEARS.

---

109. On a white marble square :—

FRANCES PEMBERTON
AGED 11 YEARS
DIED 5TH JANUARY
1842.

---

110. On a white marble square :—

SAML PEMBERTON
ESQUIRE
AGED 75 YEARS
DIED 23RD FEBRUARY
1840.

---

111. There is part of a dark marble ledger beneath the communion rails probably covering the vault of the founder.

ST. THOMAS, LOWLAND.

In 1706 the Parish Church was burnt by the French and £838 loss sustained. Another church in the Island was also destroyed. (*B.T. Leeward Isles*, Vol. XII.) The present building is cruciform and stands on a small eminence facing St. Kitts, with delightful views across the Narrows.

PARISH REGISTER.

Transcripts of Baptisims and Burials for the years 1733 and 1734 were printed in *Caribbeana* I., 233.

There are fragments from a volume which ran from 1740 to 1827. Among these is a sheet of baptisms of 1769 :—

Sarah a Mulatto woman, belonging to Richard Oliver, also Rowland and William mulatto children of ditto.

—19. Thomas William son of Thomas Washington by his wife Mary aged 14 months.

Nov. 4, Archibald Thompson son of ditto, aged 4 weeks.

Then follow a few entries of 1770 of Huggins & Parris. Signed on the back by John Bowen, Rector.

Several burials for 1768, 1769 and 1770 occur.

Funerals continued by Wm. Scott cover the years 1771—82.

1772, April 25. Sophia Gardiner, daughter of Thomas Washington by his wife Mary, aged 6 weeks, buried.

1773, June 11. William Senhouse, son of John Bertrand by his wife Elizabeth, aged 9 months, buried.

On another sheet are baptisms for 1774-76.

1776, April 11. John, son of John Bertrand by his wife Martha, aged 4 months, baptised.

Several entries of Washington, Thomson, Scarbrough, Gardner, Pinney occur.

1782 continued by Tho. Washington (? a churchwarden).

There are a few Marriages for 1770.

The following memorandum is explanatory.

" Nevis. Whereas the Gentlemen of the Vestry expressed to me a desire that the Parish Register, greatly impaired by time and accident, should be fairly transcribed into a new volume ; I do hereby certify that I have faithfully complied with their requisition, having truly and exactly copied the foregoing entries from the original Register. Wm. John Julius, Rector."

1 April, 1784, attested by the two churchwardens.

Later is another note :—" Taken from a private book of the late Rev. Wm. Jones 1787-1790."

From 1791 the Baptisms, Marriages, and Burials are all entered on the same page and the record is fairly complete from this year.

Sam¹ Wm. Harman, Rector signs in 1797.

Sam¹ Lyons, Rector, signs in 1804.

1809, Dec. 20. Thomas Martin, Esq., buried.

1824, Feb. 24. Thomas Arthurton, Esqr., buried.

(Sam. Lyons Arthurton of Nevis was of Codrington College in 1843).

1824, May 11. At sea, on board Sloop " Lady Jane." I, William Henry Rawlins, clerk in Holy Orders, and Curate of the Parish of St. Ann, Sandy Point do certify that I solemnized the marriage of John Fra : Arthurton with Jane Maria Lyons both of the Island of Nevis.

1827, Jan. 1. Robert Mulhall, Esqr, buried.

In 1827 three parchment covered volumes were provided and the entries made on printed forms.

1829, Aug. 18.   John Crowe, Lieutenant in the 93 Reg^t Foot and Frances Elizabeth Strather spinster of St James Windward were married.

Very few whites appear now in the Registers, but numerous slaves.

RECTORS.

Cradock Wells, 1716—27. (*Nevis Records*, p. 263), Rector for 10 years (*Caribbeana* III., 340).

William Wharton, 1735, died Feb., 1737.   Rector also of St. John's, 1729. (*Ibid*. I., 94).

John Bowen, 1770.   Rector of St. John's, 1767.

William Scott, M.A., 1767—1782.   Rector also of St. James', went out 11 July, 1764. died 24 Sept., 1782, aged 47.   Monumental Inscription No. 125.

William John Julius, 1784.   Later Rector of St. Ann, Sandy Point and St. Paul, Cabesterre, St. Kitts'.   Licensed by the Bishop of London 21 Sept., 1781. Will dated 22 June, 1810, p. 1810.   (425 *Collingwood*).

William Jones 1787—90.   Rector of St. Johns and died 1800.

Samuel Wickham Harman, 1797.   Later Rector of St. John's, Antigua, where he died in 1827 aged 58.

Samuel Lyons, 1804.   Rector of St. John's, Antigua, 1802-3.   Rector again in 1825.   Lost at sea in the Brig " Underhill," Nov. 1827.

Daniel Gateward Davis, 1824.   Rector also of St. Paul's, 1813.   Later Bishop of Leeward Islands.

John Hendrickson Laurence, B.A., died 19 Oct., 1836, aged 35.   Monumental Inscription No. 114.

James Bovell, M.D.   Rector also of St. John's, died 1880, aged 62. Monumental Inscription, No. 163.

Charles A. Shepherd was Rector here before removing to St. Kitts.

There are only five tablets.

112.   In south Transept on west wall, white on black marble :—

SACRED TO THE MEMORY OF
SARAH BELL,
WIDOW OF PHILIP P. CLAXTON
SHE DIED ON THE 8TH SEPT., 1837,
AGED 25 YEARS
HER REMAINS ARE DEPOSITED
BY THE SIDE OF THOSE OF HER BELOVED HUSBAND
WHOM SHE SURVIVED ONLY A FEW MONTHS
THIS TABLET IS ERECTED
BY PETER THOMAS HUGGINS ESQ^R
TO PERPETUATE THE MANY VIRTUES
OF A MOST AFFECTIONATE CHILD.

---

113. West wall of north Transept, white on black marble :—

In the Aisle of this Church
lie the remains of SARAH, the late Wife of
the Honorable SAMUEL LAURENCE of this Island
She departed this life on the 31ᶠᵗ day of December 1823,
in the 53ʳᵈ year of her age
after a protracted illness, leaving a large family
to lament their loss ;

---

114. North wall of Chancel :—

SACRED | TO THE MEMORY OF THE |
REVᴰ JOHN HENDRICKSON LAURENCE, B.A.
LATE RECTOR OF THIS PARISH
WHO DIED AFTER A SHORT ILLNESS ON THE 19ᵀᴴ OF OCTOBER 1836,
AGED 35 YEARS.
(Erected by widow).

Eldest son of Samuel Laurence of Nevis, esq., matriculated from Exeter College 18 May, 1820, aged 18 ; B.A., 1824.

1823, Dec. 31. Sarah Laurence, the wife of Samuel Laurence, Esqʳᵉ. (Bur. Reg.).

1825, Feb. 17. Lockhart Gordon, Junior, and Anne daughter of Samuel Laurence, Esqʳ

1826, Feb. 9. Honᵇˡᵉ Samuel Lawrence.

Edwᵈ Laurence æt 20, ex Insula de Nevis, W. Indies, was admitted to Peterhouse, 1 July, 1828.

On 26 Nov., 1823, Edward William Laurence of St. Peter's House, Cambridge (aged 15) third son of Samuel Laurence of Nevis, W.I., Esq., was admitted at Lincoln Inn. (*Peterhouse Admission Book*, p. 434).

---

115. On the south wall of Chancel is a white marble cross on a black shield :

PETER T. HUGGINS
DIED NOV. 7, 1874,
AGED 42 YEARS.

---

116. On the east wall of south Transept :—

IN MEMORY OF
PHILIP PROTHEROE CLAXTON
SON OF ROBERT CLAXTON, ESQᴿ
OF THE CITY OF BRISTOL
HE WAS A RESIDENT MERCHANT OF THIS ISLAND FOR
SEVERAL YEARS AND WAS BELOVED AND RESPECTED BY
ALL WHO KNEW HIM. HE DIED SINCERELY LAMENTED
ON THE 14ᵀᴴ JANUARY, 1836,
AGED 31 YEARS.
AND HIS REMAINS ARE BURIED IN THIS CHURCH YARD
THIS TABLET IS ERECTED BY HIS AFFLICTED MOTHER

His father, of Park Street, Alderman of Bristol died at Almondsbury co. Gloucester, 20 June, 1812, aged 58. Monumental Inscription in the Mayor's Chapel. His mother died at Westbury-on-Trim, Jan., 1841, aged 72.

Butler Claxton of Nevis must have been nearly related. See pedigree in *Caribbeana* VI., 41.

1830, July 17. Philip Protheroe Claxton, Gentleman, of St. Thomas' Parish and Sarah Bell Huggins, Spinster of the same parish, third daughter of Peter Thos. Huggins, Esq., Licence.

On the west wall of the south Transept are two old ledgers, fixed flush in the wall for their better preservation :—

117.   Blue marble, the bottom corners gone :—

> HERE LYES THE MIROVR OF EACH MARTIALL MIN*
> RELIGION WHO CONFIRMED AND REFIND
> IN ALL HIS ACTIONS, WHO WAS FORTVNATE
> AN ATLAS TO *VPPORT THE WEIGHT OF STATE
> THIS ILANDS SAFGARD AND HER FOES DECREASE
> THE FLOWER OF ARMES AND THE TOWER OF PEACE
> NOW NEVIS MOVRNE READING THIS EPITAPH,
> HERE IACOB RESTETH AND HERE LYES YOVR STAFFE
> (Space here and lower down) :—
> HERE LYETH THE BODY OF CAPTAIN IACOB LAKE
> ESQVIER LATE GOVERNOVR OF THIS ILAND NEVIS
> WHO DEPARTED THIS LIFE IN OCTOBER, 1649

Memorial Stones of this date are excessively rare in the West Indies. Two others are in St. Kitts—those of Governor Sir Tho. Warner, 1648, and of Capt. Sam. Jefferson, 1649. See *Caribbeana* I., 190. Lake was one of the first settlers in 1628 and was Governor in 1648. In 1635, then aged 30, he had a licence to go to Barbados. (*Hotten* 52).

---

118.   Adjoining No. 117 is a white marble ledger :—

> HERE LYES YE BODY OF MRS ELIZABETH ∽
> LAKE DAVGHTER TO IACOB LAKE ESQ LATE
> GOVERNOR OF THIS ISLAND OF MEVIS WHO
> DEPARTED THIS LIFE YE 18TH DAY OF THIS PRE
> SENT IVNE 1664 BEING AGED FOVRTEENE
> YEARES AND MOVNTHS NINE ∽
> (space here)
> A pious, Vertuovs, Blamelesse, Spottlesse maid
> By Cruell Death was Suddenly Betraid
> Of Sweetest life (alas) a Barbarous Crime
> To Cropp a flower) so Sweet so neare ye prime
> Let zoilus Carpe) I may not pre termit
> Her Admirable worth her pregnant witt.
> Modest She was Chaste dutifull and Staide
> Not provd not Scornefull (yet) a perfect maid
> Her parents onely Joy this Islands grace
> In heauen sure shall bee her resting place

---

*flaked

Cease Brinish teares : forbeare your greuious moane
A happy Change tis a Cælestiall throne.
Prepared is what Comfort doth this giue
To pay a debt, to dy, and yet to liue

1667, April 30. Mrs. Elizabeth the wife of Mr. Jacob Lake (bur. St. Michael Barbados).

Eliz. Stapleton of Nevis used a seal on her deed of 1750 with the single arms of Lake thereon :—*A bend between six crosses crosslet fitchée.*

The two old memorial slabs to Govr. Capn. Jacob Lake and his daughter were removed by Canon Shepherd from the aisle in the south Transept of S. Thomas' Church, Lowland, where they had been placed by the late Hon. P. T. Huggins, and built in an upright position in the Wall of the Church.

(Note by Canon Shepherd).

Mr. Huggins had removed them from an old Quaker burial ground at Pollards. There was another Quaker ground at the corner of the road leading up to Tower Hill. (*Mrs. Burdon's Handbook*, p. 214).

In the floor of the passage from the door of the south Transept are the following five ledgers, all their tops being partly hidden by pews.

119. In a sunk oval is a Jacobean shield with mantling :—

Crest : and Helmet covered over.

Arms : *On a bend between three mullets as many swans.* (Russell).

The inscription of twenty-two lines is much flaked and also broken across the middle.

HEIC jacet sepvlt

. . . .

. . . . .omin . . . . .

. . . . .COBVS

. . . . . . .M. . . . . . .

S. . . . .

. . . . . . GV. . . . . . .

R . . . . .ncis

. . . . .isimus

. . . . .Dien

July

. . . . .o q. . o

. . . . .Dom. MDCLXXX X II

VIVIT POST

. . . . .S Iames who of his

. . . . .for her th . . d Gouer . .

. . . . three . .nder

. . . . sp . . . . . . of youth and . . . . .

When . . . nds King, his Friends and Covn . . .

to ho. . . . . fairely . . . . .Esteem

Oh how lamented must be Rv . . . . . all

Who lived belov'd must Dye Depllor'd By all.

Sir James Russell, Junr., Knight, made his will at Nevis 16 July, 1688, proved 4 July, 1688.

See *Caribbeana* II., 272 for the monument in Bristol to his uncle Sir James Russell, Knight, the Elder.

120.   Blue marble ledger :—

Is Mᴿᴵˢ Mary Morton Fal'n Asleep
And is There one That can Forbear to Weep
Who Knew Her and The Covrse of Life she Led,
Which Mak's her name to Live tho she be dead
She was Devovt, and Zealovs in Her Place ;
she did advance God's Worship : Equal Pace
Likewise she held in Works of Charity,
The Genvin Prodvcts of Her Piety
of This Worlds Goods, God Gave to her Great Store :
Which she Imparted Freely To The Poore
Strangers Her Hovse did Harbovr, Freqvently :
According To Each On's Necessity
Tho Many of Her Sex Have Nobly Done
Yet She from Most of Them The Garland Won
She Liv'd in Honovr and She Died in Peace :
And Now From All Her Labovrs She doth Cease
And Here interrd Within This Tomb she Lies
Vntil She Hear That Voice, YE DEAD ARISE.
Tho she be dead, she stil surviv's Her Fate
A Pattern Which We Ovght To Imitate
Dispergit, dat Egentibvs
Ivstitia Eivs Perstat In Æternvm
Psal. cxii : ix
obiit Die 2º Septemb : Annº J663
Ætat Svæ 49

Canon Shepherd when Rector, recovered the first line by taking up the flooring of the pew.

Sir Francis Morton, Colonel of a Regiment, President and Judge was Knighted 26 March, 1679.   His will was made in London, 26 June following (88 *King*).   He bequeathed to the Parish of St. Thomas 15000 lbs. and 5000 lb. for communion plate and was buried on July 9 in St. Mildred Bread Street, perhaps in the Crisp vault.   The above Mary was doubtless his wife.

---

121.   White marble ledger :—

In a sunk depression at the top is a Jacobean transitional shield with mantling above and wreaths below.

Crest : ? *An eagle between two wings couped* (the head hidden by flooring). *over wreath and helmet.*

Arms : *Within an annulet a bull's head cabossed erased* ; impaling, *Or, on a chief, three covered cups.* (Butler).   (The Or, may be only punch marks for effect).

Hic Situs est
THOMAS PYM Armiger, Vir dignifsimus : In hac
Insulâ (Nevis) erata Consiliis Regis Georg II. fidelis
Regi, Amator Patriæ, sincerus Amicus, peramans Maritus,
Philanthropus : Terrestriam, pro Cæleste, Vitam reliquit
23º die Novem : Anno Dom : 1743 Ætat. 42.
Si omnium qui norunt quidquam adversus Mortem
valerent, viveret.

See his pedigree in *Caribbeana* III., 50.

---

122. Brown ledger :—

ELIZABETH PETERSON
born the 15th March 1727,
and departed this Life
the 1ſt November
1793.

Daughter of Wm. Peterson of the Spring plantation by Elizabeth Williams his wife, daughter of Michael Williams, Esq.

---

123. White marble ledger :—

In sunk circle a Jacobean transitional shield with mantling.

Crest : hidden. Half a helmet is visible.
Arms : *A stag statant.*

Here are the Remains of WILLIAM JONES, Eſq ;
who departed this Life the 21ſt Day of May
]753, Aged 48 Years
His Widow, being deſirous to shew her Reſpect
to her deceaſed Huſband, hath directed the
following juſt Inſcription :

Mr JONES, altho' without any Advantage of a paternal Eſtate or Education, took early Care | to forward himſelf in the World by the | Recommendation of his own Behaviour. | And so well ſucceeded in Quality of a Merchant | as to become the moſt conſiderable one in this | Iſland : during which Time he maintain'd a | fair Character, liv'd in good Credit, and, by | keeping yᵉ beſt of Company, as well as by reading . the beſt of Books, he had acquired such a | competent Knowledge as render'd him very uſeful | to the public, whilst living and dy'd a worthy | Member of the Council of NEVIS.

These three following are in the central passage of Nave.

124. White marble ledger :—

Under this Stone are the remains of
JAMES SMITH Junr
Grandson to JAMES SMITH of Crew
in the County of Cheſhire
was born in St. Chriſtophers
the 10 : day of Auguſt 1750
and departed this Life
the 10 : day of December 1771
in the 22ᵈ Year of his Age

James Smith, of the Parish of St. Thomas, Lowland, Esq. Will dated 29 Oct., 1778. My daughter Sarah wife of Alex. Baillie Esq., at Inverness £300 a year. Mary widow of my late brother John Smith of co. Lancashire. My late wife. My late son James Smith. Bridgwaters. My plantations in St. Thomas called the Windwill, Mount Pelier and Stuarts, Hams, Williams, Canoe Gutt, Greenland to my grandson James Smith Baillie. (323 *Warburton*).

Testator's wife Emma died in 1767, aged 52.   Monumental Inscription at Westbury-upon-Trim, co. Gloucester.

1771, Dec. 11.   James Smith, Junr aged 21 years.   (Bur. Reg.).

1778, Nov. 6.   James Smith, aged 69 years.

1762, Jan. 7.   Alexander Baillie and Sarah Smith.   (*St. John's Register*).

1767, Oct. 15.   Dr. James Smith sworn a Member of Council.   (*Minute Book*).

1772, Nov. 30.   John Browne to be of the Council *vice* James Smith deceased

---

125.   Dark blue marble ledger :—

Sacred to the Memory of
The REV^D WILLIAM SCOTT, M.A., Rector
of the Parifhes of Saint Thomas, and
Saint James, in the Ifland of Nevis ;
who died on the 24 day of September
1782 ; Aged 47.
And to the Memory of
Mrs Sufanna Scott his Wife, who died
on the 22 day of October 1793 ;
Aged 52.

1782 (blank).   The body of The Revd William Scott aged (blank).

1768, Feb. 29.   The body of Mrs. Sarah Scott.

---

126.   On the floor near the communion step is a white marble lozenge :—

M^RS SARAH LAURENCE
died 31^ft Decr 1823
in the 53rd year of her age.

CHURCHYARD.

To the south side are two stone vaults with ledgers and no inscriptions.

127.   Fragment of blue marble ledger near the south door :—

HERE LYETH Y BODY O.
WILLIAM MILLS WHO
THIS LIFE THE 23 OF
ANNO DOMINI]6 . .

This lettering is of the style 1680-1700.

---

128.   White marble ledger :—

In sunk circle a Jacobean shield and mantling.

Crest : *A griffins head erased* over wreath and helmet.
Arms : *A cross.*

To the Memory | of |
Mr JASPER WALL Jun[r]
of this Parifh, who departed
this life the 26th of April 1714,
Aged 37 Years.
He was a Kind Brother, a good
Neighbour, and a Sincere Friend

Jasper Wall Jr., was evidently son of Lieut. Jasper Wall who was a Member of Assembly here in 1687. On the death of the former, Tobias the next brother succeded, who died at Southampton in 1744. Will (95 *Pinfold*) See Monumental Inscription in St. Olaves Hart Str. He died 5 July, 1744, aged 58. Mary his wife died 25 Jan., 1729, aged 30. (*Misc. Gen. et Her.* 5 Series II., 234). There were three sisters who then became co-heiresses : 1-Lucretia married John Mills, 2-Bridget, married Wm. Woodley ; 3-Anne married —. Newth.

Arms of Wall : *Argent a bend between three wolves' heads couped Sable.*

See *Antigua* III., 256.

---

129.   Stone ledger over a stone vault :—

HERE LYETH Y[E] BODDYES
OF TWO CHILDREN OF M[R] IOSEPH
MARTYN AND DORETHY HIS
WIFE BOTH NAMED EDWARD
Y[E] ELDEST DIED MAY THE 6
ANN[O]]678* Y[E] OTHER THE 6
OF IVLY]679

Mr. Joseph Martyn of Love Lane, London, merchant, was named in 1705 in the will of Philip Brome of Nevis, Esq.

---

130.   White marble slab :—

Here Lyeth the Ashes of
Aron Chapman Esq., who
was one of the King's Coun=
cil in this Island & he de=
parted this life the 15th day
of March in the 41 year of
his Age and in y[e] year of
our Lord God]693 to the
Great greif of his Friends
And the unspeakable Lofs
of this Island of Neuis.

His name appears in the list of Council on 21 Nov., 1692. (*Calendar of State Papers* 2631).

His election to the Assembly was objected to 3 June, 1687 (*Ibid.* 1290).

On 5 Oct., 1683 he and Tho. Biss were named in connection with the release of a sloop confiscated by the Governor of St. Thomas. (*Ibid.* 2087).

---

* 8 altered to 9 or 9 to 8.

131.   Blue marble ledger :—

In a sunk circle a lozenge-shaped shield with Jacobean Mantling.

Arms : *On a bend three pheons.*   (Helme).

P. S.

Mortale quod habuit D. CHRISTIANA BROME, D. ROBERTI | HELME filia, Gillinghamiæ prope Shaftsburiam in Comitatu | Dorfettenfi nata (Stylo Angliæ) ffeb^r 25 1657 in certan | Spem Gloriosæ Refurrectionis, hic deponitur.
(three lines)
Bis nupta ; primum AARONI CHAPMAN Mercatori in hac | Infula infigni et honesto ; postea PHILIPPO BROME, Armigero | S.R. ad Africam negotiantis Procuratori integerrimo Viro | Monarchie et Ecclesiæ Amglicanæ (quoad Vires) semper | addictifsimo. (Ten more lines of eulogy.   She died 10 Nov. " anno suo Climacterico magno."   Monument erected by her friend Mary Pinney).

I sent the above to Canon Mayo and it appeared in Somerset & Dorset *Notes & Queries*, Vol. XIV., 154.

1652-3.   Vicesimo primo die Martii Christiana Helmes filia Roberti Helmes baptizata erat. (*Parish Register* of Gillingham).   Probably the year 1657 in the Inscription should read 165J.   There is in Gillingham Church a tablet recording her death 1 Nov., 1720 aged 68.   See pedigree of Helme in *Caribbeana* V., 41.

---

132.   Next to the above is a blue marble ledger :—

Here Lyeth ye Body of PHILIP
BROME Esqr who Departed
This Life ye 15th Day of Decemb^r
1705 Aged 52 Years.

The above three vaults are alongside each other.

Robert Helme was a Merchant of Nevis in 1676, aged 30 in 1680, Agent for the Royal African Company, till 1685.   Mr. Tho. Helme of Gillingham was described in 1705 as only brother and heir-at-law of Robert Helme.   Major Wm. Helme of Antigua, 1691, apparently brother of Thomas and Robert Helme died about 1703 leaving a daughter and heiress, Mary, who married in 1708 John Pinney of Nevis.

The will of Philip Brome, Esq., was dated at Nevis, 8 Dec., 1705, sworn 4 Jan., 1705-6.   (196 *Barrett*).

He mentions his wife Christian Frances Chapman, Mrs. Mary Helme of London, and his parents of Ile Abbotts, co. Somerset, bequeathed £50 to the Parish of St. Thomas and d.s.p.   See pedigree of Helme in *Caribbeana* V., 40.

There is now a row of twelve stone vaults all with ledgers.

Beginning at the south end :—

133.   Sacred to the Memory of
LYDIA,
the Widow of MAYSON WILSON
of Liverpool ;
Born on the 25th September 1782
died on the 20th July, 1852.

134.

SACRED
TO THE MEMORY OF
JOB EDE
OF CLAYFIELD LODGE
SOUTHAMPTON
ESQUIRE
WHO DIED
ON JESSOP'S ESTATE
IN THIS ISLAND
ON THE 1 OF JULY 1844
AGED 63 YEARS.

1813, Feb. 25. Monday was married Job Ede, Esq., late of the Island of Nevis, to Catharine Maria, eldest daughter of Lieut.-Col. Williams, of Falmouth, and grandniece of Mrs. Bulkeley, of Sidney Place in this city. (*Bath Chronicle*).

1844, July 1. In the Island of Nevis, Job Ede, Esq. of Clayfield Lodge, Southampton. (*Gent. Mag.* 334).

He was at Eton, 1789-95. (*R. Austen-Leigh's List*),

See Monumental Inscription to him at Milbrook, Southampton.

---

135. Slate slab :—

OUR FATHER
PETER THOMAS HUGGINS
BORN JAN^{RY} 1ST 1787
DIED FEB^{RY} 4TH 1857

---

136. Slate slab :—

Sacred to the Memory of
JESSY wife of the Honble PETER THO. HUGGINS
Born 14 Novr 1789 ; died 2nd Octr 1851.

---

137. Dark stone :—

SARAH BELL CLAXTON
Widow of P. P. CLAXTON
And daughter of P. T. HUGGINS, Esq.
of this Island :
died 8th Septr 1837
Aged 25 Years.

138.

PHILIP PROTHEROE CLAXTON
Died 14TH January, 1836,
Aged 31 Years.

---

139. Marble ledger :—

IN MEMORY OF
MARY CLAXTON
THE BELOVED WIFE OF
CHARLES KENNEY,
WHO WAS PREMATURELY CUT OF
BY FEVER
ON THE 16TH DAY OF DECEMBER 1840
IN THE TWENTY-THIRD YEAR
OF HER AGE.

140. Slate ledger :—

BENEATH THIS STONE
REST THE REMAINS OF
HENRY HARDING EsQRE
MANY YEARS COLLECTOR OF
H.M. CUSTOMS IN THIS ISLAND
WHO WAS DROWNED ON HIS
PASSAGE FROM ST KITTS HERE,
ON THE 13th DAY OF SEPTr 1843,
AGED 37 YEARS.

1830, July 17. Henry Harding, Esq., Collector H.M. Customs of St. Paul's Parish and Jessy Huggins, spinster, of St. Thomas' Parish, second daughter of Peter Huggins, Esqr. Lic.

141. Slate slab :—

In Memory of
MADELINE
youngest Daughter of the late
HENRY HARDING ESQ.
and grand daughter of the late
PETER THOS. HUGGINS ESQ.
of Montravers
Ob. Nov. 18 A.D. 1869 Æ. 29

142. Lozenge of slate :—

IN | MEMORY OF | ALICE ROPER | 2ND DAUGHTER OF | THE LATE HENRY | HARDING | DIED JUNE 15TH | 1879.

143. Lozenge of slate :—

IN | MEMORY OF | JESSY KENNY | 2ND DAUGHTER OF | THE LATE HONBLE PETER | T. HUGGINS OF | MOUNTRAVERS | DIED JUNE 21st | 1880.

144.   White marble slab, very fine work, ornamented at the angles :—

In a sunk oval a Jacobean shield with mantling :—

Crest :   *Out of a coronet a unicorn's head,* over helmet (no wreath).
Arms :   *A chevron between three pears.*

Subtus eſt depoſitus Viator
Vir Honoratus RICARDUS ABBOTTUS Armigeri

etc. in Latin.   (Lower down the slab is the English Translation,
as follows) :—

Stay Traveller ! and Reflect a little
Here lyes Interr'd
The Honoured RICHARD ABBOTT Esq.
And near Him his Dearly Beloved
Son CHARLES
Whoſe Death Alaſs ! tho' Untimely to Him,
Ought not to be Immoderately Lamented
By his Wife, & other Condoling Relations
As if That had Shorten'd his Fathers Life
Who having Govern'd this Island 8 years.
And Faithfully diſcharged his Duty
In Civil and Military Affairs
Reſign'd his ſoul to God
Novemb^r :]4th A.Ætat : 64
His Son dy'd Octob^r : 23^d A.Ætat : 26
Both A.D. 1724
This Small Monument of her Great Love
to Her moſt Indearing Huſband and
moſt Dutifull Son was erected
By ANN ABBOTT

Richard Abbott was a Member of Assembly, 1688 and as Major elected for the north-west Division 1693, and as Lieut.-Col. for the Parish of St. Thomas in 1694-5.   In 1697 he was a Member of Council.   In a letter of 1702 he used a seal with the above arms.   In 1711-12 he was appointed Brigadier-General.   In 1712 he was in command when the French captured the Island.   (See pedigree in *Antigua,* I., 1.).

---

145.   Stone ledger on stone vault :—

Hunc dum ſpectas ELIZABETHÆ
Tumulum, Viator, Placentis et Teneræ
Conjugis (JACOBI BROWNE) non ſis
immemor, integrâ tamen Ætate ad
Gaudia in Cœlis pro Piis repoſita,
abreptæ Anno ſcilicet Viceſimo
quarto et Octavo Janvarii Die ſub
mortem Vigeſimo 173⅔

James Browne Esq., in 1726 devised " Brownes " in the Parish of St. James to his son James.   The former and his father James were both entered in the Census of 1667-8.

---

146. Slate slab :—

OUR DEAR BROTHER
EDWARD MELVILLE HUGGINS
BORN 4ᵀᴴ MAY 1845,
DIED 31ˢᵀ OCTᴿ 1869,
ELDEST SON OF THE LATE
HON. THOMAS HUGGINS.

147.

OUR DEAR SISTER
LUCY ISABELLA HUGGINS
BORN 9ᵀᴴ NOVᴿ 1848,
DIED 30ᵀᴴ OCTᴿ 1869,
SECOND AND UNMARRIED DAUGHTER
OF THE LATE
HON. THOMAS HUGGINS.

148. Slate slab :—

THOMAS HUGGINS
OF NEVIS
FOR MANY YEARS A MEMBER OF COUNCIL HERE
BORN 27ᵀᴴ JULY 1820,
DIED 14ᵀᴴ SEPTᴿ 1869

149. Slate slab :—

IN MEMORY OF
ANNIE
THE BELOVED WIFE OF
HONᴮᴸᴱ THOMAS HUGGINS
AND DAUGHTER OF THE LATE
DAVID MELVILLE ESQᴿᴱ.
OF NOTTINGHAM
BORN JANUARY 15ᵀᴴ 1823,
DIED JULY 21ˢᵀ 1864

150. Slate slab :—

OUR | BELOVED BROTHER | CHARLES PINNEY HUGGINS | BORN OCTᴿ 2ᴺᴰ 1829, | DIED OCTᴿ 15ᵀᴴ 1859.

151. Grey granite obelisk, on east face :—

SACRED | TO THE MEMORY OF | ROBERT HUTTON | FIFTH SON OF JOHN HUGGINS | THORNLIEBANK, SCOTLAND | WHO DIED IN THIS ISLAND | 6ᵀᴴ JANUARY 1869 | AGED 22¼ YEARS. |

152. Stone ledger :—

SACRED
TO THE MEMORY OF
ELEANOR
THE BELOVED WIFE OF
THE REV^D T. B. NIBBS,
DEPARTED THIS LIFE
ON 5TH JAN^Y 1880

In the Wesleyan Burial Ground at St. John's, Antigua, is the tomb of the Rev. Tho. Barry Nibbs, Wesleyan Minister, who died 7 September, 1897, aged 83. Mr. Barry Nibbs was buried in 1756, at St. George, Angitua. I cannot place Tho. Barry Nibbs in the pedigree.

---

153. Ledger on stone vault :—

Richard Smith died 3^d July, 1789.
Aged 44 Years
Francis Smith died 28th Jany 1790
Aged 42 Years.
Jane Smith relict of Therry Smith
of Liverpool, has placed this Stone
in tender refpect to the Memory
of their worthy and beloved Children.

---

154. Slate slab :—

PETER THOMAS HUGGINS
BORN 1832, DIED 1874.

---

155. Slate lozenge in slab :—

IN | LOVING MEMORY OF | ELIZABETH HUGGINS | CALLED TO HER REST | AUGUST 28TH 1895 |

---

156. Stone ledger :—

IN MEMORIAM
EDWARD JOHN HUGGINS
BORN 6TH APRIL 1825
DIED 14TH JUNE 1878

---

157. Slate lozenge in a slab :—

IN | AFFECTIONATE | REMEMBRANCE OF | HELEN HUGGINS | CALLED TO HER REST | 24TH MARCH 1891 |

---

158.   White marble ledger :—

IN MEMORY OF
JULIA HUGGINS,
of " MOUNTRAVERS "
AT REST 24ᵀᴴ JUNE 1910

She was the last of her family in Nevis.   I have some letters from her.

---

159.   Stone vault :—

IN LOVING MEMORY OF
PETER THOMAS HUGGINS, M.D.
WHO DIED SEPT. 18, 1897
AGED 51 YEARS 11 MONTHS
AND 23 DAYS

---

160.   Granite block :—

MARGARET BLANCHARD | ONLY CHILD OF | PAITFIELD & EMILY MILLS | BORN AT NIAGARA, CANADA | DIED IN NEVIS OCT. 8, 1897 | AGED 13 YEARS.

He married in 1882 at Niagara, Emily Nash.   They were both of Nevis in 1902.

---

161.   East of Churchyard.   Broken white marble column :—

IN | AFFECTIONATE REMEMBRANCE | OF | NORMAN BRUCE CHALLENOR | WHO ENTERED INTO REST | ON 19ᵗʰ SEPTᴿ 1882 | AGED TWO MONTHS |.

---

162.   Grey Granite obelisk :—

IN LOVING MEMORY | OF | THE REV. JAMES BOVELL M.D. | FORMERLY OF CANADA | AND | FOR MANY YEARS | RECTOR OF Sᵀ PAULS, AND | THIS PARISH | WHO DEPARTED THIS LIFE | 16 JANUARY, 1880 | AGED 62 |

On the north face :—

ALSO TO | JOHN HERBERT HENDERSON | AND | JAMES BOVELL CONNELL | INFANT GRANDCHILDREN | OF | JAMES BOVELL.

James Bovell son of James of Barbados, Esq., matriculated from Oriel College, 21 June, 1802. aged 16, married 1811, Miss Applewhaite and died 1816. John Bovell married 1817, Miss Applewhaite

---

163.   Stone ledger on stone Vault :—

IN | AFFECTIONATE REMEMBRANCE | OF | MARY AUCHINLECK | WHO DIED | 13ᵀᴴ JULY 1881.

164. Small broken column and on its base :—

ALAN GUY | BORN 14TH FEB. 1888 | DIED 25TH NOV. 1888 | ALSO OF GEOFFREY EDWARD | BORN IN ENGLAND 21ST AUGUST 1889 | DIED THE 18TH NOV. 1889.

Lower down on a flat stone :—

IN LOVING MEMORY OF | INFANT | CHILD OF | JOSEPH BRIGGS | MARY EDITH BRIGGS—(NEE BARNES).

---

165. Granite flat tomb with white marble cross cut thereon :—

WILLIAM S. DANIELL, DIED OCT. 17 1910, | AGED 65 YEARS |

---

166. Stone vault, with iron cross :—

IN LOVING MEMORY OF | GRACE M. INNISS | AND HER SON | W. B. PEMBERTON   (no dates.).

---

167. Stone cross :—

TO THE DEAR MEMORY OF | JESSIE | WIFE OF AUGUSTUS BONYUN | WHO DIED 11TH FEBRUARY | 1887 | AGED 19 YEARS |

---

168. Fragment of blue marble ledger with Inscription of nine lines the 1st, 3rd, and 5th illegible.

> . . . . . .
> . . . . . . Randolph
> . . . .
> . . . . . . 23 of August
> . . . .
> And also the Body o . . . . ..
> Daughter of the abov . . . . .
> And Frances Iory who. . . . .
> . . . .]6 . .

Col. Joseph Jory of Nevis, merchant, 1673, Member of Assembly 1678, Member of Council 1682, Agent 1700-1719, died at Bethnal Green 24 Aug., 1725, married Frances daughter of Col. Randolph Russell, Governor of Nevis. He sealed a letter in 1700 with these arms :—*A double-headed eagle displayed* (Jory) ; impaling, *on a bend between three mullets as many swans* (Russell).

On another fragment of the same style as the above is the date " 1685," and " 30 " and " Mrs Ann Io . . . probably Mrs. Ann Jory.

---

169. A large blue marble ledger in five pieces near east wall of Church, only the year " 1725 " being visible.

WESLEYAN BURIAL GROUND, CHARLESTOWN.

As the planters were not dissenters there are no notable names here.

170. Blue slate ledger :—

𝕾𝖆𝖈𝖗𝖊𝖉 | TO THE MEMORY OF | THOMAS WAITSTILL STONEMAN | OF YARMOUTH NOVA SCOTIA | WHO DEPARTED THIS LIFE | 26 NOVEMBER, 1847, AGED 23 | HE WAS TAKEN ILL ON HIS VOYAGE | TO THE WEST INDIES AND DIED OF | CONSUMPTION SHORTLY AFTER HIS | ARRIVAL IN THIS ISLAND.

---

171. On a broken slab :—

Here lieth the Body | of |
JOSEPH HARRAGIN ISHAM
Son of
THOMAS and ALICE C. ISHAM
Who departed this Life
Augt the 13th
1805.

---

172. On a dirty stone :—

TO IOHN JOSEPH ROBINSON 1842.

---

173. White marble slab over stone vault :—

SACRED | *to the memory of* | REV^D WILLIAM FLETCHER TURTLE | *Wesleyan Missionary,* | Born February 9th, 1821 | *fell asleep in Jesus at* | *Charlestown, Nevis* | February 3rd, 1865 | *Also of* | *his Infant Son* | WILLIAM WESLEY | Born January 15th | Died October 8th 1854 |.

---

174. White marble slab :—

SACRED | to the memory of | MRS. ELIZABETH LUCAS | born on the Island of | St. Eustatius, | and departed this life | on the Island of Nevis | Aug. 11, 1845 |. Æ. 80.

---

175. Slate headstone :—

ERECTED | IN MEMORY OF | THE REV^D JOHN BELL | WESLEYAN MISSIONARY | WHO DIED AUGUST 16th 1839 | *Aged* 26 *Years.*

---

176. Inside the Chapel, on the north wall, are two tablets :—

SACRED TO THE MEMORY OF THE
REV^D JAMES COX
WESLEYAN MISSIONARY FOR MANY YEARS GENERAL SUPERINTENDENT
OF THE MISSIONS IN THE ANTIGUA DISTRICT
WHO DEPARTED THIS LIFE MAY 30TH 1859, AGED 58 YEARS.

177. On the east wall :—

SACRED TO THE MEMORY OF | ELEANOR, | THE BELOVED WIFE OF THE
REV. HILTON CHEESEBROUGH | WHO DEPARTED THIS LIFE JULY 30TH 1846,
AGED 39 |
SHE WAS THE MOTHER OF EIGHT CHILDREN, OF WHOM TWO | MARGARET ANN,
AND GEORGE ROBINSON | DIED IN ST. JOHN'S ANTIGUA, AND WERE BURIED
IN THE | WESLEYAN GRAVE YARD OF THAT CITY,
ALSO SARAH ROBINSON WHO DIED IN NEVIS | OCTOBER 9TH 1847, AGED 10
MONTHS.

There is a fair sized Jewish Burial Ground at Charles Town, with many stone tombs. I copied fifteen inscriptions, and sent them in 1923 to Dr. Abrahams, the Director of Publications of the Jewish Historical Society of England, who passed them on to Mr. Wilfred S. Samuel, then preparing a paper on Jewish Colonists in Barbados in 1679-80. My original list has been mislaid.

Owing to representations made as to the neglected state of the cemetery, the Legislative Council voted £20 towards fencing, and the Jewish Board of Deputies has raised a fund for its maintenance, a similar collection having been made in 1880.

St. KITTS.

The Island of St. Christopher, or as it is now invariably styled, St. Kitts, is a long oval in shape, about 23 miles long and five miles wide, with an area of 68 square miles. In the centre is a range of mountains, of which Mount Misery is 3,711 feet above the sea. Nevis is separated from it by the Narrows, two miles across.

St. Kitts was first settled by Thomas Warner, who, fitted out by Ralph Merrifield of London, Merchant, landed on 28th January, 1623-24 with 15 men. On 13th September, 1625, he was commissioned by the King as Lieutenant of the Islands of St. Christopher, Mevis, Barbadoes (error for Barbuda), and Montserrat, which he had discovered and began to plant. Several Frenchmen having also settled, a division of the Island was made on 28th April, 1627, the English retaining the central portion, and the French being allotted the two ends. On 2nd June, 1627, a patent was issued to James Hay, Earl of Carlisle, for a grant of all the Caribbees. On 29th September, 1629, the Earl commissioned Warner as Governor of St. Christopher *alias* St. Christovall. In October, 1629, the Spaniards captured the island and scattered the colonists, but Sir Thomas Warner, then in London, resettled it. The cultivation of the sugar cane was introduced here about the year 1643. Before then tobacco was first grown, then indigo, then cotton.

In 1666 war broke out and the English, being defeated by the French, capitulated and many persons left the island. In July, 1666, Lord Willoughby's fleet was destroyed by a hurricane. In June, 1667, General Henry Willoughby landed large forces, but was severely defeated. By the Treaty of Breda of 21st July, 1667, the English were restored to their part of the colony. In 1689 the English were again driven out by the French, but the following year Major-General Thornhill with 3,000 men captured the whole island. By the Treaty of Ryswick in 1697, the French territory was restored to them. In 1702 the French again capitulated, to Major-General Hamilton, and by the Treaty of Utrecht of 1713, the whole Island was finally confirmed to the English. Apart from hurricanes the Colony progressed considerably until 1782, when it was again captured by the French, but was restored next year by the Treaty of Versailles.

No colony has had such vicissitudes and changes of ownership as this one, and a large volume would be required to record its history.

Rochefort wrote in 1658 : " The English have also built in this Island five very fair Churches, well furnish'd within with Pulpits and Seats, of excellent Joyners work, of precious wood. Till the late time, the Ministers were sent thither by the Archbishop of Canterbury to whose Diocess it belongs." (*Davies* 24).

In 1677, or earlier, the West Indies were in the jurisdiction of the Bishop of London and he continued to send out the clergy until the Colonial bishoprics were constituted.

Pere Labat in 1700 thus alludes to two of the English Churches :—" Je vis aussi en passant les deux Temples que les Anglois ont à la Cabesterre. Si leur Religion est aussi simple que leurs Temples, on peut dire qu'elle l'est beaucoup.

Ils etoient au milieu d'une savanne, tous deux à peu près de même grandeur, c'est-à-dire, d'environ quarante pieds de long sur dix-huit à vingt pieds de large. Au bout opposé à la porte, il y avoit une longue table, avec une armoire á côté, et un fauteuil. Tout le reste étoit rempli de bancs à dossier, avec une allée au milieu, le tout sans ancuns ornemens de qulque nature que ce pût être." (*II*. 189).

As to the clergy he noticed that they received little consideration :—"Il y avoit chez le Major Cripts (Crisp) un jeune Ministre, qui avoit déja perdu deux femmes depuis environ trois ans qu'il étoit dans l'Isle. Il paroissoit fort empressé pour en recouvrer une troisiéme. On le railla beaucoup sur le peu de soin qu'il prenoit de les conserver." (*Ib*. 191).

The earliest census of 1678 was printed in *Caribbeana* II., 68, and there were then four parishes :—Trinity, Palmeto Point ; Christ Church, Nicola Town ; St. John's Capistar, and Sandypoint ; and three divisions :—St. Thomas, Middle Island, Half Way Tree and Kayon with 695 white men.

The Census of 1707-8 was printed in *Caribbeana* II., 132 and there were then only 462 white men, but as the names are not under parishes it is impossible to say if the lists are complete. Oldmixon wrote in 1708 that there were five parishes, three on the south side and two on the north side. (First Edition II., 226). Soon after 1713, St. Peter's, Basseterre and St. Mary, Cayon were formed.

ST. GEORGE, BASSETERRE.

The French built a fine Town, under the Cannon of the Citadel of Basse-Terre. . . . There's a large Church . . . . formerly in the Hands of the Capuchins but in the year 1646 . . . they were dismissed . . . and the Jesuits superintended church affairs. (*Oldmixon* 1st. Ed. 1708, II., 226).

In Du Tertre's map of about 1667 the church of " Nostre Dame " is drawn.

Pere Labat wrote in 1700, that there was only one ˏ(French) parish church for the whole of Basseterre, which was in the town. It was 130 feet long by 36 feet wide, with two chapels forming transepts. The walls were from three to five feet thick and the building very strong to resist hurricanes.

The English during the war used it as a guard-house and placed cannon in it. (*II*. 188).

Previous to 1713 the whole of the Basseterre quarter was French. It is impossible to say if the present site of the Church was also that of previous ones.

Soon after 1713 the English transferred the seat of government from Old Road Town to Basseterre. The Rev. John Anderson wrote in 1719 :—" A church has not yet been built at Basseterre."

By Acts of 1722-4, two more new parishes were created out of the French territory, viz.: St. George's and St. Paul, vestries constituted and churches built. (In *Moll's map* of 1732 a church is shewn).

The present Church, a handsome stone building in the Early English style, stands in a large churchyard, at the top of the town. It consists of a nave of nine bays, transepts, aisles, apsidal chancel and a tower at the south side, on the face of which are two circles, a carved human head surmounted by the date " 1670 " being in the one, and " REBUILT 1856-9 " in the other. This building was gutted by the fire of 1867 and again rebuilt. In 1834 the tower was only a few feet higher than the nave. (*West Indies Sketch Book*, II., 5).

Archdeacon Caunt possesses an old water-colour sketch of the interior previous to 1867.   This shows thirteen tablets all of which were destroyed except the two broken ones Nos. 1 and 2 of my list.   I also noticed an engraved portrait of the late Bishop Gateward Davis.

PARISH REGISTERS.

The parishes of St. George and St. Peter, Basseterre were constituted out of part of the French Basseterre quarter.   The present Register dates from 1747, and the names of both parishes head the first page, leading one to suppose that the livings were usually held by the same rector.   John Bernonville signs as Rector to 30th May, 1760.   Jno. Clarkson, Curate, signs from 1760-65.   Edwin Thomas, M.A., signs as Rector on 19th January, 1765.   The Burials commence in 1747, the first few edges ragged, but the writing good.

Marriages also commence in 1747, the early pages rotten and nearly destroyed.   Baptisms commence 7th May, 1747.   All the above consist of loose sheets and terminate in 1787 when there is a gap to 1795.

In *Caribbeana* I., 301 & 355 appeared a Transcript of Burials from 3rd January, 1743 to 11th October, 1745 and on page 358 a Transcript of Baptisms from 3rd January, 1742-3 to 13th October, 1745.   The old book from which these transcripts were copied no longer exists.

The second volume commences in 1795 and is properly bound.   The entries only relate to St. George's so perhaps the livings were then held by two separate rectors.

The names of the following families frequently occur :—

Armitrading	Emra	Newton
Colhoun	Fahie	Rowland
Cottle	Hardtman	Tyson
Crooke	Hindman	Vanderpool
Duport	Manning	Wattley
Earle	Mardenbrough	Wylly

The registers are kept in a good iron safe built into the wall of the church.

RECTORS OF ST. GEORGE & ST. PETER, BASSETERRE.

Walter Thomas, M.A., Oxford.   Rector, 1738 (*Caribbeana* III., 340). Minister of the Road 1721-5 Member of Council in 1743, buried 28 March, 1747 at Palmetto Point.

Probably identical with Walter, son of Francis Thomas of Llangates (?) co. Car. pleb. Jesus College matriculated 26 July, 1714, aged 18, B.A., 1718, M.A. 1720 (*Foster*).

John Bernonville.   Rector, 1747-60.   Went out 30 May, 1733.   Rector of St. Philip's, Antigua, 1733-46.

(John Clarkson, Curate 1760-65).   licenced by the Bishop of London, 30 September, 1760.

Edwin Thomas, M.A., Rector 1764. Licenced by the Bishop of London 11 September and went out 22 December, 1747. Rector of St. John's and St. George's, Gingerland, Nevis, 1750—13 December, 1764. A parcel of his letters (1769-71) at Fulham Palace. Buried 19 June, 1789, aged 69. Rector 25 years. Married at St. John's 20 October, 1748, Elizabeth Bridgewater, and three children there baptised.

A son Robert was baptised 13 Jan., 1755 at St. George's, Basseterre. His widow, Elizabeth was buried 13 September, 1798.

William Thomas signed as Minister from 1787, succeeded Edwin Thomas in 1789. Licenced by the Bishop of London 19 May, 1783. As son of Edwin Thomas of Nevis matriculated from Christ Church, Oxford, 25 October, 1774, aged 16. (*Foster*). He last signed 17 May, 1794 and died in England by a fall 14 April, 1795.

W. Davis, minister, signs 1792, 1793, and to February, 1794. Mr. Newman was curate in 1795.

Robert Pemberton, Rector, 1795—1812. Son of Robert Pemberton of Nevis. At Eton 1762-67, matriculated from Queen's College, Oxford, 16 December, 1767, aged 18. Licenced 22 December, 1785 to St. Paul and St. George, Nevis (*Caribbeana* III., 325). Curate of St. Thomas, Middle Island, 1786, Rector of St. James, Nevis, 1787-95. Buried here 3 Sept., 1812, aged 63.

Daniel Gateward Davis, Rector, 1826. Son of the Rev. Wm. Davis, Rector of Cayon. Baptised there 1 Jan., 1788, matriculated from Pembroke College, Oxford, 17 May, 1808, aged 20, B.A. 1814, M.A. 1823, D.D. 1842. First Bishop of the Leeward Islands, 1842-57, died in London. He married 16 December, 1813 at Figtree, Nevis, Ann Claxton who died 16 November, 1820, aged 52 and was buried at St. Paul's, Nevis, of which he was then Rector.

Francis Robert Brathwaite, M.A., Rector 1843 and Archdeacon of St. Kitts. M.A. Lambeth, 1843. Member of Codrington College, 1830. Still Rector 1852.

George Meade Gibbs, M.A., Rector 1879. Member of Executive Council. Archdeacon 1862. Retired to England 1891.

Henry Redmayne Holme, M.A., Rector 1882-91 Acting Archdeacon. Bishop of Honduras. (*M.I.* No. 3).

A. W. Watt, 1899—1911. Incumbent of St. George, Semington, 1911-23 ; Vicar of Ludgershall 1923.

R. de M. Dodsworth, B.A.,acting Archdeacon 1891-95.

Frederick Caunt, Rector 1910. Of St. Augustine's College, Canterbury, 1887. Ordained priest 1890 by Bishop Branch. Rector of St. Thomas and St. Paul, Nevis, 1890—1899. Rector of St. Thomas, St. Kitts 1901—1910. Archdeacon of St. Kitts and Canon of St. John's, 1906.

At the west end of the Nave are two shattered mural tablets which have been cemented together and repaired as far as possible.

1. The one to the south has a column in the centre, on the sinister side a man-of-war, on the dexter side a bastion with cannon, etc., signed " J. BACON, Junr., Sculptor, *LONDON*."*

----

* See another monument by Bacon in 1803 at Trinity Palmetto Point.

S.M.
of
WILLIAM HENRY SANDERSON
Efq^{re}
an Officer
in the Royal Navy
of GREAT BRITAIN
who was
born in this Ifland
on the 4th Day of Auguft
1788
Having entered
(at the attainment of
his tenth Year)
into that Profeffion
where a Field was difplay'd
to hid active Mind,
for the Exercise of
youthful Ardor, and
undaunted Energy :
Under the prompt and steady
Influence of Zeal
for the Service of his
KING and COUNTRY ;
he exhibited Talents
that would have graced
a Manhood more mature
and eftablished for himself
a brilliant Reputation

---

2. This must have been formerly a very handsome monument. It consists of a square tablet below surmounted by a pyramid. The marble much cracked and portion lost, especially the upper part of the pyramid.

On the pyramid is the following mutilated inscription :—

(Several of the top lines lost)
. . . . .Infant
. . .at Gu . . .al . pe
. . . . Aged 6 Ye. . .
And w . . . bu . . . .d at h. . . poft
DU BAR
and . . . . . . .error Bomb Vef. . . .
in . . . . Ifland
on the ^h Octob . . 179 . .
Aged 29 Years
and is Int . rrd under this Stone

Below on the square tablet is a spade shield with " DD " on the dexter side of it and " AD " on the sinister one.

Motto : JAM . . . . . .   (JAMAIS ARRIERE)
Crest : *On a chapeau a salamander.*
Arms : Quarterly of four, I. *Argent a human heart ensigned with an imperial crown on a chief Azure three mullets* (Douglas).

II. Quarterly of four, I. *Azure a lion rampant* (Galloway).
  2. *Or a lion rampant debruised of a bendlet Sa.* (Abernethy).
  3. *Argent three piles Gules.* (Wishart of Brechin).
  4. *Or a fess checky Azure and Argent debruised of a bend Sable charged with three buckles.* (Stewart of Bonkill).

III. Quarterly of four.
  1. & 4. *Gules three cinquefoils.*
  2. & 3. *Argent a lymphad.* (Hamilton).

IV. *Gules a lion rampant a bordure Argent charged with ten roses.* (Dunbar of Baldoon).

1796, Oct. 29. (Christian name unknown) Douglas, Capt. of H.M. Bomb Ketch, Terror, aged (blank) buried.
  1796, Nov. At St. Christopher's, the Hon. Capt. Dunbar Douglas, son to the Earl of Selkirk (*Gent Mag.* for 1797, 80). He was fourth son of Dunbar Hamilton the fourth Earl by Helen fifth daughter of the Hon. John Hamilton and grand-daughter of Thomas sixth Earl of Haddington. He was born 9 July, 1766 and died at St. Christopher 29 October, 1796 Alexander his next brother born 12 December, 1767 died at Guadaloupe 7 June, 1794.

---

3. On a brass on the north side of the west wall of the Nave :—

IN LOVING MEMORY OF HENRY REDMAYNE HOLME, M.A. | BISHOP OF HONDURAS AND FROM A.D. 1882 TO 1891 RECTOR | OF S^T GEORGE'S AND ACTING ARCHDEACON OF S^T KITT'S. | THE FIGURES OF S^T MARK AND S^T LUKE HAVE BEEN PLACED | IN THE ABOVE WINDOW BY HIS FORMER PARISHIONERS AND | FRIENDS AS A MEMORIAL OF HIS DEVOTED MINISTRY.

---

4. In the north aisle :—

SACRED TO THE MEMORY OF | JOSEPH HENRY BOON, | OF THIS ISLAND | WHO DIED AUGUST 24, 1879, | AGED 68 YEARS | AND OF HIS SON | WILLIAM SIDNEY BOON | WHO DIED IN CALCUTTA OCTOBER 14, 1871, | AGED 18 YEARS |

There is a Boon Mausoleum in the churchyard of Trinity, Palmetto Point.

---

5. Latin Inscription under the east window to :—

GEORGE ARTHUR COLLINS, B.A., of Queen's Coll., Oxford, who died Jan. 1886, aged 29.

As third son of Henry of Whitehaven, Cumberland, gent., Queen's Coll., matriculated 3 June, 1876, aged 19 ; exhibitioner 1876, B.A. 1880. (*Foster*).

---

6.   On the east wall of the south aisle :—

SACRED | to | the Memory of | THE HONOURABLE | JAMES SAMUEL BERRIDGE | FOR MANY YEARS PRESIDENT OF THE COUNCIL, | AND OF THIS ISLAND ; | WHO DIED ON THE 5ᵀᴴ NOVEMBER 1885, | AGED 79 YEARS |

7.   On a Brass adjoining :—

IN MEMORY OF | SIR JAMES ROBERT LONGDEN, G.C.M.G. | BORN 7ᵀʰ JULY 1827 | DIED 4ᵀʰ OCTOBER 1891 | ERECTED BY HIS WIFE ALICE EMILY.

In the West Indies, he was President of the Virgin Islands, 1861 ; Lt.-Gov. of Dominica 1865 ; Lt.-Gov. of British Honduras 1867 ; Gov. of Trinidad 1870 and of British Guiana 1874.   K.C.M.G. 1876, G.C.M.G. 1883.   He was a son of John R. Longden of Doctors Commons.   There is also a monument to him in the Cathedral at Port of Spain, Trinidad.

On the floor of the south Transept is a row of seven fine old ledgers laid side by side, the organ resting on their lower ends and so covering up portions of the Inscriptions :—

8.   On a much cracked stone :—

Here lye the Bodies
of REBECCAH & MARGARET
ROWLAND Daughters
of RICHARD & ELIZABETH
ROWLAND of Bafseterre
Alfo the Body of RICHARD
ROWLAND their Son
A : D : 1738
Here Alfo Lyeth the Body of
ELIZABETH ROWLAND Wife of
RICHARD ROWLAND who Departeᵈ
this Life the . . . of Jvly A : D : 1741
(Organ floor cuts here)

The Hon. Richard Rowland married (perhaps secondly) Margaret daughter of the Hon. Tho. Bridgwater.   She was buried 1 June, 1753 and he remarried in 1757 Mrs. Anne Ogilvie widow of Essequibo.   He dated his will at Greenwich 10 June, 1761 (265 *Cheslyn*) and named his son Francis, daughter Margaret and grand-daughters Anne and Elizabeth Wells.

See Nos. 45, 139, and under Sandy Point.

9. Blue marble, very bold Jacobean shield with mantling :—

Crest :*An eagle with wings displayed* over wreath and helmet.
Arms : *on a chevron, between three mullets, as many escallops.*

> . . . . .re Lyes Tho⁸ Blacket
> (Organ floor cuts the second line)

Probably one of the Blackets (now Baronets) of Newcastle, as the above is their coat-of-arms.

———

10. Much damaged blue marble ledger.

On a sunk oval is a Jacobean shield with mantling (the shield being placed at an angle) which is unique for the West Indies).

Crest : *An heraldic tiger ? bezantée or pelletée* over wreath and helmet.
Arms : *A similar tiger.*

> Here lyeth the Body . . . .
> GEORGE TAYLOR
> late of this Ifland Gent
> (The Organ cuts the fourth line)

In 1652 Capt. Nicholas Taylor was appointed a Commissioner by Cromwell to collect debts of sequestered estates in St. Christopher.

Thomas Taylor and Capt. George Taylor were here in 1654. Nicholas Taylor was of St. Johns, 1677-8.

Elizabeth, daughter of Col. John Estridge, by her first husband—Taylor had two sons John and Joseph, living in 1699.

Samuel Okes Taylor and John Taylor were both estate owners in 1753.

George Taylor of St. George, Basseterre, gent. Will dated 15 June, 1728. By deed of 23 February last I conveyed all my estate to Benjamin Markham of St. Anne's, gent. on trust. (Vol. *A* 2). By deed he also conveyed a plantation of 98 acres to Tobias Wall, Esq., as security for £2000.

Nicholas Taylor married 22 October, 1734 at St. Peter's, Basseterre, Elizabeth Fenton, an heiress, and had three sons, 1—George of Carshalton Park died 30 June, 1814, aged 78, Will (445 *Bridport*). 2—John of Carshalton Park died 9 July, 1832, aged 82, whose daughter and heiress, Anne, married Joseph Estridge. 3—Rev. William Taylor.

1747, Dec. 18. John, son of Nicholas and —. Taylor baptised, buried him 25 December.

1751, Nov. 28. Samuel James born 10 December, 1748, and John born 17 November, 1750, sons of Nicholas and Parnel Taylor, baptised.

———

11. Blue marble ledger :—

> Here Lieth the Body of
> MR. PAUL DE MARSAL,
> who Died the 21ˢᵗ of September 1758
> AGED 57 YEARS.

———

Louis De Marsal a sufferer by the late invasion of the French received a debenture dated 25 March, 1712.

John De Marsall of St. Peter's, Basseterre, planter. Will dated 13 April, 1739. My wife Hester. My sons James. . . Zachariah and Peter £300 c. each (? my daughters) Mary and Hester £400 c. each. My son John. My brother Paul. Sworn 30 April 1739. (*St. Kitts' Records*, vol. G., No. 1816).

Mary De Marsall, widow. Will dated 28 Feb., 1738-9. My son Paul. My grand-daughters Frances and Mary Ann Duport. All residue to my daughter Susanna wife of Isaac Duport. (*Ibid*, No. 1826).

Lewis Daniel De Marsal. Will dated 7 June, 1750. My uncle Paul De Marsal £150. My mother Martha wife of Francis Des Fountains £50 a year. (Several cousins). Sworn 21 June, 1750. (*Ibid*, vol. P., No. 4346).

Isaac Duport, died Jan., 1780, aged 85. Will (490 *Oxford*) Mrs. Duport died 17 May, 1781, aged 83.

BURIALS.

1749, Aug. 21	Mary De Marsal
1750, June 8	Lewis De Marsal.
1752, June 3	James De Marsal.
1755, Oct. 12	Daniel Demarsal.
1758, April 26	Peter De Marsal.
1758, Sept. 22	Paul de Marsal.
1759, Oct. 3	John Demarsal
1770, Aug. 8	Hester De Marsal, 62.
1774, March 5	Elizabeth De Marsal, 54.

MARRIAGE.

1755, June 30.   Simon Duport to Esther Demarsal

---

12. Blue marble, much worn and scaled :—

In sunk oval a Jacobean shield with mantling :

Crest : *A tower* over wreath and helmet.
Arms : Worn away.

. . . . e lye . . . . .
. . . A B F . . . .
departed this life Jul . . . Fou
. . .ed Thirty . . . . Year
. . kew . . the Bod . . er dav . .
(The Organ cuts the sixth line).

---

13.   In a similar oval with a Jacobean design :—

Crest : *Out of a coronet a demi ostrich* over wreath and helmet.

Arms : *Or, a lion rampant between three crosses croslet* part of the shield and inscription much flaked.   (King, of Devonshire and Towcester, county Northampton).

Here lies Int . . . . . of
BENJAMIN KING of . . . . .nd Efq.
who departed this Life . . . . . of Dec^r
Anno Domini]7.0
in the Fortyfifth Year of his Age.

The year is doubtful, the third numeral is 0 or 6.   1760 seems too late for the Jacobean style, but an old slab in stock and out of fashion may have been sent out.

The organ only rests on the corner of the slab.

1749, May 28.   Benjamin, son of Joseph and Elizabeth King.   Bapt.

1753, Benjamin King, esq., one plantation in Trinity Palmetto Point (*Baker's Map*).

A copy of the above inscription in the *New English Register* in which it is stated that Daniel King, junr., of Lynn, Mass, born about 1636 was in 1687 a resident merchant on the Island of St. Kitts.   (*Vol.* 46 p. 84).

There was a Benjamin King, Esq., of Antigua who died in 1758, but not apparently connected.

1760, Dec. 23.   Benjamin King, Esqr.   Buried.

1772, Jan. 2.   Joseph King, Esq., of the island of St. Christopher, to Miss Giles, daughter of Daniel Giles, Esq., merchant of New Broad-street-buildings. (*T. & C. M.*, 55 ; Gent. Mag. 46).   As Mary, wife of Jos. King, she was party to a close roll in 1786.

Benjamin King of St. Christophers, Esq.,   Will dated 28 November, 1760. Wife Sarah £300c. a year, dau. Elizabeth £1500 st. at 21.   Bro. Jos. King, £50 c. a year.   Sister-in-law Mrs. Frances Lowrey.   All residue to son Joseph.   Sworn 5 January, 1761.   (*St. Kitts' Records*, No. 6551).

1793, Aug. 2.   At Taplow, Joseph King, esq., son-in-law to Daniel Giles, esq., deputy-governor of the Bank.   (*Gent. Mag.*, 772).

---

14.   Blue marble, at the end of the row and touching the south wall :—

Here Lyes the B.dy of
(*Sic*)   Mr IOHN UANDERPOOLE
who departed this life . . . . 3^d of Aug^{ft}
In the Year of 1740
and in the . . . . .fecond
Year of his Age
Also the Bodies of F.ANC . . . .
Daughters of IOHN & . . . . .
VAN . . . . RPOO. . . . FR . . .
May y^e . .1737 in y^e . . . . . . .Age
ELIZ^o Died Nov ye 5th 1738 in ye 21^{ft} Year of

John Vanderpool in his will dated 2 Aug. and sworn 12 Nov., 1740, names his wife Elizabeth devised his plantation to his son Samuel and bequeathed to his other children George, John, Wm., Mary, Martha, Rebecca and Ann £1000 c. apiece. (*St. Kitts' Records*, No. 2075). There are numerous entries in the parish register of this parish as well as in those of St. Thomas and Christ Church. Some of the family were in Nevis.

15. Immediately end on to No. 14 is a blue marble the dates very uncertain :—

HERE LYETH Y^E BODY OF IOHN WILLI . . . .
LATE OF THIS ISLAND MERCH. WHO DEPA. . . . . .
THIS LIFE THE XXI DAY OF OCTOBER MD . . . . .
IN THE X.XIII YEAR . . . . . . .GE
ALSO TWO OF HIS C . . . . DR . . .
. . ARY

ALSO

The . .odies of Magdalene & Doroth .
Cochrane, Daughters of Thomas . .
Ann Cochrane who died in their in
fancy Ann :]780.

John Williams of Basseterre, Merchant, wife Ann, my brother Robert. Will dated 20 Oct., 1739. Sworn 13 Nov., 1739.

1780, Sept. 26. Magdalene, daughter of Thomas and Anne Cochrane, aged 19 months., buried.

1780, Nov. 24. Dorothy, daughter of Thomas and Anne Cochrane, aged 3 months.

16. Adjoining No. 15, end on to No. 13, and nearly all under the organ is a blue marble ledger of late eighteenth century style. No name nor date discernible.

There is another blue marble beyond this but with Inscription worn completely away.

17. Copy of Inscription on a tablet placed in this church before its destruction by fire :—

This Tablet is erected by THOMAS BERKELEY E^{SQRE} of London, to the memory of his much respected father HENRY BERKELEY Esqre who was born in this Island in January, 1734, and was the son of MAURICE BERKELEY Esqre by Miss TOBIN of Nevis.

MAURICE BERKELEY descended from MAURICE DE BERKELEY, one of the branches of the ancient and illustrious House of BERKELEY, of the County of Gloucester, married in the year 1732 Miss TOBIN, a daughter of the very respectable family of TOBIN of the Island of Nevis, and with his Lady came out to the West Indies, where he did not long encounter the climate. He died leaving two Sons HENRY & MAURICE. HENRY was the father of seven Sons and three daughters, of whom

THOMAS is the youngest of the Sons, MAURICE died unmarried. The high character for honor and integrity upheld in this colony by HENRY BERKELEY is universally acknowledged by all its inhabitants, and this humble memento is offered by his son as a tribute of gratitude to his memory for having shown so virtuous an example to his posterity. (See pedigree in *Caribbeana* V., 17).

---

18. Ledger near north side of Nave :—

Sacred | TO THE MEMORY | OF JOHN LEWIS, | A NATIVE OF EAST LOTHIAN | SCOTLAND, | WHO DEPARTED THIS LIFE | JANUARY, 25th 1837, | INTERRED 32nd YEAR | OF HIS AGE.

---

19. Lofty stone and brick mausoleum. On white marble on the face are :—

Crest : *A bird* (head and one leg lost).
Arms : *Argent a saltire engr Sable between four escallop shells.*
(? Berridge).

---

20. Headstone :—

SACRED TO THE MEMORY | OF | CHARLES CUNNINGHAM JONES ESQRE | OF THE COLONIAL BANK WEST INDIES | WHO DIED OF FEVER AT BASSETERRE ST KITTS | ON THE 11th OF FEBRUARY, 1856 | IN HIS 37th YEAR |.

---

21. Headstone Cross :—

S. M.
The Revd
Charles C. W. M. Sm . . . . . .
Curate of this Parish
who died June MDCCCLV
Aged XXXV333 Years.

---

22. Similar headstone. Gothic lettering, nearly illegible.

Alice Eleanor Jermyn
aged . . . years . . . months
died at sea & was buried off St Kitts
. . . . MDCCCLXV
William Edward Jermyn
aged

---

23.   White marble ledger :—

In Memory of | MARIANA | Daughter of | *Alfred and Sarah Anne Jones* |
Born 23rd April   } 1845
Died 22nd October }

Mrs. Jones was a daughter of Fred. Huggins of (? Nevis) who died at New-
haven, U.S.A., before 1848.   She died in England in 1894, aged 81.   Her children
were—
     1—A daughter born 1837 at Charlestown, Nevis.
     2—A daughter, born 1840, married — Couchman and of Bedford in 1910,
aged 70.
     3—Arthur Fred., born 1842 at Olivees near Basseterre.
     4—Clara, born 1844 at Olivees.
     6—Mariana, born 23 April, and died 22 October, 1845.
     5—Alfred Vivian, born 1846, B.A., Oxford.
     7—Rev. Wm. John Webber, born 1850 at Greenland, Basseterre, B.A.,
Oxford, 1877 ; my informant 1910.
     8—Alice, living in 1910.

24.   White marble ledger :—

SACRED | TO THE MEMORY OF | CHARLES ST JOHN WILKINSON | WHO
DEPARTED THIS LIFE | ON THE 23RD DAY OF NOVEMBER 1843 | AGED 22 YEARS |

25.   Ledger over vault enclosed by iron railing :—

Owing to the height of the fence it is difficult to read the inscription.

SACRED TO THE MEMORY | OF | MRS SUSANNA BERKELEY | WHO DEPARTED
THIS LIFE | ON THE 7TH OF MAY 1826 | AGED 53 YEARS |.

26.   Headstone :—

Beneath | THIS STONE LIE | THE MORTAL REMAINS OF | JANE ELIZABETH
RAND | SHE WAS BORN IN BASSETERRE | ST CHRISTOPHERS | THE 13TH OF
DECEMBER, 1804 | DIED THE 4TH DAY OF AUGUST 1836 | NEAR THIS SPOT | ALSO
LIE THE REMAINS OF | SARAH YOUNG | WHO WAS BORN SEPTR 20TH 1795 | AND
DIED MAY 17TH 1837 |

27.   Sacred | to the Memory of | Matthew Cole Cleghorn who | departed this
life on the 4th of | November, 1832, in the 20th | Year of his age | *Also* | Pletcher
Robinson Taylor | born in Tortola Octr 14th 1809 | died in St Kitts Feby 12th
1841| *Also* | The Honourable Ralph Bush | Cleghorn late President of the |
Island of Nevis who departed | this life on the 7th of March | 1842, aged 37 Years.

Ralph B. Cleghorn was born here, and at the age of 5 was taken by his father
for education to England, returned in 1823, married in June, 1824, directly after
which his father died at sea.   He then proceeded to London, returned again the
end of 1825, and opened a store, which at first produced an income of £1200 c.

Espousing the cause of the slaves he manumitted 15 of his own and rendered himself so unpopular that his business suffered. In 1829 he was elected from among the free coloured people to be their delegate and went to England returning in December, 1830. He has been put in the Commission of the Peace and now begs for a government post. (*Long letter to Zachary Macaulay*, dated 29 June, 1833, in the Editor's possession).

---

28. White marble ledger :—

SACRED | TO THE MEMORY OF | GRACE GILBERT | WIFE OF THE | REV. T. M. CHAMBERS, M.A. | WHO DIED | APRIL 5TH 1856.

---

29. Lofty iron railing with a cast-iron upright iron plate fixed thereon :—

SACRED
TO THE MEMORY | OF |
HARRIOT COOK
WHO DEPARTED THIS
LIFE SEPTEMBER 20th 1823
AGED 38 YEARS.

---

30. Lofty stone sarcophagus. On white marble, north face :—

SACRED
TO THE MEMORY OF
H. E.
CHARLES THORNTON CUNNINGHAM ESQUIRE
LATE LIEUTENANT GOVERNOR OF ST CHRISTOPHER'S,
AND OF THE LEEWARD ISLANDS
WAS IN THE 36TH YEAR OF HIS AGE AND IN THE FULL VIGOR OF LIFE
OVERWHELMED BY THE SUDDEN VIEW OF THE PORTRAIT OF
A RECENTLY DECEASED AND MUCH BELOVED SISTER
EXPIRED IN A MOMENT ON THE 14TH DAY OF JANUARY, 1847.

His engraved portrait hangs in the Library.

---

31. A large mausoleum east of chancel has no name.

---

32. White marble vault. On the top slab :—

Sacred | to the memory of | *WILLIAM TORREY* Junior, | who was born January the 24th 1767, | and departed this life | July the 2d 1804 | ALSO | *WILLIAM TORREY* Senior, | who died the 8th day of June, 1803, | Aged Seventy five years |.

On the north face :   *WITHIN THIS VAULT*
are deposited the remains of
JOHN ROBINSON THURSTON
Doctor of Medicine
who was born in the Town of Newport
in the State of Rhode Island, U.S.A.
on the twenty-fourth day of April A.D. 1774
and departed this life on the seventh day of May 1819
HEREIN
likewise are interred the remains of
ESTHER
daughter of Doctor John R. Thurston
who was born on the 24th day of December, 1816
and died on the 21st day of April, 1819

At the west end :   IN THIS VAULT
repose the remains of
CHARLES HODGSON
who was born in the
town of Driffield Yorkshire
ENGLAND
on the sixteenth day of June
A.D. 1787
and departed this life on the
sixth day of June, 1831.

---

33.   Square Roman altar :—

In Memory of T. . . McMahon
of the County of Kilkenny in
. . . . .Member
. . . . .he departed
this life ye 30th Novr 1811 in
the 67 Year of his Age

(Gap in Register from 11 June 1810 to 1 August, 1812.
1839, Feb. 21.   In Berners Street, Anne, third daughter of Terence McMahon
of St. Kitts. (*Gent Mag*. 442).
1845, Sept. 8.   In Bathurst street, Hyde Park Gardens, aged 84, Mrs. Eliz.
Dalrymple McMahon, late of St. Kitts.   (*Ib*. 434).

---

34.   Ledger over stone vault (flake) :—

. . . Memory of
. . . . . . *D. BURLINGHAM*
. . . . . Son of
. . . . *ANN BURLINGHAM*
of Evesham, Worcestershire,
ENGLAND,
Members of the Society of
Friends.
Hexlanded here on the 23rd of April
being too ill to proceed to
Jamaica whither he was going
for the benefit of his health
and died the 29th day of
April 1838
in his 25th Year.

---

35. Stone vault east of Church .

Sacred to the Memory of
MR JOHN WICKENDE . .
late Merchant in Basseter . . .
in the Island of St. Christoph . . .
a native of Rochester
in the County of Kent
who departed this life
the 5th August 1825
aged 31 years

(Gap in Register 2 August, 1825, to 9 February, 1826).

---

36. Stone vault :—

SACRED
to the Memory of
JOHN SPAN Second Son of
SAMUEL SPAN Esqr
of Briftol
who departed this life
on the 7th. day of June
1821,
In the Twenty-first Year
of his Age
Universally beloved and regretted

1793, July 18. At St. Vincent, Mr. Andrew Span, son of Samuel Span, Esq., merchant of Bristol. (*Bath Chronicle*).

1796, Nov. 2. At Clifton, John Span, Esq., merchant of Bristol, to Miss Dorothea Munro, only daughter and heiress of Hugh Munro, esq., of Carriacou, in the Government of Grenada. (*Gent. Mag.*, 965).

Sanuel Span, Senior, died in Bristol, 2 December, 1795. Will proved in 1796. (40 *Harris*). He refers to his plantation in Grenada.

1808. Samuel Span was killed in a duel in Trinidad.

1811. Samuel Span of St. Vincent. Will. (511 *Crickitt*).

1814, Dec. At Stapleton, Gloucestershire, aged 16, Samuel, son of the late Samuel Span, esq., of Bristol. (*Gent. Mag.* 610).

1821. Samuel, second son of Samuel Span of Bristol, Esq., died 7 June, aged 20.

BLOXWORTH, CO. DORSET.

Sacred to the memory of OLIVER MᶜCAUSLAND SPAN, of the Bengal Army ; eldest son of the late OLIVER Wᴹ SPAN, of Trinidad in the West Indies, and of KATHERINE his wife. He was born July 31, 1827, and died Aug. 8th, 1857, in the fort of Agra. (*Hutchins* I., 182).

---

37.   On a small loose fragment :—

> SACRED
> TO THE MEMORY
> OF ANNA MARIA
> DAUGHTER OF TH .
> HONORABLE
> GEORGE ESTRIDG . .
> BORN JULY . .
> 1834 DIED. . . . .

1840, Feb. 28.   On Wednesday last, Anna Maria, only daughter of the Hon. George Estridge, Esq., aged 5 years and 7 months.   (*St. Christopher Gazette*). This was one of the oldest families in the Island.

---

38.   East of Chancel.:—

> WITHIN THIS TOMB
> LIE THE REMAINS OF
> ISAAC DUPUY ESQ^RE
> WHO DIED
> SEPTEMBER 21st 1829

He was Member of Council in 1826, an Assistant Justice of the K.B. & C.P. and assistant baron of the Court of Exchequer.

1753 . . . . ac Dupuy to Elizabeth Thomas by Lic.

1754, Dec., 23.   Frances daughter of Isaac and Elizabeth Dupuy, born 12 September, bapt.

1756, Oct., 25.   Frances Dupuy buried.

1759, June 6.   Elizabeth Dupuy buried.

---

39.   Stone vault :—

> **In Memory**
> of RICHARD MARPLES DELANEY
> Son of DANIEL & MARY DELANEY
> who departed this Life 31^ft March 1757
> in the 2^d Year of his Age
> Alfo the Body of DANIEL DELANEY
> Son of DANIEL & MARY DELANEY
> who departed this Life 26th Nov^br 1757
> in the 4th Year of his Age
> Likewife the Body of MARY DELANEY
> Wife of DANIEL DELANEY
> who departed this Life 9th May 1783.
> in the 63^d Year of her Age.

1748.   John Delaney to Elizabeth Queen by banns.

1762.   Richard Dawes and Elizabeth Delaney.   Lic.

BAPTISMS.

1754, Nov. 10.　Daniel, son of Daniel and Mary Delaney, born 19 Oct.

1755, Dec. 28.　Richard Marples, son of Daniel and Mary Delaney, born 16 Oct.

1762, Oct. 2.　George son of Daniel and Mary Delaney, born yᵉ 23ᵈ Sept. ult.

1776, April. ―― son of Wᵐ decᵈ and Mary Delaney, born 27 Aug., 1773.

1780, Nov. 23.　Mary, daughter of Thoˢ and Mary Delaney, born 3 Sept., 1778.

BURIALS.

1757, April 1.　Richard Marples Delaney, an Infant.

1757, Nov. 27.　Daniel Delaney, an Infant.

1775, Dec. 2.　Wᵐ Delaney, aged 46.

1776, Aug. 15.　Henry, son of Wᵐ and Mary Delaney, aged 6.

1780, Aug. 28.　Thoˢ Delaney, aged 2.

1780, Dec. 30.　Mary, daughter of Thoˢ and Mary Delaney, aged 2.

1783, May 10.　Mary Delaney.

1790, Nov. 23.　Samˡ Delaney, aged 35.

ST. ANNS, SANDY POINT.

BAPTISMS.

1724, Dec. 27.　John, son of Daniel Delaney by his wife Anne.

1729, Jan. 5.　Anne, daughter of Daniel Delaney and his wife Anne.

1730, March 1.　William, son of Daniel Delaney and his wife Anne.

1731, Aug. 25.　Daniel (born Augᵗ 17, 1731) son of Daniel Delaney and his wife Anne Delaney.

1732, Oct. 1.　Mary (born Sepᵗ 23, 1732) daughter of Daniel Delaney and his wife Anne Delaney.

1735, March 2.　James (born Feb. 9, 1735) son of Daniel Delaney and his wife Anne Delaney

1736, Oct. 17.　George (born Oct. 7, '36) son of Daniel and Anne Delaney.

1738, Aug. 2.　Darby, son of Danˡ ―― Delaney.

1745, Oct. 27.　Elizabeth (born Oct. 21, '45) daughter of Danˡ and Elizᵗʰ Delaney.

BURIALS.

1731, Nov. 4.　Kennelly, son of Daniel and Ann Delaney.

1734, Feb. 20.　Mary, daughter of Daniel and Anne Delaney.

1735, July 4.　Margaret Delaney.

1738-39. ―― Delaney's son.

1790.　Jas. Delaney, Senʳ, Esq., of St. Kitts also John Wᵐ Delaney of St. Croix, subscribers to Peterkins Planting.

1800, Aug. Lately.　At Liverpool, James Delancy (sic) Esq. of St. Kitts, to Mrs. Phipps Weston, widow. (Gent. Mag. 795).

1803.　Lately at St. Kitts, aged 73, Daniel Delaney, esq. (Ibid. 1294)

―――――

40.　Blue marble :―

Above in a sunk oval is a Jacobean shield with mantling.

Crest : *A demi-lion rampant reguardant couped, in its paws an anchor.*
Arms : *Three helmets within a bordure engrailed Argent.*

(Halliday of Wilts and Somerset. *Burke's Armory*).

Here lies Interred the Remains of
MR ALEXANDER HALLIDAY late of
this Ifland Merchant who Exchanged
this life for A better on the Jst day of
October 1754 Aged 23 Years & 11 Months
To whose Honour'd Memory
his Brothers JOHN and WILLIAM paid
this Tribute of their unfeigned Love.

1754, Oct. 1.   Alexander Halliday buried.

1757.   William Halliday, marry'd to Jane Wilson by L.   She was daughter of Richard Wilson, Chief Justice of St. Kitts.   Her marriage bonds were dated 30 Nov. 30 1757.

1759.   July 26.   William Halliday, Esq., at St. Kitts.   (*Gent. Mag.* 497).

1810, Oct. 7.   In George Street, Manchester Square, Mrs. Halliday, widow of the late William Halliday, Esq., of the Island of St. Christopher.   (*Ib.* 493). John the other brother was I think identical with John Halliday of Antigua, the ancestor of Lord Tollemache.

---

41.   This and the next two vaults are placed on one long platform :—

Here lie the Remains of JOHN EARLE,
the Elder of this Ifland, who departed this
Life the tenth day of November
Anno Domini 177J,
in the fiftieth Year of His Age.
Here also lie the Remains of Six of His
Children who died in their Infancy
And His *Daughter MARY PITCHER* who
* . .rted this Life the 28 day of June
Anno Domini 1772
. . . the twenty first Year of Her Age
. . . . lie the Remains of *BARBARA H. EARLE*
Wife of *John Earle* who departed this
Life the J March, 1781, Aged 26 Years.
In Cœlo Quies.

1771, Nov. 10.   John Earl, 49, buried.

John Earle born 14 May, 1722, married 20 Dec., 1745 at St. Mary Cayon Elizabeth Burt, who was born 16 May, 1726.

1771, Sept. 12.   Isaac Pitcher and Mary Earle married.   She was daughter of John Earle, and was buried 29 June, 1772, aged 21.   Her husband born 1744, died 1822 at 22 Queen Square, London.

John Earle, junior, born 20 February, 1747-8, died 3 Oct., 1807, aged 60, having married 9 April, 1778 at St. Margaret Pattins Rood Lane, Barbara Haliburton Mathie, born 27 April, 1755.

---

* The left edge of the 9, 10, 11, and 12 lines has been broken off and lost.

42. White marble slab :—

here lies the Body of
GEORGE PENISTON Esquire
who departed this life
January the twenty third 1820
Aged forty eight Years.

---

43. Marble slab :—

Sacred to the Memory of
SAMUEL WOODLEY Esquire
who departed this Life November
11th 1795 in the 63rd Year of his Age
This Marble is placed here by his
Affectionate Daughters

Of a well known family. See pedigree in my *History of Antigua.*

BAPTISMS.

1767, Aug. 2. Elizabeth, daughter of Samuel and Sarah Woodley, born 21 July.
1770, June 27. Mary, daughter of Samuel and Sarah Woodley, born 28 Oct., 1769.
1774, April 3. John, son of Samuel and Sarah Woodley, born 2 April.
1775, Dec. 17. Joseph King, son of Samuel and Sarah Woodley, born 24 Nov.
1777, May, 18. Lucretia, daughter of Samuel and Sarah Woodley, born 5 April
1779, May 23. James, son of Samuel and Sarah Woodley, born 24 Dec., 1778

BURIALS.

1780, June 15. Sarah, wife of Samuel Woodley, 38, buried.
1795, Nov. 12. Samuel Woodley, Esq., aged (blank) years, brought from St. Peter, Basseterre.
This Samuel is not mentioned in any of the family wills. He may have been younger brother of William the Governor-General, or else illegitimate.

---

44. East of Chancel. White marble flat slab :—

Here Lyeth the Body of
JAMES WARD Esqr
who departed this Life July 27th 1757
Aged 56 Years.

There were Wards in Nevis. See Bookplate of Henry Ward Townley. (*West Indies* Book-plates, No. 700).

---

45.   White marble slab over vault :—

Here Lies
the body of
WILL^M FENTON WELLS
Son of W^m & E_{LIZ}^h W_{ELLS}
who departed this Life
the 12th Day of April 1758
Aged Four Years
Also the Body of ANSTANCE WELLS
Daughter of the above
W^M & ELIZ^H WELLS who departed
this Life the 29th Day of May 1759
Aged nine Months
Alfo the Body of ELIZ^H WELLS
Wife of the faid W^M W_{ELLS}
who Departed this Life
the 29th Day of June 1759
Aged Forty two Years.

1792.   In the West Indies, William Wells, esq., only brother of the Rev. Robert Wells, Rector of Penmaen, co. Glamorgan.   In a series of more than 48 years, by a sedulous attention to commerce (the nature of which few men understood better) he acquired an immense fortune in money and landed property in the island of St. Christopher's.   (*Gent. Mag.* 963).

Mrs. Elizabeth Wells was daughter of the Hon. Richard Rowland who in his Will of 1761 names his grand-daughters Anne and Elizabeth Wells.   See No. 8

BAPTISMS.

1747, Sept. 23.   Richard, son of Wm. and Anne Wells.   N.B.—He died the next day.

1754, Dec. 17.   Wm. Fenton son of Wm. and Parnel Wells, born 1 June.

BURIALS.

1747, Sept. 24.   Richard infant son of Wm. Wells, Esq.
1752, Oct. 25.   Elizabeth Wells a child
1753, Oct. 26.   Peter Wells
1757, April 2.   William Wells an Infant.
1758, April 13.   William Wells a child
There is no record of the burial of Anstance
1759, June 29.   Elizabeth Wells.   Oct. 5.   Hannah Wells.
1761, Sept. 29.   William Wells, Senior.
1767, Jan. 3.   Sarah Wells.
1767, Jan. 3.   Anne Gibbon, daughter of the said Wells.
1767, Jan. 7.   Mary Wells, daughter of Sarah Wells, 8 years.
1767, Oct. 27.   Miles Wells, aged 27.
1770, July 27.   Wm. Wells by the Parish.

TRINITY, PALMETTO POINT.

1783, March 3.   William, Mulatto son of the Hon. William Wells, born March 1, 1775.

Grace, daughter of the Hon. William Wells, born Jan. 2, 1777.
Nathaniel, son of the Hon. William Wells, born Sept. 10, 1779.

46. Large altar tomb. White marble slab on top :—

On a sunk oval is a Jacobean shield with mantling.

Crest : *A mower with his scythe* over wreath and helmet.

Arms : *Argent a cross Patonce.*

> Here lieth the Body of
> THOMAS PILKINGTON Efq^r
> who departed this life October
> the 19th 1740 in the 56th
> Year of his Age
> Also PARNEL PILKINGTON wife
> of the Said Thos who Departed
> this Life Septm^r the 6th 1748
> Aged 109 Years
> Also MARY STEWART, who Depa=
> rted this Life Septem^r the 22^d 1751 :
> Aged 44 Years.

The age 109 must be an error, as she was probably younger than her husband and had a daughter, Parnel born in 1731.

1748, Sept. 6. Parnel Pilkington, widow, buried.

1751, Sept. 22. Mary Steward, buried

Parnel Pilkington of St. Christopher, widow. Will dated 18 April, 1747. My son Thomas Pilkington 5 guineas. My son Wm. Bates Pilkington, my loving husband Thomas Pilkington, my sons James Pilkington and John Pilkington £200 each. My daughter Elizabeth, wife of Nicholas Taylor £50. My daughter Parnel Vanderpoole £300. Sworn 8 Oct., 1748. No. 4009 St. Kitts. There are several land deeds of hers.

Thomas Pilkington of St. George, Basseterre, planter. Will dated 17 Oct., 1740. My wife Parnel £1000, my eldest son Thomas, my 3 sons William, James, and John. No. 2079.

John Pilkington married (settlement dated 3 Dec., 1742) Mrs. Sarah Hardtman, widow. (*Caribbeana* VI., 105).

1787. At Carshalton park, Surrey, William Bates Pilkington, esq., of the Island of St. Christopher. (*Gent. Mag.* 550). I saw no tablet to him in the church. Carshalton Park was the residence of Mr. George Taylor of St. Kitts.

---

47. Blue marble ledger :—

> HERE LIETH INTERRED THE BODY
> OF MR THOMAS WEBLEY WHO
> DEPARTED THIS LIFE THE 4TH DAY OF
> AVGVST MDCCXLII AGED XXXVII
> LIKEWISE ANN THE WIFE OF
> MR THOMAS WEBLEY WHO DEPARTED
> THIS LIFE THE XVIIITH OF NOVEMBER
> MDCCXLII AGED XXXI.
> LIKEWISE THOMAS SON TO THOMAS
> AND ANN WEBLEY WHO DEPARTED
> THIS LIFE THE XVTH OF JUNE
> MDCCXL AGED VI YEARS.

---

48.   White marble ledger :—

WILLIAM PATRICK HODNETT,
AGED 17 YEARS.

---

49.   Slab on earth :—

In Memory | of | JOHN JOSEPH FLETCHER | Son of | RICHARD FLETCHER | And | JANE MARY | His Wife | He died 3rd Janry 1791 | Aged 8 Weeks | Alfo LOUISA MARTHA their | Daughter who died the 8 : day | of Febry 1792 Aged 9 weeks.

BURIALS.

1791, Jan. 3.   Joseph, infant child of Richard Fletcher, aged 3 months.

1792, Feb. 9.   Louisa, child of Richard and Jane Mary Fletcher, aged 27 months.

1795, Aug. 11.   Richard Fletcher, Esq., brought from Trinity, Palmetto Point, aged —

1795, Sept. 21.   Martha, daughter of late Richard Fletcher, Esq., and Jane his wife brought from Trinity, Palmetto Point, aged —

---

50.   Marble slab on earth :—

Here lies the Body of
Jane Rofcrow who departed
this life the 17th Day of May
1749 In the 28th Year of her
Age

1749, May 18.   Jane, Wife of Thomas Roscrow, buried.

---

51.   Jacobean shield with mantling in circle :—

Crest : *A mailed cubit arm couped holding a shield* over wreath and helmet.
Arms : *Argent three lions rampant reguardant.*

Here Lyeth Interr'd the Body of
Mrs SARAH TYSON
Wife of Mr THOMAS TYSON
who departed this life 24th of Novbr
1738, in the 45th Year of her Age
And alfo feven Children

	SEABORWHITE (*sic*)
	THOMAS
	FRAYSSE
Namely	IOHN
4 Sons & 3 Daughters	SARAH
	SARAH ye fecond
	MARY

Margaret Tyson aged 27 was entered in the census of 1707-8. The family subsequently became very numerous and several members occupied high positions.

---

52.   A blue slate slab :—

IN MEMORY OF
Richard Hall Son of
James and Eleanor Hall
who departed this life the 2nd
of September 1793 aged 6 Years
2 Months and 13 days

1793, Sept. 2.   At St. Peter's, Richard Hall, aged 6, buried.   (Bur. Regr.).

---

53.   Grey marble.   Mortar has been mixed on the right corner of the first
three lines :—

Here lieth the B. . . .
MICHAEL EBB. . . . .
Sugar Baker who D. . . . .
This Life the 26 of October
Anno Domini 1765
And in the 45 year of his
Age *may he rest in Peace.*
AMEN.

1765, Oct. 27.   Michael Ebberley.   (Bur. Reg.)
1766 (Later than Oct.) 23.   John Ellis and Sarah Ebberley, widow.

---

54.   White marble ledger :—

Here Lies the Body of Jn. Beavor Esqr of
Kingſale in the Kingdom of Ireland late of
the Iſland of Tortola who departed this
Life the 31st July 1768
in the 58th year of his Age
ALSO in this *VAULT* is Interred the
Body of Mrs HONOUR BEAVOR of
the Iſland of Montserat.

1768, July 30.   John Beaver, aged 58.   (Bur Reg.).

---

55.   Headstone :—

William Dansey
departed this Life
the 23 August 1782
Aged 17 *Years.*

---

56. Small ledger. Jacobean shield with mantling in circle :—

Crest : *A tower.*
Arms. *A chevron between three towers.*

About twelve lines very indistinct.

St. Chriftophers
Under this. . . . .
. . s the Body of CHRIST
. . . D . . . . . . .H . . . , . .D. . . . . . .
and fon of DANIE. . . . .MAR. . . .
. . . . .of Westalington
in yᵉ County of Devonshire
. . . . . Mafon
. . . . . . yᵉ . . . of July
. . . . . .Months . . . . .days
Died yᵉ 12 of Iune 1736 (?6)
Aged 8 Months & 18 days.

West Alington one mile from Kingsbridge, a sea-port in S. Devon.

———

There is also another Inscription on the south face, partly buried :—

In Memory
of JAMES DAVIS and LVCRETIA DAVIS
who Departed this Life 1789.

———

There is a modern cemetery in Basseterre close to Government House which I did not enter. It was probably here that a monument was erected at the public expense to the late Sir Robert Bromley, Bart. It consisted of a Calvary cross and steps in Greek white pentelikon marble from Athens, with a border of similar marble to enclose the grave. As a further tribute to his memory, the people of St. Kitts-Nevis have caused a tablet to be erected at Stoke Church, Notts. It is of classic design, the frame being hand-coloured English onyx alabaster, with a white marble plate on which the inscription is engraved in black letters, surmounted by the Bromley coat of arms and crest in colours. The inscription reads : " In memory of | Sir Robert Bromley, 6th Baronet, | of Stoke, Newark, and of Ashwell, Rutland, | who was born at Stoke on January 4th, 1874, | and died on May 13th, 1906, at Springfield, St. Christopher, | in the Presidency of St. Christopher and Nevis, | where he administered the Government | from the 27th October, 1904, to the day of his death. | This tablet was erected by the people | amongst whom he lived in the Leeward Islands | as a slight recognition of his great ability | and his earnest efforts for the welfare | of all classes in the above Presidency."

———

ST. MARY, CAYON.

" Spooners " is to the south and " Cunninghams " to the north of the village. The Church is in a very good state and is one of the best cared for in the Island.

RECTORS.

Archibald Cockburn, 1728. Rector also of Christ Church, Nichola Town. Minister at St. Kitts in 1714 and 1728.

Joseph Barnes, 1792 and 1806. Also Rector of Christ Church, Nichola Town Rector of St. Peter's, Basseterre, 1824-25.

John H. Laurence, 1826. (*Almanack*).

Wm. Gardner Bradley, B.A., 1852.

In 1852 St. Mary and Christ Church were merged into one ecclesiastical parish. As first son of William of Atherstone, co. Warwick, cleric, he matriculated from Brasenose College, Oxford, 11 Dec., 1838, aged 18; B.A., 1842.

1852, Jan. Lately. The Rev. Wm. Gardner Bradley, Rector of St. Mary, Cayon, St. Christopher, &c. His father was Rector of Nether Whitacre, co. Warwick. (*Gent. Mag.* 105)

Charles Cummins Culpeper, 1879. See under St. Peter.

He was of Anguilla and a member of Codrington College, 1848.

Henry Bascom Hughes, B.A. (S.P.G.). 1895. M.I. No. 60

On the south wall of Nave are three tablets and one brass.

57. IN MEMORY OF | JAMES GEORGE | INFANT SON OF G. J. FRASER | WHO DIED ON THE 19TH MARCH 1840, | AGED 3 YEARS & | 10 MONTHS |.

58. IN MEMORY OF | ANN SMITH | THE BELOVED WIFE OF JOHN DELAP WILSON | AND NIECE TO THE HONBLE ROBERT CLAXTON | SOLICITOR GENERAL OF THE ISLAND OF ST KITTS : | WHO DIED AT MILFORD IN HAMPSHIRE, | ON THE 20TH OF JANUARY 1836 | AGED 24 YEARS |.

(See pedigree of Claxton in *Caribbeana* VI., 43).

---

59. Above are masonic compasses, etc. :—

Jn Memorp of | GEORGE REID, | A NATIVE OF SCOTLAND ; | WHO DIED ON DUPUYS ESTATE, | SEPTEMBER 12TH 1860, | AGED 26 YEARS.

(11 lines. Resident of 3 years, erected by brother masons).

---

60. Brass, raised letters :—

To THE GREATER GLORY OF GOD
AND IN PIOUS MEMORY OF
HENRY BASCOM HUGHES,
FOR 15 YEARS PRIEST OF THIS PARISH
THE NEW LAMPS WERE PLACED
THROUGHOUT THE CHURCH
BY PARISHIONERS AND FRIENDS
R. I. P.

He was a native of St. Vincent and a member of Codrington College in 1874.

---

61.   Matrix of Brass Cross on floor :—

62.   On the brass Eagle :—

"**For the word of God and in pious Memory of James W. and Louisa A. Hill**"

63.   Thick ledger under Font, raised one inch above floor :—

IN MEMORY OF
FRANCIS WILSON
FIFTH SON OF
JOHN WILLIAM
DELAP WILSON ESQ^R
WHO DIED MAY 8TH 1833
AGED 19.

The Font of grey marble looks late 17th century.

64.   Blue marble ledger next No. 63 flush with floor :—

HERE LYETH Y^E BODY OF
IOSEPH IORY FFOCHE
GENT : WHO DYED IANUARY
THE XXXTH MDCCXX$\frac{IV}{V}$ AGED
XIX YEARS AND VIII MONTHS

Col. Joseph Jory was sometime of Nevis and died 24 August, 1725, intestate at his seat Albro' Hatch in Barking.   Frances his niece and heiress married 1—John Foche of Albro' Hatch and 2—in 1728, Col. Martin Bladen, M.P., who died 15 February, 1745-6.   She died 14 August, 1747, and her heiress and executrix was Mrs. Mary Helden wife of the Hon. John Helden of St. Kitts, later of Egham, co. Surrey.

Henry Foche was admitted a fellow of St. John's College, Cambridge, 23 March, 1712-13.

A pedigree of FFoche was recorded in the *Visitation of Kent A°* 1663-8 signed by "Hen. FFoche" of Canterbury.   See also the Arms from the *Visitation* of 1594 in *Misc. Gen. et Her.* 5S. vol. V. p. 58.

65.   Stone ledger :—

Here Lyeth the Body
of SARAH BROWN who departed
this Life the 16th of October 1719
in the 71^b Year of
her Age

66. Ledger next preceding :—

Here lie the Remains of
SELINA FRANCES the beloved
and ever to be lamented Wife of
the Honourable
JOHN DELAP WILSON
President of the Council
of Saint Christophers
who died in childbed on the 3rd of September *(no year)*
Aged 36 Years   *(mortar here)*
Also are Interred near this spot
GERTRUDE and EUGENIA
his two Infant daughters.

Mrs. Wilson was sister to Dr. Davis of Bath.

---

67. South of Church.   White marble slab over stone vault :—

SACRED TO THE MEMORY
OF
JOHN BROWN EsQ^R
WHO DEPARTED THIS LIFE
JAN^{ry} 26th 1824 AGED 48 YEARS
ONE OF HIS MAJESTYS JUSTICES OF
THE PEACE FOR MANY YEARS IN
THE ISLAND OF SAINT CHRISTOPHERS

---

68. Blue marble ledger of which the lower part is cracked, over stone vault :—

Here are Depofited the Remains of
Mrs ELIZABETH THOMSON
who was the only Daughter of the
late ROBERT DALZELL Efq^r and
wife of ROBERT THOMPSON Efq^r
She departed this Life April 8th]772
Aged 28 Years
Also the Remains of M^{rs} ANN DAL
ZELL Widow of ROB^T DALZELL
Efq^r dec^d and Mother of M^{rs}
THOMPSON who departed this life
Augt 8th 1786 Aged 75 Years.

See a letter from Robert Thomson, President of this Island, in *Gent. Mag.* for 1801, p. 652.

1816, March 2. At Charles Thomsons, esq., Portland-pl., in his 78th year, Robert Thomson, esq., many years president of St. Christophers and acting governor of the Leeward Islands. (*Ib.* 372).

1832, Jan. 10. At the Savoy, C. Thomson, esq., Attorney-gen. of St. Kitts, and eldest son of the late Charles Thomson, esq., to Maria, only daughter of N. Byrne, esq., of Lancaster Place. (*Ib.* 78).

---

69.   Narrow ledger over stone vault :—

Sacred
TO THE MEMORY OF
GEORGE REID
THIRD SON OF GEORGE REID ESQ
OF HALLCROSS MUSSELBURGH,
SCOTLAND,
WHO WAS BORN AT MUSSELBURGH,
13TH SEPTEMBER, 1834,
AND DIED ON DUPUYS ESTATE
ST. KITTS AFTER A FEW DAYS ILLNESS
ON THE 12TH DAY OF SEPTEMBER 1860
AGED 26 YEARS.
Erected by his father and only surviving sister.

---

70.   Loose stone on which mortar has been mixed :—

HERE LIES THE BODY OF
JOHN W. DELAP WILSON
MANY YEARS PRESIDENT
OF HIS MAJESTYS COUNCIL
OF ST CHRISTOPHER
WHO DEPARTED THIS LIFE
SEPTEMBER 13TH 1825
AGED 49 YEARS.

Son of Richard Wilson of Marylebone by Margaret Halliday his wife and great-grandson of Richard Wilson of Cayon, Chief Justice of St Kitts. He was appointed Member of Council in 1801 and was President in 1821.

---

71.   Headstone :—

Sacred
to the *Memory* of
Henry Sprott Planter a
native of Scotland, who
departed this Life January
2nd Anno Domini 1822
Aged 56 Years.
Erected by his daughters.

William Crooke late of St Christophers now of Marylebone, Esq.,   Will dated 17 July, 1805.   To my niece Elizabeth Sprott, wife of Henry Sprott of St. Christophers and daughter of my sister Mary Wood £1000.   (*Caribbeana* V. 317). Adam Sprott, Esq., and Mrs. Mary Sprott were living in 1790.

---

72. On a white marble ledger over a stone vault enclosed by iron railing, two corners of the stone missing and railing broken—much neglected. :—

SACRED
TO THE MEMORY OF
ELIZABETH MARY FAUNTLEROY,
THE WIFE OF
THOMAS TURNER,
WHO DEPARTED THIS LIFE
ON THE
21ST DAY OF MARCH 1841,
IN THE
27TH YEAR OF HER AGE

73. Headstone :—

HERE | IS DEPOSITED | THE REMAINS | OF | JOHN BVRNE | DEPARTED JUNE | 22nd 1805 | AGED 20 |

74.

HERE
LYETH THE BODY
OF M^{RS} MARGARET
ROGERS' WHO DEP
ARTED THIS LIFE
MAY 1ST 1782 AGED 32
YEARS ALSO THE
BODY OF MR IOHN
COOPER WHO DE
PARTED THIS LIFE
NOV^{R} 12TH 1787 AGED
20 YEARS

75. White marble :—

DEDICATED
To the memory of
MR ALFRED FAILLE
Born in Lille in 1841 ;
Died in S$^{t.}$ Christopher
the 3rd February 1854

76. White marble :—

DEDICATED
To the memory of
MR A. FAILLE
Born in Lille in 1813 :
Died in St Christopher
the 26th January 1854

77. North of Nave, headstone :—

IN
Memory of Iane
Anny Daugh : of
Pavl Mc Pharson by
Iane Crosley his wife
Who Dyed *Jany* 24th
1756 Æ 4 mounths.

78. Headstone broken and loose :—

SACRED
TO THE MEMORY OF
EBENEZER D. JOLLEY
WHO DIED 3RD AUGUST 1859
AGED 6 YEARS

CHRIST CHURCH, NICOLA TOWN.

This parish is just beyond Cayon and about eight miles from Basseterre. The Church has a tower with spire to the north of the chancel.

RECTORS.

Archdeacon Cockburn, 1728. ?Alexander Cockburn who went out 10 October, 1710.

James Ramsay, Rector, 1761-81, went out 28 Nov., 1761. Rector also of St. Johns. Several of his letters of about 1771 are at Fulham. Lt.-Col. Phipps also has some as well as the Rector's family bible. He was born 25 July 1733 at Fraserburgh, Aberdeenshire, and became a naval surgeon before taking holy orders. From 1781 until his death 20 July, 1789, he was Vicar of Teston co. Kent. He married in 1763 Rebecca Akers of Christ Church. Eight children were baptised here.

John Julius Kerie, 1826 and of St. Johns. (*Almanac*).

Son of the Hon. Jedediah Kerie by Elizabeth Mary Julius, born 1785, matriculated from University College, Oxford, 18 October, 1806, aged 21, B.A. 1810, M.A. 1815.

Ebenezer Elliott, B.A., Rector 1852. (*Almanac*).

79. On square white marble tablet over the western entrance arch of the Nave :—

SACRED | TO THE MEMORY OF | HENRY CHARLES GREENE, | ESQUIRE | *LATE OF NICOLA TOWN* | WHO DEPARTED THIS LIFE | ON THE 7TH DAY OF AUGUST 1840 | IN THE 19TH YEAR OF HIS AGE.

1840, August 7. At St. Kitts, aged 19, Henry Charles, fourth son of Ben. Greene, of Russell Square and Bury St. Edmunds. (*Gent. Mag.* 446).

80. On a small brass tablet on south wall of Nave :—

IN MEMORY OF | LUCRETIA HARRIS, | SEPT. 21ˢᵀ 1912, 81 YEARS | WHO GAVE HER ALL TO THE | GLORY OF GOD AND THE PONGAS MISSION | R.I.P.

80A. South side of Churchyard, white marble slab on stone vault enclosed by iron railings rusted and broken :—

SACRED | TO THE MEMORY OF | SARAH LYNCH, | WIFE OF | JOHN EARLE TUDOR, | BORN MAY 1ˢᵀ 1818 | DIED AUGUST 18ᵀᴴ 1863.

---

81. On a second white marble ledger low down :—

$\mathfrak{Sacred}$ | TO THE MᴱMORY ᴼF | JOHN EARLE TUDOR | DIED MAY 7ᵀᴴ A.D. 1865 | AGED 60 YEARS.

1840, Jan. 3. On Friday night, at Conyer's Estate, Mrs. Mary Tudor, aged 60 years. Relict of the late Samuel Tudor, Esq. (*St. Christophers' Gazette*).

John Earle in his Will dated 1805 names his daughter Mary Elizabeth Tudor wife of Samuel Tudor.

---

82. Stone Cross, low iron rail on stone curb—smashed :—

SACRED TO THE MEMORY ᴼF | MARY JANE | WIFE OF REGINALD HARPER | *OF THIS ISLAND* | WHO DIED 30ᵀᴴ DEC., 1875, AGED 37 YEARS | AND OCTAVIA CHRISTIANA FURLONGE | *HER SISTER* | WHO DIED 28ᵀᴴ FEBʸ 1876 AGED 36 YEARS.

1819, Feb. 16. At St. Kitts, aged 36, Cornelia-Elizabeth wife of Thomas Harper, Esq., Secretary of that Colony. (*Gent Mag.* 485). The Furlonges were of Montserrat and Antigua.

---

83. At east of Chancel are three good stone vaults, the first two enclosed by iron railings, the third by wooden ditto :— Metal letters.

IN | LOVING MEMORY OF | WILLIAM GREENE | BORN JUNE 6ᵀᴴ 1824 | DIED SEPᴿ 18ᵀᴴ 1881 |

---

84. Granite cross :—

RESTING IN HOPE | THE BODY OF | PAGET AUGUSTUS WADE | BORN JANUARY 17 1849 | DIED DECEMBER 25 1911.

85.

SACRED | TO THE MEMORY OF | HENRY CHARLES GREENE | ESQUIRE | *LATE OF NICOLA TOWN* | WHO DEPARTED THIS LIFE | ON THE 7ᵀᴴ DAY OF AUGUST 1840 | IN THE 19ᵀᴴ YEAR OF HIS AGE |

86.   On a little white marble coffin-shaped slab over brick vault.   On oval a cherub's head and wings :—

In Memoriam
CAR : LAVAL MOLINEUS   (Sic)
Infan : Ætat : Tri : Ann :
Hoc Sepulcrum
Posuere
Afflicti Parentes
Obiit 30th June 1787
Eheu Lector
Memento Mori.

See pedigree of Molineux in *Caribbeana* III., 2, in which the name of this child does not appear.

---

87.   In the middle on a slate slab over stone vault in perfect condition :—

Here Lyeth Interr'd the
Body of M^{RS} MARY CRISP Late
wife of IOSEPH CRISP of this
Ifland Efq who departed this
life Ian^y 27th 1730 Aged 38
Alfo the Bodys of SAMUEL
SHERMAN Efq Father of the
above f^d MARY CRISP, & CORNELIA
BROZETT her Sifter (wife of
Major IAMES BROZETT) with her
Niece ANNE and her Sifter in law
ELIZABETH BROZETT.
Near this Place alfo lyes the
Bodys of MR CALEB CRISP
and ANNA HIS Wife

See pedigree of Brozett in *Caribbeana* I., 4.   Joseph Crisp was son of Caleb and Anna.   Caleb was dead in 1708.   Margaret Caleb daughter of Joseph and Mary married 1—John Willett and 2—about 1727, Charles Laval Molineux.

---

88.   White marble cross within curb :—

Cecil Thomas | Crisp Molineux Montgomerie | of Garboldisbam, Norfolk. | born May 20th 1846, died April 17th | 1901.

Nos. 86, 87, and 88 are enclosed by a wooden fence. Major Geo. Fred. Molineux Montgomerie the late owner of the plantations left the Island in the boat which took me ashore in 1914 so our meeting was a short one.   He was killed 22 Oct., 1915 in France having rejoined the Grenadiers.

---

89.   Headstone :—

Sacred to the memory | of Mifs Elizabeth Curtis | who departed this Life 18 Nov^r | 1840 (?) Aged 60 Years.

ST. PETER'S, BASSETERRE.

This Church is a large square building, whose age it would be difficult to determine, but the Rector, the late Canon Yeo, told me he thought it was probably the old French one altered or rebuilt, and that might well have been the case, for the altar is to the north.

The present Rector, Canon C. A. Shepherd, writes :—" The Church is believed to be an old French one, or French government building, afterwards converted into a church, and connected with the French Governor's residence at " Fountain " by an under ground passage.   In Labat's map published in 1724, which is a touched up copy of Du Tertre's of 1667, is marked " Logis de Mr de Poincy," and close to it " Eglise des Carmes."

Down to 1795 the living was always held with St. Georges.

RECTORS.

William Davis, 1795—1824.   He received the bounty 26 Jan., 1791.   Was acquitted of the murder of a slave in 1813.   He interviewed the Bishop of London in Jan., 1815.   His son Daniel Gateward Davis became Bishop of the Leeward Islands.

Joseph Barnes, 1824—1825.   See under Cayon.

William Fraser, 1826—1852.   See No. 91.

Edward Hyndman Beckles, 1853—1858.   Consecrated Bishop of Sierra Leone in 1860.   He was of a Barbadian family.

T. M. Collins, 1858—1860.   (Officiating Minister).

Charles Cummins Culpeper, 1860—1871.   Rector of Cayon, 1879.

George Edward Yeo, 1872, till his death in 1914.

Charles A. Shepherd, 1915.   Rector 1895 of St. Paul and St. John, St. Kitts, later Rector of St. Paul, Charlestown, Nevis, then Rector of Old Road, St. Kitts. A cousin of Dean Shepherd of Antigua.

Henry Curll Shepherd, 1920, of St. Edmund Hall, Oxford, B.A., 1912. Curate of St. John's, Antigua, 1915-1917.   Rector of St. Pauls', Antigua, 1917— 1920.

---

90.   West wall of Nave :—

Sacred to the Memory of
ULICK BURKE Esq[r] Planter of this *Island*
Born in the *County* of Galway in *Ireland*
who died on the 17th of May, 1808
in the 69th Year of his Age.

Ulick Burk of co. Gallway now in St. Christopher.   Will dated 10 Jan., 1739.   My brother John Burk £10.   My wife Mary and four children Thomas, Bartholomew, Mary and Monica all executors.   Patrick Burke of St. Christopher Executor.   (*St. Kitts Records* No. 1983).   See No. 146.

---

91. West wall :—

SACRED TO THE MEMORY OF
ANNE MYRA,
SECOND DAUGHTER OF
CHRISTOPHER PICKERING ESQ^R
OF THIS ISLAND
AND WIFE OF
THE REV^D WILLIAM FRASER
RECTOR OF THIS PARISH
WHO DEPARTED THIS LIFE
AFTER A FEW HOURS ILLNESS
ON THE 11TH OCT^R 1832,
IN THE TWENTIETH YEAR OF HIS AGE.

1806, Feb. 19.   Christopher Pickering and Jane Ann Basden ; by Lic.

East wall of Nave has two brasses and two tablets.

92. Brass :—

In Loving Memory of
Wm C. S. Rapier

THIRD SON OF THE LATE

Sir Robert Rapier, Bart

OF MILLIKEN AND NAPIER

who died on 26th September, 1900
Aged 42

There is a stone to him in the Churchyard.

General William Napier of Culcrench, born 1712, married Jane daughter and heiress of James Milliken of Milliken, Renfrewshire and St. Kitts, by his wife Joan, daughter of Alexander Mc Dowall of Garthland and died 1780, leaving one son Robert John Milliken Napier who took the name of Milliken. (See *Baronetages*).

---

93. Crest : *A stork.*

Arms : Quarterly, 1 and 4, *A stork close.*   (Mathew)
2 and 3 *Azure in chief two mullets* (? Van Leemput) ; Impaling : Quarterly of 4, 1 and 4, *Argent a fess in chief three torteaux* (Dering) ; 2 and 3, *Argent a saltire* (Dering).

Motto : EQUAM SERVARE MENTEM.

SACRED to the MEMORY of
DANIEL BYAM MATHEW, ESQ^R
of CAYON, and PENNITENNY of this Island
who departed this Life
the 26TH of APRIL A.D. 1838, Ætatis suæ 82.
(Son of Daniel Mathew of Felix Hall in Essex ESQ, and Grandson of General William Mathew, Governor of the Leeward Islands)
He married ELIZABETH, Daughter of
SIR EDWARD DERING ;
of SURRENDEN-DERING, in KENT, Bar^t
by whom HE had Issue DANIEL DERING,
and MARY ELIZABETH, who married WILLIAM THO^S ROE ESQ^R
(Commiffioner of the Customs also High Steward of the Savoy, &c., &c., who died the 25th of APRIL A.D. 1834).

This Tablet is erected to his Memory by his only Daughter the above Mary\Elizabeth Roe, of Withdean in the County of Suffex, | and his Sister Louisa, Widow of the Rt. Honble James Lord Gambier | of Iver Grove, in the County of Bucks (Admiral of the Fleet) | who died the 19th of APRIL A.D. 1833.

He was married at Lambeth Palace 21 Sept., 1784.   Daniel Dering Mathew the only son died s.p. in 1856.

See pedigree in *Antigua* II., 252, *and West Indian book-plates*, p. 78.

---

94.   Brass with Head of deceased engraved thereon :—

IN MEMORY OF
ELIZABETH PRATER BRANCH
BELOVED WIFE OF
WILLIAM JOHN BRANCH, M.D.
AND DAUGHTER OF
JOHN FRANCIS GREENIDGE M.D.
SHE WAS BORN AT BELLE FARM
BARBADOES
ON THE 5TH OF FEBRUARY 1846
AND DIED AT BASSTERRE S^T KITTS
ON THE 16TH OF OCTOBER 1880

Dr. W. J. Branch (brother of the late Bishop Branch) died 6 March, 1914, aged 75.

The Greenidges were of Barbados.

95.

SACRED
TO THE MEMORY OF
SOLOMON ABRAHAM WADE,
BORN JUNE 15TH 1806,
DIED AUGUST 17TH 1881
BURIED IN THE CEMETERY, BROMLEY,
KENT, ENGLAND.

The Reredos was erected in memory of the late Hon. Thomas B. Hardtman-Berkeley, C.M.G., born 14 Jan., 1824, died 6 Nov., 1881.   There are many eulogistic lines.

CHURCHYARD.

96.   Blue marble ledger over stone vault west of chancel :—

Here lyes the Body of
ELIZABETH BRIDGWATER
wife to THO : BRIDGWATER
ESQ^n who departed this
life May]6 : 1739 Aged 63.

He was Member of Assembly 1710, nephew and heir of Mrs. Susannah Cole 1733, of St. Kitts, and was buried at St. George's 9 July, 1744.   Will dated 23 June and sworn 12 July, 1744.   See pedigree in *Caribbeana* V., 210.

---

97. East of churchyard :—

WITHIN THIS TOMB
LIES THE BODY OF
SARAH,
THE BELOVED WIFE OF
JOHN SLACK
WHO DEPARTED THIS LIFE 19TH AUGUST 1874
AGED 45 YEARS

98. White marble ledger next to preceding :—

Here lies *CHRIS*ᴿ *MARDENBROUGH*
Son of *CHRIS*ᴿ *& MARGARET MARDENBROUGH*
died . . . Nov. 1761
Aged 2 Years & 9 Months
Alfo *GILES MARDENBROUGH*
their Son who died 17 Novʳ 1767
Aged 7 Years
Alfo *ELIZABETH* their Daughter
who died 16ᵗʰ Novʳ 1767
Aged 5 Years
Alfo *MARGARET MARDENBROUGH*
Wife of *CHRIS*ᴿ *MARDENBROUGH*
who died 2ᵈ Decʳ 1770
Aged 30 Years
Alfo *ELIZABETH BROWN*
Sifter of *RHODA MARDENBROUGH*
who died 18ᵗʰ Octʳ 1790
Aged 57 Years
Alfo *SUSANNA MARDENBROUGH* Daughter
of *CHRIS*ᴿ *& RHODA MARDENBROUGH*
who died 15ᵗʰ May 1794,
Aged 10 Years

99.

Underneath Lay the Bodies
Of *GILES MARDENBROUGH*
who died the 25ᵗʰ June 1774
Aged Eight Months
Of *GEORGE WRIGHT MARDENBROUGH*
who died the 18ᵗʰ June 1775
Aged Two Months.
Of *MARGARET WRIGHT MARDENBROUGH*
who died the 29ᵗʰ Oct., 1779
Aged Nine Months
Of *GILES MARDENBROUGH*
who died the 13ᵗʰ Augvft 1785
Aged Two Years & Four Months
All the Offspring of
CHRISTOPHER & RHODA MARDENBROUGH
Alfo beneath Lays the Body
Of *RHODA MARDENBROUGH*
Wife of *CHRISTOPHER MARDENBROUGH*
who died the 5ᵗʰ March 1791
Aged Thirty nine Years

1756, Sept. 25. Christopher Mardenbrough marry'd to Margaret Wright (St. Peters).

1755, Dec. 6. Dr. George Wright. (Bur. Reg. St. George, Basseterre).

---

100. Archer also gives the following in abbreviated form which I did not see :—

CHRISTOPHER MARDENBROUGH of this island was born June 1, 1734 and died Sept. 17, 1806. This stone is erected to his memory by his grateful children.

---

101. East side of the Church-yard. On a grey granite cross :—

SACRED | TO THE MEMORY | OF | CHARLES JAMES BRANCH, D.D. | FOURTH BISHOP OF ANTIGUA | BORN OCT. 7, 1834 | IN BARBADOS | CONSECRATED JULY 25, 1882 IN LONDON | FELL ASLEEP AUG. 31 1896 IN Sᵀ KITTS.

See his father in *Monumental Inscriptions of Barbados*, No. 408. He was a member of Codrington College in 1853, held various livings in the West Indies and was Archdeacon when consecrated Bishop Coadjutor in 1882, succeeding Bishop Jackson. He came to St. Kitts to be treated by his brother the late Dr. W. J. Branch but his illness proved fatal.

The nine following which I had omitted to take, Canon Shepherd kindly sent me Oct. 1915 :—

102. On stone cross :—

To the beloved, the cherished
the unfading memory of
Axel Hamilton Berridge
Born April 28th 1847
Passed away April 15th 1883
Alice Georgina
His devoted wife
erects the symbol of our Holy Faith

---

103. Stone cross and slab :—

Sacred to the memory of
Arthur Axel Hamilton Berridge
The dearly beloved infant of
Axel Hamilton and Alice
Georgina Berridge
who departed this life
on 3rd September, 1875
Aged 4½ months.

104. Flat marble slab :—

In
loving memory
of
our dear Father
L. T. Jones
who departed this life
June 17th 1903

105. Marble cross :—

In memory of
Wm. E. S. Napier
3RD son of the late
Sir Robert Napier, Bart.
of Milliken and Napier
died 26th Sep. 1900, Aged 42.

106. Marble cross :—

In memory of
George Wattley
who died October 19th 1869
Aged 44
In loving memory of
our Mother
Elizabeth Maria
widow of George Wattley,
who died November 27th 1902
Aged 75

There are many entries to the Wattleys at St. George's, Basseterre and Trinity, Palmetto Point.

107. Marble headstone :—

In memory of
Thomasin Greenidge
wife of
R. H. Clarke
died Aug. 14, 1906

108. Marble cross :—

In loving memory
of
William Walter Clarke
Died 5th February, 1884
Aged 21 Years
And his infant brother
John
23rd October 1875

109. Marble cross :—

In loving memory of
George Cecil Yeo
Born Nov. 24, 1870—Died July 23, 1904

He was son of the late Rector, Canon Yeo.

---

110. Marble cross :—

In loving memory of
Henry Charles Wade
born March 30th 1844
died Octr 5th 1882

ST. JOHN'S, CAPISTERRE.

The building consists of a plain Nave with a tower at the west end. There is no Chancel :—

RECTORS.

Vacant, 1728.

Mr. Davidson, Rector of St. Paul's, wrote to Governor Mathew :—" The next parish to me designed for Mr. Willet's tutor, Mr. Demany. . . that young gentleman's uncle John Willet, Esq., no date. 1734-5 Letter from John Dumeny. (*Fulham Palace Records*).

Temple Henry Croker, 1790 M.A. 1760. Writer. A native of Cork, scholar of Westminster School 1743, also admitted to Trinity College, Cambridge.

As son of Henry of Saresfield Court, co. Cork, pleb. matriculated from Christ Church, Oxford, 25 November, 1746, aged 17 ; B.A. 1750, Rector of Igtham, Kent, 1769-73. Bankrupt. Printed four sermons in St. Kitts 1790. See *N. & Q.*, 12 S.X. 391 and 13 S. I. iii. (*D.N.B.*)

John Julius Kerie, 1826 and of Christ Church. (*Almanac*).

Edwin Elliott and officiating Minister of St. Pauls, 1852. (*Almanac*).

Soon after 1852 St. John and St. Paul were merged into one parish.

Walter Pemberton, 1879. (*Almanac*).

Son of Rev. Jos. Herbert Pemberton, Rector of St. John's, Nevis, baptised 1827, of Codrington College 1846, died at Alphamstone Rectory, co. Essex in 1901.

Chas. A. Shepherd, 1895.

Joseph Emry, S.P.G., 1914. Rector of St. Paul's, Antigua, 1895.

111. On the north wall is a finely carved white marble scrolled tablet :—

P. M. S.

MARIÆ WILLETT

Iohannis Stanley

de Infula Nevis Armigeri

ex Uxore Ejus Debora Hill

Filiæ Pofthumæ

Iohannis Willett de hac Infula Armigeri

Conjugis (eleven lines omitted)

Nata fuit Iº die februarij MDCXCII

et XXXI Ætatis nondum Expleto

XXV die Novembris MDCCXXIII

Puerperio immaturo obijt

et Mortales Ejus Exuviæ una cum Infantule

Iuxta Parentum Mariti fui Cineres

Prope Hunc Murum fepultæ

Immortalitatem manent

Ens Entium Miferere Noftri.

See No. 117 for her sister Elizabeth wife of Henry Willett.

The above John Willett remarried, Margaret by whom he left two daughters and co-heiresses, Elizabeth wife of the Hon. William Ottley and Margaret Willett. Mrs. Willett was in 1736 wife of Charles Laval Molineux of Christ Church. See pedigree of Stanley in *Caribbeana* III., 364, and of *Willett* II., 290.

---

112. North wall of Nave. Black and white marble :—

Above a cross and SERVIRE DEO SAPERE

IN MEMORY OF

— WITH THE COMMUNION SERVICE —

JOHN WENTWORTH GOULD, ESQ.

BELLE VUE

WHO DEPARTED THIS LIFE

17TH JULY 1869, AGED 69

AND OF

SARA MARIA GOULD,

HIS WIFE

WHO RESTED FEBRUARY 6TH 1870

THOMASINA BRYAN,

12TH MARCH, 1872

Samuel Gould of this parish had two sons, 1—John who married twice, and died s.p. 2—Samuel, who married Miss Richards and had one daughter who married Mr. St. Clair and died s.p. in America. (Note by Mr. Winston St. Claire of Canada, July, 1918).

---

113. On the south wall. Black and white marble :—

SACRED
TO THE MEMORY OF
HERIOT CAINES MAILLARD
WIFE OF
WILLIAM ANTHONY MAILLARD, ESQ^RE
OF THIS ISLAND
WHO CALMLY RESIGNED HER SOUL
INTO THE HAND OF HER REDEEMER
ON THE 2ND OF AUGUST, 1825,
AGED 30 YEARS.

1839, Oct. 4. In this Town, on Sunday last, Mr. William Maillard. (*St. Christopher's Gazette*).

Jeremiah Maillard of St. Christopher, gent. Will dated 28 Oct., 1741. My wife Catherine and 5 children Peter, Philip, John, Abram and Mary Maillard. My mother, Mary Maillard. Sworn 4 Dec., 1741. (*St. Kitts' Records*, No. 2260). See No. 126.

Richard Rawlins born 1764, married 4 Sept., 1788, Elizabeth Vanderpool Maillard, born 1767, she was buried 3 Sept., 1835.

---

114. On the Keystone over the Entrance Arch of the Church :—

D. Percival
C. W.
july 25
1764

Davis Percival, Church Warden. The year 1764 is doubtful. It may be 1754.

---

115. On the corner stone of the Churchyard wall is :—

HENRY WILLETt (*sic*)
NOV.]2 .]73]

SOUTH SIDE OF CHURCHYARD.

116. White marble let in to a large stone building, its arched entrance being filled up :—

ESTRIDGE'S
MAUSOLEUM

There is a good description of a visit in 1834 to " Estridges " in the parish of Christ Church, in the *West India Sketch Book* II., 70. The estate had one of the finest works in the Island.

---

117.   Grey marble slab over a stone vault :—

In a sunk oval is a Jacobean shield with mantling.

Crest :   *Out of a ducal coronet a cock*, over helmet.
Arms :   *Three bars gemelles and in chief as many lions rampant.*

Here Lyeth the Body of
ELIZABETH WILLETT
Late Wife of
HENRY WILLETT ESQ^R
and Daughter of
Coll : IOHN STANLEY of NEVIS
who Departed this Life in
Child-bed y^e]2th of *August*]725
Aged 34 Years 5 Months & 5 Days

She was married 18 Sept., 1718.   Her husband was aged 27 in 1707 and
died in 1740.   See pedigree in *Caribbeana* II., 290.

118.   A similar grey marble slab on a stone vault :—

In sunk oval a Jacobean shield with mantling.

Crest :   *An owl* over wreath and helmet.
Arms :   *A chevron between three owls.*

Here Lies WILLIAM WOODLEY Efqr
who Departed this Life the 2^d Ianuary
1738, in the 63^d Year of his Age
He was a Tender Hufband, a Kind Father,
a Good Neighbour and a Sincere Friend
with him Lye his two Sons,
IASPER WOODLEY, who Died the 29th Iuly
1735 in the 28th Year of his Age
and TOBIAS WOODLEY, who Died the]^{ft}
March 1734, in the 20th Year of his Age,

In his will dated 17 Nov., 1738, he names his wife Bridget and left to his
son John his plantation here and to his son William one in St. Peters.   (*St. Kitts'*
Records No. 1750).   See pedigree in *Antigua* III., 256.

119.   On a lozenge-shaped stone over a stone vault :—

IN | Memory of | Eliza Dawson | who departed | this life 7 October | 1821
Aged 76 Years |

120. White marble slab over stone vault, enclosed by low iron rusted and broken railings. Metal letters :—

SACRED | TO THE MEMORY OF | MAJOR THOMAS LYNCH, | 48th REGI-MENT, | WHO DEPARTED THIS LIFE | 12th DECR 1860 | AND OF SALLY JANE, his wife | THIS MEMORIAL IS PLACED HERE | BY THEIR SORROWING DAUGHTERS | ALSO OF | WILLIAM B—, ESQRE | WHO RESTED 29TH DECR 1862, | AGED 32. | THE LOVED AND LAMENTED | HUSBAND OF | THOMASINA B— |

(I unfortunately omitted the surname—*Editor*.)

121. Square stone set on a stone vault :—

> IN MEMORY OF
> PETER E. BLANCHET
> AND WIFE
> GEORGIANA
> WHO BOTH REST HERE
> 1844.   1862.

ST. PAUL'S, CABESTERRE.

This parish was constituted by Act of 22 June, 1724, out of part of the old French Cabesterre quarter.

The Church is a small plain building without chancel or tower standing in a picturesque situation facing St. Eustatius. The rectory abuts on the west of the church-yard.

RECTORS.

— Davidson. Temp. Governor Mathew.

William John Julius 1792—1810, also Rector of St. Annes. Licensed by the Bishop of London 21 Sept., 1781. In his will dated 22 June, 1810, he describes himself as Minister of St. Anne, Sandy Point and of St. Paul, Cabesterre, and left all his estate to the Hon. Jedediah Kerie late of St. Christopher, now of Bath. Proved 30 Aug., 1810. (425 *Collingwood*).

John Hutchinson Walwyn, 1826, with St. Anne's. Rector of Gingerland, Nevis, 1815—1817.

122. On the north wall :—

> THIS TABLET IS RAISED IN HEARTFELT GRIEF
> FOR THE LOSS OF A MOST DEVOTED
> AND MUCH LOVED SON AND BROTHER.
> TO THE MEMORY OF
> WILLIAM HENRY, SECOND SON OF
> REVD JOHN HUTCHINSON WALWYN, DECEASED
> AND ANNE, HIS WIFE
> DEPARTED THIS LIFE ON THE 18TH DAY OF AUGUST 1845
> AGED 28 YEARS
> HIS BODY WAS LAID IN THE TOMB OF THE FAMILY IN THE CHURCHYARD OF
> ST JOHN'S, CAPISTERRE.

Thomas Wallyn was entered in the census of Nevis in 1677.

Mr. John Wallwin was buried at Middle Island, St. Kitts in 1757.

William Wallyn of the same parish died 11 Nov., 1792, aged 74.   Ann Hutchinson his wife died 1 Oct., 1785, and several of their children were baptised 1744-68.

John Hutchinson Wallwin married 11 June, 1776, Ann Hutchinson Rawlins.

———

123.   On the north wall :—

M. S.
WILLIAM STEPHENS ESQUIRE,
WHO DEPARTED THIS LIFE
ON THE 7TH DAY OF MAY, 1830,
IN THE 74TH YEAR OF HIS AGE
HE WAS BURIED NEAR THIS SPOT
BY THE SIDE OF HIS SON WILLIAM,
WHO DIED ON THE 28TH DAY OF DECR 1827,
IN THE 20TH YEAR OF HIS AGE.

He was in 1825 a J.P. and Coroner.

———

124.   On the west wall under the gallery, south of entrance door :—

IN THIS VAULT ARE DEPOSITED THE REMAINS
OF
FRANCES GEORGES THOMAS
WIFE OF JOSEPH RAWLINS THOMAS ESQUIRE,
LIEUTENANT IN THE ROYAL NAVY
(Six lines.   Erected by her husband).
ON THE 10TH DAY OF JUNE 1817, AGED 23 YEARS
ALSO FRANCIS ANN THOMAS
THEIR INFANT DAUGHTER, WHO JOINED HER PARENT
IN A STATE OF ENDLESS BLISS ON THE 7TH DAY OF
SEPTEMBER 1817, AGED 8 MONTHS

Lieut. Thomas married secondly at Trinity, Palmetto Point, 10 Nov., 1825, Miss Mary Burke Thomson and had a daughter Emily baptised there 5 Sept., 1830.   He later became a special magistrate in Jamaica where he died 30 May, 1839. (*Gent. Mag.* 438).

———

125.   White marble over a stone vault the surface very flaked :—

In a sunk circle is a Jacobean shield with mantling :—

Crest : *A cubit arm holding a sword* over wreath and helmet.

Arms : *A cross between four fleur-de-lis.*

MARY Wife of THOMAS FENTON
lies Here entombed. She lived & died
A. . . .
A. . . .   Wife . . . .
A tender Mother & dear. . . . .
Ob. Oct^ris 30]73 . . . Aged . . . . .
Here alfo lies her younge . . . Son
James a Sober & promifing youth
Ob. Dec^ris 28 17.2 . Ætatis 23

See *Caribbeana* I., 79 for notes of this family. A Capt. Thomas Fenton was buried at St. John's, Nevis, 25 April, 1734. The arms are apparently those of Fenton of co. Nottingham.

---

126.   Blue marble ledger :—

Here lieth the Body of
WILLIAM BLACKBURN of Morley
in Yorkfhire, who Departed this Life
March the 16th 173⁹ in the Forty Firft
Year of his Age
Near this Place   (*sic* nothing else)

Six more vaults have no Inscriptions.

---

127.   White marble cross enclosed by wooden railings west of Nave :—

3n **Loving Memory** | of | GEORGE HENRY BURT | Born 17TH MAY 1787, DIED 1851 | ALSO OF | GEORGE HENRY BURT | *GRANDSON OF ABOVE* | BORN 2ND MARCH 1837, | DIED 30TH DEC. 1867 |

1809, March 14 George Henry Burt and Eliza McTear by Lic. (St. George, Basseterre).
He was of " Brothersons " and Speaker, ninth and youngest child of Thomas Burt of St. Kitts (died 1804, aged 64) by Catherine daughter of Milliam Musgrave of Montserrat
G. H. Burt, the grandson was a Lieut. in a West Indian Regiment.
Mrs. Stephens, wife of Mr. Stephens, who keeps the Seaside Hotel in Basseterre, at which I stayed, is his daughter. I also met there her elder sister Miss Burt. This family cannot prove any connection with the older one of Nevis of whom was William Mathew Burt, Governor of the Leeward Islands.

---

128.   White marble cross :—

3n | **Loving Memory of** | JOHN WORGAN MARSHAL | WHO LOST HIS LIFE NEAR THIS SPOT | IN THE STORM OF | AUGUST 27TH 1881 | AGED 21.

---

129. A fragment of a slate or blue ledger stands upside down near the entrance path. About three feet is exposed. In a sunk circle is a Jacobean shield with mantling. Crest : *A bird* over wreath and helmet Arms : *A chevron between three birds with feet.*

Owing to this stone having been partly buried in the earth I wrote for further information to Mrs. Burdon, wife of Major Burdon the Administrator of St. Kitts, who replied on 28 May, 1919, that Mr. Arthur Davis, the churchwarden, had caused the half-buried upright stones along the path to be removed in 1916, and this particular one had been preserved on account of its fine coat-of-arms, and thrown on the grass. Mrs. Burdon had the stone washed and forwarded a rough sketch of the coat. The birds are not martlets but resemble choughs. The remainder of this stone with the inscription has been lost. Unfortunately owing to the charge being a common one it is impossible to identify the family.

ST. ANNE'S, SANDY POINT.

St. Anne's, one of the original English parishes, contains the Town of Sandy Point, situated on a bay, guarded by Fort Charles (now used I think as a leper asylum). The great rock fortress of Brimstone Hill, 750 feet above sea level, is also about a mile off, and when it was fully garrisoned, many of the officers resided in the adjacent town.

By Act of Legislature, the inhabitants were allowed to erect houses within the fortifications, to which their families could resort in time of invasion.

The Church is of the usual plain type, with a Tower at the west end. It stands on rising ground, close to the sea, facing St. Eustatius, and is surrounded by a large church-yard. See a view in *Caribbeana* I, 73.

RECTORS.

David Bethune, 1724-30. (*Caribbeana* I, 42). And of St. Pauls, had been rector at Montserrat in 1714.

John King, 1753-63. Buried in 1763, minister of this parish 10 years. Went out to Antigua 1750,

William Julius, 1797.

Lewis Brotherson Verchild, 1810—1818. First son and heir of James George Verchild, educated at Eton 1793, died about 1818, after eight years' work here. (*Ante* III., 212).

John Hutchinson Wallwyn, 1822., and of St. Pauls, 1826.

John Penny, — 1840.

1840, Sept. At St. Christopher, aged 35, the Rev. John Penny, Rector of Sandy Point in that Island and Chaplain to the Garrison. (*Gent. Mag.* 670).

John Archer Gittens, 1852, of Barbadoes, and of Codrington College, 1830.

Noel Branch, 1879. Baptist Noel Branch was of Codrington College, 1865.

H. M. Pigott, 19...

130. Above is an urn and below it, behind the organ :—

" AVCTO SPLENDORE
RESVRGO."
" FVENTES D'ONOR "
" NIVE " " PENINSVLA "
" BLADENSBVRG "

also a bugle with " 85 " inside the handle.

TO THE MEMORY OF
LIEUTENANT THOMAS CHRISTOPHER MYTTON LETHBRIDGE
OF H.M. 85ᵀᴴ OR THE
KINGS LIGHT INFANTRY REGIMENT
WHO DIED AT SAINT KITTS ON THE
31ˢᵀ OF MARCH 1844
AGED 23 YEARS

Below is his Crest : *Out of a mural crown a demi-eagle displayed charged on the breast with a leopard's face cabossed.* Arms : *Over water a bridge of five arches embattled on the centre arch a turret in chief an eagle displayed*, also the badge of Ulster. Motto broken off and lost, the left wing of crest is also missing.

---

131. A dark marble slab fixed on the east wall of the Chancel to the north of the altar :—

Sacred | to the Memory of | MARY ANN FAHIE | died on the Twentieth day of November, 1810 | Aged 39 Years |.

See pedigree in *Caribbeana* IV., 266.
In the Hodge Act of 1790 she was described as Mary Ann Fahie late Mary Ann Pasea (one of the grand-daughters of Bazaliel Hodge Senior, of Tortola, Esq.), but her parentage not given. Her husband Richard Augustus Fahie was Member of Council in 1802, and they were married 14 Jan., 1788, she then being 17 ; so that she was probably a daughter of Mr. Pasea by Miss Hodge and not as shown in *Caribbeana* III., 302.

---

132. On a brass on the south wall of the Nave :—

Motto above, TRUTH and below, SPES MEA IN DEO.
1—Crest : *Out of a mural crown a demi-eagle displayed.*
2—Crest : *Out of a Coronet two arms in armour holding a leopards face.*
Arms : Quarterly of 4.
1—Lethbridge
2—*Gules a chevron engrailed between three leopards' faces* (Periam).
3—*Argent three stirrups within a bordure Or, charged with roundles.* (Buckler)
4—*Sable on a fess between three eagles' heads couped as many mullets.* (Giffard).
Supporters.—*Two ravens.*
Badge of Ulster in centre point of shield.

THIS TABLET WAS ERECTED IN MARCH, 1869, AS A
RECORD, THAT THE HANDSOME MONUMENT IN THIS CHURCH
TO THE MEMORY OF
L^T Thos Christopher Mytton Lethbridge
BY HIS BROTHER OFFICERS, OF THE 85TH KINGS LIGHT
INFANTRY, WAS THE ELDEST SON OF SIR JOHN HESKETH
LETHBRIDGE, Bar^T OF SANDHILL PARK, SOMERSETSHIRE,
WHO HAS APPENDED THE FOLLOWING LINES TO HIS
LAMENTED SON'S MEMORY.

1844, March 31. At St. Kitts, Thomas Christopher Mytton Lethbridge,
Lieut. 85th Light Infantry, eldest son of John Hesketh Lethbridge, and grand-
son of Sir Thomas Buckler Lethbridge, Bart., of Sandhill Park, Somersetshire.
(*Gent. Mag.* 670).

133.   On a small brass :—

In Memory of | RACHAEL C. VANHORN SAYERS | The Beloved
Wife of | JOHN TUCKER SAYERS | of the Island of Saint Christopher
planter | who departed this life | January 1st 1857 | Aged 39 Years |
she left her devoted husband and nine children | to lament her loss |

134 :—

sacred | to the memory of | MAJOR JOHN GORDON | late of | the
47TH REGIMENT | who died at S^T kitts | on the 16TH of march 1843 | aged
35 years | (Four lines, erected by brother officers).

135 :—

In | memory of | HENRY GILBERT | BURGESS, esq^{re} | of the
ordnance dep^T | eldest son of | henry w^M burgess esq^{re} | of chelsea,
middlesex, | died april 21st 1848, | aged 25 years his remains lie near |
this spot.

1848, April 21. At St. Kitts, aged 24, Henry Gilbert Burgess, of the
Ordnance Department, eldest son of the late Henry William Burgess of Sloane
Street. (*Gent. Mag.* 110).

The above four tablets are on the south wall of the Nave.

136.   On the north wall of the Nave east of the door, grey and white marble,
above is an Urn :—

Sacred to the Memory of
MARY, the Wife of MICHAEL MAILLARD, Esqr
of this Island MERCHANT
who departed this life September 2nd 1808 aged 52 Years
(Five verses of four lines each, signed JOHN MAILLARD).

137.   North wall of Nave, white marble on black :—

IN MEMORY | OF | ELVIRA COX | THE AFFECTIONATE WIFE | OF | JAMES THOMAS WAITH ESQUIRE, | OF THE ISLAND OF BARBADOS | WHO DURING THE FIRST REIGN OF | MALIGNANT CHOLERA IN THIS ISLAND | DIED ON CHRISTMAS DAY AT THE AGE OF 40 YEARS | 1854.

In the Church-yard are three loose broken marble ledgers placed against the boundary wall. They must have been taken out of the floor of the Church as they are in such perfect preservation though cracked across.

138.   In sunk oval a Jacobean shield with mantling, very perfect cutting :—

There is no Crest over the helmet.

Arms : *A chevron between, in chief two crescents and in base a sword erect point upwards between two stars of six points.* (Not in *Burke's Armory*).

Here lyeth yͤ body of WILLIAM
WOODDROP who deceaſed
15 day May 1687
Alſo here lyes yͤ bodyes of
MARGARET WOODDROP & BARBARA
WOODDROP Daughters of the
said WILLIAM WOODDROP ſenior
deceased
Alſo yͤ body of BISKETT*
WOODDROP Son to WILLIAM
WOODDROP Junior who depart
ed this life the 16 day of
Auguſt 1705.

1697, Dec. 30. William Hamilton of St. Christopher, Merchant, Exor in Trust of Mr. James Woddropp, late of this Island, deceased, and Attorney to Mr. William Woddropp, Senior, Merchant in Glascow. Power of attorney to John Esdaill. (*St. Kitts' Records*, p. 93).

Wm. Woodrop, Senior, Esq., 22 Feb., 1728, lease of his plantation of 140 acres. (*Ibid* 69).

See the Parish Register of St. Thomas, Middle Island, lately printed as a supplement of *Caribbeana* Vol. IV.. for many entries.

139.   In a sunk circle a Jacobean shield with mantling :—

Crest : *A hand holding a scroll* over wreath and helmet.

Arms : *A pile wavy, a crescent at centre point of chief.* (Rowland of Egham and Barnes, co. Surrey bears *Sable, a pile wavy Argent. Burke's Armory*).

CHARLES ROWLAND ESQᴿ
Was born the 9 of October]654.
Died yͤ]5 of   †   ber 1723
Aged 69 Years
Also, SARAH Daughter of the
said CHARLES ROWLAND was
Born the 6th day of December
]697 and died January ye 2]
]7]2 aged]5 Years.

---

* The name may be BIRKETT.   † Broken across here.

1707-8. Charles Rowland, Esq., aged 65. *Census.*

1729, Nicholas Rowland, Gent., and Mary his wife parties to deed of 16 August. (*A*. No. 104).

1743. Abraham Rowland by Mich. Williams party to deed of 19 October. Thomas Rowland, planter. Will dated 12 Dec., 1748. Wife Elizabeth. Several children born before marriage. Brother Charles Rowland. Sworn 17 January, 1748-9. (No. 4045).

1753. St. Ann, Sandy Point. Charles Rowland, Esq. and Thomas Rowland Esq., each one plantation. (*Baker's Map*).

---

140. North portion of the Church-yard. Large marble ledger :—

In Memory of
SAMUEL HARRIS Efq^r & his two Children
he departed this life January 8, 1773 Aged 74
was a Sincere Friend and a very Honest Man
SARAH PAYNE HARRIS his Eldeft Daughter
Aged 7½ Years Died 15th April 1773
REBECCA JOHN HARRIS the Youngeft Daughter
Departed this life 18th April 1773 Aged 5 Years
having Survived her Sifter but three Days
She was a most Amiable Child
Both having Died of a Putred fore Throat.

---

141. South portion of Church-yard. The next three are ledgers :—

In Memory of
Mrs MARY WOOLFORD,
who departed this life
the 27th September 1796
Aged 60 Years.

---

142.   **here Lieth the Body of**
MR FRANCIS CONWAY who *Departed*
this *Life* the 30th *March*, 1769
in the 34th Year of his Age.

---

143 :—

Here lies Interr'd | JAMES BISSE ye Son of* | THOMAS BISSE Efqr who Departed | this life the 23^d day of June in the Year 1746, Aged 20 Years.

Thomas Bisse, Esq., valued Godwins in 1699. Thomas and Elizabeth Bisse had several children baptised at St. Mary, Cayon, 1724-28 (*Caribbeana* I., 40). Mary, daughter of James Bisse, senior, married Codrington Burt.

I think there were Bristol Merchants of this name trading to Antigua in the seventeenth century. A pedigree of this family has been deposited by Lt.-Col. Pook in the custody of the Society of Genealogists of London at 5 Bloomsbury Square.

---

* The second line was cut afterwards.

144. Broken ledger. The right side partly gone :—

Sub hoc marmore Chir . . . . . .
Exuviæ conduntur *GULI* . . . . . .
Qui infavste cecidit *Ani*
Óculo dextro perfora . . . . .
Septimo die Ma. ij . . . . . .

145. Ledger worn and the corners broken off and missing :—

. . e lyes the Body of
. . . ANN BLAKE . . . lias BO . . IN
. . . e of Mʀ PATRICK . . LAKE FITZ PE. . . .
. . . R in the County of GALLWAY JRELA. . .
who departed this . . . the . .ᵗʰ day . . .
Fe . . . . y 17$\frac{1}{2}$$\frac{1}{9}$
in the . .ᵗʰ
(2 or 3 illegible lines here)
BLAKE FITZ PE . . . .of CUM. . .
In the County of Gallway in the. . .
. . . . .of this Island who
. . parted this life the 7ᵗʰ day of March
1744 Aged 68 Years

I examined this stone late in the afternoon and again at noon. The sun was too strong at noon, and the lettering showed up better in the evening.

The above Inscription has been fortunately preserved by Betham in his *Baronetage* published in 1803 (III, 374), though he omits the name of the parish or island :—

" Here lies the body of Mary-Anne Blake, alias Bohun, the wife of Patrick Blake Fitz-Peter, of Cummer, in the county of Galway, in Ireland, who departed this life the 18th day of February, 1720, in the 38th year of her age.

Here also lies the body of the above-mentioned Patrick Blake Fitz-Peter, of Cummer, in the county of Galway, in the Kingdom of Ireland, late of this island, departed this life the 7th day of March 1744, aged 68 years." The surname Bohun is evidently an error for Bodkin. Mary Ann, only child and heiress of Andrew Bodkin of this island who died 1689, married Patrick Blake as his first wife and they were the grand-parents of the first baronet.

There are several large land deeds dated 1685 relating to the transactions of Andrew Bodkin, gent. (1st Book *A*. I., p. 198).

146. White marble ledger over a stone vault :—

In a sunk circle on a festooned shield

Crest : *A cat o' mountain sejant.*
Arms : *Or, A cross Gules in the 1st quarter a lion rampant.*
Motto : UN ROY UN FOY UN LOY.

Rowland Garvey Burke, Efqʳ
The only Son of
Patrick Burke Efq : and *Elizabeth* his Wife,
Died in this his *Native Ifle*, 20ᵗʰ June, 1780
Aged 22 Years.
(Twelve lines A. Father, Mother and Sister surviving.)

147. Blue slate slab over stone vault :—

In Memory of
STAFFORD ANTHONY SOMARSALL,
Son of RICHARD & RACHAEL SOMARSALL
who departed this Life January 5th 1809
Aged 33 Years 6 Months and 28 Days
(Eight lines A. Mother, Wife and Child surviving.)

Stafford Somersal and Elizabeth Adams were here married 8 August, 1731. Richard their seventh child born 1st and baptised 8th Oct., 1750, married at Middle Island parish 7th March, 1772, Rachel, daughter of John Manning.

148. White marble slab :—

In a sunk oval a Jacobean shield with mantling.

Crest : broken off, over wreath and helmet.

Arms : *three bars embattled and counter-embattled on a chief as many roundles* (Emra). Impaling, *a chevron between three bugle horns and on a chief as many charges* now worn away. (Burt).

In this Vault
Lie the Remains
of
MRS CATHERINE MATHEW EMRA
late Wife of
The Honble IAMES EMRA of the Ifland of NEVIS EsQR
and Daughter of
The Honble WILLIAM PYM BURT of this Ifland EsQR
OBIIT XI : NOV : 1745 :
ANNO ÆTAT : 25º

Daughter of Chief Justice Burt of St. Kitts by Louisa youngest daughter of Governor Sir Wm. Mathew. She was married 8 May, 1741. In St. Pauls, Charlestown, Nevis, is a Latin Monumental Inscription to James Emra Esq., died Sept., 1733, aged 58. His son and heir James married secondly, 13 July, 1749, Rachel, daughter of William Yeamans of Antigua, Esq., in which island he died 28 Dec., 1759, aged 37. Monumental Inscription at St. Peter's, Parham.

The Nevis family is extinct but there are descendants of the Emras of St. Kitts not apparently or else remotely related to the former.

See pedigree of Burt in *Caribbeana* V., 89.

In the *Visitation of Essex* of 1634 is a pedigree of Emery or Amery with Arms : *Argent three bars nebuly Gules, in chief as many torteaux*—granted in 1628.

149. Next to above is a very long Monumental Inscription on a blue marble ledger :—

Within ye Vault are Buryed
The Honble ABEDNEGO MATHEW Lt Governour of ys Island
who dyed ye 18th of April]681. Aged 52 Years.
Dame CATHERINE MATHEW Relict of His Excellency
Sr WILLIAM MATHEW Knight second Son to ye above
named ABEDNEGO MATHEW & Capt Genll of these Islands

who dyed ye 28th of December]7]3. Aged 48 Years.
ANNA MATHEW Daughter of ye Honble THOMAS
HILL Lt Gen^ll of these Islands & Lt Governour of y^s
Island & first wife of ye Honble WILLIAM MATHEW eldest
Son of ye above named Sr WILLIAM MATHEW I.^t Gen^ll
of these Islands & Lt Governour of y^s Island who
dyed ye 26th of July]715. Aged 29 Years.
ANNE MATHEW Daughter of ye Honble MICHAEL
SMITH Lt Governour of Nevis & sometime Commander in
Chief of these Islands second wife of y^e above nam'd
WILLIAM MATHEW who dyed y^e 5th of April]730
Aged 3] Years.
ANNE MATHEW Daughter of y^e above named
WILLIAM MATHEW by y^e above named ANNE
MATHEW his second wife who dyed y^e]4th of Feb^ry
]7$\frac{30}{29}$ Aged 6 Days
ABEDNEGO BURT third Son of WILLIAM PYM BURT
Esq : & LOUISE y^e Youngest Daughter of y^e above
named S^R WILLIAM MATHEW who dyed y^e 25th Day
of June 1730 Aged] Year & 6 Months
MARGARET BURT Daughter of WILL^M PYM BURT
and LOUISE BURT Born April y^e 16th 1736
died March y^e 25th 1739
EDWARD BLAKE BURT fifth Son of W^M PYM BURT
and LOUISE BURT died March ye 27th 1739
Aged 4 Years 3 Months & 21 Days.
SUSANNA MATHEW PHIPPS fifth Daughter of
WILL^m PYM BURT & LOUISE BURT and Wife of
FRANCIS PHIPPS Esqr died Decr 17th 1748. Aged 24 Years.
ABEDNEGO VANLEMPUT BURT fourth Son of
WILL^m PYM BURT & LOUISE BURT
died Decr ye 2^d 1752 Aged 22 Years.

1726, Dec. 11.   Penelope, daughter of Lieutenant General Mathew, baptised.
1730, April 6.   Wife of Lieutenant General Mathew, buried.
1707-8, March, 9.   William Mathews, Esq., of St. Anne's, Westminster,
Bachelor, 23, and Anna Hill of Richmond, Surrey, Spinster, 21 ; at Stepney,
Paddington or St. Bartholemew the Great.   (Marriage Licence—Bishop of
London).   See pedigree of Mathew, Burt, and Smith in *Antigua* and *West Indian
Book-plates* and of Burt in *Caribbeana* V., 89, and of Smith IV., 291.

Daniel Smith, Lt.-Governor of Nevis will dated 1722.   My daughter Anne
wife of William Mathew, Lt.-Governor of St. Christopher.   On the stone she is
styled daughter of Michael but the Will is an authentic record.

Dame Catherine, Sir William's first wife, was styled Catherine Remée alias
Van Leemputt, maid-of-honour to Queen Mary.   She was married at Kingston-
on-Thames 28 Sept., 1682.   The surname appears in the parish register of St.
Paul, Covent Garden, where Remigeus sonn of Lewis Vanlimput was buried,
24 March, 1656.   Mary a daughter on 18 June, 1658, Remigeus on 9 Nov., 1675,
and Anna Maria daughter of Nicholas on 2 Feb., 1675-6.

---

150.   On a headstone :—

JAMES HAYWOOD
Aged 17 Years 6 months
Died of the Yellow Fever
10th June 1794.

151. White marble ledger on the top of a large vault :—

Within this Vault lye the remains of
THEODORE V. GEORGES Efquire
Who departed this Life,
Anno Domini 1763 Aged 73 Years.
As alfo Thofe of Mifs ANN GEORGES
His Youngeft Daughter
Who died Anno Domini 1764 Aged 26 Years.
Within this Vault are likewife Depofited
the remains of
JOHN D. FAHIE Efq^r
Who died October 18th Aged 55 (*sic* no year)
As alfo thofe of his Son
GEORGE M. FAHIE
Who died Anno Domini 1774 Aged 20.
Here likewife are Depofited the
Remains of M^{rs} ANN GEORGES
Wife of the Honorable Wm P. GEORGES
Chief Juftice of this *Ifland*
Who departed this Life
July 12th 1793 Aged 44 Years
ST. GEORGE'S, BASSETERRE.

BAPTISMS.

1772, Nov. 25. Caroline Louisa, daughter of Wm Payne and Ann Georges, born 12 July, 1772.

1793, Jan. 18. Caroline, daughter of — Georges &—his wife, about 3 weeks old at Trinity, Palmeto Point.

1794, Dec. 27. Henry St. John, son of Wm. Payne Georges and Ruth his wife, born 11 Sept.

See pedigree of Georges in *Caribbeana* III., 304.

John Davis Fahie son of Anthony Fahie Senior, by Elizabeth Molineux was living in 1760. See pedigree of Fahie in *Caribbeana* IV., 266.

---

152. In a sunk oval a Jacobean shield with mantling :—

Crest : *A wild boar* over wreath and helmet.

Arms : *In centre a leopards head erased between three stars of six points* ; impaling, *ermine on a saltire a leopard's face.* (Georges, see *Burkes Armory*).

The coat of Georges should have been on the dexter side.

Conditus hic Jacet
SAMUEL GEORGES (honorabilis Domini GULIELMI GEORGES
Filius et Dominæ ÆLIZABETHÆ DELAJAILLE Uxoris ejus apud
Go, fe oriundi in agro Santonienfi in GALLIA defunct :) qui vitâ
decefsit XIV Octobris, Anno Dom. MDCXCIX Ætatis XL.
Sub eodem tumulo Requiescunt
SAMUEL GEORGES Prætor (Filiusejus) qui Obiit XXIII Augufti
MDCCV Ætatis XX
Prætorque GULIELMUS GEORGES (Filius natu Secundus ejus)
qui decefsit XVII die Februarii, MDCCXX Ætatis XXVI.
SAMUEL GE ORGES (THEODORI GEORGES Armigeri Filius et SARÆ

Uxoris et Nepos Prædicti SAMUELIS GEORGES Senioris) Obiit
Qui XIV die Novembris MDCCXXVI Ætatis VII Menses.
Renata Lovisa (SAMUELIS GEORGES Senioris Uxor et THEO ;
VANELBURGH Armigeri filia) Quæ Obiit X die Aprilis
MDCCXXXVI Ætatis LXIV.
JOHANNES GULIELMUS GEORGES (Filius THEODORI GEORGES
et SARÆ Uxoris) Qui vitâ decefsit IV die Septembris
MDCCXXVIII Ætatis II.
SARA (THEODORI et SARÆ GEORGES Prædicti filia) quæ Obiit
XVI die Septembris MDCCXXXII Ætatis VI.
CATHERINA (THEODORI et SARÆ GEORGES prædicti filia) Quæ
vitâ decefsit XXXI die Januarii MDCCXXXIV Ætatis IV.
SARA (THEODORI GEORGES Prædicti Uxor et filia JOHANNIS
ESDALE Senioris et ANNÆ Uxoris ejus de Infula Sancti
Chriftopheri) quæ vita decefsit IX die Maii
MDCCXXXV Ætatis XXVIII.
Alfo MARTHA fecond Wife of the above THEODORE GEORGES Esqr died
Feb^{ry} 6th 1739. Aged 25 Years.

Will of Samuel Georges Senior (in French) . My wife Renee Vandrelburg
My children (not named). Recorded in 1700. No. 180.
" Agro Santoniensi " must be the ancient Province of Saintogne, the chief
town of which was Saintes on the river Charente between Angoulême to the east
and La Rochelle to the West, all the above territory being now in the Department of Charente.

---

153. White marble ledger, flaked on the right :—

Here Lyeth the Bodys : of Benjamen Clifton . . .
Grace his wife : she departed this Life :
the 16 :]720 : Aged 50 years : and he . . . june
the 17 : 1733 : Aged 68 years.

ST. JAMES, NEVIS (*Caribbeana* I., 235)

1740, Dec. 16. Frances Clifton daughter of Benjamin Clifton deceased,
Quaker, aged 19 years, baptised.
1743, Aug. 26. Mary Clifton, daughter of Benjamin Clifton, deceased,
Quaker, aged 17 years, baptised.
1744, Oct. 12. Henerit : Clifton, daughter of Benjamin Clifton, deceased,
Quaker, aged 16 years baptised.
1744, Dec. 23. James, Clifton son of Benjamin Clifton, deceased, Quaker,
aged 20 years, baptised.

---

154. Blue marble slab on stone vault :—

In Memory of
M^{RS} MARY SOMARSALL Wife of
ANTHONY SOMARSALL
the Elder Esquire of this Parifh
who Departed this Life Feb^{ry} 25th 1795
In the 88th Year of her Age.

Her husband was probably brother of Stafford and died 11 January, 1796,
aged 80.

---

155. White marble headstone :—

Here lies the Body of
ANN AMORY
Daughter of Stafford Somarfall
and Wife of William Amory
She was Born February the 9th
1739
And departed this Life
February 2d 1760
Aged 2] Years

---

156. Mausoleum. On the keystone :—

A. Co . . . .
Decemb . . .
1800

---

157. Ledger :—

To the Memory of
ELIZABETH FRANCKEN
who departed this Life
Decr 14 . . . . .Domini 1801

Parker Bennett Francken of this parish married Parker sister of William
Crooke, Esq., and had a son William Henry and a daughter Jane both minors in
1805.

---

158. On an iron plate fixed on railings. No stone :—

SACRED TO T. C. M. LETHBRIDGE Lt 85th Lt INFANTRY | DIED SUNDAY MARCH
31, 1844.

---

159. White marble ledger on tomb enclosed by iron railings :—

SACRED | to the memory of | MARY | the wife of | JAMES HARRIS Esq. |
Stipendary Magistrate | Born 25th October 1792 | Died 27th March 1848 |.

---

160. White marble ledger on brick vault :—

In sunk oval a shield in the early English style.

Arms : *Fretty on a chief three leopards' faces.* (Liddell).   Impaling, *A pheon
between three escallopshells.* (Not in *Papworth* or *Burke*).
No crest.

Here Lyes the Body of
ANNE Late wife of WILLIAM LIDDELL
of the Jsland S^T CHRISTOPHERS MERCHANT
Daughter of WILLIAM GERRISH of the
Jsland MOUNTSERATT ESQ^r by MARY his
wife who departed this Life FEBRUARY 25TH
J719 in the 24th year of Her Age.

Geo. Liddell of Montserrat, Esq. Will dated 17 Dec., 1695, wife Mary, son William a minor, daughters Elizabeth and Margaret wife of William Blundell, son George all est. and sole exor. (120 *Bond*).

1708, Geo. Liddell of St. Christopher, married Jane Clayton relict and Execurtix of Richard Clayton. Robert Clayton is son and heir of Richard Clayton.

1710. Geo Liddell, Esq., a Member of the General Council.

1725. Wm. Liddell, Esq., seals a deposition with the single coat of Liddell as above. Col. Liddell died at Montserrat 7 July, 1733, from injuries in a hurricane.

1726, Aug. 22. William Liddell, Esqr and Jane Cochrane. St. Anthony, Montserrat.

William Gerrish, formerly a Member of Council, and Collector of Customs of Montserrat, was a Merchant in London, 1739, and died 21 June, 1741, aged 67. See *Antigua* III., 214.

---

161. White marble headstone :—

Here lies the Body of
WILLIAM JOHN BRAGGER
Son of William and
Thomzain Bragger
who was born
October 8th 1738
and died February 3^d
1759
Aged 20 Years
and 4 Months

1738, Aug. 22. Baptised John William son of . . . . . Bragger.

---

162. Ledger :—

𝕾𝖆𝖈𝖗𝖊𝖉 | TO THE MEMORY OF | JOHN C. CARTER | OF BARBADOES | ORDNANCE STOREKEEPER | OF THIS ISLAND | WHO DEPARTED THIS LIFE | ON THE 2^D APRIL 1842 | AGED 58 YEARS |.

---

163 & 164 are white marble ledgers :—

IN MEMORY OF FORDYCE LUXMORE | WIFE OF CAPT. THO^s C. LUXMORE | *ROYAL ENGINEERS* | WHO DIED ON BRIMSTONE HILL | 16TH JULY 1839 | AGED 27 YEARS |

ALSO OF | FORDYCE JOHNSTON | LUXMORE | THEIR DAUGHTER | WHO DIED 23RD AUGUST 1837, | AGED 2 MONTHS.

1839, July 16.   On Sunday morning the 14th instant, at Brimstone Hill, the Lady of Capt. Luxmore, Royal Engineers, of a son.   (*St. Christopher Advertiser*).

164 :—

HERE LIETH THE REMAINS OF | MARGARET DOWSE | WIFE OF | SURGEON DOWSE | 4ᵀᴴ REGᵀ | WHO DEPARTED THIS LIFE 10ᵀᴴ JUNE 1836, | AGED 43 YEARS.

Some few modern inscriptions I did not take.

ST. THOMAS, MIDDLE ISLAND.

Sometimes called St. Thomas in the Middle Division.   This is another of the original English Parishes.   Captain Tho. Warner and the first settlers cast anchor in the bay here, where there is good shelter from the prevalent trade wind ; and a permanent stream of fresh water, Black River, (sometimes fetched by the inhabitants of St. Eustatius) continues to flow into the sea.   The earliest settlers naturally looked out grants of land close at hand.   Wingfield Manor, and Godwins Manor, remind one of Suffolk, the native county of Warner, Jeaffreson and others.

The town which sprang up was called the Old Road *i.e.* roadstead, and became the seat of government, remaining such until shortly after the French quarters were captured in 1713, when offices were built in 1728 at Basseterre and officials moved there.   The parish register with list of Rectors has been printed as a Supplement to *Caribbeana*.   Views of the Church appeared in Vol. II. 204.

Ten of the following Monumental Inscriptions mostly abbreviated, appeared with many notes in *Caribbeana* II., 204.

165.   In the floor of central pasage close to the communion rails is a black marble ledger :—

SIR CHARLES PAYNE
KNIGHT and BARONET,
MAJOR GENERAL of
HIS MAJESTYS
Leeward Carribee ISLANDS
Dyed the 21 Day of December
1744
Aged 62 Years

1697-8, March 22.   Patent to Capt. Stephen Payne for 60 acres.   (*St. Kitts' Deeds*, 1st Book, A. 1., p. 36).

1729, April 2.   Abraham Payne, Esq.   (*Ib.* vol. A., No. 79).

Abraham Payne of St. Christopher, Esq.   Will dated 24 August, 1738.   To my wife Frances £150 at once the use of my chariot and horses and ⅓ of the proceeds of my plantation.   My cousin Stephen Payne, my two daughters, Elizabeth and Jennet £1000 each at 18.   All residue to the child my wife goes with if a boy, but if a girl all to my daughters.   My father Sir Charles Payne, Jeremiah Browne, Joseph Phi. . . (Phipps) and Ra. Payne, Esqʳᵉ, exors and Guardians and £20 each.   By the Hon. Joseph Estridge, President, sworn 21 October, 1738.   (*Ib.* vol. G. No. 1716).

1742, June 7. Nathaniel Payne of Newport, Rhode Island, Esq., for £832 c. paid by Sir Charles Payne of St. Christopher, sell to him certain slaves. (*St. Kitts' Deeds* Vol. I., No. 3079).

Sir Charles Payne, Knight and Baronet. Will dated 3 June, 1743. My wife Jannatt, my coach and horses, and half the profits of my estate. The plantation of her brother Gillies McArthur, Esq., deceased of St. Ann to my son John. My brother Nathaniel Payne, my brother Abraham Payne, deceased, my late sister Bass. My daughter Jannatt Sharp £500. My daughter Elizabeth Orton £1500. My daughter Ann Brotherson £1500. My grand-daughter Jannatt Buckley £300. My grand-daughters Mary and Sarah Buckley £100 each. My grandson Charles Payne Sharp £1000. My grandson Charles Brotherson £500. My two younger sons to be educated in Great Britain. My son Charles Payne land in Nevis and 55 negroes. My late daughter Sarah Buckley. To my son John, the estate in St. Ann's I purchased of my brother Nathaniel Payne and 55 Negroes. My son-in-law, William Buckley, Esq. My son Gillies (? eldest son and heir) Sworn 4 March, 1744-5. (*St. Kitts' Deeds* No. 3403).

The early history of the Paynes is a blank Capt. Samuel Payne was of this Island in or before 1656 and in 1673 ; Capt. Philip Payne was here in 1669 and 1673 and they may have been brothers. Col. Stephen Payne whose parentage is unknown was born about 1660, became Member of Council 1704, and was aged 47 in the Census of 1707-8. He was probably father of 1, Abraham born about 1680 ; 2, Charles born about 1682, first baronet ; 3, Nathaniel.

The above notes are all additional to the pedigree in *Antigua* III, 7.

St. Anne's, Sandy Point

Baptisms.

1725-6, Feb. 4. Elizabeth, daughter of Captain Nathaniel Paine and Christian.

1725, July 18. Charles, son of Sir Charles Payne and Lady Janet.

1727, July 23. Abraham, son of Captain Nathaniel Paine and Christian.

1730, Sep. 17. Janet, daughter of Colonel Nathaniel Payne and Christian.

1732, June 10. John (born May 3, 1732) son of Sir Charles and Lady Janet Payne.

1753, Feb. 22. Anne (born Oct. 7,'52) daughter of Willett and Elizth. Payne.

1734, May 12. John, (born Oct. 20, 1733) son of Nathaniel and Christian Payne.

1737, Aug. 16. Charles, son to Abraham and Frances Paine.

1750, May 27. Jospeh Somers Paine (born April 25, 1750) son of Joseph and Mary.

Marriages.

1733, Oct. 24. Henry Sharpe and Janet Payne by Lic.

1747, Feb. 1. Captain Peter Hall and Mrs. Christian Payne.

St. Thomas, Middle Island.

Burials.

1737, May 1. John son of Nathaniel Payne, Esq., and Christian his wife.

1738, May 9. Charles, son of Abraham Payne, Esq., and Frances, his wife.

1738, July 25. Abraham Payne, Esq.

1738, Dec. 15. Jane, daughter of Abra. Payne, Esq., deceased and Frances his wife.

1738 Dec. 19. Elizabeth, daughter of Abrah. Payne, deceased and Francis his wife.

1744, Dec. 22. Sir Chas. Payne.
1746, Apr. 6. Col. Nathaniel Payne.
1752, Oct. 6. John Payne, Esq.
1758, June 11. Willett Payne, Esq.
1766, Dec. 13. Lady Jane Payne.
1774, Oct. 25. Cha. son of Sir Gillies and Lady Janet Payne.

MARRIAGE.

1758, Nov. 8. The Honorable Henry Brouncker, Esq. and Mrs. Elizth.
Payne, widow.

ST. GEORGE, BASSETERRE
BURIALS.

1759, Nov. 2. Mrs. Margaret Payne
1762, Dec. 8. The Honble. Ralph Payne, Esqr.

MARRIAGE.

1761, Nov. 9. The Honble. Ralph Payne, Esq. and Lucretia Ottley
by Licence.

---

166. White marble ledger to south of the preceding. In sunk oval is a
Jacobean shield with mantling :—

Crest : *A star of six points* over wreath and helmet.
Arms : *A chevron between three like stars.*

Here lies interred yᵉ Body of Captⁿ
IOHN POGSON of Horncaſtle in the
County of Lincoln in the Kingdᵐ of
Englᵈ who departed yˢ life yᵉ 29ᵗʰ day
of May]686
allſo HESTER his wife who departed yᵉ 30ᵗʰ
day of 9ᵇᵉʳ]696
And wᵗʰ yᵐ lies interred their two Grand
Sons namely
FREEMAN POGSON who departed yᵉ 24ᵗʰ
day of Iuly 1704 when but 3 months old
And IOHN POGSON Junʳ who departed
Iune yᵉ 20ᵗʰ 1720 in yᵉ 23ᵈ Year of his Age

See pedigree in *Caribbeana* I., 8, and IV., 143.

---

167. White marble ledger touching the preceding :—

COLLᴺᴸ IOHN MᴬᶜARTHUR
departed this Life April the 4ᵗʰ
]704 Aged 56 Years.
MAIᴿ GILLIES MᴬᶜARTHUR
Son to Iohn Mᵃᶜ Arthur died Aug :
23ᵈ :]722 Aged 28 years
IOHN MᴬᶜARTHUR Son to
Gillies Mᴬᶜ Arthur died Octobʳ 3ᵈ
1719 Aged] Year & 4 Months.
ANN Mᴬᶜ ARTHUR Daughter
to GIllIES MᴬᶜArthur died Augᵗ
22 :]720 Aged 6 Days
SARAH ALLETTE MᴬᶜARTHUR
Daughter to GIllIES MᴬᶜArthur died
Ianuary]6 :]72¾ Aged] Year &
5 Months

Of Col. John McArthur, Governor Christopher Codrington wrote 10 Nov., 1701 :—" I have a very gallant but a very silly man for President . . . I am satisfyed with my old Scotch man at present, for he's as brave a man as lives and as watchful an officer." (*Col. Cal.*, p. 604).

There is a letter of the President dated 28 January, 1701-2 to Gov. Codrington. (*Ibid* 92).

1732, Jan. 30. Mrs. Sarah McArthur, widow, buried.

---

168.   Plain white marble tablet over the west door :—

> This Monument
> is Erected to the Memory of
> Sʳ CHARLES PAYNE *Barᵗ*
> who Dyed
> Decᵇʳ 23ᵈ 1744
> Aged 63 Years

Above is a rococo shield of white marble with no arms on it.
He married about 1710, Janet daughter and co-heiress of William McArthur and sister and heiress of Gillies McArthur.

On the south wall of Nave are these three tablets :—

169. Brass—

In Memory of the Rev. Henry Jeremiah Dyson, Vicar of Barking, in Essex, who died in the zealous discharge of the duties of this Parish, on the 27th day of March, 1854, aged 31 years and of his Wife Matilda, who died on the 26th day of March, 1854, Aged 35 years. (Erected by a Father).

Second son of Francis of Tedworth, Hants, clerk, Merton College, matriculated 3 March, 1842, aged 18, B.A. 1845, Fellow of All Souls 1847-52, M.A. 1850, Vicar of Barking 1851. (*Foster*).

---

170.   White marble tablet :—

> IN MEMORY OF
> JAMES DEAN ROGER, ESQ.
> OF THIS ISLAND,
> WHO DIED AT BRIDGE OF ALLAN, SCOTLAND
> ON THE 4ᵀᴴ NOVEMBER 1870,
> AGED 72 YEARS

---

171. White Marble tablet :—

IN MEMORY OF
ROBERT OLPHERTS ESQUIRE
WHO DIED OF FEVER JUNE 9TH 1840,
IN THE 39TH YEAR OF HIS AGE
MR OLPHERTS CAME FROM ENGLAND TO THIS ISLAND
IN THE YEAR 1834 HAVING RECEIVED FROM HIS MAJESTY
THE APPOINTMENT OF A STIPENDIARY MAGISTRATE.

1839, Aug. 13. At Carrick Brae, Sandy Point, on the 3rd instant, the Lady of Mr. Stipendiary Justice Olpherts, of a son. (*St. Christopher Advertiser*).
There was a family of Olpherts of Belfast.

---

172. At the west end of Nave are two stained glass windows. The one to the south has :—

1. Crest : *A greyhound's head erased and collared Or.*
2. Crest : *A demi-heron couped, in its beak an eel.*

Arms : *Or, on a fess Sable between three crosses pattée as many pellets.*
Motto : VIRTUTIS PRÆMIUM.

ERECTED IN MEMORY OF MRS SUSAN WILLSON BY HER AFFECTIONATE HUSBAND AND SON.

CHURCHYARD.

The Churchyard slopes rapidly down from the Church to the high road. The entrance path with an avenue of palms divides it into two portions. The following stones are in the eastern half.

173. On a thick slab, the right top corner and both bottom corners renewed. In a sunk oval :—

Crest : *A man's head affrontée couped,* over a wreath and a knight's helmet, with mantling.
Arms : *A bend engrailed between six roses, three and three* . . .

M. (S.)
AN EPITAPH VPON TH. . . . .
.OBLE & MVCH LAMENTED GENT SIR
THO WARNER KT LIEVTENANT
GENERALL OF YE CARIBEE
IELAND & GOVERR OF YS
IELAND OF ST CHRISTR
WHO DEPARTED THIS
LIFE THE 10 OF
MARCH 1648

First Read then weepe when thou art hereby taught
That Warner lyes interr'd here one that bought
With losse of Noble bloud the]llustrious Name
Of A Comander Greate in Acts of Fame
Traynd from his youth in Armes his Courage bold
Attempted braue Exploites and Vncontrold
By fortunes fiercest frownes hee still gaue forth
Large Narratiues of Military worth
. . ritten with his swords poynt but what is man
. . . the midst of his glory and who can
. . . . re this life. A moment since that hee
. . . . . by Sea and Land so long kept free
. . . . t mortal stroakes at length did yeeld
. . . . . . ace) to Conqueringe Death the field
. . . fine Coronat

The slab has been replaced on the top of the original stone tomb and a wooden structure erected over it by the government to protect it from the weather. The tomb stands in the south-eastern corner of the site of the old church, of which the foundation on the eastern side measured eleven paces and the northern twenty paces but there were no traces of the other sides. Mrs. Wigley of Spencer House, Basseterre, an old resident, told me that when a child she used to attend service in the old church, and recollected seeing the tomb in the interior.

In the public library I saw a framed copy of the inscription undated, but nineteenth century, and of no value, together with a pen and ink sketch of the slab showing the cracks. See plate in *Caribbeana* I, 164 and notice in the *D.N.B.*

---

174. Blue marble ledger on stone vault :—
Here Lyeth the Body of
EDITH OTTLEY
wife of DREWRY OTTLEY late of this
Island Merchant who departed this
Life the 2ᵈ day of September 1725
in the 39ᵗʰ year of her Age
with Five of their Children viz.
RACHEL, KERIE, IOHN, MARTHA
& EDITHA OTTLEY
Here also Lyeth the Body of
ALICE OTTLEY
Second Wife of the Said
DREWRY OTTLEY who departed this Life
the 4 : Day of September 1738
in the 29ᵗʰ : year of her Age
with three of their Children viz.
CÆSAR, EDWARD, & MARY who all died young

Drewry Ottley the first, settled in St. Christopher about 1707, was Treasurer 1714, and was buried in St. Martin-in-the-Fields. Will dated 1759, p. 1760 (436 *Lynch*).

Drewry Ottley the second, his eldest son, was also of the parish of St. Thomas and married here 22 May, 1733, Margaret daughter of Colonel James Weatherill of Antigua. She was buried at St. John's, Antigua, 20 January, 1746, but her husband was buried here 15 March, 1751. Their children were baptised here or in Antigua.

Drewry Ottley the third, succeeded his grandfather and died 18 September, 1794, at Teddington. Drewry Ottley the fourth was named in the Will of his great grandfather. See a pedigree in *Antigua* II., 370.

I do not know the parentage of Edith the first wife. The second was Alice Cæsar daughter of Cæsar Rodney of Antigua, baptised 21 October, 1708, who married 12 February, 1722, John Panton, junior. He died intestate in New England and she obtained administration 10 January, 1727 and soon after remarried D. Ottley. (See pedigree of Panton in *Caribbeana* IV., 381).

175.   White marble ledger on brick vault :—

Here lyeth Interr'd the Body of
IOHN HELDEN Son of IOHN HELDEN of
this Ifland Esqr who departed
this life the 7th of Iune 1722 Aged
2 Years 2 Months and 19 days

The father aged 31 in 1707-8, was Member of Council and Collector of the Customs, left this Island in 1730 and died at Egham, co Surrey 11 Feb., 1738, where there is his vault. (See *Caribbeana* II., 207, and III., 375). Mary, his wife, was heiress and Executrix of Mrs. Frances Bladen who was niece and heiress of Col. Joseph Jory of Nevis and widow of the Rt. Hon. Col. Martin Bladen, M.P., a commissioner of trade and plantations.

---

176.   In sunk oval is a Jacobean shield with floriated work all around it in the Early English style.

Crest : *In a ducal coronet a plume of five ostrich feathers, thereon wings.*
Arms : Quarterly of 4 :
1—? *A chief invecked* (no trace of cups).
2—*Traces of three charges.*
3—*a saltire.*
4—*A lion rampant and a chief*, impaling, *three fishes hauriant.*
Motto : PRESSUS EXTOLLOR.

A Latin inscription of twenty-one lines very indistinct which I have translated as follows :—

Sub hoc marmore requiescit MARGARITA Uxor THOMA . | BUTLER, Armigeri &c. (Several lines follow difficult to decipher).

Margarita her daughter who was sent to London for her education died there 13 Dec., 1721 of small-pox in her 8th year, and was buried in the Crypt of the the Church of St. Andrew, Holbourn, and her mother died 29 Nov., 1727 aged 38. Stone placed by her Husband Thomas Butler.

I was told that the Rev. K. M. Gillie, Rector of St. Mary's, Antigua had a daughter buried in this vault.

The pedigree of Colonel Thomas Butler of Nevis was printed in *Caribbeana* II., 60, but this Thomas Butler of St. Kitts appears to be another person. The arms are probably similar.

1729, Aug. 10.   Thomas Payne, son of Thos. Butler & Sarah his wife, bapt.
1730, Feb. 14.   Thos Payne, son of Thos Butler, Esq. & Sarah his wife, buried.
1731, Aug. 7.   Thomas Butler, Esq., buried.
1734, July 18.   Mr. William Buckley & Mrs. Sarah Buttler, widow.

1735, May 16.   Jane, daughter of Mr. William Buckley & Sarah his wife by Mr. Thomas, bapt.

1738, Sep. 15.   Sarah, wife of Wm. Buckley, Esq., buried.

She was daughter of Sir Charles Payne of this parish, 1st Baronet and was evidently second wife of Thomas Butler.

---

177.   The broken lower half of a white marble slab on stone vault, the left hand top corner having been broken off and lost :—

. . . . .onate Hufband |
. . . . .lgent Parent |
. . . . . . sincere Friend |
Who departed this Life Septr 25th 1796
Ætate 61.

1796, Sept. 26.   Buried The Honorable Archibald Esdaile from Palmetto Point.   (Burial Register).

In 1879, the late Mr. N. Darnell Davis, C.M.G., noted this inscription as " Sacred to the memory of the Hon. Archibald Esdaile, Esquire, late Commander-in-Chief of the Leeward Islands, etc."

By a curious coincidence Mr. N. D. Davis was staying with his cousin Mr. Benj. Davis at " Lamberts " near by, while I was engaged transcribing these Monumental Inscriptions in 1914.

---

178.   Headstone :—

𝔍𝔫 𝔐𝔢𝔪𝔬𝔯𝔶 𝔬𝔣 | Rebecca Iohn Lees (*sic*) the | Infant Daughter of | James Lee Efqr and | Rebecca Phipps his wife | who Departed this Life | the 20th of April In the | Year of our LORD 1789 | Aged 4 Years.

1789, Jan. 5. (*sic*) Rebecca Lees, infant daughter of James and Rebecca Lees from Sandy Point, buried.

---

179.   Marble ledger on brick vault :—

Here lies the Body of
JOHN HENNIS the Son of
JOHN and MARY HENNIS
who departed this Life Auguft
the 24th 1758 Aged 17 Years
and Seven Months

---

180.   East of Avenue, just above J. Helden.   In sunk circle a Jacobean shield with mantling :—

Crest : *A wyvern out of a coronet* on helmet.   No wreath.
Arms : *A lion rampant between six crosses croslet.*

<blockquote>
Here lyeth Interr'd the Body of
Doct^r IOHN HUTCHINSON
late of the Parifh of S^T THOMAS MIDDLE ISLAND
who Departed this life the (10th day* of) April 1735
in the Fourtieth Year of his Age.
Here alfo lyeth the Body of
MARY
the Davghter of BENJAMIN MARKHAM Efq^r
and Wife of the aforefaid IOHN HUTCHINSON
who Departed this life the 26th Auguft 1733
Aged 28 years.
And four of their Children.
</blockquote>

In 1697 the Hon. John Hutchinson signed as Chief Justice and in 1701 as Speaker.   The above coat (with *Party per pale Gules and Azure*) is that of Hutchinson of Alford, Lincolnshire, of which place a John Hutchinson was baptised in 1633.   See the Diary of Governor Hutchinson of Mass. and Lincolnshire, p. 534.

There is a transverse crack across the fourth and fifth lines.

BAPTISMS.

1730, May 6.   Mary, daughter of Dr. John Hutchinson, and Mary his Wife, born March 16, 1730.

1731, Oct. 11.   Sarah, daughter of Dr. John Hutchinson and Mary his Wife, born March 9th,

BURIALS.

1733, Aug. 26.   Mrs. Mary Hutchinson, wife of Dr. John Hutchinson.
1733, Sep. 3.   Mary, daughter of Dr. John Hutchinson.
1733, Sep. 10.   Sarah†, daughter of Dr. John Hutchinson.
1735, Apr. 10.   Doctor John Hutchinson.

———

The following are all west of the avenue of palm trees.

181.   Blue marble ledger cracked in two places :—

In sunk oval is a Jacobean shield and mantling with helmet on wreath, but no crest.

Arms : *On a chevron between three annulets as many annulets* (*sic*).

———

* Noted in 1879 by the late Mr. N. Darnal Davis, C.M.G.

† This entry does not appear in the transcript of the parish register which has been printed.

Here Lies in Certain hope
of a Blefsed Refurrection
WILLIAM COVENTRY
late of the Parifh of
Sᵀ Thomas Middle Ifland Merchant
who departed this Life Auguft the
16ᵗʰ 1734 Aged 53 years
To his Memory therefore
John Manning Merchant
who Married his only Daughter Dutifully
Infcribes this Monument.
In this Tomb alfo is repofited the Body
of his Grandfon
John Battry Manning
who departed this Life September
the 27ᵗʰ 1734 Aged One Year
Seven Months and ten days

See pedigree of Manning in *Caribbeana* I., 242.
1734, Aug. 10.   Captain Coventry (Wm.).   (Buried).
1739, Aug. 28.   Mr. William Coventry of Basseterre and Elizabeth daughter
of Wm. Hart, Esqr.   (Trinity Palmetto Point).
Miles Coventrie, aged 18, sailed for St. Kitts in 1635.

---

182.   A small brass plate :—

ROBERT
OLPHERTS
ESQUIRE

---

183.   Blue marble ledger cracked down the centre.

In sunk oval a Jacobean shield with border of leaves.

Crest : *A sphinx passant, in the dexter foot a rose leaved* no helmet.
Arms : *A chevron between three horned sheep, a chief chequy.*   (Lambert of
Bucks and Owton, Yorkshire).

Here lyeth the Body of
MICHAEL LAMBERT, Efqʳ
Majʳ General of the Leeward Iflands
and fometime
Lievᵗ Governour of Sᵗ Chriftophers
He dyed the 6ᵗʰ day of March 172¾
In the 70ᵗʰ year of his Age
Here alfo lyeth the Body of
FRANCES *his youngest Daughter*
and Wife of Charles Pym Efqʳ
who dyed the 9ᵗʰ day of Novʳ 1724
In the 20ᵗʰ year of her Age

1757, May 5.   Madam Priscilla Lambert widow.   (Bur. Reg.).
See *Caribbeana* II., 206.   In an inventory of 1745, of the effects of Col.
James Weatherill of Antigua occurs " A painting of Major Gen. Lambert £10,"

possibly the above who was his father-in-law. On the other hand as it was entered next to a painting of Oliver Cromwell it may have related to one of the latter's generals.

Michael Lambert was entered as English in the census of 1678. His wife's surname is unknown. He made his will 1 March, 1723-4, but it is not in the P.C.C. He owned the New Invention of 106 a. in the French quarter and the College of 200 a. Leaving no son his estates descended to his daughters as co-heiresses. 1—Susannah, married firstly, Richard Holmes, Member of Council, died 1725 ; married secondly, John Douglas, will dated 1747 (359 *Strahan*) ; Her will dated 1750 (323 *Greenly*). 2—Margaret, married Col. James Weatherill of Antigua and was buried at Middle Island 18 Sept., 1751. 3—Frances, married Charles Pym.

184. Inscription framewise. The right hand top corner broken off and lost :—

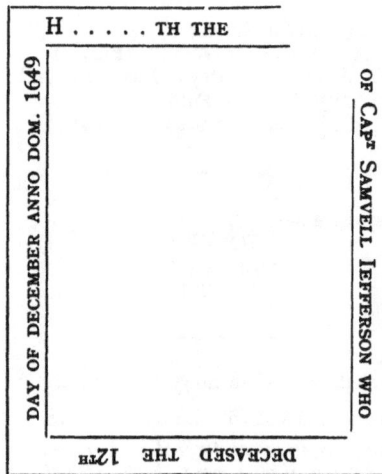

```
H . . . . . TH THE
```

DAY OF DECEMBER ANNO DOM. 1649

OF CAPᵗ SAMVELL IEFFERSON WHO

DECEASED THE 12ᵀᴴ

He was brother to Colonel John Jefferson, Sir Thomas Warner's Lieutenant, and owned the Red House plantation. See *Antigua* II., 106.

185.

Under this Marble
is buried
amidſt the tears of his friends
DAVID EVANS
the ſecond and beloved ſon of
DAVID and BEATRICE EVANS
He was born the 16ᵗʰ day of Septʳ 1796
He died the 19ᵗʰ day of Novʳ 1812

186.   Stone ledger.   Inscription rather indistinct :—

To the Memory
of M^{RS} MARY WALKER
the Wife of *Cap^{tn}* JOHN WALKER
of the City of *LONDON*
and Daughter of M^R ROB^T TAYL . R
of Kingſton upon Hull in Yorkshire
who departed this life the 3^d of
July 1785 in the 45th Year of her Age

---

187.   Ledger lower down the hill :—

Crest and spade shield, no arms visible.

Here lies
(one line illegible)
CAPTAIN JAMES COLQUHOUN
of THE *ROYAL REG^T* OF *FOOT*
ELDEST SON of ROB^T COLQUHOUN *ESQUIRE*
of CAMSTRADAN *DUNBARTONSHIRE*
Who in the service of his King & Country *FELL*
A sacrifice to this Climate on the 30th May 17 . 1 (?1761)
AGED XXXV.
(Ten lines by ANN COLQUHOUN his sister).

Walter Colquhoun of Camstradan died in Antigua in 1802.
William Colquhoun was Member of Assembly in St. Kitts in 1678. Robert,
treasurer, in 1754 by Frances Mills his wife left a son William McDowall
Colquhoun and three daughters.

---

188.   Blue marble ledger on stone Vault :—

Sacred to the Memory of
M^{RS} ELIZABETH BURT
Wife of EDWARD BURT of this Island Merchant.
She departed this Life Oct. 22, 1809
In the 41st Year of her Age.
(Seven verses of four lines each).

This Edward does not appear in the pedigree of Thomas Burt noted under
No. 117.

---

189.   Marble ledger :—

Here lieth the body of
MARY BASDEN
Wife of *RICHARD BASDEN*
who departed this life Sepr 16th 1790
Aged 37 years 1 month and 6 days

1771, Feb. 10.   Captain Richard Basden and Mary Woods.

---

190.   On the north face of a white stone vault under No. 188, in a decorated oval is a representation of a draped reclining woman with a skull and cross bones at her feet.   The stone on the south face has also been carved but is worn away.

----

191.   The following blue marble ledger was unearthed by Canon Shepherd after my first visit and I looked at it on Sunday, 22nd March, 1914.   It is on the west side of the Avenue :—

Here lyeth the bodyes
of Coll⁰ STEPHEN PAYNE who departed
this life the J0ᵗʰ day of Sepᵗʳ 1711 in the
(*sic*)   51ᵗʰ year of his Age
And also of his sons STEPHEN and
SAMUEL PAYNE who departed this life
in the 7ᵗʰ and 10ᵗʰ years of their Age

----

192.   This stone had to be well scrubbed before I could read the inscription :—

Here lies Interred the Body of Mrs. Sufanna
The Wife of Cap. Iames Phipps of yᵉ Ifland
Of Sᵗ Chriftophers & only Daughter of
Cap. Robert Clar . e late of yᵉ faid Ifland
Deceafed who departed this life yᵉ 17 Day
Of October in yé yeare of our Lord 1686
In the one & thirtieth yeare of her age

Where the " k " of Clarke should be the stone is chipped.
Her husband was killed in 1689 at the French attack.   See **pedigree of** Phipps in *Caribbeana* I., 68.

----

193.   South of Nave.   Cast iron plate on a stone vault :—

Sacred to the Memory | of |
JOSEPH PHILLIPS EVELYN
BORN IN BARBADOES 1828
DIED ON WINGFIELD ESTATE
Sᵀ KITTS OCTOBER 10ᵀᴴ 1869
Aged 41 years

TRINITY PALMETTO POINT.

The church is small, standing on an eminence abutting on the high road. See a letter from Mrs. Bromley about the neglected state of this churchyard in the *West India Committee Circular* for 5 November, 1912.

LIST OF CLERGY.

1836—40	G. Sealy	1898—'01	W. Hooker
1841—69	R. H. Barrow	1901—10	Fred Caunt
1869—89	T. A. C. Armbrister	1911—12	W. K. Livingstone
1891—96	Fred Thomas	1913—14	C. A. Shepherd
1896—98	A. C. Waller	1915—	L. R. V. Spinks

Canon Shepherd was Rector of this parish as well as of St. Thomas.

Rev. Thomas Lake in 1630 was Rector of Palmetto Point.

1637, Sept. 30. John Featly, clerk, sets forth that the late Earl of Carlisle conferred upon him the Rectory of Palmetto Point which Joseph Moore has ever since enjoyed with another living of greater value. (*Col. Cal.* p. 258).

See his memoir *Caribbeana* II., 7. He went out in 1625 with Warner and was ye first preacher and was Rector of St. Thomas, Middle Island until 1632. In 1643 he was Rector of St. Thomas and Palmetto Point, but was in England 1646.

There are three tablets on the north wall of nave and a brass on the east wall of the Chancel :—

194. IN MEMORY OF | WILLIAM SWANSTON | WHO DIED | ON THE 6TH DAY OF JANUARY, 1852 | AGED 56 YEARS | ALSO | TO THE MEMORY OF | CAROLINE I. P. SWANSTON | THE BELOVED WIFE OF | THOMAS SWANSTON | WHO DEPARTED THIS LIFE | ON THE 12TH DAY OF JULY 1858, | IN THE 60TH YEAR OF HER AGE |

195. SACRED TO THE MEMORY OF | ELIZABETH AND SUSAN DAVOREN | DAUGHTERS OF JAMES AND MARY DAVOREN | THE FORMER DEPARTED THIS LIFE ON THE 2ND OF JANY 1821, | AGED 9 YEARS | THE LATTER ON THE 13TH OF THE SAME MONTH | AGED 6 YEARS.

1821, Jan 3. Elizabeth Davoran, aged nine years ; 1821, Jan. 14 Susannah Davoran, aged six years only daughters of the Honorable James and Mary Johnson Davoran, of the Canada Estate, St. Peters. (Burial Register).
R. G. Davoren, M.D. was a Member of Assembly in 1840.

196.

BENEATH THIS PEW ARE DEPOSITED THE REMAINS OF
HENRIETT ELIZABETH CLEMENTS HENRY,
Daughter of
NICHOLAS CLEMENTS & ELIZABETH HENRY,
WHO DEPARTED THIS LIFE ON THE 11TH OF
OCTOBER 1829, AGED TWO YEARS

197.   **In Memoriam**

ROBERT HAYNES BARROW, Priest, 35 Years Rector
of this Parish : Born 5th Oct. 1811. Died 30th May 1875.
Laid to Rest in this Nave with three of his Children
ALSO
FANNY GORDON WILLIAMS BARROW (née Trew)
Wife and Mother Born 2nd Oct. 1818. Died 5th Jan. 1886.
Laid to Rest in Chiswick Churchyard, England.

1841, July 13. Rev. Rob. Haynes Barrow, Rector of Trinity, in St.
Christopher, to Fanny Gordon Williams, daughter of Henry Trew, Collector of
Customs at Jamaica and formerly of Chichester. (*Gent. Mag.* 423).

In the floor in front of the communion rails is a white stone without any
name covering his vault (so the sexton said).

CHURCHYARD.

198. In the south portion. A very large mausoleum without name said to
belong to the Boone family, but Mrs. Bromley says it is the Rawlins vault.

---

199. Blue marble ledger over stone vault. The right hand top corner
of the slab is missing :—

Here lies the Body of S. . .
Manning Late of this Isl^d W. . . . .
Departed this Life March]6 172 .
In the 52 Year of his Age
Also Joanah . . . .anning his Wife
Died May 19th 1722 In the 39
Year of her Age
and of their Children Viz
Wm Christ^n Ann Maryann Saml
and Rebecca Manning

This inscription is undoubtedly to Samuel Manning and not to John, as
given by Mr. N. D. Davis (*Caribbeana* I., 241 & 347). I examined the stone on
two occasions to make sure—The missing corner cannot be found anywhere.
Samuel Manning was of this parish at the Census of 1707-8, then aged 35. The
year of his death in the third line was according to Mr. N. D. Davis 1725, but the
5 is no longer visible. Joanah was probably daughter of William Battry and
grand-daughter of Edward and Jone Battry, because Ann Battry aged 28 was
entered in 1707-8 with Samuel Manning (probably as his sister-in-law) and one
of his sons was baptised Battry Manning.

---

200. Blue marble ledger close by. Broken in two places length ways :—

Here lyeth Inter .d the Body of
Mrs IONE GU . . HEN Wife of
Mr HOSEA GUIL . EN Daughter of
Mr ZECHARIAH & MARY RICE Deceased
who Departed this life y^e]8 of Sepr 1722
In the 44 Year of her Age
Here lyeth also four. . their Children

See *Caribbeana* II, 358, where Guilmen and Price were incorrectly given.

The following was recently accidentally unearthed by Canon C. A. Shepherd after I left the Island.

201.   On a dark stone slab in perfect order :—

Here lyes Interred The Body
of Mrs : Ione Battry
Widow Relict of Mr. Edward
Battry Decst (an Antient
Inhabitant of this Island)
who departed this life the
9th day of August Anno
Domⁿⁱ 1706 In the 82^d year
of her Age.

The Canon also writes :—An old disused silver paten and chalice have " The gift of Joan Battry to ye Parish Church of Trinity Palmetto Point."

William Battry lately dying, by will, appointed certain Exors who are all dead.   Administration of his estate is now granted 14 May, 1695 to Joane Battry his Mother and Grandmother of his children.   (Recorded 9 Aug. 1701, p. 88). He was entered in the Census of 1678 as of this parish and was Lieutenant of Charles Fort, 1689.

ST. ANNE'S, SANDY POINT.

1747, Nov. 14.   Peter Battery (born Oct. 20, 1747), son of Peter Battery and Annaple Myers, baptised

1751, Oct. 27.   Anne Dorothy (born Oct. 6, 1751), daughter of Peter Battery and Annaple Myers, baptised.

Mr. Edward Battry was of this island in 1656.   In 1672 he claimed for a plantation with houses sold to M. de Prayle.   (*Col. Cal.* p. 397).

He was of Palmetto Point in 1678 and entered as English.

Capt. Peter Batterie was in 1680 in command of Statia (*Col. Cal.* p. 563) and in 1686 at Nevis (*Ib.* p. 189).

---

202.   Large Blue marble ledger on brick vault :—

Above in sunk oval a skull and cross bones.

Here Lyeth Interr'd the Body of
JOHN BOURRYAU ESQ^R
who was born the 11 day of Octob^r]662
& Departed this Life the 6 Day of AUGUS^T   (*sic*)
1728 Aged 66 Years

See pedigree in *Caribbeana* III. 252.   His will was dated 29 July, 1728.   He left a widow Mary who signed a release of her legacy of £2000 on 23 January, 1728-9, and two sons Zachariah and Edward.   She was buried here 1 Oct., 1744 as appears by the entry at Basseterre and Edward on 3 September, 1744.

---

203.   Blue marble ledger :—

Here Lyeth the Body of
MR IOHN HART late of this Parifh,
who departed this Life the 27th April 1731
In the 32^d year of His Age
And alfo His Children SARAH & IOHN
who Died young

Probably brother of William No. 203. Nevis.   William Harte will dated
30 April, 1700.   My two sons William and John all lands, daughter Sarah Harte,
my wife.   Sworn 5 August.   Recorded at St. Kitts p. 179.

---

204.   Just above this is a large blue marble ledger with an ornamental
surround over brick vault.   It has a crack across, below the inscription :—

Here lies the Body of
MR WILLIAM HART
late of this Parifh who
Departed this life July
ye 28th 1742 in the 47th Year
of his Age
Also four of his Children
SARAH MARY and BENJAMEN
who Died Young JOSEPH
who Died Novr ye 11th 1739
Aged 14 Years

William Hart planter.   Will dated 27 June, 1742.   Wife Sarah.   My four
daughters Sarah, Mary, Margaret, and Susannah £300 each.   My son-in-law
William Coventry.   My daughter Elizabeth Coventry £200.   My two sons
William and John.   Sworn 10 September, 1742.   (*St. Kitts' Records* I. 3084).

---

205.   Stone vault surmounted by an ornamented headstone, the work
very rough :—

Sacred
To the Memory
of
Henrietta Willett
BELOVED Wife of D. Willett
who DEPARTED this life Aug.
12th 18.0 ÆT 29 YRS.

These Willetts were probably coloured.

---

206.   An old stone vault with stone slab and marks of oblong plate now
missing :—

---

207. Remains of a handsome stone monument formerly surmounted by an urn now lying on the ground. On north end " J. BACON jun^r | Sculptor | LONDON 1803."

A column is in the centre flanked by military trophies. The Inscription which is on the column is much worn :—

> . . . . .of the late Captain JOHN GARVEY
> . . . . .H.M. 3 Reg^t of Foot or Buffs
> (Sixteen more lines illegible).

On the west face or back are traces of the commencement of many lines, no date being visible anywhere.

1773, Feb. 21. John, son of Lucas and Ann Garvey, born November 5, 1772, baptised.

There are many other entries from 1735 onwards.

1797, June 21. George Frederick, Baron Pfeilitzer and Anna-Mauduit Garvey by Licence. (St. George, Basseterre).

1802, April 25. Captain John Garvey of His Majesty's 3rd Regiment or Buffs, buried.

1806, Aug. 4. Baroness Pfeilitzer, niece of William Mauduit, esq., of Lincolns-Inn Fields, and only sister of Lucas Garvey, esq. of the Island of St. Christopher. (*Gent. Mag.* 782)

Lucas Garvey of St Christopher, Esq., Will dated 24 Nov., 1812. To a mullatto boy called Anthony reputed son of my late brother Captain John Garvey deceased of H.M. 3rd Regiment of Buffs £1000. My late sister Ann Baroness Pfeilitzer Proved 16 September, 1815, testator late of Marylebone deceased. (503, *Pakenham*).

Israel Mauduit, F.A.S. & R.S., merchant in Clements Lane, Lombard Street died 14 June, 1787, aged 79.

---

208. North of the Church on a large stone platform is a stone vault with ledger on the top :—

> Here lyeth Interr'd the Body of
> ANTHONY WHARTON Efq^r
> who departed this Life November 4th 1758
> In the 57th Year of His Age.

By Elizabeth his wife he had two sons Aretas died 1806. Will (179 *Pitt*) and Anthony and three daughters Rebecca married 1759 Capt. James Young, Mary married John Julius, and Elizabeth married Ravel Kerie. See his book-plate No. 701 See *Caribbeana* I., 78 for William Wharton.

---

209. The three following graves are enclosed by a low wall :—

> Red granite tomb.
> SACRED TO THE MEMORY OF
> THOMAS SWANSTON, ESQ^{RE} M.D.
> DIED 18TH DAY NOVEMBER, 1873
> AGED 80 YEARS.
> AFTER A RESIDENCE OF OVER 50 YEARS
> IN THIS ISLAND.

Greyfriars Churchyard, Edinburgh. Monumental Inscription to William Swanston, Esq., late of St. Christopher, died in Edinburgh 7 July, 1820, aged 55 (p. 127).

---

210.   Grey granite tomb with cross lying on it :—

IN MEMORY OF AGNES MARGARET
LOVING AND BELOVED WIFE OF W. W. REID
WHO DIED AT DUPORTS
ON THE 17TH MAY 1874 AT THE AGE OF 45 YEARS

---

211.   Red granite pedestal surmounted by a white marble cross :—

IN MEMORY OF | HELEN ALICE SWANSTON | SECOND DAUGHTER OF
THE LATE | JAMES SWANSTON | OF MARSHALL MEADOWS | IN THE CO. OF |
BERWICK-UPON-TWEED, ENGLAND | WHO DIED IN THIS ISLAND | ON THE 19TH OF
FEBRUARY 1869, | AGED 22 |

BAPTISMS.

1737, Sept. 20. Elizabeth, daughter of Anthony and Elizabeth Wharton, born March 3rd.

1739, Nov.   1. Rebecca, daughter of Anthony Wharton and Elizabeth his wife, born January 31st, 1738.

1741, Aug.   6. Christopher, son of Anthony Wharton and Elizabeth his wife, born 3rd.

1744, Feb.   17. Mary, daughter of Mr. Anthony Wharton and Elizabeth his wife, born September 17th.

1746, Oct.   23. Henry, son of Mr. Anthony Wharton and Elizabeth his wife, born September 11th, 1745.

1749, June   4. Anthony, son of Mr. Anthony Wharton and Elizabeth his wife, born May 28th.

MARRIAGE.

1754, May   25. Ravell Kerie and Elizabeth, daughter of Anthony Wharton, Esq.

BURIALS.

1746, Dec.   10. Henry, son of Mr. Anthony Wharton and Elizabeth his wife.

1758, Nov.   5. Anthony Wharton, Esq.

1765, Sept.   18. John Wharton

1775, Dec.   22. Mary Wharton

1779, July   6. Mary Wharton

1793. Aug.   8. Mrs. Elizabeth Wharton, aged 87 years from Basseterre.

GRENADA.

Grenada lies 68 miles south-south-west of St. Vincent, to which it is linked up by a long string of small islands, the Grenadines, of which Carriacou, and all those to the south, belong to the first named.

The island is 21 miles long by 12 miles broad and contains 133 square miles or about 76,500 acres ; it is mountainous and very fertile and beautiful.

It became an English possession by the Treaty of Paris on 10th February, 1763, was retaken by the French on 4th July, 1779, and restored to the English by the Treaty of Versailles on 19th September, 1783.

In 1780 a hurricane caused enormous damage, and in 1795 an insurrection of the slaves and French inhabitants resulted in great destruction of property. Sir W. Young estimated that in each case one third of capital was lost.

Paterson's map of 1780 founded on a survey of 1763, gives six parishes, viz. :—St. George, St. David, St. John, St. Mark, St. Patrick, and St. Andrew, the Island of Carriacou being a separate parish.

By Act No. CI of 1807 the island, instead of being divided into four benefices, was divided into two, the one to consist of St. George, St. John and St. Mark, the rector to reside in St. George's ; the other to consist of St. Patrick, St. Andrew, and St. David, the rector to reside at St. Andrew's. The Island of Carriacou was to form one benefice.

Among the numerous provisions of this Act it was enacted that the pages of the parish register were to be numbered. Each entry was to be also numbered and signed by the Rector and Clerk, but the latter's attestation was afterwards repealed.

By Act. No. CLXVII of 1825 four benefices were created, viz. :—1, St. George's ; 2, the united parishes of St. David and St. Andrew ; 3, St. Patrick's ; 4, the united parishes of St. John and St. Mark.

St. George, the chief town, is built on a promontory on one side of a small landlocked harbour. The position is one of the most picturesque in these beautiful islands.

Fort George on the bluff at the entrance is now used as a signal or police station. Over the entrance arch is cut 1710, and there are several Georgian cannon still mounted on the stone platform. Pere Labat states that this fort was built in 1706 by M. de Cailus the Engineer General (II. 140).

Close to the citadel and on the ridge stands the Scotch Presbyterian Church, then up the hill is the English one, and just beyond, the Roman Catholic one.

A modern tunnel connects the harbour with the bay portion of the town. The Record Office and Library are on the quay.

The town was burnt down in 1771 and 1775 and partially in 1792. Many of the present houses are of brick and look fairly old, dating probably from the last conflagration. Sir W. Young noticed in 1792 the numerous brick buildings.

I landed here several times for a few hours when passing up and down the Islands, and found time to transcribe the tablets in the churches, but nothing more. Of hundreds of well-known officials and planters who died here, there appear to be no memorials, as far as I could discover.

A view of St. George's in 1819 from one of a pair of aquatints appeared in *Carribbeana* I., 97. Three lithograph views in 1833 may be seen in *Four years' residence in the West Indies,"* p. 352, and two others in Andrews' *Illustrations of the West Indies,* vol. II., not dated, but later than 1852.

ST. GEORGE'S.

This Church was probably erected soon after 1763. Sir W. Young wrote in 1792 : " The church is plain, with a handsome steeple, and a clock given by the present Governor Mathews."

H. N. Coleridge wrote in 1825 : " The church had no roof when I was there, but the plan of a new building was already prepared, which was to retain the old spire and its present excellent situation."

Act No. CLXXV of 1826 refers to the church lately erected in the Town of St. George.

The following clergy licensed by the Bishop of London went out to Grenada, but where beneficed I know not—

George Bowdler, 13th September, 1764.
John Cuming, 4th January, 1770.
John Findlater, 18th June, 1771.
Rees Lewis, 31st October, 1785.
Joseph Dent Gilmore, 10th November, 1801.

RECTORS.

John Wingate.

1789, Lately. In the Island of Grenada, the Rev. John Wingate, rector of St. Georges. (*Gent Mag.*, 955).

. . . . Dent, 1792.

March 25. The clergyman, Mr. Dent, read prayers, etc. (*Sir W. Young's Tour*, p. 297).

Francis McMahon. 1807 until his death 22nd November, 1827. He was Rector of George Town, Demerara, June, 1796 to April, 1807. (See No. 6)

John Crawford Barker, 1829—41. 13 years Rector here. Died at Tortola 26th December, 1841, aged 51. (See No. 21 for his wife's grave and No. 5 for his own tablet).

John Nibbs Garland ? 1841-48. Entered Codrington College in 1830 from Antigua. Baptised at St. Philip's 20th February, 1810, as son of Richard and Sarah Coleborn Garland. (See No. 20 to his wife and daughter in 1845).

James Alexander Anton. 1848-85, of Codrington College, 1830. Canon. Died 13th September, 1885, aged 75. Rector 37 years. (M.I. No. 4).

. . . . . Walton. 1914.

IN THE CHURCH.

1. South wall of Nave, near Organ, east end :—

Bust at top supported on the dexter side by a negro and on the sinister side by a white man.

SACRED
TO THE MEMORY OF
JOSEPH MARRYAT, ESQUIRE
OF THE CITY OF LONDON, MERCHANT,
MEMBER OF PARLIAMENT
AND AGENT FOR THIS ISLAND
WHO DURING A PERIOD OF THE UTMOST IMPORTANCE
TO THE WELFARE
AND INTEREST OF THE WEST INDIA COLONISTS
ZEALOUSLY AND ABLY ESPOUSED THEIR CAUSE
ASSERTED THEIR RIGHTS,
AND VINDICATED THEIR CHARACTER
FROM THE CALUMNY AND MISREPRESENTATION
OF THEIR ENEMIES,
IN GRATEFUL ACKNOWLEDGMENT
OF HIS EMINENT SERVICES, AND IN ORDER TO
PERPETUATE THE REMEMBRANCE OF THE SAME,
THE LEGISLATURE OF GRENADA
CAUSED THIS MONUMENT TO BE ERECTED
A.D. 1824.

1824, Jan. 12. Aged 67, Joseph Marryat, Esq., of Wimbledon House, M.P., etc. (*Gent. Mag.* 373).

See account of the Marryats in *Misc. Gen. et Her* 4th S. Vol. III., pp. 336-48, where there is an illustration of the above monument.

2.

ERECTED BY THE MEMBERS
OF THE VOLUNTEER ARTILLERY CORPS
TO THE MEMORY OF
WILLIAM THOMAS TOBIAS HARROLD, *Bugler*
AGED 18 YEARS
AND
JOHN ATHERLEY CALDER, *Gunner,*
AGED 20 YEARS
who lost their lives, by the accidental explosion of the portable magazine, on Sunday, January 5th, 1862, whilst engaged in firing minute guns at Port George on the occasion of the death of His Royal Highness, Albert, the Prince Consort, The Bugler was killed on the spot and his comrade died of his wounds thirteen days after the explosion.

3.

TO THE MEMORY OF
The Late ALEXANDER COCKBURN, ESQ^R, M.D.
WHO IN FULNESS OF YEARS,
AND WITH THE REFLECTION OF A LIFE WELL SPENT,
DEPARTED FROM THIS, FOR A BETTER WORLD,
ON THE 8TH OF NOV^R 1815 ; AGED 76.

(9 lines. A Magistrate and Member of Council).

1816, June. At Grenada, aged 76, Hon. Alexander Cockburn. (*Gent Mag.* p. 638).

In his will he describes himself as of St. George Town, Esq., physician and surgeon, refers to his son George buried there and his wife in St. Andrews, bequeaths to his son Walter his Plantation called Florida in the parish of St. John. Gives Wm. Cockburn of Revolution Hall £500. List of slaves on Florida and Retreat. Proved 1817. (414 *Effingham*).

4.

SACRED TO THE MEMORY OF
Rev : Canon JAS. ALEX^R ANTON
WHO DIED SEPTEMBER 13TH 1885,
AGED 75 YEARS
RECTOR OF THIS PARISH FOR 37 YEARS.

5.

SACRED TO THE MEMORY OF
The Reverend JOHN CRAWFORD BARKER,
A NATIVE OF THE PRINCIPALITY OF WALES,
WHO DEPARTED THIS LIFE AT TORTOLA
ON THE 26TH OF DECEMBER 1841, AGED 51 YEARS.
HIS MINISTERIAL LABOURS IN THE WEST INDIES
EXTENDED TO A PERIOD OF MORE THAN SIXTEEN YEARS
DURING THIRTEEN OF WHICH HE WAS RECTOR OF THIS PARISH
RURAL DEAN OF GRENADA, AND GARRISON CHAPLAIN.

6.

Sacred
TO THE MEMORY OF
THE REV^D FRANCIS M^C MAHON,
WHO AFTER DISCHARGING THE DUTIES
OF RECTOR OF THE PARISH OF S^T PATRICK
FROM 1784 TO 1794,
OF S^T JOHN AND S^T MARK IN 1795
WHEN THE INSURRECTION BROKE OUT,
(FROM THE MASSACRE OF WHICH
HE WAS PROVIDENTIALLY SAVED)
AND OF S^T GEORGES FOR THE LAST 21 YEARS
DIED 22^D NOV^R 1827,
AGED 68 YEARS.

7.

SACRED TO THE MEMORY OF
OWSLEY ROWLEY, ESQ[R]
WHO DEPARTED THIS LIFE ON THE 5TH DECEMBER, 1854, IN HIS 73RD YEAR
OF A REFINED AND REFLECTING MIND AND OF STERLING PRINCIPLES HE DISCHARGED
DURING A PERIOD OF 54 YEARS THE ARDUOUS DUTIES OF COLONIAL SECRETARY
CLERK OF THE COUNCIL REGISTRAR AND CLERK OF THE RESPECTIVE LAW COURTS
IN THIS ISLAND WITH IMPARTIALITY, ENERGY AND UNTIRING ZEAL
ALSO TO THE MEMORY OF CHRISTIAN, HIS WIFE,
DAUGHTER OF ISAACH HORSFORD ESQ[RE]
WHO DIED IN SEPTEMBER, 1853, AGED 76 YEARS.

8.

IN MEMORY OF
THE HON[BLE] GEORGE GUN MUNRO,
SENIOR MEMBER OF HIS MAJESTY'S COUNCIL,
ASSISTANT JUSTICE OF THE SUPREME COURT OF JUDICATURE,
AND PUBLIC TREASURER OF THE COLONY OF GRENADA,
HE DEPARTED THIS LIFE
ON THE 5TH DAY OF NOVEMBER, 1829,
AGED 50 YEARS.

Below—Crest : *An eagle with wings raised.*
Arms : *Argent an eagle's head erased.* Motto : " DREAD GOD."

See *Caribbeana* I, 76 for Monumental Inscription to Capt. Matthew Munro of this Island.

Barkly Justin Gun Munro from Grenada was at Codrington College in 1848 (*Bindley*).

9.

TO THE BELOVED MEMORY
OF A MOST AFFECTIONATE AND DUTIFUL CHILD
FRANCIS PROBY PELHAM STEWART-MACKENZIE,
LIEUTENANT IN THE 71ST HIGHLAND LIGHT INFANTRY,
AND FORT ADJUTANT OF GRENADA,
WHO WAS CUT OFF IN THE 24TH YEAR OF HIS AGE,
BY YELLOW FEVER 21ST DECEMBER, 1844.
THIS TABLET IS ERECTED BY
HIS SORROWING MOTHER.
HE WAS THE SECOND SON OF THE LATE
RIGHT HON[BLE] JAMES ALEXANDER STEWART-MACKENZIE.

(buried at Fort Adolphus).

See *Peerage* under Galloway and Seaforth.

---

10. North wall of Nave beginning at east end :—

SACRED TO THE MEMORY OF
THE REV^D WILLIAM HEATH, M.A.
FORMERLY FELLOW OF KING'S COLLEGE, CAMBRIDGE,
AND FOR MANY YEARS ASSISTANT MASTER OF ETON COLLEGE,
HE DIED ON THE 26TH OF NOVEMBER, 1838, AGED 51 YEARS,
AFTER A RESIDENCE OF SIXTEEN MONTHS IN GRENADA.

---

11.   INSCRIBED BY FRATERNAL AFFECTION,
THIS TABLET
IS SACRED TO THE MEMORY OF CATHARINE DICKINSON,
WIFE OF NODES DICKINSON, ESQ^R SURGEON TO THE FORCES IN THIS ISLAND,
(died) ON THE 8TH SEPTEMBER, 1813,
AGED 27 YEARS

See her vault in the Scotch Churchyard.

---

12. Above is an eagle and four young. Signed " WESTMACOTT, Junr.,
Fecit, London " :—

Sacred to the Memory | of |
MATHER BYLES, ESQ^R
who was Born at Boſton in N. E.
and Died
Friday the 17TH day of December, 1802
In the 38TH Year of his Age
erected by his brother BELCHER BYLES.

In 1795 he was Secretary to Lieut.-Governor Ninian Home.

Rev. Mather Byles (Missionary at Christ Church in New England) D.D. by diploma 6th April, 1770, died 1788. (*Foster*).

Mather Byles went out to New England 30th June, 1768, son of Mather Byles, Rector of Christ Church, Boston, born 12th January, 1735, died 12th March, 1814. (*Fothergill*).

---

13.   TO THE MEMORY OF
SARAH, WIFE OF JOHN KIPPING, ESQ^R :
WHO DIED ON THE 22ND OF DECEMBER, 1820,
AGED 56 YEARS.

---

14. SACRED TO THE MEMORY OF THOMAS JAMES POWELL, AND SAMUEL HARRISON, D.A. COMMISSARIES GENERAL, | THE FORMER DIED THE 17TH OF SEPTEMBER, 1817, AGED 26 YEARS, | AND THE LATTER THE 8TH OF OCTOBER FOLLOWING, AGED 22 YEARS.

(Buried at the Military Burial Ground, Hospital Hill).

1817, Oct. 8. At Grenada, aged 31, Samuel Harrison, Esq., Deputy-Assistant Commissary-General to His Majesty's Forces. (*Gent Mag.* 562).

---

15.   Sacred to the Memory of
        ISAAC HORSFORD Esquire and MARY ANN his Wife
               who were born in the Island of Antigua,
      but were resident in this Colony for more than half a Century
                  wherein at different periods | He |
    Filled the important Offices of Collector of H.M. Customs for the Port of
                              Grenville |
             Member of the Honourable House of Assembly,
          and Colonel of the Sᵗ Andrews Regiment of Militia,
                                          She (died)
               upon the 31ˢᵗ day of January, 1827, aged 77 years.
    And he upon the 4ᵗʰ day of June, 1830, at the patriarchal age of 87.

    Evidently son of Geo. Horsford of Antigua by Henrietta, daughter of Colonel John Sawcolt ; baptised 21st August, 1743, as Isaac Lucas. His brother William was also of Grenada in 1780. Capt. Yeamans Horsford was here in 1795. See pedigree in *Antigua* II., 86.

---

    16. The following three tablets are on the west wall of Nave near the font. On a tablet ornamented with military trophies :—

                           In Remembrance
                         Of thofe Brave Men,
                       OFFICERS and PRIVATES
                        In His Majefty's Service,
                     And Inhabitants of this Colony,
                 Who loft their Lives in Defence of it,
                         During the Rebellion
                       That existed in the Years
                            1795, and 1796,
                      (Moft of whom were cut off
                       In the Flower of their Youth ;)
                       The Legiflature of *Grenada*
                       Have placed this Tablet here,
                      As a Record of their Gratitude
             To the Memory of the unfortunate Sufferers :
                             A.D. 1799.
                 The Names of our Fellow-Colonifts,
                   who died at that eventful Period,
                      (Either in the Field of Battle,
         Or of Difeafes produced by exceffive Fatigue)
                          Are too numerous
                  To be infcribed within the Compafs
                             Of this Stone ;
                           And the Selection
                   Of any Individuals amongft them,
                        Would be Injuftice
                           To the Others.

---

17. At the top is an Urn and on each side a kneeling woman :—

SACRED To THE MEMORY OF

His Honor *Ninian Home,* Efq^re Lieutenant Governour, etc., etc.,

A. Campbell,	M. McCarthy,	W. Gilchrist,
J. Farquhar,	P. Cumming,	C. McCarthy,
P. Fotheringham,	A. Ker,	R. Davis,
G. Rose,	F. Johnstone,	J. Rice,
G. Walker,	P. Le Pelley,	J. Shea,
S. Ought,	J. Livingston,	D. McDougall,
W. Muir,	J. Jackson,	E. H. Johnston,
R. Webster,	F. D. Carruthers,	J. Butler,
J. Wyce,		

B. Johnston,	W. Hawkes,
W. Kinnard,	J. Barlow,
H. McCoul,	J. Cuthbert,
J. T. Guy,	J. Morris,
J. R. Linton,	P. Thompson,
J. Mercer,	M. Atkinson,
E. Matthews,	J. Thornton,
R. Todd,	W. Bell,

Proprietors and Inhabitants of this Colony ;

All of whom were taken Prifoners, on the 3rd of March, 1795,

By an execrable Banditti,

Compof'd principally of white new-adopted Subjects of this Ifland,

And their free colour'd Defcendants ;

Who ftimulated by the infidious Arts of *French* Republicans,

Loft all Senfe of Duty to their Sovereign,

And unmindful of the Advantages they had long enjoy'd,

By participating in the Bleffings of the *Britifh* Conftitution,

Open'd on that Day

Thofe deftructive Scenes which nearly defolated the whole Country ;

And on the 8th of April following,

Completed the Meafure of their Iniquity,

By barbaroufly murdering

(In the Rebel-Camp at *Mount Quaqua*),

The above innocent Victims to their diabolical & Unprovok'd Cruelty,

As a Tribute of Gratitude to DIVINE PROVIDENCE,

For having refcued the Colony

From the Horrors of Rebellion, and from utter Ruin ;

As well as to tranfmit to Pofterity

A Record of the melancholy Fate of their Fellow-Colonifts ;

This Monument is placed here

By the Legiflature of *Grenada* :

A.D. 1799.

Weftmacott Junr London.

---

18. Tablet with Naval trophies :—

To the Memory
Of JOSIAS ROGERS Efquire,
Captain
Of His Majefty's Ship *Quebec* ;
Who came to the Relief
Of this Ifland,
Immediately after
The Commencement of the horrid Rebellion
Which broke out on the 3rd of March, 1795 ;
And who died
On Board of his Ship in the Harbour of *Saint George*
. On the 25th of April, 1795,
Of a malignant Fever,
Caught by his Exertions in Defence of the Colony.
The Legiflature of *Grenada*
Have caufed this Tablet
To be placed here.
A.D. 1799

His Memoir, published in 1808, contains an illustration of the above tablet.
There is also a monument to him at Lymington, County Hants. See *Caribbeana*
III., 286.

Admiral Edmund Lord Lyons married 18 July, 1814, Augusta Louisa, second
daughter of the above.

IN THE CHURCHYARD.

19. Against the south wall of the Nave, white marble :—

HERE lie the Remains
of JOHN MILLS *Efqr*
late Collector of his Majefty's Cuftoms,
for ST GEORGES in this Ifland.
He departed this Life
AUGST 15TH 1784, Aged 42 ;
& left behind a Widow,
& fix Children. (Etc.)

He was eldest son of Tho. Mills of Nevis and Enfield by Frances his wife,
baptised at St. George, Basseterre, St. Kitts, 6th January, 1742-3. Monumental Inscription also at Hitchin, County Herts.

20.

HERE LIE THE MORTAL REMAINS
OF
JULIA MARIA DOLORES,
THE BELOVED WIFE OF
THE REVD JOHN NIBBS GARLAND
RECTOR OF ST GEORGE'S PARISH
AND OF JULIA EUGENIA
THEIR INFANT DAUGHTER
THE FORMER DIED ON THE
10TH DAY OF FEBRUARY, 1845
AGED 28 YEARS
THE LATTER ON THE
19TH DAY OF MARCH AGED 5 WEEKS

21.
Here lie the mortal
remains of
ANN S. BARKER,
Wife of the
REV. J. C. BARKER
Rector of this Parifh
She died on the 30 of
April, 1829
AGED 24 YEARS.

The Sexton told me that the French were formerly buried in this south side of the church yard.

SCOTTISH CHURCH, ST. GEORGE'S, GRENADA.

By Act No. CCXVII of 1830 the old Court House Lot was conveyed to Trustees for erecting a Presbyterian Church. The organ stands at the east end. There are only two tablets in the Church.

22. On the north side of the east wall :—

In Memory of | GEORGE MACEWAN | for nearly forty years | a Medical Practitioner in this Town | for several years a Member of Assembly | and Magistrate of the Colony | who died at Edinburgh 16TH October, 1834 | (Four lines. Erected by his brother James Macewan).

23. On the south side of the east wall :—

In Memory of | WILLIAM NOBLE JAMIESON GUTHRIE | STUDENT AT LAW | BORN 13TH FEBRUARY A.D. 1854 | DIED 7TH JANUARY A.D. 1875.

IN THE CHURCHYARD.

24. On a headstone :—

CHARLES SHULDHAM FRASER | *STIPENDIARY MAGISTRATE* | DIED OCTOBER 4TH 1850 | AGED 67 YEARS.

1850, Oct. 4. At Grenada, aged 67, Charles Shuldham Fraser, esq., stipendiary magistrate for the district of St. George. (*Gent Mag.* 678).

25. On two pieces of a broken white marble slab within iron railings :—

SACRED | TO THE MEMORY OF | DUNDAS RAMSAY | A NATIVE OF ABERDEEN, SCOTLAND | AND RESIDENT OF THE ISLAND OF | . . THOMAS | DIED THE 6TH OF DECEMBER 1841 | AGED 33 YEARS.

26.   On a flat stone :—

SACRED | TO THE MEMORY OF | A. DUFF MILNE ESQ^R | ASS^T SURGEON OF | H.M.S. PIQUE, | who departed this Life on | the 13th August 1843 | at the early Age of 27 years |. (Five lines.   Erected by his brother officers).

27.   On a headstone :—

Sacred | TO THE MEMORY OF | JOHN AHMUTY ESQ^R | BARRISTER | OF THE INNER TEMPLE | LONDON | DIED 6TH OCTOBER 1786 | AGED 30 YEARS.

The Inscription looks much later than 1786.
1786, Nov.   John Ahmuty, esq., barrister-at-law, of the Island of Grenada. (*Gent. Mag.* 671).
1831, June.   Lately.   At Lymington, aged 75, the widow of John Ahmuty, Esq., of the Inner Temple, and of the Island of Grenada, barrister-at-law. (*Ib.* 573).

28.   On a slab resting on columns :—

IN MEMORY OF WILLIAM HAMILTON, | OF GLASGOW, | WHO DIED 14 DECEMBER 1836 | AGED 38 YEARS.

29.   On a ledger over a brick vault :—

SACRED | To the Memory of CATHARINE | Wife of NODES DICKINSON Esquire | *Late Surgeon to the Forces in this Island* | who departed this life | on the 8th September, 1813 | aged 27 Years.

30.   IN MEMORY OF | MARY ANN RONEY | .   (5 lines illegible).

31.   On a headstone of white marble :—

THE REV. HENRY COCKBURN | MINISTER OF THE SCOTCH CHURCH HERE | DIED ON THE 19TH JULY 1854 | IN THE 53^D YEAR OF HIS AGE | AND 16TH OF HIS MINISTRY.   (4 lines.   Erected by his widow).

32.   On a headstone :—

In memory of | JOSIAH HUTCHINGS FRITH | Born in *BERMUDA* | January 4th 1826 | Departed this life | September 4th 1850.

33.   On a ledger :—

SACRED | TO THE MEMORY OF | HELEN COUGHLAN | YOUNGEST DAUGHTER OF | DR COUGHLAN LATE STAFF SURGEON | AT HALIFAX AND NIECE | OF JOSEPH CLARKE ESQUIRE | OF H.M. CUSTOMS IN THIS ISLAND | SHE DIED REGRETTED BY | ALL WHO KNEW HER | ON THE 30TH DAY OF JULY, 1838 | AGED 21 YEARS.

34.   Adjoining the above is another ledger with a crack across it :—

SACRED | TO THE MEMORY OF | JOSEPH CLARKE | WHO AFTER SERVING AS A | LIEUTENANT IN THE 48TH REGIMENT | THROUGH THE PENINSULA | CAMPAIGN WAS APPOINTED | OFFICER OF H. M. CUSTOMS AND | DIED WHILST ON THAT SERVICE | ON THE 15TH DAY OF AUGUST, 1838 | AGED 53 YEARS.

There are several other brick vaults without slabs.

Up the hill above the Roman Catholic Church is a large burial ground which was opened after the cholera in 185·.   There are dozens of vaults, but mostly without top slabs, merely cemented over.   Either the slabs have been stolen or they were never sent out from England.   Many are in a ruinous state.   I had not time to copy the inscriptions.

ST. JOHNS AND ST. MARK.
RECTORS.

Francis McMahon, 1795.
John McTair.
Annuity granted to his infant children 2nd April, 1807.   (*Acts* p. 249).
Samuel Rous Moe.   Died 1842.
1842, May 27.   In London, the Rev. Sam. Rous Moe, Rector of St. Johns in the Island of Grenada, son of the Hon. Miles Brathwaite, of Barbadoes.   (*Gent Mag.* 215).   He was fifth son.   Monumental Inscription in Highgate Cemetery. (*Cansick* II., 154).
Chas. Gordon Cumming Dunbar, D.D.   Rural Dean and Archdeacon, 1875.
Charles Arthur, 1895.
Canon 1909.   He wrote that the Register dates from 1809.

ST. ANDREW AND ST. DAVID.

Act No. CCXXII of 1831 refers to the churches newly erected in the out-Parishes of St. Andrew, St. David and St. Patrick.

RECTORS.

Geo. Wm. Sisnett, 1875.   Of Codrington College, 1855.
A. Honbersley, 1895.

ST. DAVID.

Charles Bispham.   Curate 1875.
Frederick Francis Canarikin Mallalieu.   Perpetual Curate 1895.
Member of Codrington College from St. Kitts, 1881.   B.A. Durham.

ST. PATRICK.

RECTORS.

Francis McMahon, 1784-94.   Died 22 Nov., 1827, aged 68.   M.I. No.6.

Geo. Augustus Gentle, 1875.   Of Codrington College.   Canon and Archdeacon 1884-9 and later.

ST. PAUL AND ST. CLEMENT.

This appears to be a new ecclesiastical parish.

Geo. W. Branch.   Curate 1875 and Perpetual Curate 1895.

ISLAND OF CARRIACOU

RECTORS.

. . . Nash.   H. N. Coleridge wrote in 1825 " that a church had been built by a clergyman of the name of Nash in Cariacou (p. 114).   Probably Wm. Nash who went out to Barbadoes 17 December, 1800.

Arthur John Pilgrim Buchanan, 1847.

1847, Feb. 4.   At St. George's Church, Grenada, the Rev. Arthur John Pilgrim Buchanan, Rector of Carriacou, son of the late Capt. Colin Buchanan, H.M. 62d Regiment to Margaret Ann, daughter of the Hon. Francis Jemmitt, of Richmond Estate in Grenada   (*Gent. Mag.*).

John Connell.   Rector 1875.   ? Of Codrington College 1842.

ST. LUCIA.

HOLY TRINITY, CASTRIES.

1.   On the north wall of the Nave :—

TO THE MEMORY OF | WILLIAM PATTISON, | A NATIVE OF GLASGOW, | DIED 12 FEBRUARY, 1143, | AGED 50.

---

2.   SACRED | TO THE MEMORY OF | THE REVEREND CHARLES SIMS, | THE RESPECTED AND BELOVED PASTOR OF | THE PROTESTANT INHABITANTS OF | SAINT LUCIA | BY WHOM THIS TABLET IS ERECTED AS | A TRIBUTE OF ESTEEM AND REGARD | HE DEPARTED THIS LIFE | IN THE YEAR 1842.

---

3.   On the south wall :—

IN MEMORY OF | MARY JANE REID | DAUGHTER OF ROBERT REID | WHO DIED ON THE 31ST OF AUGUST 1852 | AGED 8 YEARS.

---

4.   On a stone fixed in the exterior of the south wall of the Chancel :—

THIS STONE | WAS LAID TO THE GLORY OF GOD | BY HIS EXCELLENCY SIR CHARLES BRUCE, K.C.M.G. | GOVERNOR OF THE WINDWARD ISLANDS | ON NOV. 25TH 1894 | REV. J. R. BASCOM, INCUMBENT | S.T. WENBORN, ARCHDEACON.

I had no opportunity to copy inscriptions in the Churchyard.

· TOBAGO.

GOVERNMENT HOUSE, SCARBOROUGH.

Copies of the four following Monumental Inscriptions were sent by Mr. Archibald Bell (now Director of Public Works in Trinidad) in September, 1917, to Mr. A. E. Aspinall and were by the latter passed on to me in August, 1921.

They are apparently inscribed on the flat stones of vaults, which together with a fifth one, containing the body of Sir William Young without inscription, stand in a fenced enclosure about 30ft. by 18ft. in the grounds surrounding the house.

Photographs of the latter taken by Mrs. Bell show a plain brick building of one floor, without verandahs, which Mr. Bell thinks was erected early in the nineteenth century.

It stands on a hill about a mile North of Scarborough and contains fine, large and lofty rooms with a quantity of good old furniture. (These inscriptions with illustration of Government House subsequently appeared in the *W.I.C. Circular*, vol. 37, p. 446).

1.

To the Memory | of
HARRIET Daughter
of Sir F. P. ROBINSON, | K.C.B.
Governor of Tobago
She died January 9TH 1819
aged 10 years
of the Malignant Fever with
which the Island was then
Afflicted.

John Robinson, President of Virginia, married Catherine, daughter of Robert Beverly of Yorkshire, and had a son Beverley Robinson, Colonel of Militia, a Loyalist who died at Bath 9 April, 1792, aged 70, having married Susanna Philipse, great grand-daughter of Frederick Philipse who owned 390 square miles near the Hudson River. She died at Bath, Nov., 1822, aged 94. Their fourth son Frederick Philipse Robinson born near New York, Sept., 1763, served in the West Indies in 1793 in the Peninsula War and Canada, K.C.B., 1815, Governor of Tobago, 1816, G.C.B., 1838, General 1841, and died 1 Jan., 1852, aged 88. (*Gent. Mag.* 188). By his first wife Grace, daughter of Thomas Boles of Charleville he had a numerous family. She died 27 May, 1806 in Pimlico. (*Gent. Mag.* 586). See the *D.N.B.*

2.

To the memory | of |
Lieut[t] F. P. ROBINSON | of |
The 4th Regiment of Foot
Aid de camp & Private Secretary
to his father
Sir F. P. ROBINSON, K.C.B.
Governor of Tobago
He died of a Malignant | Fever |
March 15th 1820
in the 21st year of his age.

3.

To the memory | of |
AUGUSTA ROBINSON
4th daughter of
Sir F. P. ROBINSON K.C.B.
She died of a Malignant | Fever |
April 19th 1820 in the 15th
year of her age

J. PELLINARI.

4.

Here lies the Body of
ANNE
The Wife of
His Excellency
Sir F. P. ROBINSON
Governor of Tobago
She died on the 6th day of | October 1823
in the 60th | year of her age after a
painful and tedious illness.

C. ROSSI, BARBADOS.

She was a Miss Fernihough of Stafford and was married in 1811 as second wife.

---

5. The vault containing the body of Sir Wm. Young, second Baronet, has no inscription. A public memorial tablet provided by the House of Assembly is in the Church at Scarborough.

TRINIDAD.

CATHEDRAL, PORT OF SPAIN.

1. On the north wall of the Nave are 16 tablets :—

Sacred |to the memory of | EVELINA MARGARET | *daughter of* | DANIEL AND ADELAIDE BASANTA | *and wife of* | MANUEL ANTONIO TORO *who departed this life* | OCTOBER 27, 1863 | AT PONCE, PORTO RICO AGED 34 YEARS AND 24 DAYS.

2. Below the preceding :—

EMILIÆ WISSETT CALVERT | QUÆ OBIIT | PRID : NON : SEPT. A.D. MDCCCLIX.| CONJUGI DVLCISSIMÆ | SORORI. AMANTISSIMÆ. | MARITVS. E. C. FRATER G. F. W. | LYCENTES | P.C.

3. A pair of tablets side by side :—

Sacred | TO THE MEMORY OF | JOHN HENRY VAN RHYN | *who DEPARTED THIS LIFE* |APRIL 8 1864 | AT PONCE, PORTO RICO

4. Sacred | TO THE MEMORY OF | ADELAIDE EMILY | AND | GRACE EVELINA | *infant daughters of* | JOHN HENRY AND GRACE LOUISA | VAN RHYN | *who departed this life* 1ST FEBRUARY 14, 1857 | AGED 2 MONTHS AND 6 DAYS | 2ND JUNE 24, 1862 | AGED 10 MONTHS AND 8 DAYS.

5. Sacred | TO THE MEMORY OF | JOHN CARR ESQRE | OF THE SILVER STREAM ESTATE | FOR MANY YEARS AN INHABITANT | OF THIS ISLAND ; | HE DIED ON THE 4TH DAY OF APRIL A.D. 1828 | AGED 47 YEARS.

THIS TABLET | IS ERECTED TO HIS MEMORY BY HIS SON | THE HONBLE JOHN CARR | OF SIERRA LEONE.

6. THIS TABLET | SACRED TO THE MEMORY | OF | ALFRED HENRY MARTIN, M.B. | OF TRINITY COLLEGE, DUBLIN, | AND SUPERINTENDENT OF | THE LUNATIC ASYLUM OF THIS ISLAND | SON OF | JAMES MARTIN ESQRE F.R.C.S.I. | OF PORTLAW | COUNTY OF WATERFORD, IRELAND | BORN 28TH AUGUST 1849 | DIED IN TRINIDAD 29TH OCTOBER 1881.

7. To the east of the north door of Nave, Gothic tablet :—

This Tablet | SACRED TO THE MEMORY | OF | **Jane Lady Hill** | DAUGHTER OF | THE LATE RIGHT HONORABLE JOHN BERESFORD OF IRELAND | AND OF HIS WIFE ANNETTE LEGONDI | OF THE KINGDOM OF FRANCE | AND WIFE OF | THE HONORABLE **Sir George Fitzgerald Hill** | OF BROOK HALL IN THE COUNTY OF LONDONDERRY IN | IRELAND, BARONET, LIEUTENANT GOVERNOR OF THIS COLONY. | **She was born** ON THE 13TH DAY OF JUNE 1769 | WAS MARRIED ON THE 10TH SEPTEMBER 1788 | AND DEPARTED THIS LIFE ON THE 2ND NOVEMBER 1836 | HER MORTAL REMAINS WERE INTERRED IN COMPLIANCE WITH | HER OWN DIRECTIONS IN THE GARDENS OF THE GOVERNMENT HOUSE AT ST ANNS.

She was niece of the first Marquess of Waterford.   Her husband was M.P., P.C., Governor of St. Vincent 1830, Lieut-Governor of Trinidad, April, 1833 until his death there 8th March, 1839, aged 75. (See long notice in *Gent. Mag.* 89)

8.   On a brass below No. 7 :—

To the loved Memory of Thomas J. Murray late of Woodbrook | **born September 28th 1804, died Novr 10th 1888, son of | the late Henry Murray lieut H.M. 57th Regt | and of | Charlotte, born November 10th 1810, died Novr 24th 1853 ; | wife of the above and daughter of the late Richard Galwey | lieut H.M. 57th Regt**

See account of this family in *Caribbeana* I., 334.

9.   SACRED | TO THE MEMORY OF | HENRY JAMES MATSON ESQRE | CAPTAIN IN THE ROYAL NAVY | OF SEAFIELD LODGE, EMSWORTH, HANTS | ONE OF HER MAJESTY'S JUSTICES OF THE PEACE | FOR THE COUNTIES OF HANTS AND SUSSEX| HE DIED OF THE YELLOW FEVER AFTER FOUR DAYS ILLNESS | WHILST IN COMMAND OF H.M. STEAMSHIP HIGHFLYER | AT THIS ISLAND ON THE 14TH OF DECEMBER 1852 | AGED 43 YEARS |.

Below is a shield of arms cut in white marble.
Crest : Broken off and missing.   Motto : IN RECTO DECUS.
Arms : Quarterly, 1 & 4. *On a chevron sable three mullets between as many martlets* ; 2 & 3, *Per fess sable and Or a pale counterchanged three cinquefoils.*

See pedigree in *Caribbeana* I., 130.

10.   Below No. 9 :—

Sacred to the memory of | ELIZA BUSHE | the young Mother of five Infant Children, | Daughter of CHARLES GIBBONS HOBSON | of Dominica, and wife to | ROBERT BUSHE Esqr | of this Island ; | Born 1st of March 1801, | Died 20th of March, 1835.

1848, June 6. At Port of Spain, Trinidad, John Scott Bushe, eldest son of the late Robert Bushe of Dublin, to Martha Macnamara, eldest daughter of the Venerable Archdeacon Cummings, and great niece of the late Admiral Macnamara (*Gent. Mag.* 199)

11.   On a brass below No. 10 :—

To the Glory of God | And in loving Memory of | the Rev. S. Richards born Aug. 5th | 1820, died Feb. 15th 1877, for many years Rector of the | Parish of holy Trinity and Rural Dean : | and of Louisa, born July 14th 1828, died Nov: 24th 1900, widow | of the above and daughter of the late T. Murray of Woodbrook.

Samuel L. Bruce Richards student Codrington Coll. M.A. (Clergy List for 1876).

---

12.   SACRED | TO THE MEMORY OF | HENRY SCOTT | WHO DIED OF CHOLERA | ON THE 23RD OF SEPTEMBER 1854 | AGED 56   Deceased was for many years | a much respected Merchant | and a Member of the Legislative Council of this Island.

1854, Sept. 23.   At Port of Spain, Trinidad, aged 56, Henry Scott, Senior Member of the Legislative Council. (*Gent. Mag.* 639).

13.

Crest : *A griffin's head erased.*   Motto : MORS . MIHI . LUCRUM . EST.

Arms : Quarterly 1 & 4, *Paly of six Gules and Argent debruised of a bend Ermine* ; 2 & 3, *three lions passant guardant in pale.*

To the Memory of | DORA, WIFE OF THOMAS BLIGH DARRACOTT | THIS TABLET IS ERECTED. (9 lines. She sought health in Bermuda) ON THE 4TH NOVᴮ 1835 SHE DEPARTED THIS LIFE 23 YEARS | OF AGE. (Buried in the burial ground of St. John's Church, Bermuda).

---

14.   On a brass :—

Crest : *A lion rampant, in its paws an axe.*

Arms : *Argent between three hurts, on a chervon Azure a lion rampant between two fleurs de lis.*   Motto : VIRTUTE VICIT.

IN LOVING MEMORY OF | EMILIUS JULIUS WAINWRIGHT, | OF PORT OF SPAIN, TRINIDAD | BORN MARCH 29TH 1829, | DIED AUGUST 21ST 1897.

---

15.   A weeping woman below an urn.

A baron's coronet.   Arms of Harris, impaling, *Argent three garbs.*

SACRED TO THE MEMORY OF | SARAH LADY HARRIS | WIFE OF GEORGE FRANCIS ROBERT 3RD LORD HARRIS, GOVERNOR OF TRINIDAD | AND DAUGHTER OF THE VENERABLE GEORGE CUMMINS ARCHDEACON OF TRINIDAD | SHE DIED AT BARBADOS ON THE 6TH OF MARCH 1853, IN THE 22ND YEAR OF HER AGE | AND IS INTERRED IN THE CEMETERY OF PORT OF SPAIN.

1850, April 16.   At Trinidad, His Excellency the Right Hon. George Frank Lord Harris, Governor and Commander-in-Chief of that colony, to Sarah, second and youngest daughter of the Venerable George Cummins, A.M. Archdeacon of Trinidad. (*Gent. Mag.* 200)

1851, April. Lately. At Trinidad, Lady Harris, a son and heir. (*Gent. Mag.* 420).

1852, Aug. 23. At St. Ann's, Trinidad, Lady Harris, a daughter. (*Ib.* 519).

1853, March 6. At Worthing, Barbados, aged 21, the Right Hon. Sarah Lady Harris, etc. (*Ib.* 560).

16. On a brass :—

𝔍n 𝔪emory of | S𝔦R 𝔍𝔞𝔪𝔈S R𝔒B𝔈R𝔗 𝔏𝔒𝔫𝔊𝔇𝔈ℜ G.C.𝔪.G. | born 7tb 𝔍uly 1827 | died 4tb 𝔒ctober 1891 | sometime Governor of tbis Colony.

He was President of the Virgin Islands 1861, Lieut.-Governor of Dominica 1865, Lieut.-Governor of British Honduras 1867, Governor of Trinidad 1870, Governor of British Guiana 1874.

17. On the south wall of the Nave :—

Sacred | TO THE MEMORY OF | MICHAEL CUMMING | WHO DIED THE 10TH NOVR 1840 | AGED 21 YEARS | LEAVING A YOUNG WIFE | TWO INFANT SONS | AND HIS PARENTS | TO MOURN HIS EARLY DEATH |

18. SACRED | TO THE MEMORY OF | JOHN WILSON ESQ | OF GARDEN ESTATE, TRINIDAD | WHO DIED THERE | ON THE 26TH APRIL 1833, | AGED 66 YEARS.

Robert Wilson (son of Mr. Wilson who owned four plantations in Trinidad), Member of Council 1857, later Deputy Governor of the Bank of Ireland, died in Dublin, married Rose Adelaide daughter of Henry Hart Anderson of Trinidad. She had nine children of whom two sons died young, and Herbert the only surviving son a K.C. in Dublin and six daughters are living. Mrs. Wilson resided for the latter years of her life at Weymouth and died recently.

19. SACRED | TO THE MEMORY OF | LEWIS F. C. JOHNSTON ESQR | FOR MANY YEARS | A JUDGE OF THIS ISLAND | WHO PERISHED ON HIS VOYAGE | TO TRINIDAD | IN THE ROYAL MAIL STEAM SHIP | AMAZON | ON THE 4TH OF JANUARY 1852 | AGED 64 YEARS |. (Erected by his daughter).

1834, Sept. 29. At Trinity Church, Trinidad, T. R. Stansfield, Esq., Lieut. 19th Regiment of Foot, second son of R. Stansfield, Esq., Field House, Halifax, to Hannah Lætitia, the daughter of L. F. C. Johnson, Esq., one of H.M. Judges of Trinidad. (*Court Mag.* for 1835, Vol. VI.)

1842, April 25. At the Breck, near Halifax, Jane, wife of Lewis F. C. Johnston, one of H.M. Judges of Trinidad. (*Gent. Mag.* 676).

Many West Indians must have been lost in this ship, as reference to it is to be seen on tablets in several islands.

20. SACRED TO THE MEMORY OF | FREDERICK MOORE WARDE, LATE AN ENSIGN | IN HIS MAJESTY'S 1ST OR ROYAL REGIMENT OF FOOT, | AND THIRD SON OF | GENERAL SIR HENRY WARDE WHOSE MORTAL REMAINS REST IN THE | MILITARY BURIAL GROUND NEAR ST JAMES'S | BARRACKS OF THIS ISLAND.   (Erected by his parents).

1830, Nov. 27.   At Trinidad, aged 18, Ensign F. M. Warde, 1st Regiment, son of General Sir Henry Warde, K.C.B., of Dean House, near Alresford, and late Governor of Barbados.   (*Gent. Mag.* for 1831, p. 286).

———

21. SACRED | TO THE MEMORY OF | HENRY MURRAY, B.A. | A PIOUS AND WORTHY CHRISTIAN | AND AN EXEMPLARY SON AND BROTHER | BORN 28TH NOVEMBER, 1802 | DIED 3RD MARCH, 1838.

———

22. SACRED TO THE MEMORY OF | JANE CLOGSTOUN WARNER, | THE BELOVED WIFE OF | THORNTON WARNER, ESQUIRE | OF THIS ISLAND | SHE WAS BORN THE 5TH OF AUGUST 1818, | AND DIED THE 14TH OF JUNE 1839, | AT SEA ON HER VOYAGE TO ENGLAND. .

A daughter of J. Johnson, Chief Justice of the Island, she was married in 1836 as his first wife and left an only child Ashton Henry Warner, born 10 Nov., 1838, a Colonel in the Army who settled in Launceston, Tasmania.
Thornton Warner was born here 10 March, 1812, eldest son of Ashton Warner the Chief Justice.   He was educated at Harrow, entered the Colonial Civil Service and was alive in 1858.   See pedigree in *Antigua* III, 188.

———

23.   At the south door is a life size recumbent figure of the Governor reading a book.

TO THE MEMORY OF | SIR RALPH JAMES WOODFORD, BARONET | FOR FIFTEEN YEARS GOVERNOR OF THE COLONY AND FOUNDER OF THIS CHURCH | WHO WAS BORN ON THE 21ST JULY 1784 AND DIED ON THE 16TH MAY 1828 |.   (7 lines.   Public monument erected by the inhabitants).   Signed—CHANTREL, SCULP. 1839, LONDON.

In St. Clement Eastcheap, City of London, is a monument to his wife Gertrude, who died 17 June, 1796.
1812.   Downing Street, Sept. 21.   Sir Ralph Woodford, Bart., to be Governor of the Island of Trinidad.   (*Gent. Mag.* 389).
1828, May 17.   On board H.M. Packet the " Duke of York," when returning towards England, aged 44, Sir Ralph James Woodford, second baronet of Carleby in Lincolnshire and Governor of Trinidad, 15 years, etc.   (*Ib.* 373).
1834, Jan. 11.   At Trinidad, aged 29, Frederick James Gordon Hammet, second son of the late Viscountess de Rosmordue, and nephew to His Excellency the late Sir Ralph Woodford, Bart., formerly Governor of that Island.   (*Ib.* 558).

———

24. SACRED | TO THE MEMORY OF | JAMES EDWARD MURRAY | A MOST AFFECTIONATE | AND DUTIFUL SON, AND EXEMPLARY BROTHER | BORN 4ᵀᴴ OF APRIL 1814 | DIED 21ˢᵀ OF OCTOBER, 1837.

25. SACRED | TO THE MEMORY OF | MARY, | THE BELOVED WIFE OF JOHN COCKERTON | OF THIS ISLAND | ADVOCATE | SHE DEPARTED THIS LIFE | ON THE 17ᵀᴴ OF NOVEMBER, 1835 | AGED 27 YEARS | LEAVING A FAMILY OF | FOUR YOUNG CHILDREN WITH HER HUSBAND | TO MOURN HER LOSS.

26. THIS MONUMENT IS ERECTED AS A | TRIBUTE OF PARENTAL AFFECTION | BY AN AFFLICTED MOTHER TO THE | MEMORY OF HER DEARLY BELOVED | AND DEEPLY LAMENTED CHILD | ELLEN LOUISA PEACOCKE, | WHO DIED OF FEVER IN THIS TOWN ON | THE 25ᵀᴴ OF JUNE, 1838, AGED 24 YEARS | AND 10 MONTHS ; SECOND, AND | YOUNGEST DAUGHTER OF THE LATE | WILLIAM MULLINS, ESQ^ᴿ | OF BARNSTAPLE, NORTH DEVON, | ENGLAND | ALSO TO THE MEMORY OF | WILLIAM LLOYD PEACOCKE, ESQ^ᴿ | LATE CAPTAIN IN HER MAJESTY'S | 36ᵀᴴ REGIMENT, AND CHIEF | SUPERINTENDING SPECIAL JUSTICE | OF THE NORTHERN DIVISION | OF THIS ISLAND : | SECOND SON OF THE LATE | THOMAS GOODRICKE PEACOCKE ESQ^ᴿ | OF FORT ETNA IN THE COUNTY | OF LIMERICK, IRELAND AND HUSBAND | OF THE ABOVE, ONLY SURVIVING | HER LOSS NINE DAYS, HAVING ALSO | DIED OF FEVER ON THE 4ᵀᴴ OF JULY | AND ALSO TO THE MEMORY | OF THEIR INFANT SON | WILLIAM THOMAS GOODRICKE | PEACOCK ; | WHO DIED ON THE 22ᴺᴰ | OF JANUARY, 1837, AGED 13 MONTHS.

27.   An urn at the top :—

To the Memory of | MAJOR GENERAL THOMAS DUNDAS | who with great profeffional abilities | and with a mind generous and brave | fell a facrifice to his Zeal and Exertion | in the fervice of his King and Country | on the third day of June MDCCXCIV | in the forty-fourth Year of his age | His Remains were interred | in the principal Baftion of FORT MATILDA | in the Ifland of GUADELOUPE | in the Conqueft of which | he bore a moft diftinguifhed fhare | and in which he commanded at his death. | This Tablet was Erected | by a few of his Brother Officers | as a Mark of their high Efteem | for his many valuable qualities | and their regret for his Lofs.

See illustration and account of this tablet in *Caribbeana* III., 95.

28.   On the west wall of the Nave under the Gallery :—

MANFREDO LESLIE PALMES, | PARENTES HOC MARMOR FACIENDUM CURAVERUNT. | ANTIQUA STRIPE ADUD ANGLOS | AD NABURN IN COM : EBOR : ORIUNDUS | QUINQUE VIX MENSES IN HÂC INSULÂ PEREGRINATUS | XII CAL. JUN. MDCCCXXXIX | PRÆMATURÂ MORTE ABSUMPTUS EST | ADOLESCENS INGENIO MORIBUSQUE SUAVISSIMIS | EGREGIÂ FORMÂ ANIMO SIMPLICI | FILIUS FRATER PIENTISSIMUS DESIDERATISSIMUS | VIXIT ANNOS XVIII.

See pedigree of Palmes in *Burke's Landed Gentry*. 7th edition, p. 1414.

29.   On the Reredos :—

To the Glory of God | and in Memory of James Thomas | Hayes BISHOP 1889—1904.

---

30.   Beneath a window in the north wall of the north Chapel dedicated to S. Cecilia :—

A.D.M.G. JANE CUMMING DOORLY 1858-1907 | A TRIBUTE FROM CHORISTERS ETC. to their Choir Mistress.

LAPEYROUSE CEMETERY, PORT OF SPAIN.

On the east gateway is the date " 1867." There are many hundreds of memorial stones here, but there was no time to copy them. The earliest one noticed was 1838, so the above date of 1867 may refer only to the gateway.

PESCHIER BURIAL GROUND, PORT OF SPAIN.

In the Savannah, north of the Queen's Park Hotel, is a small private burial ground enclosed by a wall. It probably belonged to the Peschier family, and contains the following memorials :—

31.   To the Memory of | CHARLES PESCHIER, | NATIVE OF THE ISLAND OF GRENADA | WHO DIED AT TINIDAD | ON THE 24TH OF JULY 1850 | IN HIS 63RD YEAR.

---

32.   HERE LIES THE BODY OF | HENRY MASSY, M.D. | DEPARTED THIS LIFE | 23RD SEPTEMBER 1833 | AGED 23 YEARS. (Placed by his twin brother George).

---

33.   PANTIN ESQUIRE | Mort 31 Octobre 1862.   (Not copied in full).

---

34.   HENRY PANTIN | Agé de 45 ans | Mort 22 Janvier 1868. (Not copied in full).

---

35.   TO THE MEMORY OF | CELESTE ROSE PESCHIER | native of Grenada | daughter of the MARQUIS DE BELGENS, | and wife of the late MR HENRY PESCHIER | native of Geneva, Switzerland. | She died on the 27th of September 1817, Aged 62 Years. | (Erected by her son).

---

36.   SACRED | To the Memory of | FRANCIS PESCHIER | Died | 19th July 1852 | Aged 89 Years.

37. JOSEPH FRANCIS PESCHIER | *Died* 13*th* *May*, 1853 | AGED 69 YEARS.

Joseph Peschier was at Codrington College in 1840.

___

38. SACRED | *To the Memory of* | WILLIAM MASSEY | *Died* | 5th February 1848 | Aged 49 Years.

Several quite modern stones to " Massy " and " Dick " I had not time to copy.

___

39. CHARLES LEON PESCHIER, M.D. BORN 1ST JUNE 1810 | IN TRINIDAD | DIED 17 JUNE 1862.

___

40. Broken stone :—

DECED ... | A L'AGE DE 36 ANS | ET DORMENT A SES CÔTES | SES DEUX ENFANS, | LEWIS FREDERIC | DÉCEDÉ LE 9 NBRE 1821, AGÉ DE 2 ANS | ET CLEMENTINE | DÉCEDÉE LE 4 JANVIER 1825 | A L'AGE DE 3 ANS.

___

41. Monumental Inscription in French to Eliza Monier De Laquarrée Ganteaume, mother of eight children, died 5 May 1838, aged 31.

___

42. Broken :—

VICTOR D. C. DAMEY | DE ST BRES ... N | NE 10 MARS 1811 | MORT 16 FEVRIER ... 17

___

43. On a granite cross :—

IN MEMORIAM | KIRKMAN FINLAY | BARRISTER AT LAW | BORN NOVEMBER 22, 1843 | DIED MARCH 17TH 1883 (?)

___

44. On a cross :—

EDWARD ALEXANDER his infant son Born 24 June and Died 1st October 1879. (Abbreviated).

___

45. IN LOVING MEMORY | OF | ALEXANDER K. WIGHT | who died | 27TH SEPTR | 1866 | ALSO | OF | ROSA SOPHIA | HIS WIFE | WHO DIED AUGUST | 30TH 1889

Lower down is :—ALSO | LETITIA GEORGINA | THE BELOVED WIFE OF | R. J. MILLER | DIED 29TH AUGUST 1904 | AGE 54 YEARS.

Mr. Knox Wight, late I.C.S. resides at Exmouth and I believe is of above family.

See Monumental Inscription at St. John's, Antigua to Robert Charles son of H. K. and E. S. L. Wight, born in St. Croix, 13 March, 1849, died here 30 August 1850, also Eliz. Mary Louisa wife of H. K. Wight born in St. Croix 28 Sept., 1828, died here 17 Oct., 1853. (*History of Antigua* III, 378).

---

46. JOHN ANDREW KNOX | DIED JANUARY 4TH 1858 | AGED 30 YEARS.

---

47. CHARLES FREDERICK KNOX | DIED 21ST APRIL 1850 | AGED 40 YEARS.

---

48. CAROLINE MULLYNIX | DIED 3RD AUGUST 1848 | AGED 48 YEARS.

---

49. GEORGE KNOX | DIED 11TH MARCH 1822 | SOPHIA KNOX | DIED 3RD AUGUST 1835.

1822, March 11. At Trinidad, George Knox, esq., barrister-at-law, etc. (*Gent Mag.* 574)

George William Knox, barrister, a native of the island, was appointed Chief Justice in 1849. (*De Verteuil's Trinidad* p. 204).

---

50. Broken :—

SACRED | TO THE MEMORY OF | CAROLINE ELIZABETH PESCHIER | DAUGHTER OF DR AND M.E. PESCHIER | BORN ON THE 6 JAN. 1812 | DEPARTED THIS LIFE 6TH MARCH 1843 |. (Erected by her sponsors Caroline and D. T. Peschier).

---

51. GEORGE PANTIN | DIED 8TH OCTOBER 1859 | AGED 63 YEARS.

There are also several old broken brick vaults without names.

DEMERARA.

In 1796 the Dutch Colonies of Demerara, Essequibo and Berbice were surrendered to Sir Ralph Abercrombie but by the treaty of Amiens of 1802 they were restored. They were recaptured in 1803 by General Grenfield and Colonel Nicholson and finally ceded in 1814 to Great Britain. Many planters of Barbadoes moved with their slaves to Demerara.

ST. GEORGE'S CATHEDRAL, GEORGE TOWN.

This Church was erected and opened in 1810.

1. North Transept :—

IN MEMORIAM
HUBERT CARLTON WHITLOCK, M.R.C.S. E.,
ONLY SON OF
THE LATE HUBERT WHITLOCK, EXETER, DEVONSHIRE,
WHO DIED DURING HIS VOYAGE TO ENGLAND,
AND WAS BURIED AT SEA, 4TH JUNE, 1876,
AGED 42 YEARS.

2. Above the west door :—

SACRED
TO THE MEMORY OF
MAJOR GENERAL
STEPHEN ARTHUR GOODMAN, C.B. AND K.H.
BORN 19TH JANUARY, 1780, DIED 2 JANUARY, 1844
HE SERVED THROUGHOUT THE WAR IN THE
PENINSULA AND THE NETHERLANDS
UP TO ITS TERMINATION BY THE GLORIOUS VICTORY OF
WATERLOO
IN 1821 HE RECEIVED FROM HIS SOVEREIGN THE OFFICE (PATENT)
OF VENDVE MASTER OF DEMERARA AND ESSEQUIBO
WHICH HE HELD TO HIS DEMISE ;
IN 1823.
HE WAS APPOINTED TO THE COMMAND OF THE MILITIA.
(14 lines. Buried in Military Burial Ground at EVE LEARY).

1844, Jan. 2. In British Guiana Major-General Stephen Arthur Goodman, etc., very long notice. (*Gent. Mag.* 539)
He left a widow and eleven children. (D.N.B.)
1851, March 13. In Demerara, aged 36, Capt. Charles Arthur Goodman, Stipendiary Magistrate, late of 36th Regiment, third son of the late Maj-General Stephen Arthur Goodman. (*Gent. Mag.* 687).
1851, June 21. In George Town, Demerara, aged 24, Fitzroy John, fifth son of the late Major-General Stephen Arthur Goodman. (*Ib.* 329)
1853, Oct. 25. In Demerara, aged 18, Antonia Sophia, youngest child, etc. (*Ib.* 1854, 104).

3.   Crest : *A demi lion rampant couped, in its paws a boar's head couped.*

Sacred | TO THE MEMORY OF | J. R. F. HUTSON, Esǫ^R *M.D.* | BORN 11TH DECEMBER, 1796 | DIED 12TH OCTOBER, 1863. | WHO PRACTISED HIS PROFESSION | IN THIS COLONY FOR UPWARDS | OF 46 YEARS.

1816. " Johannes Richd Farre Hutson, Filius Natu Maximus Henrici, Medici, apud Demerary in America Meridionali."

M.D. 1817, Practitioner in Demerara (matriculated Students Glasgow University No. 9742). In 1825 Henry Hutson owned Spring Hall with 216 slaves and Spring Garden with 100.

The Ven. E. Hutson, M.A., was Archdeacon of the Virgin Islands in 1885.

The Rev. H. Hutson is Rector of St. Lucy, Barbados.

Dr. John Hutson, M.B. Edinburgh, 1883, resides at Harmony Hall, Bridgetown, Barbados.

The Right Rev. Edward Hutson, born 1873, has been Bishop of the Leeward Islands since 1910.

The Hon. Duncan M. Hutson, born 1857, barrister-at-law, 1887, K.C. 1903, died at Georgetown, 12 Nov., 1914.   (*W.I. Com. Circ.* p. 591).

---

4.   TO THE MEMORY OF
FANNY
THE FIRST-BORN CHILD OF CHARLES AND MARY WRAY
ON THE 2ND OF NOVEMBER, 1821, SHE EMBARKED
IN PERFECT HEALTH ON BOARD THE LATONA
WITH HER FATHER PRESIDENT OF THE COURTS OF JUSTICE
ON HIS VOYAGE OUT TO THESE COLONIES ;
SHE WAS TAKEN ILL ON THE 9TH
AND DIED ON THE 13TH OF THE SAME MONTH
AGED 2 YEARS 6 MONTHS.
ALSO TO THE MEMORY OF
CHARLES PITTS WRAY
WHO DIED ON THE 28TH OF DECEMBER 1822
AGED 7 MONTHS.
THEY ARE BOTH INTERRED IN THE MILITARY BURIAL GROUND
OF THIS PLACE.

He arrived 27th December, 1821, and was a barrister-at-law.

1823, Nov. 27.   At Demerara, the lady of His Honour Charles Wray, esq. a son.   (*Gent. Mag.* 176).

1827, Dec. 19.   In Suffolk Place, London, the wife of Charles Wray, esq., President of the Courts of Justice, Demerara, a son.   (*Ib.* 638)

---

5.   SACRED TO THE MEMORY OF
WALTER ROBERT D'URBAN ESQUIRE
GOVERNMENT SECRETARY OF THIS COLONY
SON OF SIR BENJAMIN D'URBAN
AND OF ANNA HIS WIFE
BATHING IN THE RIVER ESSEQUIBO
HE WAS UNHAPPILY DROWNED
ON THE 1ST OF NOVEMBER 1824
IN THE 20TH YEAR OF HIS AGE
(3 lines.   Buried in Military Burial Ground at Eve Leary).

Sir Benjamin D'Urban was Governor of the Leeward Islands 1820-25 and Lieut.-Governor of British Guiana in 1825 and Governor 1831.

6.

SACRED TO THE MEMORY OF
ALEXANDER MILNE, ESQ^R
LATE LIEUTENANT COLONEL 19TH REGIMENT
WHO DEPARTED THIS LIFE ON THE 5TH NOVEMBER, 1827
AGED 46 YEARS

7.

SACRED
TO THE MEMORY OF
CHARLES AUGUSTUS DEAN ESQ^{RE}
CAPTAIN OF THE LIGHT INFANTRY COMPANY
OF H.M. 67TH REGIMENT
ELDEST SON OF RICHARD BETENSON DEAN ESQ^{RE}
CHAIRMAN OF THE BOARD OF CUSTOMS
· OF THE UNITED KINGDOM
HE WAS BORN ON 27TH SEPTEMBER, 1808
AND DIED AFTER A SHORT ILLNESS
AT GEORGE TOWN, DEMERARA
ON 21 JANUARY, 1839
BELOVED AND LAMENTED.

1839, Jan. 21. At Demerara, Capt. Charles Augustus Dean, 67th Regiment, eldest son of R. B. Dean, esq., Chairman of the Board of Customs. (*Gent. Mag.* 446). See his grave in the military ground No. 71.

8.

SACRED TO THE MEMORY OF
PETER ROSE
A NATIVE OF SCOTLAND
AND FOR UPWARDS OF HALF A CENTURY
A COLONIST OF BRISTISH GUIANA
HE EARLY ATTAINED AN INFLUENTIAL POSITION
AND TOOK A PROMINENT PART
IN EVERY THING CONNECTED WITH THE PUBLIC PROSPERITY
FOR MANY YEARS HE WAS A MEMBER
OF THE HONORABLE THE COURT OF POLICY
AND MANAGER OF THE COLONIAL BANK
BORN ON 1ST JANUARY, 1787
DIED AT GEORGETOWN 9TH SEPTEMBER 1859
AGED 72 YEARS

1819, June 16. Peter Rose, esq., of Demerara, to Huntly, daughter of Wm. Gordon, esq., of Aberdour, Aberdeenshire. (*Gent. Mag.* 83).

---

9. Over the east door :—

Crest and Arms of Carmichael.   Arms : *A fess, etc. military flags.*

HIS EXCELLENCY MAJOR GENERAL JOHN MURRAY
AND THE HONOURABLE COURT OF POLICY
IN THE NAME AND ON BEHALF OF THE INHABITANTS
OF THIS UNITED COLONY
HAVE DEDICATED THIS MONUMENT TO THE MEMORY
OF HUGH LYLE CARMICHAEL ESQ^R
MAJOR GENERAL OF HIS MAJESTY'S FORCES
WHO DEPARTED THIS LIFE DURING HIS GOVERNMENT
ON THE 11TH DAY OF MAY, 1813
AGED 49 YEARS.
AS AN OFFICER HE WAS BRAVE AND LOYAL,
AS A GOVERNOR ZEALOUS AND INDEFATIGABLE

1813, May. Major-General Carmichael, commander of the Forces at Demerara. (*Gent. Mag.* 194).

---

10.   White marble bust on a pedestal.

SACRED | TO THE MEMORY OF | MAJOR GENERAL | SIR JAMES CARMICHAEL SMITH | BARONET | C.B., K.M.T., K.S^TW. | APPOINTED | GOVERNOR OF BRITISH GUIANA | 1833 | DIED 4 MARCH 1838 | AGED 58 YEARS. | ERECTED BY PUBLIC SUBSCRIPTION.

1838, March 4. At Camp House, Georgetown, Grenada, aged 58, Major-General Sir James Carmichael Smyth, Bart., of Nutwood, Surrey, K.C.H., C.B., K.M.T., and K.St.W., Governor of British Guiana and Demerara. (*Gent. Mag.* 212).

A more elaborate inscription may be seen on the monument in the Hall of Colony House, Berbice. (*Colonial Report*, p. 79).

---

11. On the east wall of north transept.

Crest : *A talbot statant with a rope around the neck.*
Arms : *Or, on a chevron Gules, between three leopards heads of the second, as many trefoils of the first.*
Motto : JEN OUBLIERAY JAMAIS.

IN MEMORY OF | JOHN NOBLE HARVEY, ESQUIRE, | BARRISTER-AT-LAW ; | DIED 29TH SEPTEMBER, 1854, | AGED 46 YEARS |

---

12. On the east wall of the north Transept :—

Crest : *A stag's head couped.*   Motto : " SEMPER PARATUS."

In Loving Memory of
CHARLES MONTAGUE JONES,
AND ELIZABETH HIS WIFE,
FOR MANY YEARS RESIDENT IN THE COLONY,
WHO, AFTER AN EARTHLY UNION OF NEARLY
53 YEARS DIED IN ENGLAND THE FORMER ON
THE 12TH AUGUST 1898, AGED 77 YEARS AND 5 MONTHS,
THE LATTER ON THE 13TH JAN^Y 1899,
AGED 78 YEARS & 10 MONTHS

13. South Transept, east wall :—

TO THE MEMORY OF
THOMAS DOUGAN,
OF PLANT^N MIDDLESEX IN THE COLONY
OF ESSEQUEBO, AND FOR SEVERAL YEARS
COLONEL OF THE MILITIA OF THAT COLONY
LATTERLY HE RESIDED IN GEORGETOWN
COLONY OF DEMERARY
AND HELD THE OFFICE OF POLICE MAGISTRATE
(DIED) ON THE 12TH DAY OF MAY 1840,
IN THE 52ND YEAR OF HIS AGE

Thomas Dougan, junr., died at Demerara in August or September, 1792.
Thomas Dougan senr., died there in 1797. William Dougan died at Martinico in January, 1802.
Robert Dougan, Esq., late of Tortola now in Great Britain. Will dated 6 January, 1806. To my brother John Dougan late of Tortola now in Great Britain all my estate and Exor. Codicil dated 26 March, 1807. To my nephew Thomas Dougan of Demerara, Esq., my plantation there. Proved 1808 (553 *Ely*).

---

14. Over east door of south Transept :—

SACRED TO THE MEMORY OF
JOSEPH BEETE ESQ^RE
WHO SAIL'D FROM THIS RIVER IN JUNE 1814,
FOR HIS NATIVE ENGLAND
AND DIED AT BATH ON THE 12TH OF JAN^Y 1813,
IN THE 61ST YEAR OF HIS AGE.

See account of his Monumental Inscription in Bath Abbey in *Caribbeana* II., 233, and *West Indian Bookplates* No. 277.
Robertus Crosbij Beete, Demerary, Indus, Occid. 15 Sept., 1832. (*English graduates at Leyden*).
1815, Feb. 2. On 14th inst. in Henrietta Street, Joseph Beete, esq., late of the Colony of Demerara. (*Bath Chronicle*).

---

15. Gothic Tablet :—

Sacred | TO THE | MEMORY | OF JAMES LUGAR A.M. | ARCHDEACON OF DEMERARA | AND TWENTY FIVE YEARS | RECTOR OF THE PARISH | OF S^T GEORGE | WHO DEPARTED THIS LIFE ON THE 26TH DAY OF MAY 1853, | AGED 67 YEARS |

1853, May 26. At Barbados, West Indies, whither he went for the benefit of his health, aged 67, The Venerable James Lugar, M.A., Archdeacon of Demerara, where he had been a resident thirty years. He was brother of Messrs. R. and J. Lugar of Ardleigh, Essex ; was of Sidney Sussex College, Cambridge, B.A. 1822. (*Gent. Mag.* 207)

---

16. Above the window :—

SACRED | TO THE MEMORY OF | JOHN WALKER THOMPSON ESQ^RE | LATE PROPRIETOR OF PLANTATION PERSEVERANCE | ESSEQUIBO | IN WHICH PART OF THE COLONY HE HAD RESIDED | FOR NEARLY 37 YEARS | HE DIED IN THIS CITY AFTER A FEW HOURS ILLNESS | ON THE 21ST SEPTEMBER 1866 | AGED 52 YEARS AND 9 MONTHS |

17. 𝔍n 𝔐emory of | WILLIAM WYNN KENRICK | CHIEF GOVERNMENT COMMISSIONER | OF MINES FOR THIS COLONY, | DIED AT MORAWHANNA, SEPTEMBER 14TH 1892 | AGED 55.   (Erected by his friends).

18. SACRED | TO THE MEMORY OF | CAPTAIN WILLIAM PEAKE, | THE BRAVE AND HIGHLY RESPECTED COMMANDER | OF HIS MAJESTY'S BRIG PEACOCK| WHOSE DEATH WAS GLORIOUS AS HIS | LIFE WAS HONORABLE | ENGAGED IN UNEQUAL COMBAT WITH THE | AMERICAN SHIP OF WAR HORNET | A CANNON SHOT IN MERCY TERMINATED HIS EXISTENCE | ALMOST AT THE SAME MOMENT THAT HIS | GALLANT VESSEL CONSIGN'D TO THE DEEP | GAVE A WATERY SEPULCHRE TO THE REMAINS OF | HER LAMENTED CHIEF |
TO COMMEMORATE | THE GLORIOUS BUT FATAL ENGAGEMENT | WHICH TOOK PLACE ON THESE SHORES | ON THE 24 DAY OF FEBRUARY 1813 |.   Erected by His Excellency General Carmichael).

He was brother of Sir Henry Peake, Knight, Surveyor of the Navy 1806—1822. (Archer 424).

19.   Very high up is a shield :—

Crest : *A hand holding a crown or mitre.*
Arms : *Gules three wolves heads erased.*
Motto : VIRTUTIS . . .   MERCE

SACRED TO THE MEMORY OF
GEORGE ROBERTSON ESQUIRE
NATIVE OF LONDON
(AND NEPHEW OF THE LATE HONBLE JAMES ROBERTSON
CHIEF JUDGE OF THE VIRGIN ISLANDS)
BORN 2ND APRIL 1793 DIED 26TH FEBRUARY 1843
FOR THIRTY-TWO YEARS AN INHABITANT OF THIS COLONY
THE LAST SIX OF WHICH HE AS ITS ORIGINAL MANAGER
DEVOTED TO THE ESTABLISHMENT OF THE BRITISH GUIANA BANK.
HIS REMAINS ARE INTERRED IN BOURDAS CEMETERY

20. SACRED | TO THE MEMORY OF | H. B. MAGGEE ESQRE | WHO DEPARTED THIS LIFE | 12TH FEBRUARY 1843 | AGED 60 YEARS |

There are four brasses near the west door of the south Transept :—

21. IN MEMORY OF | SIR JAMES ROBERT LONGDEN, G.C.M.G. | BORN 7TH JULY 1827 | DIED 4TH OCTOBER 1891 | SOMETIME GOVERNOR OF THIS COLONY. |

22. On a Brass above the door :—

Arms : *Or, within a bordure engrailed Sable, an eagle displayed* ; impaling, *Sable on a chevron between three long crosses Or as many lions heads erased.* (*Austin*).

This Tablet is placed here by Josias Booker of Liverpool and this Colony in fond memory of his devotedly attached Wife Mebetabel Wickham, second Daughter of the Right Revᵈ Willᵐ Piercy Austin, D.D., Lord Bishop of this Diocese and Eliza Piercy, his Wife. Born in London 1st April, 1841. Died in Liverpool 2ⁿᵈ May, 1867, aged 26 years. Her remains rest with those of her two Infant Brothers, in the Church-yard of St. John's, Redland, Clifton.

23. On a Brass above the Longden one, in Gothic lettering :—

Crest : *A swan with wings raised.*
Arms : Quarterly 1 & 4 : *Argent, two towers in chief and a demi griffin couped in base* ; 2 & 3, *Per saltire Argent and Gules two escallops in fess, as many lions faces in pale.*
Motto :—" DEO NON FORTUNA."

Sacred to the Memory of Josias | Booker of Liverpool and Allerton | Lancashire who first landed in this Colony | A.D. 1815, and to the last took a warm interest | in its welfare. He departed this life at Allerton, | June 12ᵗʰ A.D. 1865 aged 71 years and his | mortal remains are deposited in the Churchyard | of St. George's, Everton, Liverpool.

See his bookplate F. 3042. Crest.
The Rev. Arthur Wellington Booker, M.A. Oxon, his fifth son was Vicar of Croxton Kerrial, Northants in 1882. (*Foster*).

24. On a fourth Brass (Gothic) :—

In Memory of George Booker | of Liverpool and Warrenside, | New Brighton, Cheshire for many years | intimately connected with both the Landed and | Mercantile interests of this Colony. | Died at Warrenside, October 11ᵗʰ 1866 aged | 68 years and is buried at the Parish | Church Over Kellet, Lancashire.

25. On a small Brass on the north wall of the Nave under the Hymn Frame :—

TO THE GLORY OF GOD AND | IN MEMORY OF | GORING EVANS DALTON | SON OF E. T. E. & R. C. DALTON | FOR MANY YEARS A VESTRYMAN OF | Sᵀ GEORGES, DIED IN ENGLAND 1898 | ALSO OF HIS INFANT SON | EDWARD HENRY GORING DALTON, DIED 1884.|

26.   On a small Brass on the Hymn Notice Frame on the south side :—

TO THE GLORY OF GOD AND | IN MEMORY OF | EDWARD THOMAS EVANS DALTON | POSTMASTER GENERAL OF BRITISH GUIANA | AND OF | RACHAEL CATHERINE DALTON, BORN GORING HIS WIFE | FOR YEARS PARISHIONERS OF ST GEORGES. ALSO OF | ALFRED STUART DALTON | CHARLES DALTON | EDWIN PERCY DALTON | REGINALD DOUGLAS DALTON | THEIR CHILDREN WHO WERE BORN AND DIED IN THIS PARISH |.

---

27.   Window east wall of north Transept :—

IN MEMORY OF FREDERICK ELLIOT DAMPIER
FOR 39 YEARS STIPENDIARY MAGISTRATE
DEMERARA DIED JULY 1ST 1890 AGED 60 YEARS

---

28.   Window east wall of Baptistry :—

Arms of the See and ditto impaling ; *Gules on a chevron engrailed Or, between three swans rising, as many bees.*   (*Swaby*).

TO THE GLORY OF GOD AND | IN MEMORY OF SARA ETHEL | THE DEARLY LOVED | DAUGHTER OF THE | RIGHT REVD WM PROCTOR | SWABY, D.D. BISHOP OF GUIANA | WHO DIED AT SEA NOVR 11TH | 1893 AGED 20 YEARS.

The Angel holding the water has the same inscription at base.

Dr. Swaby was afterwards for many years Bishop of Barbados and a few weeks before his death Archbishop of the West Indies.

---

29.   Window west wall of north Transept :—

TO THE GLORY OF GOD AND IN MEMORY OF WILLIAM HENRY WOODROFFE WHO DIED NOVEMBER 6 1909.

---

30.   Window east wall of south Transept :—

ERECTED TO GEORGE ANDERSON FORSHAW | BY HIS LOVING WIFE AND CHILDREN.   (No date).

---

31.   Pulpit :—

TO THE MEMORY OF RICHARD MICHAEL JONES HOUSTON AND HIS WIFE LUCRETIA AND THEIR SON BOVELL.

---

32.   On the Brass Eagle :—

IN MEMORY OF FRANCIS WOLLASTON HUTTON SON OF THE | REVEREND
H. F. HUTTON, RECTOR OF SPRIDLINGTON IN THE COUNTY | OF LINCOLN AND LATE
AN ENSIGN IN THE 21ST REGT R.N.B. FUSILIERS | WHO DIED ON THE 16TH DAY OF
APRIL 1864, AGED 18 YEARS.

---

33.   On the Iron Screen :—

A.M.D.G.

THE FRONT PORTION OF THIS SCREEN WAS ERECTED
IN THE YEAR 1893 BY LOUISA WOODGATE JONES
IN AFFECTIONATE REMEMBRANCE OF HER PARENTS
WILLIAM ROBERTS NOV. 9TH 1805, AUG. 19TH 1876 &
MARY ANN ROBERTS NOV. 27TH 1809 JULY 17TH 1892
WHOSE SOULS GOD REST.

On the front of the Screen are two shields.

The one to the north side having the arms of the See impaling : *Gules a chevron Or, between three long crosses.*   (*Bishop Austin*).

The other to the south side has the arms of the See impaling the arms of Bishop Swaby.

The oldest Register is a brown leather volume marked " B " on the cover, and styled " Register of Marriages and Baptisms for the Colonies of Essequebo and Demerary, 1796." It contains no marriages. The first baptism is on 6 June, 1796. Each entry is signed by Francis McMahon. Each page is numbered as far as 196, June 1804. There are thirty-one more folios, some loose, and the last entry is on 4th April, 1807. Some few pages are frayed but otherwise the register is complete and in good condition.

Another brown leather volume, smaller than the above, is marked "A" it contains baptisms from 6th June, 1796 and is also signed F.M. to 17th April, 1807. The Dean and I checked several entries with those in " B," and as they coincided we came to the conclusion that the two volumes contained the same entries throughout. From a letter of about the year 1830 it appears that the Rev. F. McMahon took the above two volumes with him to Grenada and after his death they were purchased from his Executors for 70 dollars. From the tablet in St. George's, Grenada it appears that he died 22nd November, 1827, having been Rector 21 years. It is a pity the Marriages and Burials are missing.

The third volume has no cover. The first baptism is on 27th October, 1807 signed " W. G. Straghan, A.B.;, Minister." The first marriage is dated 26th April, 1807 and burials begin the same year.

ST. ANDREWS SCOTCH CHURCH.

Church opened in 1819. There are fourteen tablets within which I have noted and one granite pedestal outside to a minister which I did not note.

						Age.
34.	Hugh McCalmont	...	...	...	1838	37
35.	Van Kinschot ...	...	...	...	1868	—
36.	Henry Cunard Stevenson, M.D.	...	...	1876	38

						Age.
37.	Charles Harrison	...	...	...	1861	34
38.	Alex. Mackenzie, LL.D.	...	...	...	1828	58
39.	Archibald O. S. Smellie	...	...	...	1904	31
40.	Rev. Tho. Slater	...	...	...	1905	76
41.	James Struthers, D.D.	...	...	...	1858	57
42.	Rev. A. G. Simsom, A.M.	...	...	...	1830	28
43.	James Turner, son of Coll James Turner (see will of Coll Turner of Tobago in *Carribbeana* III., 295)			...	1837	—
44.	Geo. R. Bonyun, M.D.	...	...	...	1853	42
45.	Wm. Hayley	...	...	...	1878	—
46.	Rev. Æneas Gunn	...	...	...	1830	37
47.	Hugh Rogers	...	...	...	1839	53
48.	John Mackinnon (loose under the stairs)			...	1852	28

See Notes on this Church by J. Graham Cruickshank of Georgetown. (*W.I. C. Circular*, Vol. XXVII 170).

MILITARY BURIAL GROUND,
EVE LEARY or KINGSTON.

This is behind the old barracks near the sea wall and is clean and tidy. During a very hurried visit I only had time to take the names and dates.

49. Georgina Elizabeth, wife of Capt. Neame, 16th Regiment, died 1st November, 1866, aged 21, of yellow fever.

50. Charles Platt, Lieut. 16th Regiment, died 10th November, 1866, aged 27.

51. C. M. Rodney Reyne, Lieut. 2nd Batt. 16th Regiment, third son of Colonel Reyne, born 1837, died 1866.

52. Walter Ferrier Riddell, Ensign 2nd Batt. 16th Regiment, died 3rd November, 1866, aged 21 of yellow fever.

53 Eliza Earle Wolseley, died 21st March, 1851, aged 51.
John Henry Wolseley, second son of Wm. Bertie Wolseley, died 11th November, 1840, aged 20.
Eliza Jane Bourne, sister of John Henry Wolseley, and wife of the Rev. John Fred. Bourne, died 15th December, 1848, aged 20.

1851, March 21st. In Demerara, aged 51, Eliza Earle, wife of W. B. Wolseley, esq., Acting Governor's Secretary of British Guiana. (*Gent. Mag.* 687). She was daughter of Wm. Daniell of Montserrat, barrister-at-law, and was married 11th July, 1818. Her husband was born in 1797, son of Capt. Henry Wolseley by Charlotte Elizabeth his wife, only daughter of Major John Delap Halliday of Antigua.

54.   Joseph Jules Xavier Dupovy, Capt. French Navy, born 1813, died 3rd October, 1853.

---

55.   Sarah Antonia, wife of Laurence Fitzgerald and daughter of Colonel Stephen Arthur Goodman, born 1809, died 2nd October, 1838.

---

56.   Maxwell Mills Legati, died 1849.   Dux 3rd legion.

---

57.   Frances Elizabeth Spooner, died 25th July, 1851, aged 40.

---

58.   Mrs. Antonia Gone, died 24th November, 1835, aged 64

---

59.   Harriet, daughter of the late John Wilkes, Esq., and wife of Wm. Bough President of the Courts of Justice, died 7th January, 1822, aged 46.

She was a natural daughter and her father bequeathed her £2000 in his will but he died insolvent.

---

60.   Frances Elizabeth, daughter of Lt.-Colonel S. A. Goodman, died 20th September, 1825, aged 6.

---

61.   John Mervin Nooth, Lt.-Colonel, Royal North British Fuziliers, C.B., died 23rd August, 1821, aged 59.

---

62.   Francis Wollaston Hutton, Ensign 21st Royal North British Fuziliers, died 16th April, 1864, aged 18.

---

63.   Margaret Louisa Dalyell.

---

64.   Elizabeth, wife of Lt.-Colonel Hare of 27 Enniskilling Regiment, died 12th January, 1825, aged 26.

1825, Jan. 12th.   At Demerara, Elizabeth, wife of Lt.-Colonel Hare, C.B. 27th Regiment.   (*Gent. Mag.* 286).

---

65. Anne Maclean, wife of Capt. Maclean of 27th Regiment, died 24th April, 1825, aged 46.

---

66. Mary Rawson, wife of Lt.-Col. Bush, K.H., 1st West India Regiment, died 1st October, 1841, aged 51.

1841, Oct. 1st. At Eve Leary Barracks, Demerara, Mary Rawson, etc. (*Gent. Mag.* for 1842, p. 118).

---

67. Eliz. . . . OVE. . . Fort Adjutant, eldest daughter died 6 July, 1837, aged 33, leaving a husband and five children.

---

68. Charles Simon Doyle, M.D., surgeon to the Forces, died 30th October, 1836, aged 48.

---

69. Maria Louisa, wife of Capt. John Smyth, R.E., died 21st January, 1833.

1833, January 21st. At Demerara, Mary Louisa, wife of Capt. John Smyth, Royal Engineers, third daughter of the late John Plumptree, esq., of Fredville, Kent. (*Gent. Mag.* 479).

---

70. Charles Grey, Ensign 1st West India Regiment, fourth son of William Grey, Esq., died 29th June, 1842, aged 22, a native of Stockton on Tees, County Durham.

---

71. Charles Augustus Dean, Capt. 67th Regiment, born 27th September, 1808, died 21st January, 1839. See his tablet, No. 7.

---

72. Walter Robert D'Urban.

---

73. Catherine, widow of Maj.-General Sir A. Goodman, C.B., K.H., died 1855.

---

74. Charles Arthur Goodman, Capt. 36th Regiment, born 1814, died 13th March, 1851.

Fitzroy John Goodman, born 1821, died 21st June, 1851, aged 24.
Antonia Sophia Goodman, born 1835, died 25th October, 1853.

75. Evryna Dorothea, died 6th September, 1828, aged 6, daughter of Lieut. J. and A. Robinson, 60th Rifle Corps.

---

76. Fanny Ann Loinsworth, died 10th February, 1826, aged 4.

---

77. Major-General Stephen Arthur Goodman, C.B., K.H., born 19th January, 1780, died 2nd January, 1844.

---

78. Charles Hunter, Capt. Royal Artillery, died 24th June, 1856, aged 28.

There were also many vaults without inscriptions and a few with worn out ones.   One or two of children I did not take.

BURIAL GROUND OF PENAL ESTABLISHMENT AT MASSARUNI.

This ground is on a hill above the river, enclosed and in good order. I copied the most important inscriptions ; others to the various warders, etc. had to be omitted owing to shortness of time.

There were inscriptions to several persons drowned in the rapids.

79. Brass on stone vault :—

LOUIS DANIEL BEAUPERTHUY

M.D. of Paris

Born at Guadeloupe

Died September, 1871

Aged 64 Years

He partly discovered the mosquito carrying of fever.

---

80. IN MEMORY | *of* | PATRICK HORAN | THE SUP^T APPOINTED | TO THIS DEPARTMENT | ON ITS FOUNDATION | DIED 28 JULY 1844.

---

81. Headstone :—

In Memory of | LIONEL PARKS, ESQ. | (No dates).

---

82.   IN MEMORY OF | *James A. Christie, Esq.* | POST OFFICE, DEMERARA | who was drowned in the | *Keosterbrake Rapid* | on the 19th September, 1865 | *Aged* 79.

83.   IN MEMORY | I. B. VAN WATERSCHOODT | INSPT. GEN^L OF POLICE | and ACT^G RES^T COMM^R | H.M.P.S. | Died 26TH M^{CH} 1852 Aged (blank) y^{rs}

84.   IN MEMORY | of | CAPT J^{NO} ALLISON | AGED 27 | DIED 10 o . . . 76

85.   Headstone ornamented with compass and square :—

In Memory | of | CAP^T JOHN H. DELAP | *A* | *native of* | Nova Scotia | of British Barque | " Trident " | who died at | Massaring British Guiana | June 13th 1868 | aged 29 years.

86.   IN MEMORY OF | *Captⁿ Poustie* | *of the* Barque ROSANNA | who died 7 Octr 1862 | *Aged* 50.

87.   IN MEMORY OF | *Mary Chase & Ruth* | TWIN CHILDREN | *Revd E. Christian, Chaplain* | H.M.P.S. | Ruth died 18 Novr 1862 | *Aged* 6 *Mths* | Mary died | 23 Novr 1862 | *Aged* 6 *Mths, 5 dys.*

88.   𝕴𝖓 𝕸𝖊𝖒𝖔𝖗𝖞 𝖔𝖋 | ELIZA ANN LYNDON | DAUGHTER OF | 𝕮𝖑𝖆𝖚𝖉 𝖆𝖓𝖉 𝕽𝖆𝖈𝖍𝖊𝖑 𝕶𝖊𝖗𝖗 | Born 1ST January 1862 | Died 16TH September 1862 | Aged 8 months 15 days.

89.   Brass on stone :—

𝕾𝖆𝖈𝖗𝖊𝖉 | TO the Memory of | CLAUDE KERR | Captain 3RD West India Regiment | Superintendent of His Majesty's Penal Settlement | From 1862 to 1871 | Born 7TH February 1826 | Died 3RD February 1871. |

Louis L. Kerr, son of the above, born in British Guiana in 1863, entered the police force in 1888, became Deputy Inspector General, and in 1911 Inspector General in Mauritius, where he died 7 November, 1914.   (*W.I. Com. Circ.* p. 591).

90.   IN MEMORY OF | *Geo. E. Morehouse* | CAPT OF THE BARQUE | ANNE FRANCES | *Native of Sandy Cove* | *Digby Nova Scotia* | Died 14TH March 1865 | Aged 23.

BOURDA BURIAL GROUND, VLISSINGEN.

There are many hundreds of stones here as this was the chief town cemetery. The Governor and I walked through it the day I left and the earliest date we saw was 1822.

---

91. On a modern plate fixed on an old vault :—

Adrien Abraham Alexander Tinne | Assistant Secretary of the Court of Justice | and Policy in the Colony | Born 28th July 1785 | Died 21st August 1815

P.F. Tinne, as Secretary to the Court of Policy, signed the Capitulation in 1803.

ST. PHILLIPS.

This church is not yet 50 years old and contains no tablets. It stands in a very large empty church yard, older than the building, from which many stones seem to have been removed.

ST. SAVIOUR'S.

This is the Chinese Church and contains no Monumental Inscriptions. Outside in the yard on a granite monument :

92. Pierre Louis de Saffon | Born in France in the year 1724 | and | Died in Demerara in August 1784 |. The Revenue of His Estate | after other bequests he Bestowed | In Perpetuity on the Maintenance | of ten poor Destitute Orphans | Until Attaining the Age of 16 years |. The First orphan was educated | At the Saffon School | On the Selection of the | Honble The Supreme Court of Justice | In the year 1825. (*Colonial Report*, p. 80).

ROMAN CATHOLIC CATHEDRAL.

93. Sacred | To the memory of | STEPHEN CRAMER ESQ. | Died the 8th of March, 1830 | Aged 58 years. (*Ibid*).

This fine building was completely destroyed by fire and the site was bare at my visit. A new church has been since erected.

Mr. James Rodway the Librarian published articles on the churches, etc. in the *Argosy* of 4th April, 1903. He said that in early days service was held in the House of the Court of Policy.

In the Library and Museum I saw a small square stone inscribed as follows :—

94. DE'ER SAMVEL | BECKMAN OD | ER | FT DEN 10 | DECEMBER | IN HET IAER | 1707.

He was Commander of Essequebo from 1690. The stone was brought from " Plantation Fortuin."

FORT ISLAND ESSEQUIBO RIVER.

This is situated about fifteen miles from the mouth. It was formerly the seat of government and the brick fort here on the river bank mounted forty cannon but was decaying in 1799. (*Bolingbroke* p. 133).

I landed here in a boat with the Governor and Colonial Secretary.

The so called Church is a plain oblong structure massively built and was once the Court of Policy Hall.

In the floor were three slabs on one of which I think was a coat of arms, but there was no time to copy the inscriptions, which I here give with others from the *Colonial Report*, drawn up by Mr. Alleyne Leechman.

---

95. Hier Legt Begraven | Den Wil Edele Gestrenge Heer | Johanes Backer Commandant | En Capitin Luytenant | Den Militie Benerens Raad | Der Beijde Collegien | Over De Colonie Essequebo | Cum Annexis | overleeden Den 19 February, 1772 | Geboren In Doornick | In Den jaare 1737.

---

96. Hier Legt Begraven | Lawrens Gerhardus Lodewyck Backer | Geboren Te Rio Essequebo | Den 2 November 1767 | En Overleden Den 1 September | 1768.

---

97. De Gedagtenisse Des | Regtvaedigen Sat Tot | Zeegeningen Syn | Hier Legt Begraven | Michael Roth | Geboren In Neurenburg | Op Den 18 February 1732 | Overleden In Rio Essequibo | Op Den 15 November 1770 | In Syne Leven Geweest | Chirugyn In Dienst Den : | Edele Geoctroyeerde | West Jndische Compagnie | Ter Caamer Zeeland.

FORT NASSAU.

98. Heer Legt Begraavenden | Jonkheer Hendrik Jan | Van Ryswyk Eenigste Zoon | Vander Weledele Gestrenge | Heer Hendrik Jan Van | Ryswk . . . Gouverneur | Generaal over de Colonie | de Berbice Rivieren | en Districkten Geebooren | den 17 Maart 1755 en | Gestorven Den 16 | Augustus 1759.

---

99. Near Fort Nassau is a stone to the three year old son of Governor Van Batenburg, Governor of Berbice 1789-1806. The Governor died at Barbados.

(See his tomb in the churchyard of St. Michaels Cathedral.—*Ed.*)

Higher up the river, about a mile above the mouth of the Teerani Creek.

---

100. Hier Rust | Helena Anna Brockhuijzen | Dochter Van | Den Wel Edelen | Gestrengen Heere | Jacobus Brockhuijzen | Fiscaal en Secretaris Van de | Colonie de Berbice Geebooren | in dezelve Colonie op den | 9 December 1784 | en aldaar overle den op den | November 1789 | Inden Onderdom Van | 4 Jaaren 10 Maanden | En 26 Daagen.

101. Hier onder Rust | Jacobus Hendrik Brockuizen | Zoon Van | Den Wel Edelen Gestrengen Heere | Jacobus Brockhuijzen | Fiscaal en Secretaris Van | De Colonie De Berbice | Gebooren in de zelve Colonie | Opden 3 September 1780 | en aldaar overleeden | opden 25 November 1787 | In de Onderdom Van 7 Jaaren | (?. lve Maanden en 22 Dagen.

DEMERARA, PLANTATION PROVIDENCE.

102. In the Buildings yard :—

Hier onder Rust | Mr. Pieter Hendrik Koppiers | ond Governeur Generaal | der Colonie Berbice etc. | Gebooren te Geisendam den 25th January 1753 | Overleiden te . . . | Demerara den 15th September 1795.

He succeeded Isaac Kaecks as Governor of Berbice in 1778, but in April, 1789 was dismissed from office " on account of his arbitrary and assuming behaviour." He then went to Demerara and became leader of the Orange party in the little revolution of 1795.

For fuller details see *Colonial Report* No. 84 on the preservation of historic sites, November, 1912.

PLANTATION, COOMACHA.

150 miles inland. (*Archer* 426).

---

103. Hier leyt begraven | monsieur Cornelis Rassche in syn | leeven, raat derer colonie,| mr planter op Markey | gebooren der 17 Nov. A° 1689 | is over-ledenden 15 May A° 1726.

---

104. Hier benenden leyt begraven syn | suster Jesabethr (R)assche geborn der 19 Juny A° 1694 | en overleden en yaer daerna |. En syn broeder Johannes Rassche | geboren der 18 Januuwary A° 1692 | en overleeden anno 1696.

---

105. Hier leyt begraven de heer | David Balle raaten | mester planter op de plantagie en | Markay is geboeren der | 15 Nov. 1692, en gerlonee de | 8 Nov. 1734.

The Obituary of the Orphan Chamber for the years 1812—21 was printed in *Caribbeana* III, 82.

BAHAMAS.

I am indebted to my correspondent at Nassau for the following information and inscriptions in 1921 :—

" You have the sum of the Christ Church memorials, but there were 'lots' which apparently were really burial grounds, and with Christ Church date from about the beginning of the eighteenth century, or earlier even.   These are alluded to in the Christ Church Registers.   But the common burial grounds and earliest were, owing to the hard rock that chiefly composes the mass of these Islands, the sandy sea shores in which hollows were easily scooped out—The 'white grounds ' as they were called.

The ' white ground ' of New Providence, at the East of the town, was one of the chief burial grounds, before the building of St. Matthews, early in the beginning of the nineteenth century, and after the arrival of the Royalists became more used.   I have not sent any of the inscriptions from this yard, and many of them have been improved off the face of the earth.

Another of these was one to the West of the Town, below and in front of Fort Charlotte facing North, and was used early.

The Hurricane of 1866, it is said, cleared the rocks of all their superjacent sand deposit, and strewed with bones the shores adjacent to the West.

The Soldiers Burying Ground within the extensive Fort Charlotte grounds, uncovered in a recent turning over of the ground for the purpose of a golf course to amuse Americans, tho' containing the remains of hundreds of British soldiers bones, showed no memorials.

During one epidemic the Christ Church Registers say that from 5th August, 1790 to 1st January, 1791, the Incumbent buried of the 47th Regiment, 232 men, women and children, and from the last of December, 1790 to 25th December, 1791, a total of 364 men, women and children.   Besides the above, people were interred in their own grounds, but the memorials left are now chiefly improved off the face of the earth. . . .

As the result of the American Revolution, it gave us Lord Dunmore as Governor, and a number of Tory Royalists came here from all the Colonies of the Continent, but no doubt the evacuation you have in mind is that of East Florida—not Carolina—in 1785 which had been ceded to Great Britain in 1763, but was handed back to Spain in August, 1784, but the evacuation by the British settlers was not completed until 1785, homes being found for them apparently in the Bahamas.

Long previous to this, indeed from the earliest settling of the New World intercourse was continuous between Bermuda, Carolina, and The Bahamas and the other Colonies.   The local records of early date are therefore of great interest to all Britishers, and these records are crying out for quick extraction of their substance.   The paper is dropping to pieces with decay, and already much is lost . . . .   These records begin from the early part of the eighteenth century but chiefly somewhat later.   One or two scattered grants of the Lords Proprietors Agents or Governors occur, but the mass of grants and regrants of lands begins with Lord Dunmore's tenure of office, and are contained in a number of volumes.

One volume of Minutes of the Court of Ordinary contains notes of value of near or about 700 administrations and probates . . . The turning out of the Vice Court of Admiralty records and the dumping of them, or a great heap of them, in the open ground, makes one gasp, though containing no doubt the germs of many a sensational plot of adventure, as they relate to the doings of pirates, privateers, wreckers, slaves, etc. . . . .

L. J. K. BRACE."

CHRIST CHURCH CATHEDRAL, NASSAU,
ISLAND OF PROVIDENCE.

The following inscriptions, transcribed by Mr. J. L. K. Brace, of Nassau. were forwarded to me 21st July, 1921, by the Rev. T. C. Dale of 29 Larkhall Rise, London, S. W. 4.

MURAL TABLETS.

1. On south wall :—

WILLIAM MOSS, Esquire, died 9 Dec., 1796, aged 45. Born at Huyton, Lancashire ; for the greater part of 24 years of his life in Georgia, East Florida, and in these Islands. Buried in front of north pulpit.

---

2. F. A. WETHERALL, died 21 Aug., 1857, aged 44. Lt Col. 1st West India Reg^t in command here ; eldest son of Lt Gen. Sir G. A. Wetherall, K.C.B. Adj^t Genl to the Forces. Erected by the Officers of the Reg^t

In the account of his father Geo. Augustus in the " D.N.B." this son is not noticed. Genl Sir Fred. Augustus the grandfather saw much service in the West Indies.

---

3. STANLEY BYNG HORNBY, 1st L^t in H.M. Royal Reg^t of Artillery died 21 Nov., 1843, in his 29TH year, leaving a wife and two children. He joined the Service in 1832, arrived in Nassau in command of a detachment of Artillery in 1834, was appointed in 1839 a Stipendiary Magistrate for the Bahamas and retired on an allowance in 1841, and then returned to England.

He married the second daughter of Joseph Thompson, merchant of Nassau. He was third son of Revd Geoffrey Hornby, rector of Bury, Lancashire, and related to the present Lord Stanley. He was buried in Potters' Field. Tablet erected by his Father-in-law. His mother was the Hon. Georgiana Bing. See Hornby of Dalton Hall in *Burke's L.G.*

---

4. GEORGINA ELIZABETH SWANN died 14 Oct., 1858 in her 18th year. Daughter of the late Capt S. B. Hornby, Royal Artillery, and wife of Revd Robert Swann. Also their son Robert George Henry who died 29 May, 1859, aged $7\frac{1}{4}$ months. (See 45 for him).

---

5. ROBERT WEAR ELLIOTT. Born 9 Dec., 1784, a native of Northumberland, sometime Member of the House of Assembly for Harbour Island and Chairman of the Chamber of Commerce, resident here for many years greatly respected; wrecked in a storm off the Cork coast, when returning from the British Islands in his Brig the " Eliza Ann " and lost with all on board 20 Nov., 1830.

His widow Eliza daughter of John McPherson, Esq. died 16 Oct., 1832.

---

6. ANDREW SETON Esq. died 20 Nov. 1830. Wrecked off the Cork coast when returning here in R. W. Elliott Esquire's Brig " Eliza Ann," with all on board. A Member of Chamber of Commerce in Nov. 1799. His relict Elizabeth died at an advanced age 22 Dec. 1835. Member of firm of John Marsh & Co. dissolved Nov., 1807, was of the firm Seton & Elliott as early as 1816.

(This Monumental Inscription is apparently on Elliott's tablet).

---

7. FREDERIC CHARLES RICHARDSON, Esq., died 4 March, 1838, aged 22. L$^{\tau}$ in 2nd West India Regiment, born at Langford, Fifehead, Somerset ; 10 months previous to his death he had married Eliza daughter of the late Lewis Kerr, many years Speaker of the House of Assembly, and subsequently Attorney General of the Bahamas.

---

8. CHARLES CAULFIELD, D.D., died 4 Sept., 1862, aged 52. First Bishop of Nassau. Consecrated 24 Nov., 1861.

---

9. ADDINGTON R. P. VENABLES, D.D., died 8 Oct., 1876, aged 49. Bishop of Nassau. Consecrated 30 Nov., 1869, died at Hartford, Connecticut, U.S.A.

Addington Robert Peel Venables eldest son of Thomas of London, Esq., matriculated from Exeter College, Oxford, 23 Jan., 1848, aged 17 ; B.A. 1848, M.A. 1851, created D.D. 4 Feb. 1864. (Foster).

---

10. MICHOLAS ICELY died 23 Jan., 1834, of Pembroke, South Wales. Midshipman, H.M.S. Thunder ; drowned with a fellow Midshipman and a Seaman off " The Brothers " rocks near Ragged Island in this Colony, and named after them. Erected by Capt. Owen and their brother officers.

---

11. JOHN SAWYER LLOYD died 23 Jan., 1834, of Pembroke, South Wales, Midshipman, H.M.S. Thunder ; drowned with a fellow Midshipman (etc. as above).

---

12. WALTER GOULD HINSON LIGHTBOURN died 1 Oct., 1842, aged 45. A native of these Islands, Lt.-Col. of the Bahama Militia, leaving a widow and children.

---

13. MARIA ADELINE ROBINS, wife of George W. G. Robins, and eldest daughter of Don Cipriana Palacios.

---

14. MARIA ADELINE PALACIOS died 26 Jan., 1844, in her 37th year. Wife of Don Cipriano Palacios, merchant here. Buried in St Matthew's churchyard.

---

15. FREDERICK CIPRIANO PALACIOS, died 26 Feb., 1851, aged 26. Ensign in the Cape Mounted Rifles, died serving with his Regiment at Port Mare, Cape of Good Hope. Only son of Don Cipriano and Maria Palacios.

---

16. CIPRIANO PALACIOS, died 26 Nov., 1879. Born at Reynosa Old Castile Spain, 16 Sept., 1789.

1845, Oct. 23. At Nassau, New Providence, Charles Rookes, Lieutenant 2nd West India Regiment to Teresa, second daughter of Don Capician (sic) Palacios of Castile Old Spain. (Gent. Mag. 1846, p. 86).

---

17. CLARA CONRAN died 2 March, 1866, on board the S.S. Calabar on her way to Africa. Buried in the Protestant Cemetery, Madeira. Wife of Colonel Conran, 4th West India Regiment, Lieut. Governor of the Gold Coast, West Africa and youngest daughter of Cipriano and Maria Palacios.

---

18. HELEN ROSS died 14 April, 1815, aged 33. Wife of Lieut.-Colonel J. G. Ross, 2nd West India Regiment. Their infant son William Patrick died 1 June, 1815, aged 1 year 7 months.

---

19. LOUISE JOHNSON died 6 June, 1856, in her 23rd year. Daughter of W(m) J(ohn) P(etly) Johnson.

---

20. 1862, Aug. Erected by the Officers and Crew of H.M.S. Peterel to their Shipmates who died of Yellow Fever at Nassau.
    Archibald Stevenson, Surgeon, aged 29.
    Dunbar, A. Jamison, Assistant Surgeon, aged 26
    John Gray, Engineer, aged 32.
    Thomas Pigeon, Gunner Royal Marines, aged 23.
    Thomas How, Gunroom Steward, aged 25
    Thomas Edwards, Boy 1st class, aged 18.
    William Brown, Boy 2nd class, aged 16
and died at sea of the same fever :—
    John South, Ordinary Seaman, aged 19.
    James Steward, A.B., aged 24.
    Jeremiah Coffer, A.B., aged 24.

J. H. Murphy, sculpsit, Halifax N.S.

---

21. Floor stone at West end of Centre Aisle :—

WILLIAM HANNAY died 18 Sept., 1784, aged 33.

22.   Floor stone Centre Aisle :—

Honble JAMES Moss died 23 Oct., 1820, aged 61.

---

23.   Floor stone in Aisle :—

THOMAS MICHAEL CARTER died 27 Jan., 1763, in his 17th year.   Son of the Revd Robert Carter and his wife Jane.

---

24.   Floor stone in Aisle :—

JOHN FALCONER, Merchant, died 3 Nov., 1793, aged 51.

---

25.   Floor stone in Aisle :—

ELIZABETH DIXON, widow, died 18 Sept., 1779, aged 54.

---

26.   Floor stone in Aisle :—

His Excellency JOHN TINKER died 10 July, 1758, aged 58.   Eighteen years Governor and Commander-in-Chief over these Islands.

---

27.   Floor stone in aisle :—

Crest :—*An arm embowed grasping a flag (apparently the colours), to right several spears a halbert and gun rammer.*

SIR HENRY MARR, Knight, died 29 Nov., 1793, aged 58.   Late Major H.M. 47TH Regiment of Foot, 40 years in the Regiment.

This gallant veteran commenced his military career under General Braddock, and was in the action in which that unfortunate officer lost his life.   (*Gent. Mag.* for 1794, p. 278).

---

28.   Floor stone in front of Chancel :—

JAMES EDWARD POWELL, Esq., died 5 Feb., 1786, aged 67.   Lieut.-Governor and Commander-in-Chief of the Bahama Islands.

---

29.   Floor stone in Aisle :—

WILLIAM Moss, Esq., died 9 Dec., 1796, aged 45.   (See No. 1.)

MURAL TABLETS.*

30. CHARLES MAURICE BODE, died 29 Dec., 1859, aged 59, a native of these Islands, attached for 40 years to the Nassau Field Artillery Company of Militia and at his death Lieut.-Colonel of the Corps, the last surviving son of the late Dr. Charles Bode, surgeon during the American Revolution of the Hessian Grenadiers, who afterwards practised Medicine in this Colony for half a century. Erected by John A. Culhart (?) his friend.

---

31. EUPHEMIA ELIZABETH ALLEN, died 8 May, 1843 in her 25th year, wife of Major James Allen, 2nd West India Regiment, and daughter of Joseph and Mary E. Thompson.

---

32. FREDERICK KNIGHT BURNSIDE, born 30 Sept., 1857, died 17 Aug., 1862. Son of Bruce Lockhart Burnside and his wife Mary Elizabeth. Later became Chief Justice of Ceylon.

---

33. Capt. WILLIAM GILLESPIE, died 3 Oct., 1799, aged 42, at Brixton Place near London, of the Ship " Thomas Gillespie." (At foot of inscription) Capt. John Gillespie. The ship apparently lost in a hurricane. (Inscription very worn).

---

34. Arms : *A chevron between three crosses botoné a fleur de lis for difference.* Crest : *A naked right forearm couped grasping a short straight sword.*

ELIZABETH JANE ANDERSON, died 1 Oct., 1841, aged 31. Wife of Honble George Campbell Anderson, H.M. Attorney-General of the Bahamas. Buried in St. Matthew's Churchyard.

He was later knighted and died when Chief Justice of Ceylon.

---

35. ANNE AUGUSTA MARRIOTT, died 7 July, 1842, aged 26. Wife of W. G. Marriott, Esq., and daughter of John Pinder, Esq. Buried in St. Mathew's, North-West corner of Burial Ground between her Mother and two infants.

---

36. MARY ANN and REBECCA J. FARRINGTON, daughters of the late William Farrington, Esq., who perished in returning from America in the S.S. " Leo," burnt at Sea 13 April, 1877. They were benefactors to Christ Church.

---

* These appear to be in continuation from No. 20.

37. Capt. HENRY HARVEY, died 19 July, 1869, aged 46, at Nassau, New Providence, Senior Officer of the Bahamas Division and Capt. H.M.S. " Eclipse." Died of Yellow Fever. Buried in the present Agricultural Grounds formerly the Eastern Cemetery. Erected by the Officers of the Ship.

---

38. JOHN EUGENE DILLET, died 9 March, 1826, at Bristol, England. A native of these Islands, and for the last ten years of his life a resident of Sierra Leone.

---

39. EMMA CLEMENTINA BLATCH, died 16 Oct., 1825 of fever. Buried at Potters' Field Cemetery. A relation of Admiral Barnett.

---

40. MARY JANE PATTERSON ALLAN, died 24 Oct., 1852, aged 26. Wife of George Allan, Esq., late of H.M. 1ST West India Regiment. Also to their infant son Charles Herbert John who died 5 Jan., 1853, aged 11 months.

---

41. JOSEPH JOHN THOMPSON, died Aug., 1837. Son of Joseph and Mary Thompson of this Island, aged 20 years and 10 months—left here, Nassau, in the Schooner " Hero," 13 Aug., 1837, on the third day after a violent storm arose which is supposed to have caused the loss of the Schooner and all on board. Erected by his parents.

---

42. JULIUS WILLIAM THOMPSON of the 1st West India Regiment, died 12 Jan., 1851, on his passage to England in the American Ship " Franconia " wrecked off Holyhead. He, the commander and five of the crew perished. Erected by his parents Joseph and Mary E. Thompson to their youngest son born 17 Aug., 1829.

---

43. EMILY ANN ALLAN, died 24 Jan., 1850, aged 22 years and 8 months, having given birth to a daughter three weeks before. Wife of George Allan, 1ST West India Regiment and third daughter of Joseph and Mary E. Thompson of this Island.

---

44. MARY ELIZABETH THOMPSON, died 9 July, 1860, a native of these Islands, in her 72ND year, wife of Joseph Thompson, merchant of these Islands, leaving a hubsand, son and daughter and several grandchildren.

---

45. On North side of Reredos base :

RevD ROBERT SWANN for 33 years Rector and Dean of this Cathedral, died at Peterborough 11 Dec., 1899.

---

46. On North side of base of Reredos :—

DR FREDERICK DUNCOMBE, churchwarden, etc., died 22 March, 1882.

CHRIST CHURCH CHURCHYARD.

47. On a slab :—

THOMAS and DEBORAH DUNCOME. Erected by their son Robert Duncome, 1802.

48. On a slab :—

RICHARD LAKE, died 3 March, 1769, aged 41.

49. On a slab :—

JOHN SHORLAND, died 4 June, 1781, aged 43.

50. On a slab :—

MARTHA O'HALLORAN, died 4 Oct., 1788, aged 28. Wife of John O'Halloran, Esq.

51. Marble tablet let in the face of an elevated monument :—

NICHOLAS and MARGARET GARNER and their children.
NICHOLAS GARNER died 4 July, 1802, aged 67.
MARGARET his wife, died 8 June, 1744 (*sic*) aged 52, daughter of Parker.
Their children ANN married Aug., 1785, Capt HAMILTON, 37th Regiment,
    and erected the Christ Church Monument.
NICHOLAS, died 24 Oct., 1766, aged 10 months.
FREEMAN, died 7 Sept., 1776, aged 3 years.
MARGARET, died 4 Nov., 1773, aged 1 year, 9 months, 11 days.

52. On a slab :—

Miss MARGARET HANLEY, died 24 Aug., 1773, aged 23 years, 10 months, 11 days. Mrs. Hanley sister to Nicholas Garner arrived from Barbados with her daughter in 1785, and sailed for Charlestown, South Carolina, 1785.

53. On a slab :—

MARGARET FARR, died 19 July, 1778, wife of Peter Farr.

ST. MATHEW'S, NASSAU, NEW PROVIDENCE.

MURAL MONUMENTS.

54. ALEXANDER HOPE PATTISON, Lieut.-Colonel of the 2nd West India Regiment, Commanding the Troops in this Colony, second son of John Pattison of Kelvin, died 11 Jan., 1835, aged 48 (?), buried with impressive ceremonial in St. Mathew's Churchyard, New Providence.   He was one of the 3rd Division and served on the Staff of Picton and at Salamanca, etc. His fellow citizens first erected a monument in the Necropolis of Glasgow, and his widow Anna, second daughter of His Honour Judge Robert Johnson erected the stone over his ashes in which also rests his nephew.

(See *Gent. Mag.* for 1835, p. 446).

1847, Dec. 9. At Paisley, J. R. G. Pattison, of 10th Foot, only son of the late Lt.-Col. A. Hope Pattison, K.H., Commander of the Troops in the Bahamas, to Isabella, eldest daughter of William Lowndes, of Arthurlie, N.B. (*Gent. Mag.* for 1848, p. 192).

---

55. Arms : *Guttée de poix a lion rampant, on a chief three escallop shells.*
Crest : *Out of a ducal coronet a camel's head.*
Motto : TACHE SANS TACHE.

ALEXANDER HOPE PATTISON, Lieut. 2nd West India Regiment, fifth son of John Pattison, Esq. of Glasgow, N.B. and nephew of Lt.-Col. Pattison, K.H., Commanding the Troops in this Colony, died of Yellow Fever at Nassau, 28 Sept., 1834, aged 21. Erected by his brother officers.

---

56. Arms : *On a bend three escallop shells.*
Motto : TRUE TO THE END.

Honourable WILLIAM WEBB, Esq., died 17 May, 1867, in his 76TH year. He entered the Customs, Bahamas in 1801, and continued in it until the Office of Collector was abolished in 1849, when the retired on an allowance. Senior Member of H.M. Executive Council of these Islands.

---

57. Rev. JOHN WRIGHT, Jesus College, Cambridge, late Rector of this Parish. Born 24 April, 1785, died 10 August, 1821. Erected by friends. He lies inside the Church.

---

58. ROBERT MILLAR, Esq., died 21 Jan., 1845, aged 58, a native of these Islands, he went at an early age to Scotland, etc. Erected by his sister Ann Millar.

---

59. ELIZABETH ANN FORBES, wife of Thomas Forbes of Nassau, merchant, died 4 Oct., 1798. Their infant son Thomas Irving Forbes died 17 July, 1797, aged 27 months and 15 days. Buried in the South-West corner of St. Mathew's Churchyard.

---

60. Crest : *An arm embowed in armour holding a scimitar.*
Motto : PRO PATRIA.

GEORGE BIRRILL, Esq., late Attorney-General of these Islands, and previously for several years Member of Council and Procureur-General of St. Lucia. Eldest son to the late Capt George Birrill of the Hon. East India Company Service, died 9 March, 1837, aged 38 at Nassau, New Providence. Buried in St. Mathew's Burial Ground. Erected by his widow. (See *Gent. Mag.*, p. 670.)

---

61. ELIZABETH S. KEMP, wife of Henry E. Kemp of Nassau, New Providence, Merchant, died 18 May, 1845, aged 32. Buried at the West end of the Church.

---

62. MARGARET ANN MARSHALL, wife of Charles J. Marshall, Esq., died 26 Oct., 1864, aged 55.

Also Charles J. Marshall only son of Charles J. Marshall and Margaret Ann Marshall died in New York City 13 Sept., 1865. Buried in Greenwood Cemetery.

NAVAL AND MILITARY BURIAL GROUNDS.

Extracts from the correspondence received from various Governors by the Colonial Office relating to the above, and forwarded to me by Mr. A. Aspinall, C.M.G. on 27 June, 1921 :—

BRITISH HONDURAS.

Government House, Belize, 29 Sept., 1920. " There is in this Colony only one old Military Cemetery, situated on the Haulover Circular Road, not far from the Barracks. This cemetery had not been used for a great many years, and had been sadly neglected." (*Signed*) Max Smith, Administrator.

ST. LUCIA.

Government House, St. Lucia, 4 Sept., 1920. " Of the three Military Cemeteries in this Colony, those at La Toc and on Pigeon Island are maintained by this Government, and are in good order. The remaining one on Morne Fortuné, is in the charge of the War Department Land Agent, and on my visit there to-day I found it in excellent condition."

W. B. Davidson Houston, C.M.G., Administrator,

(*Signed*) by Sir G. B. Haddon-Smith K.C.M.G., Governor of Windward Islands.

LEEWARD ISLANDS.

Downing Street, 12 Oct., 1920. The Governor has telegraphed " that the necessary measures have been taken to keep the cemeteries in the Colony in good condition."

BARBADOS.

Downing Street, 4 Sept., 1920. Colonel Amery answered Sir John Butcher's question in the House on 9 Aug.

BAHAMAS.

Government House, Nassau, 3 Aug., 1920. " There are no Naval or Military Cemeteries in this Colony. There are however a few graves in the Western Cemetery at Nassau." (*Signed*) H. E. W. Grant, Administrator.

BERMUDA.

Government House, Bermuda, 6 Aug., 1920. "All cemeteries and graves found by me to have been neglected have been put in order."

Jas. Willcocks, Governor-General, and Commander-in-Chief.

JAMAICA.

King's House, Jamaica, 9 Aug., 1920. " Members of the Navy and Army who die in Jamaica are buried in the Cemetery at Up Park Camp."

(*Signed*) L. Probyn, Governor.

St. Vincent.

Government House, St. Vincent, 18 Aug., 1920. "At Fort Charlotte there are two ancient cemeteries (a) one of these is at Low Point. There is no trace of any Military or Naval Burials although possibly such may have taken place. The only headstone relates to a woman who died in 1825. No burials now take place there."

(b) The other is at the Fort. Military funerals took place in it from the years 1825 to 1842, according to the headstones, but more recently it has been used as a cemetery for inmates of the Institutions now located at the Fort. There are some nine tombstones."

There have been Naval and Military funerals at St. Georges Cathedral, Kingstown Cemetery and Barrouallie and Rutland Vale Cemetery.

(Signed) S. J. Thomas, Acting Administrator per Sir Geo. Haddon-Smith, Governor.

Barbados.

Civic Circle Lyceum Club to A. Aspinall, Esq. . . ." offer to attend to the Military Cemetery at Needham's Point. Letters of 1 and 26 June, and 3 Aug., 1920, suggest railing and gates."

Trinidad.

Government House, Trinidad, 7 Sept., 1920. Sir J. R. Chancellor, Governor, forwarding letter from Col. G. H. May of 31 Aug., 1920 who reports—" The Military Cemetery on the Long Circular Road is in a very bad condition. Many of the graves have no tombstones, and in the case of those which have, the inscriptions are becoming illegible . . . There is no other Military Cemetery in Trinidad. . . . . encloses returns from

Tobago.

Scarborough Constabulary District.

Lieut. Otto Mackai	St. Andrew's Churchyard died		3- 8-1846	
Major Lawrence Graeme	,,	,,	14-12-1850	all in
Capt. Jerry	,,	,,	1- 7-1881	bad
Lieut. R. Eugene	St. George Fort		2-11-1831	con-
Ensign Selway	,,	,,	not visible	dition
Lt.-General Stapleton	,,	,,	1881	

N.B.—There are eleven tombs at St. George Fort, though nothing but letters is visible on them . . . . .

Plymouth District.

Joseph Scott, Commandant of the Island	Plymouth Town		1843	
Capt. John Scott	,,	,,	1819	broken
Cha. John Willer	,,	,,	1820	down
James Laird	,,	,,	1820	

A 5th grave stone defaced.

Grenada.

6 Nov., 1920, from Sir G. B. Haddon-Smith, Governor. " There are no Military Cemeteries in this Island, but there are graves of military men dotted about. There are four graves at Richmond Hill, two with inscriptions and two without.

(a) " Placed here by his brother officers to the memory of Lieut. FRANCIS PELHAM STEWART MACKENZIE, 71ˢᵀ Highland Light Infantry and Fort Adjutant at Grenada, who departed this life on the 21ˢᵀ December, 1844, at the age of 23 years." (According to the inscription in St. George's he was buried at Fort Adolphus. ED.)

(b) Sacred to the memory of Colour Sergᵗ T. M. RICHARDS, 92ⁿᵈ Highlanders, who departed this life on the 27ᵗʰ Sept., 1844, aged 34 years. This stone was erected by his comrade Sergeants as a mark of their appreciation.

On the land adjoining the Prison, there are no remains of graves, but there some headstones, most of the inscriptions on which are defaced. On one the following inscription is traceable :

Sacred to the memory of the late Capᵗ . . . FREDERICK . . . . . . the 3ʳᵈ Battʸ Roy. Artillery who died of Malignant Fever on the 24ᵗʰ June, 1793 aged 38 yʳˢ . . . .

There are six graves in Government House Grounds. The inscriptions on all but one, have been obliterated . . . .

To the memory of FREDᴷ NEWCOME Esqʳ who departed this life on the 25 Novʳ 1797, aged 25 years.

ST. KITTS.

Government House, St. Kitts, 9 Aug., 1920. There is only one such (Naval and Military) Cemetery in this Presidency, that under the walls of the old Fort at Brimstone Hill . . . It is well cared for.

(Signed) J. A. Burdon, Administrator, per Sir E. M. Merewether, Governor.

TORTOLA, VIRGIN ISLANDS.

Commissioner's Office, 9 Aug., 1920. " The sum of £3 is allocated in this Presidency for the upkeep of historic sites, etc.; this amount is adequate to maintain the existing Military Cemetery in this Presidency. The old Military Cemetery, which was of some considerable size, situated on the North side of Road Town, has now disappeared, owing to the sea encroaching, and is beyond reclaiming."

(Signed) Major H. Peebles, Commissioner,
pro Secretary Leeward Islands.

DOMINICA.

Government House, 18 Aug., 1920. Cemeteries containing Naval and Military graves in this Presidency are maintained in good condition, the principal of such cemeteries being the Military one on the southern slope of Morne Bruce, with an area of approximately one third of an acre.

(Signed) R. Walter, Administrator.

MONTSERRAT.

Commissioner's Office, 16 Oct., 1920. Gun Hill, long ago a military centre has no graves—nor at St. George's Fort or Shooters Hill two other former military centres.

Chateau Bel Air near the Hospital was once the chief military burial ground . . . . am removing bush . . . none yet found.

(Signed) C. A. Condell, Commissioner.

DEMERARA.

Government House, Georgetown, 12 Nov., 1920, from Sir Wilfred Collet, Governor, forwarding list of graves of soldiers buried in non-military grounds :—

Lodge Village District, East Coast District.
> Col. De Rinzy and Messrs. Pearce and Waby were buried in the Lodge Churchyard. (Belonged to the Local Militia).

Buxton and Friendship Village District, East Coast District :
> Sergt. C. S. Holder died 23-7-1920, buried in St. Augustine's Churchyard, Friendship. (Belonged to British West India Regiment).

Mahaica Country District, East Coast District :
> Edward Ramsey buried in the Wesleyan Churchyard.
> James Webb buried in the Scotch Churchyard.
> James Gravesande buried in Lot 29 Voorzigtigheid. (West India Regiment).

Eldorado Block and Country District, East Coast District :
> Job Liverpool buried in the Belladrum burial ground.
> Joseph McKenzie and Michael Letlow. (Police Force).

Den Amstel and Fellowship Village District, West Coast District :
> Col. George Foster Foster, S.M., buried in the Congregational Churchyard, Blankenburg.

Rosehall Village District Corentyne, Berbice :
> Private Josiah Brush, St. Joseph's Churchyard, Port Mourant, Berbice (British West India Regiment).

Bartica Country District, Essequibo :
> Walter Small, died 3 September, 1920. (British West India Regiment)

Morawhanna Country District, North-west District :
> Isaac Adams, Grave 337, died 26 Sept., 1920 (West India Regiment ; served in Ashantee Campaign).

Government House, Georgetown, 13 Sept., 1920, from Sir W. Collet : " There are only three Military Burial Grounds in this Colony and none with Naval Graves . . . Two of these are situated at Eve Leary immediately to the north of the City of Georgetown and the remaining ground half a mile outside the limits of the Town of New Amsterdam, in Berbice . . . . encloses report by the Director of Science and Agriculture . . . . The Burial Ground in Berbice has been neglected in the past . . .

Memorandum referred to " The Military Cemeteries at Eve Leary appear to have been in a state of neglect until the year 1891, when the then Sheriff of Demerara, Henry Kirke, Esq., M.A., induced the Government to take some steps to reclaim the main Military Cemetery from the disgraceful state it had been allowed to fall into.

THE OLD SOLDIERS' BURIAL GROUND.

Report of 1892-3. " When white troops garrisoned the colony, now many years ago, the men who died were buried in a block of land South-west of Eve Leary." It was cleared and railed and planted. " I have had a list of the few epitaphs, still left unobliterated, taken." It was formerly an unenclosed open swamp. " Evidences of graves still lie all over the ground." . . though few of the tablets remain. " Few officers appear to be buried here ; they had a burial ground of their own . . . at Eve Leary, most of the tablets being chiefly wood were used for firewood.

1. Lt-Col. Alex^r Milne, XIX Reg., died 5 Nov., 1827, aged 46.

2. Sacred | to the memory | of | THOS MOFFEE | Serg^t 49th Regiment | who departed this life | on the 9th of April, 1859 | Aged 32 years.

3. Sacred to the memory of | Pt^e J. HUGHES | Late of the 19th Reg^t | Who depated this life | on the 10th of August 1846 | Aged 27 years.

4. Sacred to the memory of | ANASTASIE BUCKLEY | Who departed this life on | the 17th of July 1844 | Aged 40 years.

5. Sacred | To the memory of | THOS. STANLEY | late Acting Colynnel of the | 69th Regiment, who departed this | life April 1835 Aged 27 years.

6. Sacred | To the memory of | ELIZABETH MADDEN | Relict of the late Corporal | JOHN MADDEN 86th Regiment | Who departed this life 18th | August 1831 Aged 32 years | Erected by Corporal Patrick Madden.

7. Sacred | To the memory of Sergeant | JOSEPH JONES | of the 47th Regiment | Who departed this life on the 30th | May Anno Domino 1842 |

In 1905 these Military Cemeteries passed under the control of the Director. (*Signed*) G. B. Harrison, Director, 11 Aug., 1920, who appends list of names on the tombs in the officers cemetery.*

John Mervin Nooth, Lt.-Col. Royal British Fusiliers ...	23 Aug.	1821
Henry Augustus Holmes	7 Dec.	1823
Walter Robert D'Urban, aged 20 years	1 Nov.	1824
Elizabeth Hare, wife of Lt.-Col. Hare	12 Jan.	1825
Anna Mac Lean	26 April	1825
Charles Henry Holmes	1 July	1825
Maria Louisa Smyth, wife of Capt. Smyth, Royal Engineers	21 Jan.	1833
Charles Simon Doyle, M.D., Surgeon of the Forces ...	30 Oct.	1836
Sarah Antonia Fitzgerald	2 Oct.	1838
Charles Augustus Deanesco	21 Jan.	1839
Eliza Earle Wolseley	21 March	1851
John Henry Wolseley	11 Nov.	1840
Eliza Jane Bourne, sister of John Wolseley and wife of Rev. John Fred. Bourne	15 Dec.	1848
Charles Arthur Goodman	18 March	1841
Fitzroy John Goodman	21 Jan.	1851
Sophia Goodman	25 Oct.	1653
Mary Rawson, wife of Lt.-Col. Bush, Commander West India Regiment and British Guiana Troops ...	1 Oct.	1841
Charles Grey, Ensign West India Regiment ...	29 June	1842
Stephen Arthur Goodman, Major-General	2 Jan.	1844
B. H. Baynes	9 June	1847
Maxwell Mills Legalti	— Sept.	1849
Frances Elizabeth Spooner	25 July	1851
Catherine Goodman, wife of Maj.-General Goodman ...	12 Feb.	1853
Joseph Jules Xavier Dupony, Capt. French Marines ...	3 Oct.	1853
Charles Hunter, Capt. Royal Artillery	24 June	1856
Elizabeth Dove, wife of Adjutant Dove	6 July	1857
Henrietta Frances (*sic*) 50 years	30 Sept.	1857
Francis Wollaston Hutton	16 April	1864

*Compare with my list ante p. 232.

Georgina Elizabeth, wife of Capt. Neame, 16th Regiment	1 Nov.	1866
Kathleen Jackson, daughter of above	23 Oct.	1866
Matilda Clary, servant	2 Nov.	1866
Walter Ferrier Riddle, Ensign 2nd Battalion ...	3 Nov.	1866
Charles Platt, Lieut. H.M. 16th Regiment of Foot ...	18 Nov.	1866
C. M. Rodney Reyne, Lieut., third son of Col. R. and Frances Myers, born 22 March, 1837	28 Nov.	1866
Emma Elizabeth Griffith, 21 years	10 March ——	
Frances Elizabeth Goodman, 6 years	— Sept. ——	
Mrs. Antonio Cone	21 Nov. ——	
Harriet Bough, 40 years		
Evryma Dorothea Robinson, 6 years, 7 days		
Fanny Ann Loinsworth, 4 years, 2 months		

20 old tombstones until (*sic*) illegible inscriptions
One new grave—Capt. A. R. Carroll 1920

MONTSERRAT.

1144/688

Commissioner's Office,
Montserrat,
16*th October*, 1920.

Sir,

In reply to your letter No. 384/3690 of the 22nd July, 1920, I have the honour to state, for submission to His Excellency the Governor, and for the information of His Lordship the Secretary of State, that I have made careful enquiry into the matter of military graves in Montserrat.

2. It was reported to me that there were some neglected graves at Gun Hill in the north of the island. As this place had been, long ago, a military centre, I went out there myself to investigate, but only found, deeply embedded in the sand, a few civilian graves, apparently those of the family of the then owner of the neighbouring estate.

3. So, too, no military graves have been discovered, either at St. George's Fort or Shooter's Hill, two other former military centres.

4. Consequently the only one time military cemetery here, is that at Chateau Bel Air, commonly called the Chateau, a little cemetery near the Hospital, which, until some 15 years since, was used for the burial of paupers from the neighbouring Poor House. This cemetery I am having done up and put into good order. So far I have not come on any military graves, but I know from the records in my Office, that it was once the chief military burial ground in Montserrat. If any military graves are found when all the bush, with which the place is overgrown, has been removed, I shall see that such graves are properly attended to, and shall take measures to ensure their being kept in good condition for the future.

I have etc.

C. A. Condell, Commissioner.

The Honorable Colonial Secretary, Antigua.

MILITARY CEMETERY, NEEDHAMS POINT, BARBADOS.

The following Monumental Inscriptions were copied in 1921 by ladies of the Civic Circle and forwarded on 19 August to Mr. Aspinall, who sent them on to me September 12th, 1921. They are all from the new portion. This list was forwarded by Mr. Aspinall to *Notes & Queries* in which it appeared, 12 S X. 23 in alphabetical order.

I noted some of the names of officers in *Monumental Inscriptions of Barbados*, p. 109.

1. GEORGE THOMPSON | Private R.M.L.I. | Died June 1st 1906 | 34 Years | Erected by Officers of | the H.M.S. Indefatigable.

2. EDWARD HAMILTON, Stoker | H.M.S. Pallas | Died 7th March 1897 | 24 years.

3. WILLIAM WARD | Capts. Steward H.M.S. Canada | Died 24th May 1862.

4. EDWARD JAMES DIXON | Able seaman H.M.S. Canada | Born at Dover, England | Died 29th May 1892.

5. G. NASH, Canteen Manager | 3rd Lanc. Fusileers | Died 16th March 1902 | Age 53.

6. Private M. TOY, No. 5854 | F. Company 4th Worcester Regiment | Died 20th May 1904.

7. No. 5814 Lance-Corporal HENRY NORTON | E. Company 4th Worcester Regiment | Died 13th October 1904 | Aged 24.

8. FRED POWER, Private | 2nd Duke of Wellington's Regiment | Died 22nd August 1891 | Age 20.

9. DAVID WHEATLEY | Sergeant of 18th Company W.D.R.A. | Died 14th August, 1892 | Age 35.

10. ALISON JAMIESON Wife of | Bandmaster A. I. McGill | Died 9th June 1888 |Aged 24 Years.

11. THOMAS W. COOK, R.N. | Boatswain H.M.S. Northampton | Killed accidently 1882.

12. Lance Corporal J. HALL | Died 1883 | Band 1st Bat. Royal Scots.

13. Gr. DENNIS FARRELL | 6/1 C.P.D. R.A. | Died October 1885 | Aged 38 Years.

14. JOHN CUMMINS, Stoker | Died 24th September 1899.

15. JOHN HENRY JAMES, Stoker | Died 27th August 1899 | Buried at Sea | H.M.S. Tribute.

16. JOHN KELLY, R.A. | Died 22nd February 1905 | Aged 70 Years.

17. HECTOR, son of J. E. & | Bandmaster A. GRAY | Born 5th May 1886 | Died 11th 1891.

18. CECIL, son of M. E. & |Sergeant R. I. HALL | Died February 15th 1893 | Aged 17 days | Also their son WALTER HENRY | Died 22nd February 1893 | Aged 1 Year & 5 months.

19. FRANK QUINN Qr Master Sergeant | 2nd Bat. Leinster Regiment | Died 6th September 1901 | Aged 34 Years.

20. GEORGE BOLTON, Stoker | H.M.S. Tourmaline | Died at sea Nov. 16th 1879 | Aged 25 Years.

21. JOHN GRAHAM BRANSCOMBE | Deputy Assist. Supt of Stores | Eldest son of JOHN BRANSCOMBE of London | Died 28th November 1867 | Aged 33.

22. HENRY FRITZ STOCHELL | Died March 30th 1872 | Aged 42.

23. Colour Sergeant M. KINSEALA, 98th Regiment | Died 15th June (sic) 1814 | Aged 44 Years.

24. Pte WILLIAM MANNING | 53rd Regiment | Died 1870 January 10th | Aged 26 Years.

25. Lance Sergt JOYN STEVENS | 53rd Regiment, Who died at Barbados | Died 1870 4th January | Aged 25 Years.

26. Private RICHARD TYRELL | 53rd Regiment who died at Barbados | Died 1870 6th January | Aged 28 Years.

27. JOHN COLEMAN | Pte in H.M. 97th | Died 1874.

28. JOHN COLLINGS | 98th Regiment | Died 1874.

29. EDWARD GREVES.

30. CARL GALLE

31. Sergt T. BENTON | 98th Regiment | Died 1875.

32. Pte PATRICK MULLANY | 35th Regiment | Died 1877.

33. Pte JOHN MCEVOY | 35th Regiment | Died 1876.

34. JAMES ABBOTT SUGMUR.

35. JAMES TAIT | Died 1885.

36. LOTTIE WORRISON | WILLIAM ERIC WORRISON | GORDON MACKAY WORRISON | children Died 1885.

37. WILLIAM HENRY RICHARD (child)| Died 1876.

38. ANNIE EMMA MAYERS.

39. GEORGE LIER and his wife | Died 1879.

40. JOSEPH JOHN WILLIAM WHINAM | Died 1885.

41. JOSEPH JOHN FOX WHINAM | Died 1888.

42. Corp. Sergt JAMES WALLACE | Died 1878.

43. Staff Sergt W. G. PETTIFER | Died 1880.

44. Corp. T. BARRICK | Died 1877.

45. Pte J. MATHEWSON | Died 1878.

46. Sergt T. HOLDER | Died 1878.

47. Pte R. BABEONE | Died 1878.

48. Pte R. LENIOR | Died 1879.

49. Pte J. WILSON | Died 1879.

50. P^te G. Richards | Died 1879.

51. Maud Lizette Marian Jones | Died 1885 | Henrietta Louise Lemoon Jones | Died 1879.

52. John Kneller | Died 1875.

53. George G. Carr.

54. Martha Craddock | Died 1878.

55. Major Baldwin.

56. Charles W. Tumner (of Deal, England) | Seaman, H.M.S. Tourmaline.

57. James Lims | Naval Schoolmaster of | H.M.S. Bacchante | Died 1880.

58. Susanna Forsyth | Died 1880.

59. George Bolton | Died 1879.

60. Ellen Louisa Doggett | Died 10th April 1876 | Aged 3 Years and 5 months. Alice Rebecca Doggett | Died 6th August | Aged 2 years | The daughters of W. & E. Doggett 35th R.S. Reg.

61. Mary Elizabeth the wife of | Sergeant Carmichael, C.M.L. | Died 10th January 1885 | Aged 34.

62. George William Spencer | Engine Room Artificer | H.M.S. Magicienne | Died at Barbados 22nd March 1893 | Aged 40.

63. William A. Dunlop, Stoker | H.M.S. Magicienne | Drowned at Barbados | 2nd June 1893, Aged 24.

64. Archibald McNeil | Seaman H.M.S. Tourmaline | Died in Hospital at Barbados | 17th May 1894 | Aged 19.

65. Alfred Geo. Beer, Stoker | of H.M.S. Intrepid | Died at the Hospital, Barbados | 19th August, 1898 | Aged 31.

66. Walter H. Marsh, Warder M.P.D. | Died 28th November, 1899 | Aged 38.

67. Stephen Mears, Band | 98th Regiment | Died 10th April, 1874 | Aged 15.

68. William Smithson, Bandsman | 1st Batt. Yorkshire Regiment | Died December 4th 1887 | Aged 27 Years.

69. W. H. Mauser, Bugler R.M.L.I. | H.M.S. Volage | Died January 27th 1888 | Aged 16 Years.

70. Miles H. Braithwaite | Late P^y M^s Serg^t | 2nd W.I. Reg^t | Died June 1st | Aged 45 Years.

71. Corp^l John Sheeny | 2nd Batt. Leinster Regiment | Royal Canadians | Died March 21st 1899 | Aged 26 Years.

72. No. 3568 P^te Bernard Lyons | 2nd Batt. Leinster Regiment | Died July 4th 1899 | Aged 25 Years.

73. P^te Timothy Hamilton | D. Co^y 2nd Batt. Leinster Reg. | Died August 8th 1899 | Aged 27 Years.

74. Lilian, daughter of | Warder A. B. Moffat, M.R.D. | and his wife | Died November 1st 1895 | Aged 5 years & 7 months.

75. No. 4890 P^te C. CALLIS | 2nd Batt. Leinster Regiment | Royal Canadians | Died April 29th 1900 | Aged 23 Years.

76. Bandsman W. J. SEIMONDS | 2nd Batt. Prince of Wales | Leinster Regiment | Died March 14th 1899.

77. LAURA AMELIA wife of | Serg^t ANDERSON, M.B.C. | Died June 9th 1897 | Aged 39 Years.

78 In memory of the men of the | 1st Batt. Leicestershire Regiment | who died while stationed at Barbados | during the years 1893-94-95 | Erected by | Capt BARNARDISTON, Officers | and Ships Company of H.M.S. Rover.

79. W. F. TEGG, A.B. | H.M.S. Pallas | Died 2nd May 1896 | Aged 22 Years.

80. HERCULES WEBSTER BAULD | Landsman U.S. Navy | Born March 18th 1878 | Died December 5th 1899 | Erected by his shipmates of the | U.S. Ship Lancaster.

81. C. NASH, Canteen Manager | 3rd Lancashire Fusileers | Died 16th March 1902 | Aged 53 | Formerly served as Officers Mess Col^r | Sergeant in the Rifle Brigade.

82. JAMES GIBBONS | Military Store Department | Died 27th July, 1883 | Aged 60 Years | Also his wife | CATHERINE GIBBONS | Died 2nd August, 1904.

83. Private THOMAS WALTON | 1st East Yorkshire Regiment | Died 12th August 1887 | Aged 21 Years | Erected by the Officers | and men of his Company.

84. In memory of | JOHN L. PARRETT, A.B. | Died at Barbados 8th July, 1900 | Aged 22 Years | Also of ALFRED WALKER, A.B. | Drowned at sea Oct. 29th 1898 | Aged 23 Years | Both of H.M.S. Proserpine | Erected by their shipmates.

86. GEORGE PACKHAM | Ord^y Seaman, H.M.S. Canada | Died 1st November 1893 | Aged 18 years and 9 months.

87. ROBERT BLOMBERO | Seaman U.S. Navy | Born in Finland, March 19th 1861 | Died February 26th 1902 | at Bridgetown, Barbados | Erected by his shipmates on | board the U.S. F.S. Hartford.

88. Lieutenant T. E. LE BLANC | First Battalion The King's Own | Royal Lancaster Regiment who | died of yellow fever at St Anns | Barbados, on the 28th | July 1881 | Aged 26 Years.

89. HERBERT T. COUSINS, D.A.C.O. | Commissariat Staff. Who died | of Yellow Fever eight days after| landing | August 8th 1881 | Aged 25.

90. Surg^n JAMES RONAYNE, A.M.D. | Died of Yellow Fever 10th Aug. 1881 | Aged 25 Years.

91. Captain E. LAWLESS, A.P. Depart. | Died August 16th 1881 | Aged 42.

92. SEYMOUR BLANSHARD PEMBERTON* | Lieut. 2nd West India Regiment | who died of Yellow Fever | 7th October 1881 | Aged 25 Years.

93. LOUISA DRUCE. The wife of | JAMES DRUCE, Military Labourer.

94. JOHN COLEMAN, P^te in H.M. 97th | who died 4th July 1874 | Aged 44.

95. P^te G. DOUGLAS, 35th Regiment.

---

* See note of his family in Caribbeana II. 40

96. WILLIAM THOMAS, | Aged 24 Years of Norwich, England | Dr H.M.S. Immortality | Went Home May 7th 1871.

97. ANGELINA HOWARD Died 1914.

98. PETER J. COCHING | 35th Regiment (No date).

99. Color Sergt ROBERT JONES | 29th Regiment | Died 1872.

100. The Officers, N.C.O.'s and men of | No. 17 Batt. Western Division R.A. | to the memory of | Gr F. SODEN | Gr R. WATERS | Sergt W. SCOTNEY | Gr D. HYDE | Gr F. SANDELL | Gr J. BRIDGER | Who died at Barbados 1885— 1890.

101. HARRIET JANE VICTORIA. Wife of | Major HOBBS.

102. Col. DONALD ALEX. FRAZER | Royal Engineers | Died 1881.   (5 Aug. Ed.)

103. ANNIE only daughter of Capt NASSAU | STEPHEN 94th Regiment and step- | daughter of Mrs DONALD A. FRAZER | Died 1881.

104. JULIA Daughter of | Sergt Major W. A. WEBB | 1st E. Y. Regiment | Died 1888.

105. ETHEL, Daughter of | Warder W. H. MARSH, M.P.D. | Died 1887.

106. ELIZABETH J. MANNS, Daughter of | B. D. N. J. MANNS.

107. ELLEN SEDNEY, EMILY KATE, Children of | Band Sergt G. A. BRYDEN | 2nd D. of W. Regiment.

108. JANE JOHNSTON, Wife of | Corp. R. JOHNSTON | 1st West India Regiment | Died 1878.

109. JOSEPH FITZHERBERT GITTENS | Royal Artillery | Son of FRANCIS GITTENS.

110. FRANK, Died August 3rd 1901 | Aged 6 Weeks | And | FLORENCE MIRIAM Died Aug. 4th 1902 | Children of ALBERT and MIRIAM M. WELL | Royal Army Medical Corps.

111. JANIE, Dearly loved child of | Major G. C. KNOCKER, D.A.A.G. | Born 2nd June, 1890 | Died 22nd March, 1896.

112. THOMAS CHARLES LANE WHEATLEY | Son of Major C. R. S. WHEATLEY, 18/7 R.A. | who died of yellow fever 14th Aug., 1881 | Aged 3 years.

113. ARTHUR STAVELEY CLIVE JUSTICE | Died July 12th 1881 | Aged 4½ Months.

114. Lieut.-Col. R. BULLEN | Royal Engineers | Died in Barbados 30th June, 1883.

115. HARRIET MARIA, Beloved wife of | Col. NICOLLS, R.A. and daughter of | Rev. C. Y. CRAWLEY, Rector of | Taynton, Gloucestershire | Born 5th December, 1840 | Died 26th July, 1881 | Also | GEORGINA HARRIET, dear child of above | Born 30th March, 1876 | Died 28th July, 1881.

116. JANE, beloved wife of S. Qr Mr Sergt | H. TAYLOR, A.S.C. | Died Sept. 12th 1896 | Aged 56 Years.

117. MARY ELINOR WARD (*née* REEDE) Died 11th August, 1881 | And of her husband | Surgeon Major ESPIRIE WARD | F.R.C.S.I. | Died 22nd August 1881 | This stone is erected by | THOS. PICTON REEDE | Father of former, and by | Dr. M. A. WARD, brother of the latter.

118. ELEANOR RADLEY, | Died 19th October, 1886 | CICELY RADLEY | Died 10th October, 1886 | Twin daughters of Capt JAS | COULTON, D.A.C.G. | Born 4th June, 1886.

119. GERALD PEARSON KING HARMAN | Infant son of | Major WALDRON E. R. KELLY | Assistant Military Secretary | Died 22nd June, 1888.

120. Col. SIDNEY BAYNTON FARRELL | Commanding Royal Engineers | Who died at Barbados 7th Sept. 1879 | Aged 50.

121. Col. DONALD ALEXANDER FRAZER | Royal Engineers | Died August 5th 1881 | Aged 52 Years | Also to ANNIE only daughter of | Late Capt. NASSAU STEPHENS | 94th Regt. and step-daughter of | Mrs D. A. FRAZER | Died August 2nd 1881 | Aged 37 Years.

122. EMMA CECILIA, Widow of Major | JAMES UNIACK, R.M. of Arraglyn | County Cork | Died at Shot Hall Jan. 12th 1881 | Aged 78 Years.

123. SARAH ELIZABETH, Wife of | Sergt W. H. WILSON | H.M. 97th Regiment.

124. MARY L. BAILY, Wife of | THOMAS BAILY | Died 1875.

125. MARY ELIZABETH, Wife of | Sergt S. E. HAYNES | 2nd West India Regiment | Died 1875.

126. E. A. DARCY | Son of E. DARCEY | 2nd West India Regiment | Died 1875.

127 SUDNEY, Child of | F. BOSHELL | Royal Berks Regiment | Died 1898.

128. Sergeant BENJAMIN CLARKE | 2nd West India Regiment | Died December 20th 1885 | Aged 41 Years.

INDEX NOMINUM.

A

Adams, Isaac, 252.
Ablart, Madam, 35 ; Wm., 35.
Abbott, Ann, 115 ; Charles, 115 ; Richard, 115.
Ahmuty, John, 209.
Alexander Edwd., 221.
Allan, Emily Ann, 246 ; George, 246 ; Mary Jane P., 246.
Allen, Euphemia Ely, 245.
Allison, Capt. Jno., 236.
Alvarez, Rebeccah, 75.
Amory, Ann, 178.
Anderson, Eliz. Jane, 245 ; Laura A., 258
Anton, Canon Jas. Alex., 202.
Archer, Julian H., 27.
Astwood, Olivia Bascome, 24.
Auchinleck, Mary, 118.

B

Babeon, R., 256.
Backer, Johanes, 238 ; Larwens G. L., 238.
Bailey, Lt. Joseph, 69.
Baily, Mary L., 270.
Baird, Emmeline, 34.
Baker, Henry Wilkinson, 94.
Baldwin, Major, 257.
Balle, David, 239.
Banks, H., 55.
Barker, Ann S., 208 ; Rev. J. C., 208.
Barnes, Ann Emma F. T., 25 ; Gill, 25 ; Mary Jane, 25.
Barrick, T., 256.
Barrow, Fanny, G. W., 194 ; Robert H., 194.
Bartlett, Elenor, 38.
Bascom, Rev. J. R., 211
Basden, Mary, 191 ; Richd., 191.
Bathgate, Arch., 52.
Battry, Jona, 195 ; Edwd., 195.
Bauld, Hercules W., 258.
Baynes, B. H., 253.
Beauperthuy, Louis Dan., 235.
Beavor, Jn., 145 ; Honour, 145.
Beckman, Saml., 237.
Bedfon, Capt. Sam., 28.
Bedingfeld, . . Francis Philip, 29 ; Hy. de L., 29 ; Selina Mary, 29.
Beer, Alfred Geo., 257.
Beete, Joseph, 227.
Bell, Rev. John, 120.
Belman, Bridgett, 99 ; Eliz., 99 ; Tho., 99.
Bellot, Hon. Ben., 23 ; Fred, 23 ; Jos., 25.
Bennett, Maria, 79 ; Hy. Og., 2.
Benton, T., 256.
Berkeley, Tho., 132 ; Hy., 132 ; Maurice, 132 ; Susanna, 134.

Berridge, Arth. A., 159 ; Axel Hamtn., 159 ; James Saml., 128.
Blackall, Georgina, 13 ; S.W., 13.
Blackburn, Wm., 167.
Blacket, Thos., 129.
Blanc, Hon.Wm. F. B., 29 ; Myra, 29 ; Selina, 29
Blanchard, Margaret, 118 ;
Blanchet, Georgiana, 165 ; Peter E., 165.
Blatch, Emma C., 246.
Birrell, George, 248.
Boddie, Maria 74.
Bode, Charles Maurice, 245.
Blombero, Robert, 258.
Bolton, George, 256 ; 257.
Bonifun, Augustus, 119 ; Jessie, 119 ; Geo. R., 232.
Booker, George, 229 ; Josias, 229 ; Mehetabel W., 229.
Boon, Joseph Hy., 127 ; Wm. Sid., 127.
Boshell, Sudney, 270.
Bostock, James, 25.
Bough, Harriett, 254.
Bourne, Eliza J., 232 ; 253.
Bourrifan, John, 195.
Bovell, Rev. James, 118.
Bowring, Wm., 69 ; Jane, 69.
Bragger, Wm. John, 179.
Braithwaite, Miles H., 257.
Bramble, Ann, 49.
Branch, Eliz. Prater, 157 ; Ch. James, 159 ; Wm. John, 157.
Brand, E. M., 49.
Branscombe, John G., 256.
Brazier, Ann, 93 ; Edwd., 92 ; Edwd., 93 ; Wm., 93.
Bridger, J., 259.
Bridgewater, Eliz., 157.
Briggs, Eliz., 81 ; Jos. Lyder, 81 ; Jos., 119 ; Mary Edith, 119.
Brodbelt, Francis, 88 ; Frances Hill, 88 ; Joseph Hill 88 ; Rich., 88 ; Sarah, 77.
Brockhuizzen, Helena Anna, 238 ; Jacob, 238 ; 239.
Brooks, Jane, 80.
Brome, Philip, 112.
Brown, Capt. Hy., 38 ; Hon. James, 13 ; Capt. James, 21 ; John, 149 ; Sarah, 148 ; Wm., 243.
Browne, Eliz., 115 ; Jacob, 115 ; Simon, 95 ; Thomas, 95.
Brozett, Cornelia, 154 ; James, 154 ; Eliz., 154 ; Ann, 154.
Bruce, Sir Charles, 211.
Brush, Josiah, 252.
Bryan Thomasina, 162.
Bryden, Ellen S. & Emily K., 259.
Bucke, Gray, Oct., 55.

www.ingramcontent.com/pod-product-compliance
Lightning Source LLC
Chambersburg PA
CBHW031503270326
41930CB00006B/219